Arab Modernism as World Cinema

This book has been made possible in part by the National Endowment for the Humanities: Exploring the human endeavor. Any views, findings, conclusions, or recommendations expressed here do not necessarily represent those of the National Endowment for the Humanities.

This project was also supported in part by funding from the University of California President's Faculty Research Fellowships in the Humanities, MR15328710.

Further support came in grants from the Committee on Research, the Arts Research Institute, and the Pavel Machotka Chair in Creative Studies at Porter College, University of California, Santa Cruz.

The publisher and the University of California Press Foundation gratefully acknowledge the generous support of the Robert and Meryl Selig Endowment Fund in Film Studies, established in memory of Robert W. Selig.

Arab Modernism as World Cinema

The Films of Moumen Smihi

Peter Limbrick

UNIVERSITY OF CALIFORNIA PRESS

University of California Press
Oakland, California

© 2020 by Peter Limbrick

All production stills and images from Moumen Smihi's films are courtesy Imago Films.

Library of Congress Cataloging-in-Publication Data

Names: Limbrick, Peter, 1967- author.
Title: Arab modernism as world cinema : the films of Moumen Smihi / Peter Limbrick.
Description: Oakland, California : University of California Press, [2020] | Includes filmography, bibliographical references, and index.
Identifiers: LCCN 2019023203 (print) | LCCN 2019023204 (ebook) | ISBN 9780520330566 (cloth) | ISBN 9780520330573 (paperback) | ISBN 9780520974333 (ebook)
Subjects: LCSH: Smihi, Moumen, 1945- | Motion pictures—Arab countries. | Motion picture producers and directors—Morocco.
Classification: LCC PN1998.3.S58584 L56 2020 (print) | LCC PN1998.3.S58584 (ebook) | DDC 791.43/75—dc23
LC record available at https://lccn.loc.gov/2019023203
LC ebook record available at https://lccn.loc.gov/2019023204

Manufactured in the United States of America

29 28 27 26 25 24 23 22 21 20
10 9 8 7 6 5 4 3 2 1

For David

CONTENTS

Acknowledgments	*ix*
Note on Transliteration	*xiii*
Introduction: Moumen Smihi, World Cinema, Arab Modernism	1
Chapter One: Radical Realities: Form and Politics in the New Arab Cinema	34
Chapter Two: The Voice of the Arabs: Smihi's Soundscapes	73
Chapter Three: *Kan ya makan*: Intertextuality and Arab Modernism	107
Chapter Four: Religion, Secularism, Modernity	144
Chapter Five: For a New Nahda: Gender, Sexuality, and Freedom	180
Notes	213
Filmography	241
Bibliography	243
Index	261

ACKNOWLEDGMENTS

This book's beginnings date back to 2007, when I served on the programming committee for the San Francisco Arab Film Festival. Watching a screener of Moumen Smihi's *A Muslim Childhood* (2005), I was captivated but realized I knew nothing of the filmmaker's other work. The festival director, Sonia El-Feki, invited Smihi to the festival, and having by then done my homework, I decided he'd make an excellent guest in my undergraduate film studies class at the University of California, Santa Cruz. Our conversations there about montage, Sergei Eisenstein, the Beat poets, and film theory certainly thrilled my students, but nothing matched Smihi's own joy at seeing the "Hitchcockian trees!" he loved so much from *Vertigo* (1958), Alfred Hitchcock's film set in San Francisco and in the redwoods of the Santa Cruz mountains. That encounter whetted my appetite to see more of Smihi's work, so in 2010—on the same day I received tenure—I flew to Tangier, where I viewed most of his films for the first time. (Some, like *Egyptian Cinema: Defense and Illustration* (1989), took longer to access, and another, *Colors on Bodies* (1972), has remained inaccessible to me because of the fragile state of its sole surviving print.)

    I returned determined to write about his work. In the course of that research and writing, I have learned so much from Smihi, it's hard to know how to thank him. He has been extraordinarily generous with his time, patient with my questions, and from the outset welcomed me as an interlocutor. I hope that what I write here might in some way do justice to the complexity and depth of his thinking and creative practice.

    This work has taken me back on many trips to Morocco and Paris and sent me deep into archives, libraries, and languages. In the process, I have accumulated debts too numerous to repay and intellectual companions too many to mention; I hope that any I unintentionally overlook here will forgive me, just as I hope they'll forgive any mistakes in the text that follows. My Arabic teachers, especially Nasser Riyadh and Maher Sabry at Pacific Arabic in San Francisco and a host of others at Qalam wa Lawh in Rabat, have instilled in me a love for Arabic that only keeps growing as I work at it. Stephan De Gery knocked my French into better shape, and Parisa Safa made the learning more fun. Livia Alexander opened her Rolodex and managed a wonderfully successful retrospective of Smihi's films, which I curated and which Kathy Geritz, Dean Otto, Mimi Brody, and George Clark welcomed to their respective institutions. That program owed much to the support of former director Noureddine Saïl and his staff at the Centre cinématographique marocain (CCM), especially Mohammed Sabiri, and Grace McKay at Electric Pictures did wonders to digitize some important but fragile prints. Seeing these films beautifully projected and then speaking with audiences about them helped refine some of the ideas in this book. Omnia El-Shakry was the most inspiring co-curator for our related symposium, "Unfixed Itineraries: Film and Visual Culture from Arab Worlds" at the University of California, Santa Cruz, in 2013, and for their support with the retrospective and symposium I especially thank Susan Gilson Miller, Emily Gottreich, Stefania Pandolfo, Neda Atanasoski, Shelby Graham, Irene Lusztig, Soraya Murray, John Weber, and all the invited presenters.

Research for the project unfolded in many places and with the help of many people and institutions. In the earliest stages of the project, Rasha Salti filled my notebook with suggestions of people to meet and films to see; her support, encouragement, and introductions were precious. In Paris, I especially thank Rabah Ameur-Zaïmeche, Ali Cherri, Eloïse Djoehana, Laurel Hirsch, Ghoson Hammod, Anne Pastor, Meyar al-Roumi, Sarah Sobol, Hélène Walland, and the staff at the Cinémathèque française (especially Laure Marchaut), the Bibliothèque nationale de France, INA, and the Centre Georges Pompidou. Time and again, Claude Pomme Brard provided warm welcomes and logistical support for my research in Paris, especially making space for me to create the beautiful frame enlargements that grace the book, and I thank le petit Louay for befriending me and his big American sibling, Esther. Thanks to Ody Roos for all his interventions and assistance with prints and production details. In Beirut, I benefited hugely from conversations and visits with Angela Harutyunyan, Lamia Joreige, Kristine Khouri, Ghassan Salhab, Tariq Teguia, and Christine Tohme.

In Morocco I enjoyed research in the CCM archives with the help of Moha Messaoui and at the Bibliothèque Nationale du Royaume du Maroc in Rabat and the Bibliothèque du Roi Abdul Aziz al-Saoud in Casablanca. Then-director Gerald Loftus and the Legation staff welcomed me at TALIM (the Tangier American Legation Institute for Moroccan Studies) on several occasions. Thanks to Khalid Bekkaoui, Jean-Noël Ferrié, Juan Asís Palao Gómez, Latifa Menaouar, and Sadik Rddad for inviting me to give talks and for being such generous hosts, and to Saïd Chemlal,

Zineb Qtb, Reda Zaireg, Abdilah Zirat and his students, and the students at the Moroccan Cultural Studies program at Sidi Mohamed ben Abdellah University in Fez for asking so many great questions. Across many trips to Morocco, I have also been privileged to enjoy the hospitality, friendship, and research collaboration of Mrimi Abdellatif; Latefa Ahrarre; Hamid Aidouni; Mohammed Alami; Saïd Amel; Cherqui Ameur; Francesco Apruzzi; Abdellah, Mohammed, and Rayan Bailoute; Georges Bousquet; Roland Carrée; Hamza Elbardai; Ali Essafi; Abderrahim Filali; Abdeladim El Ghouaouta; Maud Houssais; Mohammed Mezzine; Léa Morin; Yasmina Naji; Marie Pierre-Bouthier; Bouchra Smihi; and Abdelmajid Zeggaf. In 2012 I was incredibly lucky to meet three generations of Bouanani women all at once, and sharing couscous with Naïma Saoudi, Touda, and Ito before watching Ahmed Bouanani's films together is something I will never forget. Touda Bouanani's support, collaboration, and own artistic practice are things I continue to treasure.

Away from Morocco, I was lucky to present work from this project in a wide range of venues. Thanks to Diana Allan, Jamal Bahmad, Luca Caminati, Tarek Elhaik, Bishnupriya Ghosh, Kenneth Harrow, Will Higbee, Adrian Martin, Florence Martin, Marc Matera, Masha Salazkina, Bhaskar Sarkar, and Stefanie van der Peer for invitations to speak, and to all those who came and engaged with my and Smihi's work there and at meetings of the Society for Cinema and Media Studies and Middle East Studies Association. Others collaborated with me on panels, read work, suggested things to see and read, or supported me in myriad other collegial ways. Huge thanks to Kamal Aljafari, Samirah Alkassim, Michael Allan, Nezar Andary, Omar Berrada, Mona Damluji, Manthia Diawara, Kay Dickinson, Brian T. Edwards, Suzanne Gauch, Chris Holmlund, Priya Jaikumar, Caren Kaplan, Laura U. Marks, Larissa Sansour, Karl Schoonover, Viola Shafik, Jonathan Smolin, and Eric Smoodin.

Some of the ideas here were developed in two journal articles, "Moumen Smihi's Tanjawi/Tangérois/Tangerian Cinema," *Third Text* 26, no. 4 (2012): 443–454 (in a special issue edited by Walid Sadek; that material, copyright © Third Text, is reprinted by permission of Taylor & Francis Ltd, http://www.tandfonline.com, on behalf of *Third Text*) and "Vernacular Modernism, Film Culture, and Moroccan Short Film and Documentary," *Framework* 56, no. 2 (2015): 388–413 (in a dossier edited by Masha Salazkina). At the University of California Press, I benefited greatly from generous feedback and suggestions from Tarek El-Ariss and another, anonymous peer reviewer. Raina Polivka has been talking with me about this project for years, and it's immensely satisfying to see it to fruition with her and Madison Wetzell at the helm. Lindsey Westbrook has been a patient and meticulous copyeditor.

At UC Santa Cruz, I thank my current and former chairs and deans for their support of my work, especially leave for the two fellowships I was fortunate to enjoy, and thanks to my departmental colleagues and staff for creating such an inspiring work environment. There and across campus, the support and friendship of a host of colleagues, including Anjali Arondekar, Terry Burke, Jim Clifford, Sharon

Daniel, Muriam Haleh Davis, Mayanthi Fernando, Anna Friz, Irene Gustafson, Jenny Horne, Jonathan Kahana, Sean Keilen, Stephanie Moore, Margaret Morse, Rick Prelinger, Lisa Rofel, Thomas Serres, Shelley Stamp, and the growing UC Maghrib studies network have all nurtured this research in different ways and made Santa Cruz an ever-richer intellectual home. For research and translation work, Fabiola Hanna, Dominic Romano, and Alejandra Monteagudo were invaluable assistants. Tristan Carkeet and Dean Lyons helped bring Smihi's beautiful images to press. My PhD students Raed Rafei, Rana al-Jarbou (who also worked as a research assistant), Suzy Halajian, and a succession of undergrads keep giving me reasons to believe in this work.

Friends and loved ones helped by being here, or there, in myriad ways. In addition to those embedded in the thanks above, Jennifer Derr, Michael B. Gillespie, Brian Petty, Afzal Shah, and Marc Siegel have kept me buoyed no matter what the challenges of the moment. How lucky that Rosalind Galt turned up as the serious thinking and writing began. Everything goes better with her brilliance and love, and as a close reader of wordy drafts, she has no peer. Getting to know Adrian Goycoolea is an added gift.

Nothing will make up for the absence of David Pendleton, dear friend of twenty-four years, who died far too young as I was nearing the end of the writing. My loss is shared not just with his family and other friends, but by the Harvard Film Archive and an international film community. He was the best-read and deepest-thinking cinephile I know, and our conversations about cinema, ideas, and life in general have marked me deeply. It is my profound sorrow that he is not around to see this book finished, or to do the Smihi series we always talked about, and I dedicate this book to him, with love.

Around home, the support of Josefine Messing, Tina Schubert, Luise Stadelmann, Carola Marti, Jenny Mann, and Robert Schröder let us all get things done, and Nate Tinner came in for a three-pointer at the end. As always, my father, Warren Limbrick, my siblings, Susannah and Michael Limbrick, and their partners and kids continue to be my emotional anchor in the South Pacific. Thanks, too, to the Berkeley-Oakland-Brooklyn Bomse crew. Nothing important ever happens without the steadfast love, trust, and support of Amy Bomse, especially during this project, which took me far away on so many occasions. Last time I wrote a book, I said, "Oscar Limbrick Bomse teaches me to see and hear differently every day, and I hope Esther Limbrick Bomse never stops shaking things up." Happily, ten years on, nothing could be truer.

NOTE ON TRANSLITERATION

For transliteration of words from Arabic, I have used a modified version of the guidelines of the *International Journal of Middle East Studies* (IJMES), omitting all diacritics except for *ayn* (‘) and *hamza* (’).

I refer to the titles of Moumen Smihi's films in English in the text for the sake of readability; their original Arabic and French titles appear in the filmography at the end of the book. For other films, I use an English title first with the original language in parentheses. I have followed the same method with literary titles, except in the case of work that has never been translated or published in English; in those cases, I give the Arabic first with an English translation in parentheses.

For names of people and places, I have used the most common transliteration that might be encountered in further research; similarly, to avoid confusion, I transliterate character names from Smihi's films according to how they appear in the credits and his writings (e.g., Mohammed Larbi, not Mohammad al-‘Arabi; Larbi also more closely resembles a Moroccan pronunciation). Since French transliteration rules differ from English, this will lead to some inconsistency, but it should aid the reader given the predominance of French or French-influenced sources on the Maghrib. Hence, Taha Hussein and not Taha Husayn for the writer's name; Chefchaouen and not Shafshawan for the village in the Rif. I also defer to the transliterations that individuals themselves use: most importantly, Moumen Smihi, not Mu’min al-Smihi! An exception to this rule, including for Smihi, is in the bibliography: where a work is only published in Arabic, I use a standard transliteration of the author's name, which, in those cases, may help in further research.

All translations from French and Arabic are my own unless otherwise stated. Where I quote from films in English, I am referring to the English subtitles associated with each film where they exist, and my own translations where they do not.

Introduction

Moumen Smihi, World Cinema, Arab Modernism

In Moumen Smihi's second feature film, *44, or Tales of the Night* (1981), a short scene takes place in a village in the Rif region of Morocco during the 1920s, when the French had occupied the country and were actively subduing local populations under the guise of their "protectorate."[1] The scene is enigmatic and features an unnamed character whom we never encounter again in the film. In the sequence just prior, we have heard about the local resistance armies all over Morocco that have stymied French efforts. A few minutes later, a quote from French marshal Louis Hubert Gonzalve Lyautey appears as a title in Arabic and French that confirms: "In Morocco, we found ourselves faced with a historical and independent empire, extremely jealous of its independence and rebellious against all kinds of servitude. Here, we actually found a state and a people." Sandwiched between the signs of popular resistance and the French admission of Moroccan strength, these few shots, without dialogue, show the French being quietly escorted out of a Moroccan village.

The departing soldiers in the narrow street pass an unnamed figure performing handstands while dressed in the red silk pants and shirt of a Moroccan acrobat in the popular tradition of the Ouled Sidi Ahmed ou Moussa.[2] As he lands, he catches sight of the soldiers and stands, back to the wall, to let them pass. The camera moves from a long shot to a medium shot and we see the figure look off-screen to his right, raising a hand to shield the glare from his face as he follows their movement (fig. 1). Witness to the French defeat, this character, by his enigmatic presence, confirms the durability of Moroccans and their culture in the face of the alien presence and force of the colonizer. The actor here is Moumen Smihi, the film's director, just thirty-six years of age at the time of the film's release, and his brief appearance in this scene is his only moment before the camera in any of his feature films.

FIGURE 1. Moumen Smihi as an acrobat in *44, or Tales of the Night*, 1981.

Smihi appears again, however, in his 1993 documentary *With Matisse in Tangier*, this time as a narrator who guides us through Henri Matisse's work and its relationship to Morocco. And in the documentary *With Taha Hussein* (2015), an homage to the work of the Egyptian writer, Smihi sits in an armchair on a stage, recounting to us the importance to Arab culture of his intellectual hero. These rare on-camera appearances—the Rifian acrobat watching the defeat of the French, the narrator in the spirit of Orson Welles discussing a French artist as seen by a Moroccan, and the intellectual guide who leads us through the history of Arab culture's relationship with the West—represent some of the varied faces of Moumen Smihi's fifty-year career. Deeply invested in the popular practices of Morocco and constantly depicting them in his films, he weaves them together with the influence of regional and global languages, practices, and peoples. Resolutely local in their narratives and forms of address, his films are at the same time worldly in their engagement with other film traditions. Redolent of European art cinema in their rich images and often-experimental soundtracks, they are infected with the energy and vitality of Arab, Moroccan, and Amazigh popular cinema and culture.[3]

Smihi's work is not only radically beautiful as cinema but, together with his critical writing and reflection, part of an oeuvre that seeks nothing less than a rethinking of the relationships of cinema, culture, and modernity in the Arab world—in other words, an Arab modernism for a new Nahda. The Nahda, often translated as an "awakening" or Renaissance, was the nineteenth- and early twentieth-century movement in which Arab writers, artists, and politicians reenergized Arab culture by engaging with other languages and societies, especially Europe. Just as some recent writers have invoked the potential of the Nahda as "a historical archive of the contemporary Arab intellectual," Smihi's cinema takes up this same spirit in yearning for a new Nahda that might surmount the challenges of the present.[4] In keeping with that project of transformation, *Arab Modernism as World Cinema* is concerned with questions of modernity, modernism, and their relationship to Arab cinemas in a transnational frame. Continuing the project of other scholars who have sought to account for modernism's development outside of Europe, this book makes the argument that engagement with modernity is something that occupies Smihi's cinema and Arabic cultural production not as a belated effect of European colonialism but as an extensive project of world-making in its own right.

With the title *Arab Modernism as World Cinema*, then, I make a claim that is methodological as well as analytical. As a form, Arab modernism has been associated more with literature and art than with cinema.[5] Extending our view of Arab modernism beyond the literary and visual arts while not relinquishing its affiliations with them allows me to underscore the contribution that cinema has played in shaping Arab cultural expression, and to call for an exchange between disciplinary fields such as area studies, comparative literature studies, art history, and film studies, all of which have been critical to this project.[6] I also mean the title to argue that Arab cinematic modernism—its histories, its films, its perspectives—should be an integral part of discussions of world cinema rather than remaining marginal to it, as it has to date. While I concur with Lúcia Nagib that "a positive definition of world cinema" should allow us to take seriously all films from all places, no matter their genre, mode of production, or form, I also want to affirm a more specific relation of Arab cinematic modernism to the world.[7] I argue here that Smihi's films, like some others that I compare them to below, actually express their "worldly" aspirations as a problematic of content and form. That is, they consciously insert themselves into the world in their narrative concerns and they participate in an aesthetic that is worldly, embodying what Dudley Andrew calls a "cross-pollination that bypasses national directives."[8]

To claim that Smihi's work is part of an Arab modernism is not to create a new pan-Arab national identity, and by using the term throughout this book, I do not mean to suggest that there is a singular Arab cinematic modernism that might unify all textual expressions, no matter their provenance. That understanding is especially important with respect to the Maghrib and Morocco, which are not exclusively Arab in language or ethnicity.[9] As I will show, these films are deeply attentive to practices, languages, and cultural histories that reflect the heterogeneity of the Maghrib. What I do mean to show, however, is how Smihi's inflection of modernist cinematic practice has affiliations not only with the modernism of his Moroccan peers, grounded as they have been in the popular practices of the country, but also with the wider experiments with modernism that continue to transform other Arab cultural expressions.

Consequently, this book offers more than just a critical study of Moumen Smihi's cinema. Rather, in using his work as a kind of lever, it begins the project of "worlding" Arab cinema and wresting it from the dominant critical and theoretical frames in which it finds itself in English- and French-language scholarship: typically siloed into author or single-film studies, national cinema approaches, or accounts that privilege political narratives over all else. It moves beyond the established geopolitical axes that would restrict Moroccan cinema to the postcolonial legacies of colonial histories. This book will demonstrate that Smihi's films exceed the limits of such frames and, further, that they enable us to see how Arab cultural expression should be taken up as integral, not marginal, to theories and histories of modernism and modernity.

MOUMEN SMIHI

"I was born in Tangier. My whole life deals with this city, with the residues and effects that it left in me."[10]

Moumen Smihi was born in 1945 in Tangier, the storied city in the north of Morocco that was, at that time, still an international zone governed by a host of foreign powers. Tangier's special status was due to its historical importance as a port city and center for Mediterranean trade and for its strategic importance in the governance of the north of Morocco. Just kilometers from Spain, it had been under Roman, Byzantine, Umayyad, Portuguese, British, and Moroccan control, and it was subject to debates between the major colonial powers of Britain, France, and Spain even as France gained control of much of the country after the signing of the Treaty of Fez in 1912. Tangier's international status was affirmed in a 1923 treaty that allowed for nominal governance by the Moroccan sultan within an international administration; Spain continued to have control over other parts of northern Morocco.[11] After Moroccan independence in 1956, Tangier was slowly integrated into the postindependence state.

Smihi grew up in a corner of the medina (the old city) that was also home to the US diplomatic mission, the Tangier Legation. The Legation occupied a building gifted to the United States by Sultan Moulay Slimane in 1821; the building then became the US consulate and now houses the Tangier American Legation Institute of Moroccan Studies (TALIM). Smihi's family lived in this neighborhood until he was seventeen, then moved to the *ville nouvelle*, the city built by the French around the medina that has since expanded outward into the surrounding hills.[12] Smihi's father was a *fqih*, a religious man who had a particular role within Moroccan Islam. Not a priest, he presided over legal matters for the community and so was learned in Islamic jurisprudence (much like the character of the father in Smihi's

2013 film *The Sorrows of a Young Tangerian*). Smihi grew up speaking *darija*, or Moroccan Arabic, as his first language, but learned modern standard Arabic and French at primary school and at the *lycée français*, or French school.[13]

As Smihi describes it, he was shaped by both the Arab and international popular culture of Tangier and by the philosophical tradition taught to him at the *lycée*. At approximately twelve years of age he discovered the Arabic popular press that was distributed around the region, and available in the little café and adjacent bookstore on the Zocco Chico, a few steps from his house. Many things captured his interest as an adolescent. The monthly magazine *Kitabi* (My Book) translated and reviewed international literature; it could include Henri Rousseau's *Confessions* (1782–89) one month, Maxim Gorky in another, or even an Arabic translation of Alfred Kinsey's *Sexual Behavior* (1948). Smihi also read Taha Hussein's autobiography, *The Days* (al-Ayyam, 1929), which set the stage for his deep appreciation of Hussein as a critic, scholar, and educator.[14] At the *lycée* he was deeply influenced by his French teachers, many of whom were Sartrean progressives, supportive of Moroccan and Arab nationalism and independence. Through them, Smihi developed an appreciation for modern literature and European Enlightenment philosophy and was exposed to thinkers who would prove pivotal to him such as Jean-Paul Sartre, Henri Rousseau, Voltaire, and Sigmund Freud.

The atmosphere engendered by his teachers at the *lycée* also extended into cinema, where some of them led a *ciné club* at the Roxy cinema in the *ville nouvelle* (now the venue for the annual Moroccan National Film Festival). His first encounter with films by Federico Fellini, Kenji Mizoguchi, and Jean Renoir constituted "the beginning of cinephilia and the beginning of [his] consciousness of the movie as a new art."[15] Outside the *ciné club*, Smihi had access to even more films, including the Egyptian movies that were everywhere in the Arab world. Sneaking out of the house without his parents' knowledge (like the young Mohammed Larbi of his film *A Muslim Childhood* [2005]), Smihi would see films at the many theaters that surrounded the medina: Egyptian films at the Ciné Vox; Spanish-language films, including Luis Buñuel's, at the Cine Cervantes; and US films dubbed in French by directors like John Ford, Howard Hawks, and Charlie Chaplin at the Alcazar, right next to a medina gate. For his family and others in the area, these films were sacrilegious, with the Egyptian films featuring actresses like Shadia, Faten Hamama, and Leila Mourad, who smoked and drank and did not wear veils. Those who attended the films were similarly stigmatized. Smihi, who was captivated by these works and their challenge to local mores, was not the only one to be inspired by what cinema offered; some local Moroccan women attended the screenings unveiled, too, struck like he was by the possibilities they afforded for self-fashioning.[16] Tangier's films and theaters thus constituted a domain of Arab life and experience that proved important to his work, especially his trilogy of semiautobiographical films: *A Muslim Childhood*, *Girls and Swallows* (2008), and *The Sorrows of a Young Tangerian*.[17]

Smihi's cinephilia was furthered in the politicized environment he found in Rabat, Morocco's capital, where he attended Mohammed V University for a year in 1963–64. There he saw François Truffaut's *Jules and Jim* (Jules et Jim, 1962) and rejoiced in its *nouvelle vague* qualities. He saw his first Sergei Eisenstein film, *Battleship Potemkin* (1925), and appreciated its revolutionary sentiments in an environment where the rule of Hassan II (1962–99) involved severe repression for Moroccans (a period popularly known as *les années de plomb*, or "the years of lead," in which political dissent was forcefully policed and extinguished). In the university environment, Mehdi Ben Barka's Marxist UNFP (Union Nationale des Forces Populaires, or National Union of Popular Forces) was popular among students who rejected Hassan II's rule. Smihi, like many others, dreamed of leaving, "and the country of the dream was the country of my professors, the French professors, especially since they were telling us how French intellectuals like Jean-Paul Sartre were defending the Arab nation!"[18] He pursued scholarship opportunities in France, hoping to study poetry and literature at the Sorbonne. But what he found instead was a scholarship to L'institut des hautes études cinématographiques (IDHEC), already by the 1960s the favored destination for a generation of postcolonial African filmmakers. Several Moroccans preceded him there: Mohamed Afifi, who graduated in 1957, was the first, followed by others who became important figures in Moroccan cinema: Mohamed Abderrahman Tazi, Ahmed Bouanani, Abdelmajid Rechiche, Mohammed Seqqat, and Abdallah Rélili.

Arriving in Paris, Smihi took up residence at one of the *cités universitaires*, the college halls of residence that were organized by nationality. In the Moroccan hall, he was back in the Marxist revolutionary context that he had encountered in Rabat. But he navigated several other spaces critical to his development as an artist: IDHEC, where he trained; Paris itself, with its storied environments like the Café les deux magots, the Latin quarter, and the Sorbonne; and L'École pratique des hautes études, where he first encountered the work of Roland Barthes, whose writing has remained, like Taha Hussein's, critical to his work. He took advantage of free seminars, open to the public, offered by thinkers like Jacques Lacan, Michel Foucault, and Claude Lévi-Strauss. Further extending this para-education was the Cinémathèque française, then under the direction of its founder, Henri Langlois. Smihi increasingly found the environment of IDHEC too technically oriented at the expense of ideas, and frustratingly conservative, even racist, after the enlivening experience of his leftist teachers at the *lycée* and the radical ideas of Lacan, Barthes, and others. Indeed, he appreciated the irony of receiving a French education from French leftists in the former French colony of Morocco, only to encounter a more conservative education in the metropolitan center.

Yet his IDHEC enrollment gave him a free pass to the Cinémathèque française, which he used daily, even as his IDHEC attendance fell away. What is more, his growing passion for cinema outstripped his interest in political action fostered in the *cité universitaire*. "You know, when I left the campus the students were having revolutionary meetings—'Down with Hassan II! Long live the revolution!'—and when I came back at midnight they were still having their political meetings, but I had seen five films!"[19] Smihi thus came to feel that his métier was to be found in a revolutionary approach to cinema rather than in the Communist Party. Selling Moroccan Communist newspapers to immigrant Moroccans in the suburbs of Paris, for example, Smihi was also scouting locations for his first post-IDHEC film, *Si Moh, the Unlucky Man* (1971). Despite his resistance to political party membership, however, Smihi understood the importance of the 1968 uprisings in Paris and, like his teachers Barthes and Lacan, saw the unrest as the concretization of much of the theory he was learning. For him, Barthes's radical rewriting of textuality and ideology and Lacan's theories of the unconscious converged in the streets of Paris with actions in which he, too, took part.

Paris, then, shaped Smihi as a young filmmaker experimenting with form and extraordinarily open to influences from a range of sources while beholden to no particular political or artistic camp. His resistance to dogma and his stubborn individualism has meant that he has remained on the margins of Moroccan political movements, preferring to adopt the role of a critical intellectual. This degree of independence is borne out not only in the complexity and precision of his films but also in the precarity of their funding and distribution. Since the beginning of his career, Smihi has demonstrated an affinity for marginal modes of production that allow him to pursue projects independently even at the cost of a lack of financial success. At the end of his IDHEC studies, Smihi made *Si Moh* as part of the GREC (Groupe de recherches et d'essais cinématographiques, or Research and Cinema Experimentation Group). Created by Pierre Braunberger, Anatole Dauman, and Jean Rouch, GREC produced noncommercial films with funding from the Centre national du cinéma (CNC). Functioning in parallel to the CNC, it operated without a commercial budget and distributed its films only through universities and festivals. After *Si Moh*, Smihi made a second short film, *Colors on Bodies* (1972), about the painter and educator Arno Stern, a Holocaust survivor who set up a painting workshop for children in Paris. And while Smihi found employment working as an assistant producer and assistant director for ORTF (Office de Radiodiffusion-Télévision Française, the French public television station, now TF1), he feared he would become stuck there, salaried but in a job without creative potential. Spurred on by some of those involved in GREC, notably Braunberger and Dauman, he returned to Morocco to begin work on his first feature, *The East Wind* (1975).[20]

In Tangier, Smihi succeeded in getting funds for his first feature, cobbled together, as many of his budgets were, from a variety of sources, including two friends. Mohamed Torres, a few years older than Smihi, was from a prominent nationalist family in the neighboring city of Tetouan and had studied in Tangier and the United States. During the 1970s he was committed to trying to support a new Moroccan cinema. Mohamed Tazi (not to be confused with Moroccan filmmakers Mohamed Abderrahman Tazi or Mohammed B. A. Tazi) was, like Smihi, from Tangier although they did not know each other until they both ended up at the Moroccan house in the *cité universitaire* in Paris (Tazi was studying psychology).[21] The two men gave him a small sum of money, around 4 million centimes, "just enough to buy 16mm film and sandwiches for five weeks' shooting here in Tangier."[22] The remaining support came in the form of a crew whose wages were paid by the Centre cinématographique marocain (CCM, the Moroccan National Cinema Center). The actors were unpaid, including Leila Shenna, the lead actress. The film's total budget was only 50 million centimes [approximately US$100,000]. Thus began production on a film whose success on screens in Paris (it played for seventeen weeks there) signaled Smihi as one of the important figures in a circuit of North African filmmakers who became recognized as practitioners of a "New Arab Cinema." Yet film's success in France, and the critical reputation it garnered, was not reflected in Moroccan distribution. There it suffered the same fate as so many other Moroccan films (such as *Traces* [Wechma, dir. Hamid Benani, 1970], or later *Mirage* [al-Sarab, dir. Ahmed Bouanani, 1980]), and did not play in commercial theaters.[23] Nor was *Si Moh*, his earlier film, exhibited in Morocco. Indeed, forty years would pass before that film was programmed in the Mediterranean Short Film Festival in Tangier in 2013.

Smihi's emergence as a filmmaker must therefore be traced as an exploration of both theory and practice in an environment that stretched from Tangier to Paris and back. His training at IDHEC certainly gave him the proficiency with the medium that he was to exploit so experimentally in *Si Moh* and *The East Wind*, but the films' radical energy is more attributable to the formative environment of the Cinémathèque française and to the intellectual journey begun at the *lycée* in Tangier and continued through the seminars at l'École pratique des hautes études. Deeply engaged with structuralist theories of film and culture, and attracted since his youth to poetry and writing of all kinds, Smihi developed critical writing as an activity interposed between productions that could be years in the making.[24] During the IDHEC years, he was intrigued by the *nouvelle vague* directors like Truffaut, Jean-Luc Godard, Jacques Rivette, or Éric Rohmer, all of whom had begun their careers as writers and critics, and his circle at the Barthes seminars included Serge Daney and Serge Toubiana, who published in *Cahiers du cinéma*. Smihi began writing in French while in Paris, but upon his return to Morocco he wrote in Arabic for outlets like *al-'Alam* (The World) and *al-Itihad* (The Union), two of the more widely read leftist newspapers. Intellectually speaking, many of these articles were attempts to mediate between the West and the Arab world, following in the footsteps of his intellectual hero, Taha Hussein. In so doing, he courted controversy from those on the left who felt that to write on US or European filmmakers was to defend the imperialists. Others, he recalls, were suspicious of his writing on Freud and Lacan—Freud for his Judaism and Lacan for his intellectualism. Recalling his response to such criticisms, Smihi recounts that he invoked the rhetoric of a Gulliver returned from his travels: "Yes, it's imperialist . . . but there are fantastic directors called Josef von Sternberg and Erich von Stroheim and Charlie Chaplin and Howard Hawks and Fritz Lang and . . . and . . . you must see their films, it's fantastic, it's a new world!"[25]

While quick to characterize somewhat comically the encounters provoked by his writings, Smihi nonetheless refers to a real problem, one that Taha Hussein also suffered. Smihi's intervention into the critical domain of Morocco and the Arab world was significant for its attempt to formulate *in Arabic* concepts that had been previously articulated in other languages. The engagement with modernity pursued by Hussein and other Nahda intellectuals, however, often took shape in dialogue with and through the translations of texts and ideas that were circulating in the West (as well as other locations, like Russia and India).[26] The degree to which that engagement signified either a colonial dependency or the revitalization of culture through intellectual traffic and exchange was often debated; indeed, it underpins even contemporary debates on religion, secularism, gender, and sexuality, among other domains. For Smihi, however, the stakes were always clear: just as his personal trajectory had involved him in the Parisian debates, his writing was enthusiastically open to films and ideas from beyond the Arab world. Moreover, like the Nahda modernists, he sees that openness as an important intellectual position for reestablishing the worldliness and relevance of Arab culture and ideas, but only to the extent that the debates and explorations take place in Arabic, not simply in the imported language of the colonizers.

The point of translation and of openness to the foreign is the possibility that new ideas will enrich a cultural domain and even regenerate understandings of other Arabic-language interventions and traditions. The Syrian writer Adonis, for example, discussing the same issue in *Introduction to Arab Poetics* (1990), has argued that it is important to move beyond "a dependency on the European-American West, to compensate for the failure to invent and innovate by intellectual and technical adaptation and borrowing." Adonis asserts that borrowing and adaptation are productive and should not be dismissed; indeed, they might enable (as they did for him) a reassessment of traditions within Arab thought and poetics itself. Reading Charles Baudelaire, he confides, allowed him to discover the modernity of eighth- and ninth-century Arab poets like Abu Nuwas or Abu Tammam.[27] Smihi, while noting the enthusiastic adoption of Sartre's work through its Arabic translations and its republication in Beirut, has argued that the interventions of French structuralism were practically unknown in the 1970s, when he began writing about them from Tangier. While Sartre, adopted by Arab nationalists for his once-supportive statements on pan-Arabism, was easily assimilated, the work of other writers like Lévi-Strauss, Lacan, and Barthes was slower to be acknowledged or adopted.[28]

Nonetheless, Smihi never avoided French as a language of theoretical or artistic work, then or now. Like many other writers in Morocco, he often turned to French as a language imported with colonialism but effectively localized and made relevant by an anti-colonial Moroccan left. Not just an administrative language, French became important to artists like Ahmed Bouanani (who wrote his poetry, fiction, and criticism in French exclusively) and the many contributors of the journal *Souffles* ("in French, literally, 'breaths,' figuratively, 'inspirations'"), who, under the editorship of Abdellatif Laâbi, published twenty-two issues in French between 1966 and 1972.[29] The continued use of French did, in fact, become an issue toward the end of the journal's life. Its reconstitution in 1971 as the Arabic-language journal *Anfas* (with the same meaning as *Souffles*) not only signaled its editor's desire to commit to Arabic as an anti-imperial language and the journal's "increasing identification with ongoing liberation struggles in the Maghreb and the Mashriq," but also precipitated its censorship as the state deemed its potential threat even greater.[30] Yet *Souffles* had earlier defended the potential for French to constitute a language of anti-colonial literature, and Laâbi had called for Maghribi writers to use any languages at their disposal while remaining skeptical of all of them.[31] Another defense of French as a language of thought in the Maghrib is that proposed by Abdelkebir Khatibi, especially in his *Maghreb Pluriel* (A Plural Maghrib, 1983) and in the essay translated into English as "Double Criticism" (1985), where he advocates the strategies of "double criticism," "thought of difference," and "thought in languages," which might use linguistic plurality to decenter the West while also transforming Arab thought from within.[32] The work of translation and of thought in languages thus became an imperative for those whose practices took shape in the complex postcolonial space of Morocco.

It is within such practices that we should place Smihi. Always an ardent advocate for the use of *darija* in his films, and for the necessity of thinking in and through Arabic, he nonetheless treats French as a language of possibility both within the Maghrib and further afield. For, as Smihi himself would point out, his essayistic interventions not only challenged the conservatism (as he saw it) of an Arab world that was scarcely familiar with psychoanalysis, structuralism, or the new waves of modernist cinema. He also wrote in French to raise these questions outside of Morocco and even in France. There, too, structuralism and semiotics were often rejected by a conservative critical and academic establishment. Smihi's desire was thus to intervene on both fronts, and in both languages.[33]

INTELLECTUAL ITINERARIES

Geographically, Smihi's trajectory in his early years followed the axis of Tangier-Paris. But even if Paris generated for him new perspectives on cinema, politics, and culture through the Cinémathèque française and the École pratique, Tangier-Paris was but one of many intellectual, political, and artistic axes that Smihi followed. The discourses that mattered to him far exceeded the familiar lines of a Franco-Maghribi postcolonial route. Taking stock of his writings and recollections of this period, it is clear that Tangier functioned for him like an antenna, pulling in signals from diverse nodes in a network that was truly global. One node was the United States: Hollywood films were a strong cultural influence that marked Smihi in Tangier. But so was literature. The city was at one time or another host to Beat writers like Allen Ginsberg, Gregory Corso, Tennessee Williams, Truman Capote, Jack Kerouac, and William S. Burroughs, and it was home for its most famous long-term American resident, Paul Bowles, and for some time to Jane Bowles also. These writers mattered to Smihi, particularly Paul Bowles, with whom he developed an acquaintance and then a working relationship (Bowles introduced Smihi to Gavin Lambert, the writer, with whom he wrote the screenplay for his film *Caftan of Love* [1989], based on Bowles's translation of Mohammed Mrabet's story *The Big Mirror* [1977]).

Their countercultural spirit made a deep impression on Smihi as a youth: "My generation of Arabs coming out of the colonialism period was so excited to find in these books and minds [something] to enhance their thirst for anti-conformism and liberty. Then, America and her writers and intellectuals were a model, an ideal, the hope of our future."[34] Cairo represented another broadcast node—not only for cinema, as has already been noted, but for its writers such as Taha Hussein and Naguib Mahfouz, and for the popular culture mentioned above. Beirut was another important axis because of the dissemination of texts in Arabic from its many publishing houses, the most important in the Arab world. Tangier, then, was unusually generative of and receptive to a worldliness that remains a hallmark of Smihi's thought and his cinema. Consequently, he has always avoided a narrow or dependent relationship with French thought or culture, just as he has continued to articulate the possibilities of an Arabic-speaking world that might again be, like Tangier in the 1950s, open to multiple discourses, faiths, and languages:

> For me, to all intents and purposes a Tangerian Arab, all of that [cultural difference] is not antithetical but complementary. This space of the medina in international Tangier was really cosmopolitan. The different faith communities, European, Christian, Jewish, and Muslim lived together sometimes even in the same houses. The doors of the apartments weren't closed; they remained half-open even when their occupants were absent.... What I read as an adolescent on the Arab golden age in Baghdad or Granada or Istanbul described similar cosmopolitan situations. The Arab world has always been, all the time, multi-ethnic (Berber, Kurd, black, Turk ...), multi-confessional (we forget that in North Africa almost 30 million or more Arabs are Christian), multilingual (look at the translated manuscripts of the ancient Greeks—they are in Arabic and Hebrew, on display at the Alhambra library), and multicultural (the influences that are Byzantine, Persian, and Indian have been decisive on architecture, music, the philosophy of the first empire).[35]

As I've argued elsewhere, then, Tangier operates as the privileged site for Smihi's filmmaking—as setting, as production center, and as anchor for the generative heterogeneity of discourses that his films embody.[36] Its polyglot population and dense mix of voices and languages inform the multivocal soundspace of many of his films. And the city's historical importance as a link to the rest of the Arab world and to Europe informs not only the films set in Tangier (*The East Wind*, *Caftan of Love*, *With Matisse in Tangier*, parts of *Moroccan Chronicles* [1999], *A Muslim Childhood*, *Girls and Swallows*, *The Sorrows of a Young Tangerian*) but even the few that are not (*44, or Tales of the Night*, *The Lady from Cairo* [1991], other parts of *Moroccan Chronicles*).[37] For in those films, the intensity of perspectives and the deeply intertextual nature of their form reveals the formative years of the director's youth and his perseverance in working with its legacies.

SMIHI AND THEORIES OF AUTHORSHIP

It is through these interventions within a transnational domain of cinema and culture that I will place Smihi's contributions as an auteur, surely a contested category over the past forty years of film theory. Yet, as I will show, there is much to gain by organizing a study around Smihi's work, as there is for many other Arab or North African filmmakers. Certainly, institutional factors alone make such an approach appropriate: as Roy Armes points out, the *avance sur reçettes* (an advance based on predicted ticket sales) structure of funding used by France and Morocco's state cinema agencies typically allocates funds to a director as sole author, and many Arab directors funded in this way (Smihi included) fulfill multiple roles as writers, directors, and sometimes producers of their own work.[38] Thus, even more so than in some other film industries, the role of the director in the Maghrib takes on particular significance from the earliest stages of a film. Such a structure often involves struggle, and Smihi's conditions of production have customarily been demanding due to an uncompromising vision of what he wishes to achieve: his account of the production of his film *Caftan of Love* (fig. 2), for example, is a tale of uninterested funders who wanted recognized stars and the type of story that Smihi did not wish to deliver (and this despite the cowriting credit of the well-known writer and screenwriter Gavin Lambert).[39] More generally, in terms of a corpus of work, Smihi makes a formidable figure for an author-based study since he published essays and articles in both French and Arabic, and these, together with his edited volumes of filmmakers' essays and interviews translated into Arabic, create a network of texts that extends the scope of his writing beyond the cinematic.[40]

Beyond the immediate situation of his own production, however, addressing Smihi's work enables us to complicate a discourse that has often posed a too-stark opposition between a commercial, popular Egyptian cinema (often compared to

FIGURE 2. Moumen Smihi directs Natalie Roche on the set of *Caftan of Love*, 1989.

Hollywood) and smaller, national cinemas on an art cinema model (such as Tunisian or Palestinian). Such an opposition too readily relies on a Hollywood-versus-art binary while ignoring the diversity and differential currents within Egyptian cinema, just as it forecloses the possibilities for those inhabiting the "non-Egyptian" model ever to aspire to the status of popular cinema. Thinking critically through the situation of the Arab cinema auteur dispels any notion of the supposed homogeneity of Egyptian cinema, in which system directors like Salah Abu Seif or Shadi Abdel Salam made quite specific aesthetic interventions. Equally, addressing Smihi's work renders more complex our understanding of the relationship between modernism and the popular in the Maghrib.

Attending to the work of a single filmmaker might seem like an unusual proposition when that filmmaker does not enjoy popular recognition and widespread distribution. Although a history of Moroccan production, distribution, or exhibition is not my project, these relations—which are the subject of other studies—all affect the degree to which a filmmaker like Smihi is known internationally.[41] Beyond the difficult circumstances of production that have historically afflicted Moroccan filmmakers lurk even greater obstacles in the domain of distribution and exhibition. Despite all its critical acclaim in France, for example, *The East Wind* was never distributed in Morocco, and the same fate befell most of Smihi's later films. Reading Moroccan film and culture magazines from the 1970s on, one finds a steady stream of criticism of the egregious situation by which Moroccan films were routinely ignored by distributors who were more interested in screening US, Egyptian, or Hindi cinema, assuming that a film like *The East Wind* would never find an audience because it was shot in black and white. Bouanani notes, for example, that of the eight Moroccan films produced between 1970 and 1976 (including *The East Wind*), only Souheil Ben-Barka's *1001 Hands* (Les mille et une mains, 1972) received a Moroccan release.[42] Internationally, Smihi's films have had success at festivals, including Toulon (where *The East Wind* won the grand prize, the international critics' prize, and the *cinéma d'art et d'essai* experimental prize), Venice (where *44, or Tales of the Night* won the Venezia Genti prize for best feature film), Alexandria (a best actress award for Yousra in *The Lady from Cairo*), Berlin, Taormina, Valencia, Pesaro, Paris, and, more recently, the United States (the Arab Film Festival in San Francisco and the Arabian Sights Film Festival in Washington, DC). None of that, however, has been enough to ensure US or broader European distribution, although films like *Moroccan Chronicles* and *44, or Tales of the Night* did enjoy theatrical runs in France.

Turning to film criticism and scholarship, Smihi is hardly a well-known figure in the Anglophone domain, either; the present work is the first book-length study of the director, and there is little else written in English on his work.[43] But we would be sorely mistaken to treat that absence as an evaluative measure of his significance. The list of film cultures, films, and filmmakers that have been excluded from English-language criticism over the decades is long. Euro-American film studies, especially those written in English, have only gradually made up for lack of attention to cinemas from Asia, Africa, Latin America, and the Middle East, and even as work on these regions has begun to appear, enormous numbers of films and filmmakers remain unknown to Anglophone scholars and their readers. Smihi's visibility is considerably better in French-language criticism. His films have reliably been reviewed in French journals, especially in the 1970s and 1980s as his and others' work emerged as a new postcolonial Maghribi cinema. Interviews and essays feature across this period, too, and continue into the present.[44] In Arabic, too, he is the subject of essays and reviews, especially in Morocco in recent years.[45]

To a large extent, of course, many of these issues of visibility and circulation are bound up together: a filmmaker's visibility to Anglophone readers and viewers depends on the films' distribution and exhibition, including someone having the means to prepare subtitles and strike new prints. DVD or Blu-ray releases depend on the accessibility or restoration of film material, too, and are based on market decisions that likewise turn on existing reputation and recognition. My own ability to write about these films depended on, first, being proximate to a film festival (the San Francisco Arab Film Festival), and then on the institutional support that has allowed multiple research trips to Morocco and Paris. My decision to curate a retrospective touring program of the work was an attempt to put these films into further conversation and make them more available for audiences and scholars.[46]

Smihi's situation is by no means unique; the list of Moroccan and Arab filmmakers who are not well known in the West is long. There is precious little work, for example, on Smihi's peers and compatriots like Ahmed Bouanani, Mustapha Derkaoui, or Souheil Ben-Barka despite their important role in Moroccan film culture, nor on filmmakers of their generation further afield, like Mohamed Zinet in Algeria, Sadok Ben Aïcha in Tunisia, Tawfik Saleh in Egypt, or Khalid al-Siddiq in Kuwait. Bouanani's work has now become better known (though the films are still not in distribution) thanks to the efforts of his daughter, Touda, and the other curators and translators who have championed him. Derkaoui's landmark film *About Some Meaningless Events* (De quelques événements sans signification, 1974) remained, like the rest of his work, obscure until the intervention of curator and critic Léa Morin, who supervised its recent restoration; both Derkaoui's and Bouanani's films have since screened at the Berlinale. With the infrastructures around Moroccan cinema so historically weak (with respect to production, distribution, and exhibition) and simultaneously so rigid (with respect to what is approved for production or exhibition), it is up to these "cinematic friendships," as Laura U. Marks has termed them—the loose networks formed by filmmakers, curators and programmers, arts organizations, and researchers—to provide us with alternative visions to supplement the work that is more accessible in the West.[47] Even as important recent books by Marks, Nezar Andary and Samirah Alkassim, Suzanne Gauch, Kay Dickinson, and others have brought to light filmmakers whose work has languished in obscurity, there is no shortage of others of whom Western and especially Anglophone viewers and readers are barely aware.

One of my intentions in writing this book, then, is to reveal the aesthetic and cultural significance of Smihi's films, overlooked as much within Morocco as in the English-speaking world because of the obstacles cited here. Yet this study will offer more than a deep familiarity with Smihi alone by situating the question of authorship in a wider frame. Even as I take a single filmmaker for my focus, I resist reading Smihi's films in terms of a triumph of authorial creativity, marshaled over successive films, that should only be understood unto itself. Certainly I will attend to questions of style and aesthetics, since Smihi's films are remarkable in their varied use of cinematic languages. But at every turn I will try to convey that the importance of these films exceeds the bounds of Smihi's own creative and intellectual energies, keen as those certainly are.

In addressing such questions of language and authorship, I follow some of the more insightful and complex approaches to authorship in film scholarship. Tom Gunning's colossal book on Fritz Lang, *The Films of Fritz Lang: Allegories of Vision and Modernity* (2000), confronts the conundrum of authorship by noting that, in many respects, the field of academic film studies prematurely or preemptively adopted the dictum of Barthes's "death of the author" without fully thinking through the complexities of authorship and signification in relation to histories of cinema and with respect to discrete iterations of cinematic language, film by film. For Gunning, it is axiomatic that a contemporary study of the corpus of a single director will not seek to tie meaning too closely to authorial consciousness or biography; rather, following Barthes, Gunning signals that where authorship might yet be explored is in the ambiguous space where the author as a controlling figure behind the text disappears, to be replaced with language, signification, and the possibility of meaning and writing. Seeking to enlarge the prospects for an author-based study, Gunning writes: "The possibility of a modern author dedicated not to self-expression but to the play of discourse, particularly relevant in a medium like film where the 'auteur' rarely speaks directly in 'his own voice,' but rather indirectly through sounds and images assembled, performed and in some ways produced by collaborators, remains largely unexplored."[48]

Gunning, then, sees authorship in the post-Barthesian context as an encounter with language. Just as the literary author engages language and its multiplicities of signification, so does cinema authorship involve "an encounter with the language of cinema." In fact, authorship may reveal itself not through evidence of the creative hand of an individual but rather as the traces of that very struggle with language, staged from a position both inside and outside the film: "I would claim a director has to struggle to assert authorship, both in the making of the film and in the discourses surrounding it. An authored film shows the signs of this struggle, a struggle by which the author may discover (and reveal to the viewer) something other than her personality or individual 'history, tastes and passions.'"[49] For Gunning, Lang offers a rich terrain for such a study given his lengthy career and the number of texts (written and visual) that he left behind. Rather than treat him as an author whose creative individuality, preceding the text, is reflected in it, Gunning offers that the complexity and contradiction of cinematic language in the films offers evidence of the way that Lang's authorship is in itself the product of a creative struggle with and, crucially, within language: "The search for the author takes place in a labyrinth in which at times even the film director himself has lost his way."[50] The job of the critic, then, is to uncover something of that struggle while understanding its implications for cinema more broadly.

Smihi offers a compelling case for Gunning's revision of authorship in terms of a struggle with language. Smihi's own "encounter with the language of cinema" is one that, like Gunning's, has taken shape in dialogue with the work of Roland Barthes. Smihi's conscious embrace of intertextuality and his love for cinematic languages that, as he willingly admits, escape his own grasp is part of the intriguing promise of his work. When considered together, his films—as do Lang's for Gunning—offer the traces of a filmmaker whose preoccupations and stylistic interventions can only be considered in relation to the complexity of languages (visual, aural, musical) that his films also produce—complexities that render compromised or contingent whatever authorial intentions he might have entertained in the making of the film or in the dialogues that follow its appearance.

SMIHI, NATIONAL CINEMA, WORLD CINEMA

> *"Some of us want to create an Arab cinema that could be integrated in the entire history of cinema."*[51]

Working across the field of authorship, then, can also help create new understandings of Arab and North African cinema beyond the too-restrictive treatment of discrete national cinemas and the search for authentic postcolonial national forms. Many critical accounts in English of Arab cinemas continue to take the national as their theoretical frame, and even discussions of individual directors tend to place them still within a national context. Smihi's work can help us think through cinematic relationships that in reality escape the national and can be more fully located within the scope of the regional and the global. For this reason, just as I will work skeptically with ideas of authorship, I will also avoid reading and accounting for Smihi's films primarily in relation to something called "Moroccan cinema." If a relatively uninflected auteurism has been one prominent approach to Anglophone criticism of Arab cinemas, a "national cinemas" approach has been the other. From encyclopedias to handbooks to edited collections, much critical work in English on Arab cinema tends to understand it through the lens of national cinema, however fragile or robust that cinema might be deemed. This focus is unsurprising when the foundational popular critical discourses in many countries of the Maghrib or Middle East have been those of nationalism, encompassing both the search for an authentic national expression from the ashes of the colonial experience and the nationalism born of a resistance to contemporary forms of imperialism and globalization. Yet this book pushes against the "common sense" understanding that locating Smihi within a national cinema is the best way to understand his work. As central as Morocco is to Smihi's films, we must think through the films' relationship to broader currents in Arabic-language cinema and world cinema *as well as* their imbrication in the national.

While one might be tempted to argue that contemporary Moroccan cinema—with its increased prominence on the world stage—has recently become transnational, I contend that it has always been so, even if those relations have taken diverse and sometimes unequal forms. Even a cursory account of Moroccan film history will reveal the ways that colonialism and postcolonial independence structured cinema in Morocco as a project that was never divorced from regional or global flows of capital or ideas. Morocco, like most African countries, experienced its early cinema through the historical experience of colonialism, from the actuality films shot by Lumière operator Félix Mesguich in Casablanca to the documentary films shot by

French filmmakers during the years of the protectorate (1912–56). (Some of these were repurposed by Bouanani in his essay film *Memory 14* [Mémoire 14, 1970].) The early history of feature filmmaking, structured by French colonial relationships, nonetheless engaged Morocco in a history that was at once local in the use of Moroccan locations, and global by its address to French viewers and its participation in internationally popular genres. *The Rose of the Souk* (La rose du souk, 1930), for example, directed by Jacques Séverac, was the first film to star a Moroccan (Leila Atouna). Shot in Morocco with postproduction conducted in Berlin, it was an adventure film in the tradition of Hollywood silent adventures such as *The Mark of Zorro* (1920) starring Douglas Fairbanks or *The Thief of Bagdad* (1924) also starring Fairbanks. Exhibition was transnational, too: during World War II, urban screens in Morocco were dominated by films from Egypt and Hollywood, and films expanded the sense that Moroccans had of the world. As Bouanani recounts in his unpublished history of Moroccan cinema, "La septième porte" (The Seventh Gate): "During this time of war, famine, and rationing, the screen became more than ever an open door toward an agreeable elsewhere, a world where everything appeared easy and possible. In the Egyptian musicals, social barriers didn't exist; the adventure films, the serials, the *Tarzan* and *Jungle Jim* films, and all the cape and dagger films where Errol Flynn was king, all invaded the Casablanca theaters."[52] This is the atmosphere that Mohammed Osfour, the first Moroccan to explore the medium as a director, exploited in making his first adventure film, *The Boy of the Jungle* (L'enfant de la jungle, 1941) at the age of fifteen; soon after, his favorite location in the forest at Aïn Diab, near Casablanca, was taken over by US troops in 1942.

The founding of production studios at Souissi, funded by French capital, was another notable moment in the transnational history of production in Morocco. Souissi aimed to rival Egypt's film distribution in North Africa, and the studio produced several films between 1946 and 1948; some of the technical positions there were held by Moroccans.[53] Many of the films, like *Yasmina* (dir. Jean Lordier, 1946) or *Ma'rouf the Cairo Cobbler* (Maʿarouf al-Iskafi /Maarouf, savetier du Caire, dir. Jean Mauran, 1947), had a soundtrack in Moroccan Arabic dialect with French subtitles. This was an unprecedented attempt to present Moroccan cinema in a language that could be understood by local Moroccans, with some compensation, however, for their regional market. Smihi recalls them having a "transregional dialect drawing on *fusha* [Modern Standard Arabic] when necessary." The word for a cobbler, for example, would have been *kharaz* in Fez or *zapatero* in Tangier but the film used the standard Arabic *iskafi* for wider comprehension.[54] Despite reservations about some of the productions (largely due to the mix of Arabic dialects, which he found at times confounding), Bouanani saw in the work produced at Souissi "the will to endow Morocco with a national cinema resolutely non-Occidental in its expression."[55] The two films from this period that he singles out for praise are *The Seventh Gate* (La Septième porte, 1947) and *Desert Wedding* (Noces de sable, 1948), both directed by André Zwoboda, who was French. In keeping with attempts to compete with Egypt, *The Seventh Gate* was released in an Arabic-language version as well as in a French version. *Desert Wedding* eschewed dialogue but used a French voice-over, narrated by Jean Cocteau. Smihi regards Zwoboda's films as "small masterpieces that I would consider to be Moroccan and Arab," and the French film critic Pierre Boulanger praised *The Seventh Gate* (which was based on an Arabic story) for its realist view of Morocco mixed with a supernaturalism drawn from the Arabic story material.[56] Both films, argues the critic Insaf Ouhiba, "inscribe themselves in a cultural universe that is Arab and especially Moroccan... in that they break with the colonial discourse of the pre-war period." In *Desert Wedding*, "the European is completely evacuated from the image and is only present through the voice of the narrator, that of Jean Cocteau. Zwoboda thus inaugurates a new and original vision of the Orient and speaks his opposition to colonial domination."[57] The history of Souissi studios thus indicates the degree to which production in Morocco took shape out of the economic channels of French colonialism but was at the same time inflected by local realities along with Egyptian and US influences.

Smihi himself is profoundly aware of this history, as his essay "Mythologies Arabes" (Arab Mythologies) makes clear. As well as his assessment of the Souissi films and the history of production in Morocco, he writes of his early experiences of film exhibition and patronage in Morocco and the strong feeling that the cinema that came from Egypt *was* his cinema. Egyptian cinema offered, he writes, an

> image of the self, of "my" Arab society, even if the dialect was a bit strange. But it wasn't a radical strangeness. Egyptian was only as strange to us as the dialects of Fez or Marrakesh, with which we'd had no relationship during the colonial period. But the world of Egyptian cinema was the Arab world that was mine, certainly by language, by clothing, by architecture, by psychology, by the structure of the family (with polygamous characters). The genres of the Egyptian film intersected entirely with the culture, in the larger sense of the term, of Moroccan society.[58]

Indeed, earlier in the same essay (which suggests that the history of the reception of Arabic literature might offer parallels for the establishment of an Arabic film studies), Smihi offers that as a child from an educated family reading Arabic literature, there was no sense of national belonging ascribed to any of the books: "I didn't learn till much later the place of birth or the nationality of writers like [Abu al-'Ala'] al-Ma'arri or Iliya Abu Madi or Salama Musa: I didn't know if they were Syrian or Iraqi or Egyptian. They were points of reference, facts in the history of *Arab* literature."[59] Never a devout pan-Arab nationalist, Smihi nonetheless indicates here that the histories of cinema and circulation in the Arab world mean that one should consider the relationships between films and place through a lens larger than the national.

Of course, such an argument is necessitated more by the films themselves than by anything Smihi might say or write about them. Their images, stories, and sounds demand that we place Smihi's films in a context wider than that of Moroccan cinema alone, and that we consider this Moroccan filmmaker's work in relation to a bigger world. To identify and address the presence of Egyptian films and star images in a film like *A Muslim Childhood*, for example, not only provides insight into the contemporary environment of Tangier that Smihi's film depicts, but allows us a potentially better understanding, too, of Egyptian cinema's role in the world and how it has inflected popular culture across Arabic-speaking countries. To consider the relationship between France and Morocco as it is constructed in Smihi's *The Sorrows of a Young Tangerian* offers an opportunity to assess the intellectual legacies of France as they entwine with Arab nationalism and other political projects in the Maghrib.

In this way, Smihi's oeuvre is a lever with which to productively address a wealth of issues that escape the domain of the national. While these issues could be enumerated as discrete questions (addressing, for instance, the relationship between different sources of film funding within Europe and the Middle East and North Africa; the relationship between so-called national cinemas and other cinemas of the region and beyond; the aesthetic models and influences, both filmic and non-filmic, on cinemas of the region; or the relationship between imperial and local discourses in the colonial and postcolonial periods), they are in fact better formulated as a problematic that will occupy every section of this book. That is, *Arab Modernism as World Cinema* demonstrates that Smihi's cinematic modernism is vernacular in its local roots, Arab in its genealogy, and worldly in its aspirations. Smihi's films demand a role in a world they wish to reconfigure in the wake of colonialism's destructive force. Insisting on the possibilities for cinema to make other, new, heterogeneous worlds, Karl Schoonover and Rosalind Galt propose that we not give up on that promise even as we remain vigilant about globalizing discourses and histories.[60] Smihi himself remains close to such concerns, as when, speaking of the "double culture" that he experienced as a Moroccan living in Paris, he wrote that "it is up to us, too—the others, the non-European societies—to invent the future. Another future, perhaps."[61] In this way, he is attentive to the role that his own cinema and Arab cinema more generally might play in the creation of new possibilities, new futures, new worlds.

Smihi's cinema and writing both reflect and help constitute that radical project of cultural transformation by which Arab intellectuals and artists have sought to shape their contemporary world—the project of a new Nahda. The active role of Arab artists and intellectuals in forging local modernist trajectories still needs to be better accounted for and understood. In Morocco, for example, the 1960s and 1970s witnessed a small but vibrant literary and artistic movement that sought new modes of expression and affiliations. Moroccan painters, filmmakers, and writers experimented with vernacular forms and international avant-garde practices which they theorized in pursuit of a postcolonial modernity that was neither nationally insular nor beholden to Europe. Films like *Return to Agadir* (Retour à Agadir, dir. Mohamed Afifi, 1967), *6 and 12* (6 et 12, dir. Ahmed Bouanani, 1968), or *The Forest* (La forêt, dir. Abdelmajid Rechiche, 1970) were radical in their blending of, for example, Vertovian montage, US bebop, and Moroccan popular culture. Important work in the visual arts by Mohamed Melehi, Mohamed Chebaa, and Ahmed Cherkaoui; in letters and criticism by writers like Abdellatif Laâbi and Toni Maraini; and in the fields of sociology and philosophy by writers like Abdelkebir Khatibi and Abdallah Laroui, to name but a few, testified to the ways in which modernism was a project articulated in the Maghrib in its own terms. Journals like *Souffles*, *Anfas*, and *Intégral* were sites where debates about the politics and poetics of modernism were vigorously discussed. Similar movements could be traced in Egypt with the work of writers like Taha Hussein, who actively tried to translate his writings on literature, culture, education, and modernity into public policy. In Syria, Saʿadallah Wannous and Adonis experimented across theater and poetry, and filmmakers like Mohammad Malas and Omar Amiralay pushed the bounds of cinematic expression in dialogue with their European training but also in creatively distinct modes of visuality. These artists and thinkers rejected Western dependency just as seriously as they engaged local concerns, but their work was always in dialogue with movements and expressions across the Arab world *and* with Western ideas.

SMIHI, THE NAHDA, AND ARAB MODERNITY

For Smihi's films, this legacy is omnipresent. Indeed, his work constitutes part of the Arab world's long history of thought and critique stretching from the pre-Islamic period to the present day. While Smihi draws on thinkers like the tenth- and eleventh-century polymath Ibn al-Haytham and poet Abu al-ʿAlaʾ al-Maʿarri, the twelfth-century philosopher Ibn Rushd, and others from the Islamic "golden age," many of his intellectual affinities can be found in the period of the Nahda.[62] Some accounts of the Nahda tend to re-center Europe in its history, even implicitly tying its beginnings to Napoleon's arrival in Egypt.[63] Instead, I argue that a genealogy that sees Europe behind the Nahda's interventions effaces the agency of Arab intellectuals in their commitment to liberal thought, as they range far and wide in their thinking and influences. Take, for example, Ahmad Faris al-Shidyaq, the brilliant nineteenth-century writer whose controversial 1855 text *Leg over Leg* (al-Saq ʿala l-saq fi ma huwa al-Fariyaq) was foundational for the Nahda and has recently been published in English for the first time.[64] In her foreword to its English translation, Rebecca C. Johnson calls *Leg over Leg* "an inaugural text of Arab modernity. It is also among the most controversial: generically impossible to characterize, it is a critical, self-referential, learned, and irreverent book of observations on the lives and manners of 'The Arabs and their Non-Arab Peers' that includes scathing attacks on authority, both ecclesiastical and worldly, as well as liberal and libertine discussions of relations between the sexes." To what should we attribute al-Shidyaq's iconoclastic thought? Not, argues Johnson, to the "importation" of ideas from the West, but rather through engagement *with* ideas in Europe, *from* the site of Lebanon and *in* Arabic.[65] Similarly, in his own discussion of al-Shidyaq, the historian Fawwaz Traboulsi rejects what he calls the "spark theory" that sees Napoleon's invasion as the instigator of a process of political and cultural reform that led inevitably to the work of a writer like al-Shidyaq.[66] Traboulsi's treatment of al-Shidyaq reveals a *Nahdawi* (Nahda proponent) who was concerned to create a specifically Arab modernity through his engagement with other ideas and his deep respect for Arab language, history, and thought. By deepening our comparative inquiries, we can, in the words of Tarek El-Ariss, begin to see Arab modernity as it takes place "in *between* and *beside* East and West."[67]

Perspectives such as these should allow us a less narrow view of the encounters with Europe that were indeed part of the Nahda legacy, such as those of Rifaʿa Rafiʿ al-Tahtawi. One of the interventions of Muhammad ʿAli Pasha, the Ottoman ruler of Egypt during whose reign the Nahda flourished, was to engage further with European scientific and educational practices, for which purpose he sent delegations to Italy and France beginning in 1809. Al-Tahtawi, who was head of the student mission that set out to France in 1826, recorded his impressions for his governor in diary entries that were first published in Arabic and have been collected and translated into English as *An Imam in Paris*.[68] The significance of al-Tahtawi's writing is its particular conceptualization of the relationship between France, the object of his curiosity, and Egypt, the country and culture that he knew and from which he traveled. In France, al-Tahtawi encountered a civilization whose political and technological progress he felt to be greater than Egypt's. His aim, tied closely to the wishes of his patron, Muhammad ʿAli, was to account for that progress through observation, description, and eventually by the incorporation of what he learned into the Egyptian setting. His account ranges across a wide spectrum of emotions, feelings, and opinions, but they are characterized neither by a sense of inferiority nor by a judgmental rejection of the foreign. Al-Tahtawi understands Europe's differences as the product of political organization and practices that France developed through revolution and change. Egypt had not experienced such transformations under Ottoman rule and it was thus politics and custom that accounted for what he saw, not intrinsic cultural, religious, or ideological difference. As Elizabeth Suzanne Kassab argues, al-Tahtawi understood that "European civilization is not totally foreign to Muslims because it is based on Islamic sciences imported into Europe in the Middle Ages, and that the achievements to be learned from were the product of human effort and not the product of Christianity per se."[69]

Here, then, is a sentiment that was common to many proponents of the Nahda: that it was possible for the Arab world to learn from Europe at that particular historical moment while recognizing that Europe had earlier benefited from such exchanges flowing in the opposite direction. History would show that societies transform themselves through contact with other ideas, whichever way the vector of influence might be drawn. This belief underpinned many reformers' views that to become modern again was not tantamount to becoming Westernized. Indeed, as the historian Joel Beinin has pointed out, it would be a mistake to study the intellectual history of the Arab world in search of simplistic oppositions between what is imported and what is indigenous. "One of the defining problematics in the intellectual history of the modern Middle East," writes Beinin, "is whether new ideas and related institutions come from the West or whether they were indigenously produced. But this is a false binary. The Middle East has always already been engaged with Europe through webs of commerce, culture, religion, and empire."[70] Such webs most certainly include the intellectual back-and-forth that al-Tahtawi recognized and that ʿAli pursued, but they also include cinema, the object of this study.

For one of the things that the history of Arab cinema enacts, emerging as it did in the period of the Nahda itself, is the bridging of the same cultural spheres (Arab and European, Arab and non-Arab) that the Nahda attempted to bring together. Smihi's films bring into focus the urgency of moving beyond the primacy of postcolonial theoretical perspectives that, in seeking to identify sites of resistance to colonial power, can at times reduce dissenting Arab discourses to inauthentic copies of the West. Leyla Dakhli finds evidence of such reductiveness even in the work of the great Albert Hourani, who chronicled the development of *Nahdawi* thought in his *Arabic Thought in the Liberal Age* (1962) and where, in one passage, he addresses Ibn Rushd and his treatment by Arab journalist Farah Antun.[71] Dakhli takes issue with Hourani's discussion of Antun, whose embrace of secularization put him at odds with the religious scholar Muhammad ʿAbduh. Hourani's reading of Antun, argues Dakhli, strips Antun of the agency of his own thought, seeing his ideas as essentially "those of [French philosopher Ernest] Renan, although without the seduction of his master's voice." Antun had studied with Renan and translated his work, and the Antun who thus emerges in Hourani's account, writes Dakhli, is "a second rate, derivative thinker obsessed more with imitation and Western recognition than with the urgent context in which he was intervening." In doing so, objects Dakhli, Hourani himself reduced Antun to a victim of European superiority. "To reduce Arab cultural critics to Western intellectual influences the way Hourani framed Antun," she writes, "is no less problematic than reducing them to their religious affiliation." Dakhli argues instead that we must treat Arab intellectuals in such a way that respects what she calls their "capacity for invention," and that we might, in so doing, "consider borrowings and references from Europe and the

West as transformations, hybridizations, or self-examinations from a strategic location of distance."[72] Dakhli's warning resonates with those of many of the thinkers I will consider here, but more than that, it sets the stage for the ways that the cinema I will study performs a similar function of transformation, cross-referencing, and self-critique.

The questions raised in the Nahda, and in historical accounts of it, are intrinsically relevant for discussions of cinema, whose emergence coincided with the latter part of the Nahda. In its own "capacity for invention," Smihi's cinema demonstrates how the Nahda might be taken up and used as an archive for the present, as Jens Hanssen, Max Weiss, and Nadia Bou Ali have framed it.[73] In revealing the inspiration that Smihi takes from the historical Nahda, I am concerned to show how his films resonate with the possibility of a new renaissance or rebirth, one that is not isomorphic to that pursued in the nineteenth or early twentieth centuries (nor even that of the post–World War II Arab nationalist period, which Elias Khoury has seen as a "second" Nahda).[74] The "new Nahda" that is the horizon for Smihi's films nonetheless retains its antecedent's claims for political freedom, democratization, religious equivalence, or even secularism, and it demands political and cultural change in the present. If Smihi's films openly cite and revere Nahda figures like Taha Hussein, it is because, in his view, they risk being forgotten in a time of intensified ideological clashes that often efface the long history of dissenting thought in the Arab world, especially with respect to the role of religion in political life.[75]

It is perhaps for similar reasons that the Nahda and its legacy have come into sharper focus for many recent thinkers, with several studies devoted to addressing its historical contours and the prospects for its transformation or reemergence in the present.[76] In particular, the two volumes edited by Hanssen and Weiss (which build upon a conference on Hourani's legacy that took place at Princeton University in 2012) demonstrate, first, how the Nahda might be better placed in the history of liberal thought in the Arab world, and second, how the legacy of the Nahda might serve as a starting point for a challenge "to the unsatisfying linear narrative of a singular European modernity that diffused from Europe towards its peripheries in a modular form."[77] In the work of contemporary thinkers like those collected in Hanssen and Weiss's volumes (especially, in this context, Traboulsi, Kassab, Khoury, Dakhli, Marilyn Booth, Orit Bashkin, Robyn Creswell, and Yoav DiCapua) as well as other writers like El-Ariss, Stephen Sheehi, and Jeffrey Sacks, there emerges a complexity to the Nahda which complicates any straightforward claims to it being either a colonial imposition or a rigid template for a singular Arab modernity.[78] As Hanssen and Weiss put it, "In some ways, the struggle over the memory and promise of the Nahda parallels the debate over the virtues as well as the dangers of the European Enlightenment."[79] As with critiques of the Enlightenment, polemics on the Nahda can make bedfellows of very different critics. The idea that the Nahda was "an imposition of foreign concepts, cultures and practices" that alienated "an autonomous and authentic 'Arab' or 'Islamic' self" could unite "certain liberals, Islamists, and neo-conservatives alike."[80] But internal critiques of Arab society by leftists, who saw in the Nahda a hope for remaking Arab society in dialogue with ideas common to the West, could at times align with neo-conservative or Orientalist ideas of backwardness or cultural malaise. Despite Smihi's own love for Hussein and of the Nahda's staging of an encounter that included Europe, his films, in their complexity and their affiliations with other cinematic traditions, hold the potential to surpass the Nahda's historical narrative in search of something new and even more suitable for the present. El-Ariss's study of Arab modernity's "trials" draws upon a diverse array of texts that, he argues, undo the Nahda's East-West dichotomy and dismantle "the master narratives of European civilization and of Arab modernity alike."[81] For El-Ariss, the irruption of new modes of popular cultural production, or the incorporation of African-Arab experiences into the textuality of encounter (such as in Tayeb Salih's writings), complicate narratives of Arab modernity that hinge on a European-Arab dichotomy. In placing Smihi's cinema within broader contexts than just those of Europe versus the Arab world, I hope to show how his films use the Nahda's principles of freedom toward ever new horizons of possibility. I argue that, rather than use European modernity to explain the Arab world, we should instead follow these films in tracing what a new Nahda might make possible in the world and what it might do to for our understandings of modernity and modernism in cinema.

Accounts of Western modernity typically see it as stretching across several centuries: Marshall Berman, for example, periodizes it into an early phase, lasting from roughly the beginning of the sixteenth century to the late eighteenth; a middle period, from the start of the French Revolution in 1789 through the nineteenth century; and a late period stretching through the twentieth century.[82] Cinema's relationship to modernity thus emerges from the experience of modernization and urbanization endemic to nineteenth- and twentieth-century capitalism; it is a key technology of twentieth-century modernity. Characterized by changes in systems of production (the factory line and automation) and thus subjectivity (the experience of alienation from labor, the shock of the crowd and the city), the late phase of modernity has generally been thought of as beginning in European and US industrial centers and gradually spreading to other locations. Concomitantly, it is usual to think of modernism as an *aesthetic* response to such conditions that developed in concert with other historical shifts in European consciousness.[83]

As many thinkers—from Karl Marx to Marshall Berman to Fredric Jameson—have suggested, modernity's emergence and spread can be explained by its twinned relationship with capitalism.[84] Yet the spread of capitalist modernity was deeply entangled with colonialism. To think of modernity only with respect to the radical changes that took shape in Europe during this time ignores the extent to which such changes were made possible and sustained at great cost by Europe's "other" populations. Consequently, some theorists have argued that the underside to the Enlightenment and to European modernity was the development of colonial systems of power and knowledge.[85] As Dipesh Chakrabarty puts it, the challenge in accounting for European modernity is "the recognition that Europe's acquisition of the adjective 'modern' for itself is an integral part of the history of European imperialism within global history; and second, the understanding that this equating of a certain version of Europe with 'modernity' is not the work of Europeans alone." Rather than seeing colonialism as an aberration within a history of modernity, then, we must see it as caught up in modernity's expansive project. In light of that understanding, the task of the historian, argues Chakrabarty, "is to write into the history of modernity the ambivalences, contradictions, the use of force, and the tragedies and ironies that attend it."[86] Chakrabarty's "provincializing" project thus *emplaces* Europe and its thought, not so much contesting the importance or purchase of Enlightenment ideas, nor relativizing them as wholly "culture-specific," but rather challenging their claims to an uncomplicated universality and centrality.

The debates around such positions—and they are extensive and ongoing—typically turn on two related problematics. One is the extent to which the subject produced by modernity is a universal one and whether the associated Enlightenment ideals of truth, reason, the secular, and will always follow it. This issue is certainly pertinent to the Nahda debates, as many writers acknowledge.[87] The other problem is the degree to which modernity functions the same way everywhere. Do the terms and characteristics that we associate with the European experience of capitalist modernity work the same way across every society? The first question becomes associated with ideas of historical progress; the second, with questions of culture and difference. While such questions have elicited the most debate and controversy in the terrain of subaltern and postcolonial studies, their relevance is hardly contained within that particular area. As Chakrabarty has pointed out, they bear on a much more general question that we could frame as: "How do we make sense of the global legacy of the European Enlightenment in lands far away from Europe in geography or history?"[88] This is a question that preoccupies Smihi's cinema with respect to the specific terrain of Arabic thought, where debates around *tanwir* (Enlightenment) have intersected with broader debates about the Nahda. Addressing the interventions of the Syrian journal *Qadaya wa-shahadat*, whose writers like Saʿadallah Wannous and ʿAbd al-Rahman Munif found inspiration in the versions of universal humanism espoused by Nahda figures like Hussein, Kassab sketches a kind of "post-independence Arab Enlightenment" that might be studied comparatively alongside other Enlightenments across the Global South.[89]

Along with the call to "provincialize Europe" and question the assumed universality of its thinking has emerged a discourse on "parallel," "other," or "alternative" modernities—that is, those that take shape discrepantly in places other than

Europe and the United States. In an attempt to deal with the Eurocentrism of the historicist version of modernity (by which sites other than Europe are seen as belatedly or incompletely modern), theses on alternative modernities stress what Dilip Parameshwar Gaonkar calls "creative adaptations" to modernity's effects. Yet such adaptations, argues Gaonkar, are not voluntaristic in the way Jameson suggests: modernity is no longer centered in the United States or Europe alone, and one cannot simply pick and choose which bits of it to take. "Creative adaptation," or the practice of forging "hybrid modernities," is rather the mode by which societies now practice an interrogation of newness.[90] Moreover, while arguing against the universalist assumptions of earlier conceptions of modernity, Gaonkar nonetheless maintains that thinking about alternative modernities means neither ignoring Western discourses about it nor denying its effects:

> To think in terms of alternative modernities does not mean one blithely abandons the Western discourse on modernity. That is virtually impossible. Modernity has traveled from the West to the rest of the world not only in terms of cultural forms, social practices, and institutional arrangements, but also as a form of discourse that interrogates the present. Whether in vernacular or cosmopolitan idioms, that questioning of the present, which is taking place at every national and cultural site today, cannot escape the legacy of Western discourse on modernity. Whoever elects to think in terms of alternative modernities (irrespective of one's location) must think with and also against the tradition of reflection that stretches from Marx and Weber through Baudelaire and Benjamin to Habermas, Foucault, and many other Western (born or trained) thinkers.[91]

Gaonkar's adamant embrace of the need to think with, as well as against, the European modernist legacy is a reminder that what is at stake is not to find some other modernities that have emerged as *alternatives* to European modernity, as something wholly other to the West. It is rather to conceive of narratives of modernity that recognize creative adaptation and hybridity while also admitting the possibility of thought and influence from centers other than Europe or the United States. It is for the latter reason that Smihi's films are so instructive and so beautifully attuned to the conditions of modernity in the Arab world. Their profound dialogue with European modernity is always conducted in relationship to Moroccan and Arab discourses, too—discourses that in some cases preceded or even enabled the European modern. These films build a modernity that is never a European construction.

Accounting for modernism as a set of aesthetic practices within modernity is therefore complicated by such a position. Overwhelmingly, the tradition of Euro-American film studies has located modernism in the experimentation of European and US avant-gardes, driven by what Berman calls the giddy mixture of the utopian and dystopian found in the writing of Marx, Baudelaire, Walter Benjamin,

Gertrude Stein, and others. In confining itself to Euro-American contexts, film theory and film studies have largely ignored, discounted, or disavowed modernist experimentation that takes shape elsewhere, or at best have seen it as imitating movements and ideas more properly found in European texts. Such a logic is doubly problematic for it tends, first, to blinker us to only one kind of temporality, the "first" appearance of a Euro-American form which is then seen to be the basis for everything else; second, it thus relegates to second-class, derivative status anything that appeared after Europe. How, then, to account for cinematic modernism in the Arab world and North Africa while refusing two pitfalls: the danger of conceiving of it as an aftereffect of Euro-American culture and imperialism, and the folly of theorizing a modernism or modernity that exists in wholly separate spheres to that of the West? Keya Ganguly, in a brilliant reassessment of Satyajit Ray's relationship to international modernism, forcefully rejects the "alternative modernities" thesis, arguing that "what remains most important in rethinking the concept of modernism is to insist on its explanatory force without relativizing it in the same move." For Ganguly, to postulate something like a hybridized modernism in India, for example, one that might differ in some respects from Western modernism as it has been encountered in European contexts, is to assign Ray's films to a cultural backwater where his innovations might only be seen within an exceptionalist and culturalist narrative of belated or derivative adaptation to established Western norms. The issue, argues Ganguly, is not that modernism's terms can function only for Euro-American texts, but that, historically, modernism was so concerned with its own universality that it neglected anything outside Europe. The European modernists rendered "experiments outside Europe or the United States as derivative or, at best, complementary." Yet, Ganguly suggests, that does not mean that modernity was European, just that it had not previously addressed its own blind spots with respect to the rest of the world. A contemporary rereading of modernism "now needs to resituate what seems anachronistic or out of place as, in fact, illuminated by the same light and belonging in the same conversation that had hitherto reserved the pride of place in understanding modernity for itself."[92] The critical impulse is thus recuperative, embracing the non-Western into the light and conversation of modernity but without changing its fundamental terms.

Ganguly's construction of a firm opposition between a relativistic, multicultural, even trendy approach to modernisms and a more rigorous, singular, structural approach (following Theodor Adorno, Raymond Williams, Jameson, and the Marxist modernist tradition) strikes me as unnecessarily stark. Ray's thoroughgoing engagement with European thought and culture is beyond question (and is extremely reminiscent of Smihi's own practice). Yet whatever the global reach of capitalist modernity, Ray's participation in an international avant-garde was never practiced to the exclusion of Bengali idioms, history, or social contexts in his films; all feature as part and parcel of his engagement with modernity. We might argue that his engagement is not far from Gaonkar's claim that, in the encounter with Western modernity, "people 'make' themselves modern, as opposed to being 'made' modern by alien and impersonal forces."[93] Thus while Ganguly characterizes her position as diametrically opposed to what is broadly termed the "alternative modernities" thesis, a certain overlap in perspectives enables both her and Gaonkar to close their texts with an appeal to Jürgen Habermas's notion that modernity has always been unfinished. Gaonkar uses Habermas to account for modernism's differential site-specific negotiations outside Europe; Ganguly uses Habermas to argue that a corrective reading of European modernism should extend its unfinished reach toward the terrains it overlooked. Both writers thereby retain the sense of modernity as something unexpected in its effects and outcomes.

Miriam Hansen's influential essay "Fallen Women, Rising Stars, New Horizons: Shanghai Silent Film as Vernacular Modernism" (2000) offers further clarity on the relationships between Euro-American forms of cinematic modernism and other cinema traditions or sites. Hansen shows how Shanghai cinema of the 1920s and 1930s successfully translated the idioms of Hollywood cinema into terms that were accessible for local audiences, neither slavishly imitating or parodying the Western form nor rejecting it in favor of some notion of discrete local authenticity. Instead she shows that "Shanghai cinema of the 1920s and 30s represents a distinctive brand of vernacular modernism, one that evolved in a complex relationship with American—and other foreign—models while drawing on and transforming Chinese traditions in theater, literature, graphic and print culture, both modernist and popular."[94] Hansen's idea of vernacular modernism relies on a thorough reading of Hollywood's relationships to modernity and modernism while also drawing on understandings of the way that Hollywood cinema was received and taken up by audiences.[95] Thus, while remaining cognizant of the ways in which Hollywood was a globalizing Western technology that arrived through unequal capitalist relations (often suppressing local film exhibition), Hansen is also able to show the ways that Shanghai's own cinema enacted a process of translation by which it engaged and transformed the local in responding to the globalizing forces of the foreign modern. As I have argued in the context of Moroccan modernist cinema of the immediate postcolonial period, Hansen's hypothesis enables us to take account of the transformative forces of Euro-American modernism *and* the purchase of the local without relegating the latter to the position of backwardness and without elevating the former to a position of supremacy, with which all else must fall into singular dialogue.[96]

These debates allow us to see how Smihi's cinema is able to engage a Euro-American modernity through a process of what Hansen terms "reconfiguration and translation," without re-centering or privileging the West. Translation, indeed, is key. Just as Smihi himself delighted in the translations of foreign texts that the Nahda made possible, his films place us into the broader domain of translation that characterizes so much of the Moroccan postcolonial literary and cinema scene. Indeed, it is the messy business of translation that avoids the dangers of separate spheres.[97] If one rejects an overarching telos of Eurocentric time and influence in the search for some kind of autochthonous modernity, one risks instead a hermetically sealed Arab, non-Western, or "other" identity that has nothing to do with Western modernity. The possibility of a retreat into nationalism, regionalism, or ethnic or linguistic particularity haunts the potential project of Arab modernity, if such articulations of the modern take shape only around postcolonial difference and resistance to cultural norms and impositions from outside. What this book calls for and outlines, then, with Smihi's films as its clearest proponent, is an argument about the necessity to approach Arab cinemas and Arab culture within an internationalist, worlded, and modern frame.

The chapters that follow endeavor to bring the stunning images, sounds, and critical interventions of Smihi's films into a framework that locates them within a diversity of artistic, critical, and intellectual traditions. Among these are local, micro histories and practices—not only Arab Moroccan but also Amazigh (or "Berber")—that might be lost to audiences outside those languages or locations.[98] Moreover, the presence of those vernacular practices in the films might be equally surprising to those within an Arab or North African frame who have sometimes been quick to dismiss Smihi's experimentation as derivative of a European tradition of modernist cinema. This study will show that Smihi's films are intensely grounded in the local. But they are simultaneously part of networks that are much greater, extending into other parts of the Arab world and beyond it, too. Thus the other element of the book's intervention is to show how the films are at once embedded in traditions of world cinema and other global, hybrid modernisms. They are enthusiastically, self-consciously, and inescapably international in a way that is both polemical and radical, avoiding nativism and folklorism for the radical possibilities of the modern, yet at the same time eschewing Orientalism or a hierarchy of the European, American, or global by building their narratives and affective form from the imbrication of the global in the local, the incorporation of the foreign into the familiar, and the injection of micro-narratives and locations into the flux of worldliness.

To think of Smihi's films in this way shows us that they, like the films of some other Arab directors, should be recognized as an important part of modernist art cinema—not a singular modernist art cinema but rather one of the compelling array of modernisms that we have begun to recognize and confront beyond Europe's borders. In this sense, the book wants to contribute to the remapping of film theory in ways that dislodge its Eurocentric proclivities, opening it up to the practices of moving image culture that have previously been overlooked.[99] Indeed, this project participates in a wider, interdisciplinary effort to rethink Moroccan culture and history in global terms. For example, in *A History of Modern Morocco* (2013) Susan Gilson Miller writes against several dominant historiographical strands in Morocco, such as the search for a "pure" or essential Morocco that was untouched by the violent transformations of colonialism. Instead, she stresses the ways in which Morocco was always a space caught up in the flows of international history. Colonialism spurred hybrid epistemologies and practices, and Morocco was both an adopter of foreign ideas and an exporter of its own "through expositions, world fairs, architecture, migration, and other forms of diasporic activity."[100] On the terrain of literary and artistic history, Kenza Sefrioui's 2013 account of the journal *Souffles* also stresses its internationalist avant-garde qualities and how its authors and artists worked within such a context.[101] And the recent translation and republication of key essays from *Souffles* and *Anfas*, already cited, demonstrates the scope of these worldly, postcolonial, modernist engagements.[102] More broadly, as I have noted already, important work on Arab engagements with modernity by writers like El-Ariss offers a perspective on modernity and modernisms beyond the dichotomy of European versus Arab.[103] Robyn Creswell's work on literary modernism in Beirut uses translation to sidestep "sterile disputes about imitation and authenticity" that serve to delimit the contributions of artists of all kinds. "Beiruti modernism," Creswell writes, "cannot be understood either as the copy of a European prototype or as a betrayal of the Arabic poetic tradition."[104] Such work shows that Arab modernisms are vibrant discourses with distinct, if fragile, histories forged from the multiple and ongoing travels and crossings between Arab worlds and others, Western or not.

ORGANIZATION OF THE BOOK

Rather than being arranged chronologically or film by film, this book is structured thematically to address issues central to Smihi's work, placing it in the contexts developed above. The first three chapters focus on questions of cinematic language and form, some of which have particular resonance within the terrain of Arab cinemas. For example, realism has been a central term in the development of film cultures across the region, whether in discourses on Italian neorealism, the Arab novel, or the legacy of colonial actuality films. The first chapter, then, addresses the porous boundary between documentary and fiction that characterizes some of Smihi's early work, situating it both within the modernist experimentation with the *court-métrage*, or short film, in Morocco in the 1960s and 1970s and within similar aesthetic practices across the region, including in Egypt, whose cinema Smihi examines in his documentary *Egyptian Cinema: Defense and Illustration* (1989). In *Si Moh, the Unlucky Man* and his first feature, *The East Wind*, Smihi's deployment of realism constitutes a radical response to postcolonial realities in Morocco. The chapter places these and later films within other currents of realism that were explored within Arab cinema and beyond it. Film sound is increasingly prominent as a subject of film theory and criticism, and although little attention has been paid to it in English-language studies of Arab cinema, I argue in chapter 2 that Smihi's soundscapes are a key aspect of his cinematic modernism, making audible the social and political contexts of the worlds he represents. To listen to the soundtracks of these films—whose elements range from Radio Cairo's pan-Arab broadcasts of the 1950s to Moroccan pop stations, calls to prayer, the popular stories of the *al-halqa* tradition of storytelling,[105] Amazigh songs, and the non-diegetic music of Frédéric Chopin—is to be struck by the ways in which sound constitutes a mode of social exchange, political critique, and self-fashioning across the region. Smihi's particular attention to sound illuminates the polyglot and cosmopolitan history of Arab and North African life. Chapter 3 focuses on the rigorous intertextuality of Smihi's films to develop an argument about the multivocality of Arab culture in the postcolonial period. Whether through collaborations with (then) living writers like Paul Bowles (on *Caftan of Love*), through retrospective homage (to Matisse, in *With Matisse in Tangier*, or Taha Hussein, in *With Taha Hussein*), or through his films' multiple citations to other films within a global canon, Smihi's filmmaking divulges his roots as a Tangier filmmaker who grew up at a crossroads of languages, literary traditions, and cinematic images. This chapter explores intertextuality as evidence of the unpredictable circulation of global culture across the Middle East and of Arab cinema's place in the world.

The remaining two chapters use these observations about cinematic language to further inform an exploration of two key cultural debates in which Arab cinema has participated. So much the stuff of popular reporting but also of academic criticism, questions about religion, gender, the *hijab*, and sexual identities are endemic to contemporary discussions of the Middle East. Chapter 4 shows how Smihi's cinema uncouples the cinematic relationships between the terms "Arab" and "religion" to offer a vision of a multi-confessional, tolerant, and secular Moroccan and Arab world. In particular I show how the films engage overlooked Arab cultural and intellectual traditions in order to reconfigure the relationship of the sacred with the profane and to demand a new openness and freedom of expression. With their emphasis on local and popular practices and customs, the films reveal how culture and politics are mutable and not tied to fixed ideas about the role of religion. By situating the films within these diverse Moroccan and Arab traditions while also comparing them to the interventions of filmmakers like Pier Paolo Pasolini and Luis Buñuel, the chapter argues that Smihi's secular cinema forms an important part of a modernist cinematic culture of sacrilege, skepticism, and political commitment. Debates about gender go to the heart of the political critique prevalent during the Nahda, but gender and sexuality are also crucial to Western representations of the Middle East, whether it be in the Orientalists' fascination with what they saw as an Arab and Eastern tolerance for homosexuality, or the *opposite* stereotype now predominant: that Arab cultures abhor homosexuality and brutally repress women and queers in contrast to the West's supposedly liberal, enlightened perspectives. The fifth and final chapter offers a queer reading of Smihi's work, showing how the films enact a critique of patriarchal relations and homophobia while simultaneously asserting the power and sexuality of women and the existence of mobile relations of desire. As with their representation of religion, analyzed in the previous chapter, Smihi's films suggest to the viewer a set of alternative histories and possibilities that escape the strictures of the present. Joining his films to other, sometimes overlooked representations of gender and sexuality, this chapter reveals the work of Arab cinema in calling for a world in which gender equality and sexual expression are indices of freedom.

In following this trajectory, I answer the following questions: How, in the wake of Edward Said and the critique of Orientalism, should Anglophone film studies engage the diverse and vibrant phenomenon of Arab cinema? How can Smihi's cinema allow us to better understand the extensive traffic of images and ideas between Arab and non-Arab cinemas and cultures? What are the implications of his work for theories of postcolonial cinemas and global modernisms? While world events continue to provoke commentary on the political history of the region, analysis of cultural expression in the Arab world has generally reduced it to a function or expression of broader political movements or ideological positions, as El-Ariss and Marks have also noted.[106] In contrast, this book takes seriously the aesthetic, cultural, *and* political dimensions of Smihi's work in relation to other cinematic traditions and histories, within the region and without. This book, then, in pursuing its argument about Smihi's thoroughly worldly cinema, urges us to rethink the Euro-American limits of film theory with respect to questions of modernism and to recalibrate our understandings of Arab cinema beyond questions of authorship and national cinema. At a time when, more than ever, we need ways to work across borders, Smihi's films attest to the potential for cinema to reimagine the world.

1

Radical Realities: Form and Politics in the New Arab Cinema

Moumen Smihi's transformative approach to cinematic realism becomes apparent from the earliest moments of his remarkable first film, shot soon after he graduated from the L'institut des hautes études cinématographiques (IDHEC) in 1968. *Si Moh, the Unlucky Man* (1971) emerged directly from Smihi's encounter with cinema, politics, and theory in Paris. The film follows a Moroccan immigrant, Si Moh (short for Si Mohammed; *si* or *sidi* is an honorific in Moroccan Arabic) who wanders Paris in search of work. Paris is established in the first few minutes as a city of overwhelming visual and aural sensations. The first sequence is a montage of long shots and close-ups that includes a railway arrivals sign, clogged city streets by night and by day, a stark modernist apartment block, an outdoor fire in an oil drum, and—in the middle of it all—a long shot just a second in duration that reveals a man with a suitcase standing on an island in the center of a street as a truck rushes by. The montage of seemingly disconnected views continues as Si Moh reappears on a train platform (fig. 3), boards a bus, and then, as the film elliptically suggests his movement through the Paris streets and *bidonvilles* (slums), arrives at a small hut. There he sits with other Maghribi workers who look at postcards from their families and discuss their work conditions and prospects even as the image track cuts away under their voices, revealing spatially disconnected scenes and locations around the city. Thus far, just five minutes into this short work, Smihi's camera has captured the minutest details in stark black and white: the texture of the makeshift housing where Si Moh and his friends meet; the faces of the people in the frame; the small objects like teapots, ashtrays, and espresso cups in the cafés and rooms where the nameless characters eat and drink. Soon after, we watch Si Moh arrive at a construction site, where the camera slowly and patiently documents the movements of

FIGURE 3. Si Moh arrives in Paris by train in *Si Moh, the Unlucky Man*, 1971.

heavy machinery and materials before a brief moment of dialogue where Si Moh asks a construction foreman for work. The rest of the film continues in this manner evocative of observational documentary, placing Si Moh into an environment that looks completely unstaged but edited so that the city dwarfs and overwhelms him. The discordant, seemingly unsynchronized soundtrack adds still more to the disconcerting and confusing sense of the city that the film constructs. By the end we find Si Moh alone and seemingly despondent, falling asleep on the train in a sequence of arresting still images that freeze the action before us (fig. 4). Then, as the images move again, we see him on the steps of the Paris metro surrounded by other men who are homeless or without hope.

The film, then, places us between two poles: one the one hand, it appears as a realist or even documentary rendering of a city and some of its inhabitants; on the other, using disjunctive editing and sound as well as stark still and moving images, it constructs an alienated and fractured modern subject caught in a dystopian version of the quintessential modern city. It reveals both a documentary impulse regarding the representation of Paris and the situation of its migrant workers, while also reminding us of modernist city films like *Nothing but Time* (Rien que les heures, dir. Alberto Cavalcanti, 1926), *Berlin, Symphony of a City* (Berlin: Die

FIGURE 4. Si Moh asleep on the metro: one of many still images that Moumen Smihi inserts into the flow of *Si Moh, the Unlucky Man*, 1971.

Sinfonie der Grosstadt, dir. Walter Ruttman, 1927), or *Man with a Movie Camera* (dir. Dziga Vertov, 1929), all of which push beyond realism into a modernist construction of subjectivity. This chapter will argue that Smihi's work, from *Si Moh* onward, continually occupies this dual vision, embodying diverse modes of realism while also embracing a cinematic modernism. Working in the tradition of others who have experimented across the space between each tradition, yet turning such experimentation to his own ends, Smihi destabilizes the realist-modernist dichotomy to produce a cinema expressive of Arab subjectivities in particular spaces and moments.

To seriously account for this kind of strategy, however, one most go beyond the self-evident examples of European cinema that I've already mentioned; Smihi finds reference points in Arab cinema and culture, too. Realism, or *waqi'iyya*, emerged in Arab cinema as an attempt at a new kind of cinematic form. The development of differing modes of realism, beginning in Egyptian cinema and taken up elsewhere, is an issue that is addressed in more detail below. For the moment, however, I will argue that for Arab critics and filmmakers alike, realism constituted a formal innovation tied to the development of a cinematic language appropriate to the conditions of the Arab world. In pushing against the conventions of Egyptian commercial cinema, for example, filmmakers like Salah Abu Seif and Tawfik Saleh, beginning in the 1950s, used realism to signal an engagement with social realities that Egyptian melodrama had thus far failed to address. By showing an affiliation with movements like Italian neorealism, Egyptian filmmakers registered their determination to create new forms of cinema anticipating the "new waves" that were emerging in other places. Moreover, their embrace of a realist cinematic language aligned them with the modern forms of literature pursued by writers like Naguib Mahfouz, with which Smihi's films are also associated; indeed, Mahfouz himself was deeply implicated in this experimentation, both as a screenwriter and as a writer whose books were adapted into cinema.[1] Later, the pursuit of various modes of realism by other filmmakers in Morocco, Algeria, Syria, Kuwait, and elsewhere in the 1970s and 1980s signaled a way for their films to differentiate themselves from the dominant melodramatic form of Egyptian cinema and to articulate concerns relevant to postcolonial life within authorial discourses of exception and innovation.[2] Thus, while realism never developed as a dominant commercial mode within Arab cinema, it did become a terrain on which filmmakers indexed their commitment to new forms of representation and to addressing such issues as the aftermath of colonialism, the Palestinian question, or the state of political struggle within the region.

In all those respects the films participated in a movement that has been termed the New Arab Cinema. The term is partly a critical one, but also functioned to a great degree as a self-identification on the part of filmmakers. The interviews included with filmmakers like Youssef Chahine, Salah Abu Seif, and Khairy Beshara in Smihi's own documentary, *Egyptian Cinema: Defense and Illustration* (1989) evidence the way that some filmmakers in the 1970s and 1980s saw themselves as challenging the norms of cinema as it had been experienced in the Arab world to date through a combination of social themes, independent authorial visions, and especially experiments with form. Férid Boughedir's documentary film *Arab Camera* (Caméra arabe, 1987), which includes clips and extensive interviews with filmmakers, also traces the contours of this movement, which not only included several female filmmakers like Moufida Tlatli, Selma Baccar (both from Tunisia), and Jocelyne Saab (Lebanon), but also took gender and sexuality as prominent themes. As Viola Shafik argues, French uses of the term (such as in Claude Michel Cluny's book *Dictionnaire des nouveaux cinemas arabes* [Dictionary of the New Arab Cinemas, 1978]) tend to stress a plurality of cinemas across multiple sites, North African and Middle Eastern alike, so that one might include the Algerian *al-sinima al-jadid* (new cinema) or the Syrian *al-sinima al-badila* (alternative cinema) in Syria as examples of New Arab Cinemas; such a pan-regional scope is also the concern of filmmaker Nouri Bouzid's description of the state of Arab cinema after the 1967 defeat.[3] Smihi himself would relate all these cinemas to each other but also, crucially, to the other "new waves" that shook up film history in Europe and Asia and that influenced Arab filmmakers like him, too.[4]

While Shafik is correct in arguing that there is no singular genre or style that typifies the films of the New Arab Cinema, experiments with form often took shape around questions of realism and modernism. In the case of Smihi's films, realism creates an affiliation with other Arab filmmakers and with cinema movements that have explored new perceptions of the world. Understanding how realism has functioned across Arab cinemas thus allows us to index the extent to which other Arab filmmakers tried to engage with local realities and the degree to which they saw themselves working in conditions that were international. Such an investigation, however, will yield not a single realism but multiple versions. When Shafik argues, for example, that "Egyptian realism does not constitute a coherent ideological movement" and that it might generally be described as a "melodramatic realism," she indicates that it generally tended toward what we might call a dominant realism, the equivalent of the quotidian forms of realism that underpin much classical Hollywood cinema.[5] For Smihi, realism is not an end in itself, nor does it possess an uncomplicated relation to the real. Rather, it is one possible way of approaching a world that is complex and that defies easy representation. In that sense, his realism always pushes toward modernism and, in rejecting dominant realisms, takes cinema toward new forms of self-expression. Such tendencies are relatively rare in Arab cinema generally, but they have emerged in the work of his historical peers like Youssef Chahine, Khalid al-Siddiq, and Mohamed Zinet, and in that of contemporary directors like Tariq Teguia and Rabah Ameur-Zaïmeche. How do their realist tendencies intersect with modernist ones? How do form and politics relate? How does Smihi's work illuminate this relationship?

Rosalind Galt and Karl Schoonover have productively addressed the complexity and relation of these two terms by triangulating them with another contested one: "art cinema." Putting in question its definitions, they trace the ways that art cinema has—against some stereotypical assumptions that it is apolitical—"from its beginnings forged a relationship between the aesthetic and the geopolitical or, in other words, between cinema and the world."[6] While one could claim for it an intrinsic affinity with realism through movements such as Italian neorealism and its circulation in international art cinema markets, it has just as often been associated with modernist tendencies toward the expression of subjectivity and noncausality. Indeed, they argue, art cinema has often mediated the boundaries between these two terms, so often oppositional in film theoretical history. Consequently, "we might say that the realism of an art film is never exclusively realist, because film's narration remains always inflected by the admission of a modernist sensibility. At the same time, its modernism can never achieve absolute purity because it remains tinged by realist tendencies. Art cinema draws our attention to the persistent inadequacy of these terms, especially in their constantly melodramatic binary opposition."[7]

Galt and Schoonover's formulation of the problem is helpful in assessing Smihi's work, which demands a similar interrogation of the way that realism and modernism interact within an Arab cinematic context. Ultimately, I will argue that Smihi's formulation of an Arab cinematic modernism constitutes an active embrace of a global art cinema in the terms that Galt and Schoonover have proposed it. His work is at the forefront of Arab engagements with the complexities of cinematic language and representation, and his long career outstrips most of his contemporaries' in its consistent adhesion to such an experimentation with ideas and form. In Smihi's hands, realism becomes a malleable tool that allows the filmmaker to make a modernist intervention into the world without being beholden to a strict or predictable relationship to the real. Whether one compares Smihi's films with each other or thinks of single films, this argument holds true: in *Si Moh*, as I have begun to show, the impulse toward realism in the presentation of a migrant worker's life in Paris is complicated by the experimentation with temporality and the image, an experimentation redoubled with a modernist soundtrack that I will consider further in the next chapter. Other films, while quite different, maintain a similarly complex aesthetic: *44, or Tales of the Night* (1981), for example, combines a frequently realist aesthetic with fragmented narration and a disjunctive soundtrack.

In so doing, Smihi traverses the terrain that animated the debates on realism and modernism that occupied György Lukács, Bertolt Brecht, and other Marxists from the 1930s to the 1960s. While Smihi would reject the label "Marxist" (he chose to stay outside of identifiable party affiliations through the turbulence of the Moroccan postcolonial period), his method certainly owes a great deal to the concerns articulated by Marxist critics in those debates, particularly Brecht's rejection of what he saw as the "tyranny" of older forms of realism (favored by Lukács) in favor of new techniques that came to be identified as a kind of political modernism.[8] Indeed, the complex realism of *Si Moh*, with its modernist proclivities, could be seen to exemplify Jameson's treatment of a Brechtian aesthetic in which "the spirit of realism designates an active, curious, experimental, subversive—in a word, *scientific*—attitude towards social institutions and the material world."[9] That this characterization almost perfectly matches Smihi's self-assessment of the film as "the analysis of reality" is scarcely accidental.[10]

Yet the subversion of such a realist-modernist dichotomy is far from an academic question in Smihi's work, which conjoins realism and modernism in ways reminiscent of what Pier Paolo Pasolini achieved through a poetics that was both radical and political, as John David Rhodes has noted. "Pasolini," Rhodes writes, "is sympathetic to modernism, to its refashioning of received forms, its deconstruction of concepts, modes of address, its reflexivity, its commitment to aesthetic autonomy, its restless impatience with the world, and its appetite for critique.

However, Pasolini is also deeply, deeply committed to reference, to the relation between the work of art and the world out of which it emerges and back toward which (for Pasolini) it must invariably point."[11] Such a double commitment is what constitutes Pasolini's "cinema of poetry," argues Rhodes, an approach to political critique and aesthetics that animates the filmmaker's work. Rhodes's description of Pasolini might well apply to Smihi, especially for the manner in which he (like Pasolini) has personally articulated his methods or approaches. The discourse on the self, subjectivity, and language that Smihi articulates in an essay like "Anthropologie culturelle" (Cultural Anthropology, 1984), for example, is matched with his concern in the same essay for what he terms an "anthropological" approach to history and to the representation of popular traditions and practices; Egyptian cinema of the 1950s briefly exemplified such a concern in its adoption of realism and neorealism, he argues.[12] For Smihi, then, the work of his films is to attempt a narration of the self from the vantage point of an Arab subject while also relating something of the real social conditions and histories of the world that subject inhabits. This goal, which we witness across his oeuvre, takes shape through the engagement with and complication of realism in its various modes and practices. While also a mode of production that allows him to independently pose questions that commercial films might avoid, as was noted in the introduction, art cinema is also a mode of practice that allows Smihi to negotiate the necessary tensions between modernism and realism that animate his work.[13]

In this sense his cinema is profoundly intertextual, something that will be explored at length in chapter 3 (where I will also draw on his literary influences). But in particular, in keeping with the art cinema connections I have drawn above, I will argue that his work should also be placed within the broader domain of global modernist art cinema that emerged in distinctive contexts in the 1960s and 1970s. The adoption of neorealist techniques by radical filmmakers in the 1960s and after constituted a refusal of Hollywood's quotidian realism, a realism enveloped in melodrama, but also a rejection of the moral certainties and the particular national political context of Italian neorealism. For all that his work participates in such traditions, however, it also charts its own, very particular route. In his writings, where we can turn for sustained engagements with his practice, Smihi stresses the need for discourse on the self, for an approach that creates an Arab-Islamic aesthetic that responds to a rigorous self-questioning and that responds to history and what he terms the "provocation of the real."[14] In order to understand his aesthetic, I situate his work in terms of its own engagement of the real but also in relation to other Arab films that utilize realism as a mode.

Moreover, I point to the ways that his versions of realism are never separate from what is sometimes posed as realism's opposite: modernism. This chapter, then, isolates three currents of Smihi's practice that intersect with or transform modes of realism. The first is the legacy of neorealism in his work, which includes the type of Italian neorealist aesthetic championed by André Bazin, including a fascination with the presentation of bodies in space, and even the role of the still photographic image. The second current, which overlaps with the first in many of its visual signifiers, is a mode of realism that Smihi elaborates and that I am calling Rouchian. Influenced by his reading of Claude Lévi-Strauss and by Jean Rouch's cinematic experiments, many of Smihi's films search for images and sounds that do the anthropological work of representing a culture. This work, however, is a process of auto-ethnography, a representation of culture *to itself*. Smihi attempts to find a mode of practice that learns from the kind of colonial anthropological visions that have dominated the region while rejecting their ideological biases. What he calls for is an auto-anthropology in which Moroccan and Arab-Islamic culture might represent itself for itself and for its others, and to enact such a discourse he builds on Rouch's exploration of documentary fictions. Finally, this chapter addresses how all these engagements with the real take shape within a practice that is nevertheless resolutely modernist in its expression of subjectivities and in its desire to conjoin European and Arab modes of thought.

LEGACIES OF NEOREALISM

Returning to *Si Moh*, we see Smihi using those neorealist legacies in the way that he establishes relationships of bodies and space, of people and their environments. The actor playing Si Moh was Abdesslam Sakini, a young Moroccan whom Smihi had met in the Cité internationale universitaire in Paris.[15] Sakini was, like Smihi, a Moroccan recently emigrated to Paris, and he was at the time trying to work as an actor there.[16] Sakini's presence registers in relation to the space of the city in a manner suggestive of a documentary, not so much because of his own actions but because of the mise-en-scène around him and how it is constructed. Visually, Smihi stays close to the assumed realities of his material, preferring a visual aesthetic of immediacy and seeming authenticity over careful staging and sculpting. Thus we are given extended sequences of the construction site that allow the viewer to see its rhythms and patterns and shapes, which appear to continue unchanged even as Smihi's actor enters the scene (fig. 5). To some extent this pattern continues in later moments as Si Moh/Sakini continues to traverse Paris, eventually descending into the metro.

In Smihi's film, then, the body of Si Moh becomes an element in a mise-en-scène where the city, too, becomes a character. The film contains more shots without Si Moh than with him, constructing a discourse in which the city functions not as a "backdrop" to the movement of the character but as a location that defines him. In a 1983 essay, without mentioning *Si Moh* specifically, Smihi outlined his interest in the kind of cinema in which urban space plays a formative and definitive role, noting that in the ending of Michelangelo Antonioni's *The Eclipse*

FIGURE 5. A body in the city: Si Moh arrives at a construction site, where his presence barely registers, in *Si Moh, the Unlucky Man*, 1971.

(L'éclisse, 1962) (in the long sequence in which two lovers fail to meet at the appointed time, the space where the rendezvous would have taken place is shown in a succession of "empty" shots of streets, trees, buildings, a newspaper blowing), "it's no longer even the person *and* the city but, indeed, the city *without* the person."[17] Within this city, Si Moh/Sakini becomes not so much a character nor simply an actor, but something more akin to Robert Bresson's *actant* or *modèle*. He is between actor and character, his body and movements registering in the mise-en-scène as traces of something that has taken place before the camera. Such a strategy responds to the emphasis that Bazin placed on indexicality and, with it, the kind of relationship between bodies and space that he found especially compelling in the work of Italian neorealists like Roberto Rossellini. While, as I will argue below, the influence of neorealism may appear more thoroughgoing in *Moroccan Chronicles* (1999), *Si Moh* and *The East Wind* (1975) nonetheless generate a Bazinian interest in the body in the frame even if they reject Bazin's emphasis on duration over cutting. As Schoonover argues, "Bazin continually encourages his reader to think of the onscreen actor less as a performer and more as a filmed body. Bazin's film actor shares more with the human subjects of documentary than she does with the stage actor."[18] For Smihi, this attention to the body's presence in space and the intersection of documentary and performance allows him to register the presence of the Maghribi worker in a space to which he is intimately connected by histories of migration and colonialism. Here precisely is Smihi's attention to creating an Arab subject in the context of history and place, even if (as I will argue below) the film also diverts from its realist impulses to construct a radical view of subjectivity.

The East Wind also straddles this divide. The film (whose Arabic title, *El Chergui*, refers to the insistent easterly wind that blows across northern Morocco's coast and mountains, including Tangier) is organized around the character of Aïcha, who resists her husband's efforts to take a second wife. She turns to the aid of other women and a marabout, or holy man, who encourages her to use magical practices that will defeat him. Although the marriage never happens, Aïcha's death at the end of the film is left ambiguous, signaled as either an accident or a possible suicide. The film continues after her death, turning its attention to her son, Brahim, who attends the French school, and to the environment of the port of Tangier at the edge of the medina (the old part of the city). While Smihi has resisted a reading of the film as sociological, the work nonetheless emerges as an unprecedented investigation of the status of a Tangerian woman at the historical moment just before decolonization.[19] Indeed, the visual energy that the film excites is largely a product of Smihi's ability to take the lessons of neorealism in dramatically new directions.

Yet, like *Si Moh*, the film depends on location shooting in which the placement of the actor/character in space is a compelling part of the drama. Nowhere is this more striking than in the extended sequence in which Aïcha/Leila Shenna walks through the medina and out into the *ville nouvelle*. The camera is handheld, freed to move about the space as we cut back and forth between Shenna's movement in close-up (the camera frames her head, dramatically enclosed in a jellaba with a white face covering) and the long and medium shots of the marketplace and its activities. In these close-ups, Smihi uses a compressed space of conflicting image planes in a way that we seldom see in his work; an exception is a brief shot of Larbi in a square overlooking the medina in *Girls and Swallows* (2008), where boys playing constantly push through the foreground frame in front of Larbi, who occupies the middle ground. There, as in this shot, the conflict of planes gives an intimacy to the image through which we better understand the flow of the city. While the focus is quite literally on Aïcha, the shot, with its blurred background plane of a man's face (Aïcha actually occupies the middle ground of the shot, and at one point a passing figure intervenes between her and the camera), places her in radical proximity to other city dwellers in a manner that contrasts with her seclusion at home (fig. 6).

In the opposing long shots we see other aspects of the city: merchants preparing cooked food, women shopping for fruit or talking, traffic passing pedestrians who comb the market, and a clutch of chickens at the feet of a seller, one of which Aïcha chooses for herself. In a continued succession of unmatched cuts, the montage

FIGURE 6. Aïcha in *The East Wind*, 1975, traverses Tangier in a sequence that puts her in close relation to the city and its human environment.

moves us across several corners of the old and new Tangier, following Aïcha's progress in long shots that reveal the geography, the architecture, and the feel of the streets. Here Smihi deploys a single professional actor, Shenna (who was then still relatively inexperienced), amid a group of nonprofessionals, thus creating, along with the immediacy of location, the kind of "casual mixing" of bodies within the frame that so intrigued Bazin.[20] Smihi continued to work with this dynamic kind of casting throughout his career, notably in *The Lady from Cairo* (1991). In choosing the Egyptian actress Yousra to play Amina, who searches for success in the world of Egyptian film and music, Smihi not only represents the Egyptian studio system but directly participates in it (as he did by choosing Bashir al-Dik, a prominent writer and director, as his screenwriter). Yousra had, by the end of the 1980s when the film was shot, worked with Egyptian directors Youssef Chahine (*Alexandria, Again and Again* [1989]) and Ali Badrakhan (*The Hunger* [1986]) and appeared in several television dramas in addition to having an active career as a singer.[21] Indeed, Smihi has compared his casting of her to Rossellini's decision to place Ingrid Bergman, already a Hollywood star, at the center of several of his neorealist films.[22]

In other ways, too, *The Lady from Cairo* shows Smihi attempting what other filmmakers like Salah Abu Seif and Husayn Kamal made possible: retaining the conventions of Egyptian melodrama while inserting moments of neorealism in the mise-en-scène. For example, the early scenes of *The Lady from Cairo* are reminiscent of Abu Seif's *The Monster* (al-Wahsh, 1954), which opens with a scene of peasants working in a rural village along the Nile (milking cows, plowing fields, grinding flour) before the action moves to predominantly interior settings. Husayn Kamal's *The Postman* (al-Bustagi, 1968) also constructs a stark contrast between studio interiors, stunningly simple and beautiful in their design and shooting, and exterior rural locations. Smihi, who admires both films, begins *The Lady from Cairo* with a rural scene in which Amina, his central character, works the fields near her village, dreaming of moving to Cairo to sing and perform. Her subsequent life in Cairo is shot in the streets of popular neighborhoods as well as in the lush surroundings of an upper-class *bey* (gentleman). Within its dramatic narrative arc (the story of her rise to fame, her simultaneous exploitation by the men around her, and her tragic relationship with her brother), Smihi continues to find settings that stress the everyday lives of poor or middle-class Egyptians and presents traces of Egypt's history in the buildings and streets in which the action is set. Smihi's camera frames Amina around grand, colonial-era buildings with crumbling stucco, their walls plastered with posters and graffiti, latticed balconies covered in laundry, and trees and gardens coexisting with dusty streets and sidewalks (fig. 7), all of which capture a reality of the city; the sequences recall the city walks in Salah Abu Seif's *The Empty Pillow* (al-Wasada al-khalia, 1957) or *I Am Free* (Ana hurra, 1959). Later in the film, Smihi shoots around the neighborhood of Giza, in the vicinity of the pyramids. Here, among the desperately poor surroundings, we see the makeshift dwellings that sprout up around abandoned cars as the camera renders the harsh light and shadows in deep focus.

Aside from location shooting, however, Smihi also weaves found or archival documentary material into the narrative. This material, drawn from newsreels, television, and broadcast radio, serves to bind the melodramatic narrative to the history of Egypt. *The Lady from Cairo* covers a span of approximately fifteen years, marked in the film by the passage of time from Nasser's rule, to Egypt's defeat in the 1967 war with Israel, to the assassination of President Anwar Sadat in 1981, and finally the Palestinian declaration of independence in 1988. As I will show in the next chapter, the historical referentiality is partially achieved by sound—radio broadcast is a key element within the soundtrack of the film, and is used to signify the 1967 defeat and Nasser's subsequent resignation. But a visual realism is also achieved using found footage. For example, Smihi inserts footage of the breaching of the Bar Lev Line (*Khat Barlif* in Arabic) in 1973, when Egyptian forces advanced across the Suez Canal, breaking through the large, fortified sand hill that Israel had developed along its edge. In one shot the fortifications smoke from an attack; in

FIGURE 7. Amina navigates Cairo in neorealist sequences that show the city's texture in *The Lady from Cairo*, 1991.

another, aerial shot we see tanks advancing across the Sinai. While this footage is anchored by Amina's voice-over, it exists as a kind of non-diegetic insert in the film: it is clearly not supposed to be seen by any character in the narrative and functions as a realist commentary on the action. In this respect it differs from Chahine's use of World War II newsreel footage in *Alexandria, Why?* (1979), which he integrates into his diegesis to the point where a character, Ibrahim, throws a Molotov cocktail into a British vehicle, seen as found footage, that then explodes in a match on action. At other moments, however, the historical material that Smihi references does become diegetic: later, as Omar and Amina fight, a television broadcasts Anwar Sadat's historic visit to the Israeli Knesset (legislature), narrated by a British news commentator. Smihi thus encloses the news broadcast within the story of a dissolving relationship, marking the trajectory of his characters' lives with the events of the region. In *Girls and Swallows*, too, Smihi uses found footage, this time of the return of Mohammed V from exile in 1956, which along with a radio broadcast (voiced by Smihi) announces the fact of Morocco's independence from French rule. Again here, the role of the newsreel footage is like that of a non-diegetic insert in the film (none of the characters comment on or interact with it), even if the sound of a projector whirring almost suggests a viewer within the story world of the film.

The Lady from Cairo took Smihi further than ever before in the direction of studio filmmaking (fig. 8), with all its constraints (he referred to it recently as a "straitjacket" [*carcan*] in detailing the difficulties of the shoot).[23] It is partly in reac-

FIGURE 8. Moumen Smihi (left) with cinematographer Tarek Telemsani (second from left) and two unnamed crew members on the set of *The Lady from Cairo*, 1991.

tion to that experience of working in Egypt that Smihi, upon returning to Morocco, set about making his next film, *Moroccan Chronicles*, using 16mm film stock and smaller, more portable cameras—the antithesis of the large, more complex model of 35mm studio production. *Moroccan Chronicles* also signified a desire to turn more directly to a neorealist style in the wake of *The Lady from Cairo* and *44, or Tales of the Night*, a style that would allow Smihi to address contemporary questions of Moroccan social life through an engagement with popular practices and global economic and media flows. The film, which unfolds in three chapters set in Marrakesh, Essaouira, and Tangier, is organized within a framing tale in which a mother recounts stories to her son as he recovers from his circumcision; he is approximately seven years old. The larger story takes place in the city of Fez, where the film begins and ends with documentary-style footage that presents the city in its everyday activity: after a wide pan over the urban landscape, we cut to a traveling shot that encircles the walls of the medina before there is another cut to a wide, deep-focus shot of workers leaving a textile factory (it is hard not to think of the famous Lumière brothers actuality *Workers Leaving the Lumière Factory* [1895]). Then the camera isolates a woman who looks to be in her thirties and begins to follow her route through the city on her way home. There is a brief dramatic interchange between her and her son, Amine, who attempts to escape his impending circumcision by climbing on a roof. Avoiding the event itself, the

FIGURE 9. Amine's mother tells him a story while he recovers from his circumcision in *Moroccan Chronicles*, 1999.

camera instead performs a kind of tour of the medina before cutting back to the mother as she comforts her son, dressed in his circumcision finery with Moroccan money tucked into it (fig. 9). She begins to tell him a story that begins, as do all stories of the *One Thousand and One Nights*, "*Kan ya makan* . . . " (Once upon a time . . .). From this moment there is a cut, and we are plunged into the Marrakesh chapter of the film.

Here, a neorealist style makes plain Smihi's engagement with the popular. From a high overhead angle, the camera pans over the famed Jemaa el-Fnaa, or main square, in the medina to a ground-level shot of acrobats cartwheeling on a rug spread on the ground with onlookers all around. A sequence of impressions follows: Gnawa musicians performing, snake charmers enticing their serpents from a box (fig. 10), and more acrobats creating a stunning vertical formation. Tourists and Moroccans look on, and the camera circles to follow a man with a gray wig and then a *hakawati*, or storyteller, relating a tale. The cuts continue as we are presented with continuing visual and aural documentation of the chaotic and lively square. That sense of a city square shot in documentary style reappears in *The Medina of Paris: A Square during the Ramadan Market* (1996), a one-minute film in the spirit of the Lumière operators' films, commissioned by GREC (Groupe de

FIGURE 10. The lively popular culture of the Jemaa el-Fnaa square in Marrakesh features in *Moroccan Chronicles*, 1999.

recherches et d'essais cinématographiques, or Research and Cinema Experimentation Group, the same organization that produced *Si Moh*) to commemorate the centenary of cinema. Smihi's film unfolds in a single take from a fixed vantage point above a square in the Goutte d'Or district of Paris, an area in the Eighteenth Arrondissement that is home to a large African immigrant community. The movement of pedestrians and shoppers across the cobblestones is matched by motor scooters, a van, and a couple of cars, all of it taking place in a long shot that might remind us of the souks in Tangier as shown in *The East Wind*. As the title *The Medina of Paris* suggests, the film gives the sense of Paris as a medina or Arab city, one that has been transformed by its inhabitants by being practiced in a particular way. In its sixty-second duration, the film reconfigures the Paris that Smihi presented in *Si Moh* a quarter of a century earlier, in which the city appears completely indifferent to its migrant worker. This city, rather, is made by its Arab and African residents, shown during a minute of the month of Ramadan.

While the vibrant space of the square in *Moroccan Chronicles* might have generated any number of stories, it is at the moment we see a man with a performing monkey that we are introduced to the principal characters of the first sequence of that film. Crucially, though, this performer seems to just emerge from the crowd of the marketplace, and those who surround him look no different from the other onlookers whom we have observed in the sequence thus far. Smihi has thus extracted the beginnings of a narrative from the teeming life that he has documented with his camera, and the bleached, discolored edges of some frames (caused by the damaged film stock he received from the Centre cinématographique marocain) only adds to the effect of loose-knit documentary or even home-movie footage.

The first chapter of the film follows this monkey tamer and a group of three boys who taunt and kill the animal before being punished and forced to dance for him on a leash, just like the monkey did, in the square. The neorealist style of this chapter conceals neither the cruelties of the world of the square nor the arbitrary nature of what happens to people there. There is no narrative explanation for the boys' actions toward the monkey or their hostility toward its trainer, and we are left to surmise that there may be no motivation other than the boys' own amusement. Nevertheless, in the flatness of its approach to the story material, in which we sympathize little with the protagonist (who has himself exploited his monkey for money), the story also allows us to appreciate the full gamut of Moroccan life around the streets and the square. Inasmuch as there is exposition of cruelty, there is an equal appreciation for the carnivalesque pleasures of the space and its performances. The handheld camera moves and dodges around the old male dancer with his wig in an early part of the sequence, and isolates parts of his gyrating torso and distorted face in close-up at the end; the sound of the snake charmer's horn joins with the old man's singing and carries over into a shot of the *hakawati* telling his bawdy story about a young man having sex with his lover; cobra heads fill the frame in close-up before two other snakes are balanced on a charmer's head; and the Gnawa musicians' cymbals are framed against the vibrant costumes.[24] There is a celebration here of the *sha'abi* (popular) pleasures of the open square as it becomes a space for unbridled music, bodily expression, personal connection, and cruelty, and all these are rendered visible to us.

While more contemplative in tone, the third chapter of the film (set in Tangier) also brims with observation and neorealist immediacy. It follows an old fisherman, Ammou, who thinks he has seen a great white whale with a belly full of treasure (his whale is in fact a trans-Mediterranean freight ferry), and it is sometimes reminiscent of *The East Wind* in its presentation of the daily realities of the port and its life. In color this time, we observe the routines of mending fishing nets or splicing rope intercut with shots of trucks loading ferries that then leave the port. This chapter continues to contrast the relationship between Moroccans who are poor and immobile, like Ammou and his peers, and the global world that arrives as a fatal threat by container ship from Europe. In contrast to a cosmopolitan character like Shams in the film's second part (which I will discuss further in the next chapter), Ammou and those like him are able to experience the global only as a negative and at its point of reception, where it threatens and even destroys them.

Neorealism's function here as a practice that might reveal the relationships between the local popular and the wider world is redoubled by Smihi's own understanding of neorealism's place in world cinema. Aside from the explicit references in his writing to the interventions of Rossellini, who, while under the sign of the national, also practiced such a relation between the local and the international, Smihi's impulse to worldliness might be understood by comparing him to another filmmaker whose work also negotiates the charged postcolonial spaces of the global and the local, of popular cinema and art cinema, by engaging histories of neorealism: Satyajit Ray. Moinak Biswas's account of realism in the Indian context is instructive for our understanding of Smihi's films in the context of Arab and international cinema, in two aspects in particular. First, Biswas argues that the development of neorealism in Indian cinema was not due solely to its "arrival" in the films screened at the International Film Festival in Delhi in 1952, but was rather part of the longer history of realism in the novel, which should, he argues, be studied as an international form with multiple modalities. Biswas's account of realism in the Indian cinematic context shows that Ray was not only developing a form that was in dialogue with elements of Italian neorealism but also working out aspects of the Bengali and Indian novelistic forms that had begun to stress social realities and settings. Second, working beyond the language of origin and influence, Biswas instead treats neorealism as one of the ways that Indian cinema became worldly, with the Indian novel (itself a form that was less derivative of a European original than formative of a new phenomenon) as one of the sites of dialogue and exchange with cinema. Biswas's example of this is the film *Uprooted* (Chinnamul, dir. Nemai Ghosh, 1950), in which Ghosh (who had not, Biswas suggests, himself seen any neorealist films) managed to anticipate and develop a neorealist style. "This anticipation," argues Biswas, "and the afterlife that neorealism enjoyed in various national cinemas through the rest of the century show that its global reach is not to be understood solely through the model of 'influence.'"[25]

Moreover, as Biswas argues later, the manner in which experiments with neorealism and dialogue with the realism of the Indian novel shaped Indian cinema offers us a way to see that cinema as engaged with, rather than simply derivative of, the world: "The dialogue with neorealism . . . was one of the ways in which Indian cinema entered a global affiliation; it found an alternative mode of becoming part of world cinema—a globalism different from the one created across nations by Hollywood. The global spread of the novel form provides a broad horizon against which the dynamics of cinematic modernity would be understood."[26] Such a reading of Indian cinema helps us understand the dynamic of neorealism in relation to the work of Smihi and his contemporaries in Morocco. A film like *Spring Sunshine* (Shams al-rabiʿa / Soleil de printemps, dir. Latif Lahlou, 1970) also demonstrates a neorealist impulse in its representations of Casablanca and the life of a solitary office worker there. Mohammed Reggab's *The Barber from the Poor Neighborhood* (Le coiffeur du quartier des pauvres, 1982) shares a legacy of neorealism in its presentation of the Moroccan city and its focus on poor neighborhoods and marginalized figures. These films, along with Smihi's, owe their shape not to the slavish adoption of imposed European forms but to their directors' engagement with world cinema. Their neorealism is one aspect of their mixing of local elements and traditions with ideas and practices that were animating international art and culture and that were key to a modern society.

In Smihi's hands, however, the cinematic legacies of neorealism were also expressed in a dialogue with Egyptian cinema, which he explored extensively in his film *Egyptian Cinema: Defense and Illustration* (1989). In the 1950s a handful of Egyptian filmmakers began to investigate themes of poverty and social problems in a style that was more realistic than anything that had preceded it.[27] Generally speaking, the style of these films—by directors like Salah Abu Seif, Tawfik Saleh, and Youssef Chahine—was not consistently neorealist and existed in tension with the demands and conventions of Egyptian commercial entertainment cinema, which remained largely melodramatic and with relatively tight censorship. Chahine's *Cairo Station* (Bab al-hadid, 1958) mixes its realism with the codes and conventions of the Egyptian melodrama, and Salah Abu Seif's *Cairo 30* (1966) was postponed for many years because of the censors' refusal of his material (based on a novel by Naguib Mahfouz), which turned on the exploitative relations between the bourgeoisie and middle classes as well as the question of socialism and revolutionary activity. Abu Seif is generally regarded as the first director to extensively develop a cinematic realism, but there was precedent for his work in an earlier Egyptian film, *The Will* (al-'Azima, dir. Kamal Selim, 1939). Selim's film is set in a working-class neighborhood of Cairo and centers on a barber's son and his prospects. As Mohamed Khan points out, it addresses the social gap between salaried government officials and tradespeople, reflecting both popular attitudes regarding class and the social problems that are embedded in them. Selim's film was, according to Khan, the first to break with the tradition of song and dance in favor of a setting—an alley—that was re-created to resemble those that Selim found in his extensive research in Cairo's poorer neighborhoods. He fought unsuccessfully with the studio to name the film "The Alley," based on his belief that the social situation, not the character or his willpower, was the most important protagonist.[28] As Abu Seif, who learned his craft from Selim by working as an editor for *The Will*, pointed out, "Even though the scenes were shot in the studio, we reconstructed scenes so faithfully that everyone thought we had shot the film out on location."[29]

Abu Seif's own work went further in its aesthetic and political turn to realism. In films like *The Monster*, *Raya and Sakina* (Raya wa Sakina, 1953), or *Beginning and End* (Bidaya wa nihaya, 1960), Abu Seif developed a style that was more extensively realist in story, setting, and cinematic treatment, and his films studied the effects of poverty, corruption, and unjust social circumstances on his protagonists.[30] *Raya and Sakina*, for example, was based on the true case of two women in Alexandria who became Egypt's first serial killers. This film's realism tends toward naturalism as it develops a distinction between the moral superiority of the police and the depravity of the killers; Claude Michel Cluny, for example, argues that the Alexandria depicted in the film is Manichean in its scope, precluding a more thorough social critique.[31] But in *Cairo 30*, the visual legacy of Italian neorealism is pronounced and Abu Seif utilizes a more complex combination of mise-en-scène and cinematography than was evident in either his earlier work or *The Will*. For example, in one astonishing sequence, the camera tracks and follows his two central characters through the city, where giant billboards with cartoonish images of wealth and luxury overwhelm them, creating an ironic counterpoint to their conversation about greed and society; Abu Seif's two lovers stroll through a city whose built environment seems to communicate with them. One could easily compare such shots to those in *Bicycle Thieves* (1948), where Vittorio De Sica positions his own protagonists before walls, posters, and visually evocative parts of the city.

In these and many other cases, Abu Seif's work was bound up with the literary vision propelled by Naguib Mahfouz. While Mahfouz is primarily known as a novelist, he also authored more than twenty screenplays over a twelve-year period between 1947 and 1959 and worked extensively with Abu Seif.[32] Their collaborations with Mahfouz as screenwriter resulted in key films such as *Raya and Sakina*, *The Monster*, and *The Thug* (al-Futuwa, 1957), which Abu Seif singled out as the most direct expression of his drive toward realism: "For the first time, I underlined the importance of economic factors and I unveiled the class nature of Egyptian society. I unmasked the links that exist between the holders of capital (on the market) and the holders of political power. I suggested that the exploitation of men by other men would continue as long as the relationship between the classes was not reversed."[33] Yet in this film in particular Abu Seif develops the kind of modernist transformation of neorealism that we will see later in Smihi's work or that was present in some of the later work of Rossellini, such as his *Europe '51* (Europa 51, 1952). *The Thug* is set entirely outdoors in the markets of Cairo and develops the *futuwa*, or tough-guy, character type that Mahfouz had used in previous films, here developed as an underdog (named Hariri) played by Farid Shawqi. Abu Seif's camera quickly sets up the stakes of his exploitation, with crane shots showing the scope and commotion of the markets and their quotidian importance, and an impressive montage sequence showing how painful and grinding Hariri's work is as he pulls a vegetable cart laden with produce and sometimes people. Jump cuts show his feet taking a beating from the pavement, intercut with a donkey's legs doing the same work. After we see Hariri bandaging his feet, he sits down to eat as the camera cuts from his eating to the donkey also being fed, the two aligned by the film's discourse. Abu Seif thus develops a vision of a society marked by corruption and oppression and generates a mise-en-scène that attempts to represent that oppression starkly and effectively through the intervention of cinematography and editing. This manipulation of space and the camera's approach to it is one of the reasons why Smihi pointed to Abu Seif's work as indicative of a new kind of realism, drawing on previous models yet grounded in contemporary Arab realities that might better represent the world of its subjects.

ROUCHIAN ANTHROPOLOGIES FOR ARAB WORLDS

What have these histories of neorealism meant for Smihi, and how have they, and related forms of realism, functioned in relation to his work? Smihi himself has treated the appearance of realism in Arab cinemas as a moment in the development of cinematic self-expression. In the previously mentioned article "Anthropologie culturelle," delivered at a roundtable in Milan in 1984 and republished in his collection *Écrire sur le cinéma* (Writing on Cinema), Smihi argues that Egyptian cinema in its first few decades—the 1920s to the 1950s—was "fundamentally derivative. It copies, rearranges, parodies, or casts in a new mode the American, Italian, and French cinemas. It recycles genres: musical comedies, dramas, historical films, melodramas, respecting them or mixing them up according to its own recipes."[34] He contends that the arrival of a neorealist sensibility in Egyptian films in the 1950s was the beginning of new mode of cinema that moved closer to the expression of a cultural identity:

> Beginning in the 1950s we see, in effect, the birth of an Arab cinema that renews the links with its society, culture, and history. It is a cinema that we will come to designate, little by little, by the terms realist, neorealist, or even poetic realist: it is characterized by the kinds of subjects it tackles (social, psychological, political), by a proper aesthetic of restraint, conciseness, dramatic *déroulement*, and by the constitution of a professional world (screenwriters, directors, cinema actors, the participation of journalists and writers). It is characterized, too, by an ambition that is stated, worked on, and researched: to invent a cinema that is no longer constituted in mimicry but in an image of the self and its cultural identity, by the self.[35]

In this way, Smihi discloses the importance of the other experiments with neorealism to his own vision, citing Selim's *The Will*, Kamal's *The Postman*, Abu Seif's *Case 68* (al-Qadiyya 68, 1969), and Saleh's *Diary of a Country Prosecutor* (Yawmiyyat na'ib fi al-ariyaf, 1969), and argues for them as critical elements in the formation of a cinema that can better articulate a culture and its practices. As the rest of this chapter will show, Smihi himself developed a flexible way of working with realisms of many kinds, and his comments do not suggest that he saw it as the only style appropriate for Arab cinemas. Rather, he situates experiments with realism in cinema and the novel as generative of new practices of cinematic self-expression rather than as stylistic ends in themselves.

In pursuit of such practices of self-expression, Smihi has often invoked anthropology as a discourse that can produce knowledge of the self. Conscious of the way that anthropology has been associated with the drive for colonial control and knowledge in the Arab world, Smihi nonetheless attempts to claim it as a domain of knowledge that can inform cinema when practiced from the perspective of the insider. He has argued that in the wake of postcolonial independence, anthropology was marginalized within Arab universities and research centers because of its associations with the colonial enterprise, and sociology became predominant.[36] But in the work of structuralist anthropology yoked to psychoanalysis, such as he encountered in Paris, he finds the potential for a different reckoning with the self. I will have many occasions to return to this predilection of Smihi's in subsequent chapters, for it is one of the intellectual foundations of his work (even as that work is not reducible to such discourses), but there are particular implications of such an approach where the image and the mode of cinematic realism is concerned. Ethnographic filmmaking has, of course, been one of the sites of interaction between anthropology and cinema's encounter with the real. Smihi alludes to this when he reserves criticism for the ethnographic filmmaking that the French conducted in Morocco while at the same time recognizing that it left images of a culture in the midst of a confrontation with a violent form of colonialism. What would it be for such an ethnographic look to be mobilized in the service of the self rather than the service of the Other? How might an ethnography of the self proceed in a way not restricted to documentary images but dealing also with fiction?

Smihi finds a way through these questions in the legacy of French filmmaker Jean Rouch's *ciné-ethnography*, an experimentation that takes place through the act of filming and through the presence of the filmmaker in the midst of that encounter. Rouch's work, as Reda Bensmaïa has shown, puts in question the very notion of the insider and outsider just as it questions the genres of fiction and documentary.[37] Indeed, the encounter between filmmaker and subject was central to Rouch's practice for the way that it can destabilize the boundary usually assumed to hold between fiction and documentary reality. Steven Feld has argued that what made Rouch's work particular in the context of anthropology and documentary filmmaking alike was "his blurring of the very cinematic distinction between documentary and fiction film in favor of a more ethnographic and imaginative integration."[38] This strategy is most strikingly developed in the feature-length fictions *Jaguar* (1957–67), *Me, a Black Man* (Moi, un noir, 1958), and *The Human Pyramid* (La pyramide humaine, 1959). In *Jaguar*, for example, Rouch wanted to make a film about migration between different regions of Africa, but instead of attempting a documentary, he improvised a narrative with his participating actors and created something akin to a travelogue. The three characters, Damouré, Lam, and Illo (all their real names), begin in a village in Niger and decide to travel, ending up in Accra, in Ghana, where they make a small fortune in the huge open-air market before eventually returning to their village. Shot in 16mm, mostly without sound (voice-over narration, some of it mimicking dialogue between characters, was added later), the film's fictional frame nonetheless allowed for the exposure of aspects of the realities that he and his characters encounter.[39] In *Me, a Black Man*, Rouch continued to develop this tension between documentary and fictional narrative in the relation between the actor/subject and his real conditions of life. As Rouch put it, "We began filming in the same way we did in *Jaguar*. But in *Jaguar* the actors played roles that were not their own, whereas here I found myself facing someone who was playing his own role, his own life. Thus was constructed this bizarre dialogue with truth, this autobiography on film."[40]

It is not difficult to see the liberating influence of such interventions on Smihi's films. The dialogue between documentary and fiction that structures Rouch's work is visible in *Si Moh, The East Wind*, and to some extent in all the films, especially the Tangier trilogy (*A Muslim Childhood* [2005], *Girls and Swallows* [2008], and *The Sorrows of a Young Tangerian* [2013]), which Smihi often speaks of as works of autobiographical fiction. In a kind of afterthought to one of the interviews included in Feld's book, Rouch states: "For me, as an ethnographer and filmmaker, there is almost no boundary between documentary film and films of fiction. The cinema, the art of the double, is already the transition from the real world to the imaginary world, and ethnography, the science of the thought systems of others, is a permanent crossing point from one conceptual universe to another."[41] What such a perspective enables for Smihi is the development of films that captivate the viewer in that "art of the double," the play of likeness and difference between the pro-filmic world and the now-diegetic world on-screen. For example, *Si Moh*'s sequences in the city and construction sites are part of the fictional diegesis of Smihi's immigrant worker, but they also index the actual spaces of Paris that immigrants inhabited, including those caught in the field of Smihi's camera. Sakini's character of Si Moh has immediate referents in the real: not only the experiences of Sakini and Smihi themselves, but also those of the other migrants who populated the city in search of work. In creating a simple narrative of urban movement, Smihi reprised the real movements of the people he engaged when he sold political broadsheets in the *banlieues* (suburbs) with his leftist friends. *Jaguar*'s story of a real migration, narrated by way of a fiction about three young men who find their way from Niger to Ghana and back, is redoubled in Smihi's short film, which is equally interested in the place of migrants in relation to the spaces they must inhabit and negotiate while attached emotionally and affectively to home.

In *Moroccan Chronicles*, the opening scene of the Marrakesh chapter—set in the Jemaa el-Fnaa, as discussed earlier—offers us the same heady mix of narrative action staged within observed reality that one finds in the Accra market sequences of Rouch's *Jaguar*. Smihi's fiction, woven into the everyday life of Marrakesh that he shoots, constitutes part of the film's Rouchian strategy; it is equally noticeable in the film's third (Tangier) chapter, where Ammou and other characters interact with the activities of the busy Tangier port, and in its framing narrative, too. The final scene of *Moroccan Chronicles*, part of the framing story, takes place at the Fez train station. Amine has run away, leaving only a letter for his mother, and departs on a train bound for Tangier. Here again, Smihi shoots the area with the neorealist style that he employed at the factory and around Fez in the beginning of the film. The train station—like the factory and the card game (staged in the Tangier chapter), a site of cinema's earliest documentary experiments—is the very location for the historical phenomenon that the film analyzes: Moroccans leaving for Tangier, from where they attempt to make their way to Europe for work.

Similarly, *The East Wind*'s sequences of Aïcha/Leila Shenna in the market document the everyday realities that are unfolding constantly around the story. For the first thirty minutes of the film, we predominantly see Aïcha within the domestic sphere, in the company of other women and children. The camera stays fixed, observant, at the height of the low Moroccan couches (in a conscious nod to Yasujiro Ozu's famous tatami-level camera), and we gain an unprecedented and intimate look at a female-associated space in a Tangier setting. As the critic Abdelwahab Meddeb points out, this is a significant and radical departure from the Tangier that was well known to spectators by the 1970s: a haven for drugs and espionage, as rendered in many adventure films.[42] In contrast to these interiors, Smihi places Aïcha within exterior spaces that privilege the kind of documentary fiction that Rouch might champion. Indeed, in between two sequences I have already discussed, where Aïcha walks through the city in a neorealist observation of figure and space, is an unusual scene of staged, semi-fictional action. Having entered the *ville nouvelle*, Aïcha comes upon a garden party in the courtyard of a large mansion, populated by the international bourgeoisie of Tangier. As the British expats drink and talk among themselves in English, a title appears in French: *potins de la colonie* (colonial gossip). This is not a subtitle; it is rather a textual device that, as I have argued elsewhere, functions as an omniscient commentary on the action.[43] These figures (drawn from the actual expatriate community of Tangier, as the credits suggest) perform a kind of satire of colonial manners and pretension, discussing the quality of the gin and stories of colonial life. As the scene continues, the camera moves us around the party but cuts away to Aïcha's contemptuous stare in a sequence of shots that also serves to align her with the Moroccan servant at the party (fig. 11).

The documentary-*like* footage that Smihi constructs with his actor-models, many of them nonprofessionals, gives way at some moments to actual documentary footage. As the action moves to an outdoor fair near the beach, we observe the preparations as people go about their work pitching tents, organizing produce for

FIGURE 11. Aïcha stares contemptuously at the English bourgeoisie and their garden party while making eye contact with the Moroccan waiter in *The East Wind*, 1975.

sale, and practicing music. The camera stays with these everyday aspects of the scene even as it gradually introduces Aïcha and the other characters into it. Later, after Aïcha's dramatic death at the Hercules Grotto, the film cuts back to the port of Tangier and we have an extended sequence of shots that document the activities at the port as fishers, boat builders, and dock workers go about their various labors— grinding propellers, fixing nets, scraping boat hulls. Interrupted by a sequence of still, empty shots around the medina and then the *ville nouvelle* (with the sound of a long ship's horn or siren over) we return to the docks, where men leave their jobs and walk toward the city. This last part of the sequence, intercut with flash-forwards to Brahim at school (those shots belonging to a sequence that comes shortly after), stresses the mobility of the workers and is accompanied by sounds of their labor, along with seagulls, the wind, and foghorns. Thus while the sequence is carefully edited and constructed, it includes shots that engage directly with an everyday reality of the pro-filmic without the introduction of dramatic elements; in that sense, the material differs from earlier parts of the film such as Aïcha's walk. Here the fiction is present through the layering of sound and image and the use of editing to insert diegetic material from moments just subsequent (these in fact may be either flashback or flash-forward; we cannot be sure of the temporal logic) but the images of the port remain within the register of the documentary, furthering Smihi's embrace of ethnography as a way of seeing within Morocco.

We might continue to see a Rouchian approach throughout Smihi's work even as recently as *The Sorrows of a Young Tangerian*, in which Rouch's principle of "only one take" (the shooting method to which he claimed to adhere, whether approaching fiction or reality) meets a Bazinian fondness for duration as Smihi uses exceptionally long takes that lend a documentary quality to the image while also imparting a sense of improvisation. Here, even an actor's occasional stumble over dialogue (as appears to happen in a conversation between the teenage Mohammed Larbi and his teacher, Muriel) does not seem amiss. For all its staged beauty and its compelling narrative fiction about Larbi's negotiation of political activism in a time of a repressive *makhzen* (Moroccan state), *The Sorrows of a Young Tangerian* is something of an essay film, testing its dramatic narrative with highly staged sequences of theater, ensemble performance, and music. It is a film that encourages a distanced perspective on the action, the better to appreciate the social and political dynamics of its moment, yet it also surprises with unscripted moments that are startling in their cinematic beauty and in their revelation of a reality that threatens to overtake the fiction. For example, in a scene at the end of the film, Sidi Ahmed and Larbi travel toward the airport in the back seat of a car. There is little conversation until Sidi Ahmed takes the hand of his son, who has earlier in the film announced his atheism, and begins to pray for him. As the extremely long take and its uncomfortable moment continue, strong shafts of sunlight begin to enter the frame from the back window and the lens flares, creating a circle of purple and rainbow colors, a starburst, and a line of blurry polygonal shapes that threaten to obliterate the image. The effect, occurring completely fortuitously during the shoot, suggests not only the intrusion of a pro-filmic world beyond the scope of the fiction but also a sense of the divine at exactly the moment when it is invoked by the father.

REALISM AND MODERNISM

In an interview with Guy Hennebelle published in 1981, Smihi articulates a desire to find a cinematic discourse in a Moroccan, African, or non-Western context that is transformative and new when compared to the Euro-American classical cinema tradition. "Perhaps," he offers, "it belongs to the film-makers of societies which weren't in at the origins of the cinema's invention, to call into question the structures and types of construction of the films inherited from classical cinema. It seems to me that cinema may be a form of writing capable of regenerating a mode of thought."[44] In this comment, Smihi signals his intention to forge a new form of *ciné-écriture*, or cinema-writing, that would be expressive of the cultural, historical, and political environment that he finds himself in. At many points in the interview he grapples with the problem of how to find an appropriate cinematic language to represent the Maghrib in ways that are appropriate to its historical specificities. That he is still, however, concerned with some conception of a real is witnessed in his discussion of *Si Moh*. Arguing that he tried to avoid the sentimentalities typical of some films about migration, which he finds "obsessed with suffering," Smihi tells Hennebelle that with *Si Moh* the intention was rather to approach "the analysis of reality."[45] Here he signals his attempt to avoid exactly the "brutal humanism" that Karl Schoonover finds in many of neorealism's spectacles of pity.[46] Instead, Smihi's "analysis of reality" is suggestive of a method that does not center a spectator in a singular point of view typical to what Colin MacCabe might call a classical conception of realism.[47] To efface the spectator within a taken-for-granted and singular point of view is what the quotidian realism of Hollywood has produced, and it is for the most part what the earliest phase of Egyptian cinema also produced. Smihi's aim with *Si Moh*, by contrast, was to produce a method of analyzing some of the contradictions and complexities of Si Moh's life but through a discourse that enabled the spectator to take some distance from the action while still engaging with, as Smihi puts it, "the way in which the consciousness of an oppressed person might formulate the nature of this problem [emigration]." Thus with a simple narrative as pretext, he argues, we might better understand and reflect on how the migrant worker "decodes" the "western industrial setting" in which he is placed.[48] Crucially, however, Smihi's gesture toward representing the consciousness of an oppressed person, as he puts it, does not depend upon and nor could it countenance a singular point of view in the narration. Part of what the film reveals is the splitting and dispersal of perspectives that such a reality entails for the actual subject. Thus the film's use of montage in both image and sound, which we will explore more in the following chapter, results in a perspective on space that recognizes its alienating potential for the subject. Consciousness here is not embodied in a singular, fixed perspective but is rather the aggregate of a discourse in which the camera moves across many spaces and the soundtrack offers sounds both diegetic and non-diegetic, on-screen and off. Adopting some of the strategies of the experimental documentary form yet building a narrative that is "fictional," *Si Moh* is a fine early example of Smihi's radical approach to the question of the real by reconciling realism and modernism.

The East Wind continues this project through its refusal of a strictly linear or logical narrative development and its manner of conjoining the kind of documentary-like footage I described earlier with an aesthetic that is not reducible to realism. Just as *Si Moh* acknowledges a debt to realism while avoiding sentimentality, *The East Wind*'s images of Tangier, while reminiscent of Italian neorealism's mode of location shooting and urban representation, function differently than the neorealism of, say, Rossellini's war trilogy, or of De Sica in *Bicycle Thieves*, in that Smihi's film refuses to develop a kind of moral or humanist certainty in the face of cruelty. Its narration instead dilutes the certainty of a singular perspective through digressions, disruptions of causality, and the deployment of montage to shift scale and perspective radically throughout even as it recapitulates the aesthetic style of neorealism at the level of the shot. The tension between the aesthetics of the shot, the sometimes discordant effects of the soundtrack, and the flow of the images as established through the film's editing constitute its radically attenuated version of realism—a realism that is held in question and challenged even as it develops a perspective on the contemporary Morocco of its moment (the 1970s) and of its recent history (the period just prior to independence, when the film is set).

Such a tension is evident early in the film, which opens with a succession of spatially disconnected but conceptually linked shots that together establish the spatial coordinates of Tangier. We move in a quite logical progression from the opening shots on the outskirts of the town, to the *ville nouvelle*, and eventually, after the director's credit, to the medina. Smihi's camera then reveals the activities found in and around the medina: a small herd of goats being milked and driven through the streets, bread being baked in a community oven. Yet even as these views are established, a deliberate staging and manipulation of a mise-en-scène becomes increasingly apparent: a metal door to a bakery swings open seemingly of its own accord, an action that is repeated a little later as the camera gains unmotivated entry to the bedroom of the boy whose observations and actions will be part of the film's narration.[49] We thus become aware of someone's intervention into the reality of the mise-en-scène.

Across this long establishing sequence one can see certain hallmarks of a neorealist style. The exterior locations are seemingly devoid of dressing or staging, the mobile framings divulge handheld or improvised movements of the camera, and there is a quality to the city images that is suggestive of documentation, depiction, and contingency, those qualities valued in a Bazinian approach to neorealism over the alternatives of manipulation and staging. All in black and white, their aesthetic is gritty and unadorned. Yet as the door swings indicate, we are very much in the presence of an omniscient filmic narration that orchestrates exactly how we apprehend the real that is presented. The neorealist-styled opening shots are combined so as to produce difference and contrast rather than a slow unfurling; the montage stresses juxtaposition over continuity. Indeed, the movement back and forth between interior and exterior that ensues contributes to a sense of disorientation and fragmentation as certain scenes develop outside of strict temporal logic and with a narration that is at best attenuated, since it is sometimes tied to an omniscient perspective, but at other times seems to follow the consciousness of a character (Aïcha especially, but also her son, Brahim).

In this way, Smihi plays with the signifiers of neorealism while pushing past its limits with a modernist discourse comprised of both European and local discourses. As I have suggested above, such a mode of experimentation ties him to the broader terrain of global modernist art cinema of the 1960s and 1970s. Many radical filmmakers of the 1960s and after refused Hollywood's quotidian realism with a realism better attuned to social realities and a desire for political transformation. At the same time, while adopting a mode of representation recognizable from Italian neorealism, they rejected the particularity of the latter's national political context and discarded its tendency toward humanistic certitude in the face of fascism.

As Rachel Gabara has argued, for example, Latin American filmmakers like Glauber Rocha, widely perceived to have been formed within the legacies of Italian neorealism, came to reject it for its perceived Eurocentric qualities and the way in which it constituted another version of "second cinema." Rather than reflecting the reality of the filmmakers' society, they argued, neorealism distorted that reality through its insistence on a strong national culture—something that, Gabara explains, the Third Cinema proponents rejected in favor of regional and multiethnic affiliations as a response to the violence of imperialism.[50] Tracking this response across a range of filmmakers' proclamations, Gabara shows that while many had owed their early experiments in cinema to neorealism's possibilities for showing the world, their belief in social transformation meant that they finally settled on modes of discourse that were more interventionist and committed to the analysis and radical transformation of reality, not just its inscription. Rejecting the Bazinian view of neorealism, the Latin American filmmakers privileged the creative intervention in reality that Bazin had cautioned against. Rather than privilege duration and mise-en-scène, Tomás Gutiérrez Alea and his contemporaries understood that the transformations wrought by montage were critical for the project of reshaping reality through a new language of cinema.[51]

Such a transformative approach to reality and filmic language is well in tune with the project that Smihi himself embarked upon with his early films like *Si Moh* and *The East Wind* and that he outlined to Hennebelle in the interview cited above. Smihi and the Third Cinema filmmakers provide evidence that global art cinema modernisms took on their own characteristics that were not simply derivative of Euro-American cinematic modernism; indeed, they may have even worked in opposition to it. Third Cinema's yoking together of anti-colonial politics and radical aesthetics was seen across North Africa and the Arab world as well as in Latin America. The kind of experimentation witnessed in Smihi's work resonates not only with Latin American iterations of Third Cinema but also with the transformative rendering of reality in a film like Omar Amiralay's *Film-Essay on the Euphrates Dam* (Muhawala 'an wadi al-furat, 1970). Despite its vexed relationship with the then-new Ba'ath party's political program (which Amiralay later denounced in an essay-film sequel, *A Flood in Ba'ath Country* (Tufan fi balad al-ba'ath, 2003), Amiralay's film used a formal experimentation with documentary and montage to present a picture of Syria at the cusp of modernization in a postcolonial moment. Later films like *Everyday Life in a Syrian Village* (al-Hayat al-yawmiyya fi qaria suriyya, 1974) and *The Chickens* (al-Dajaj, 1977) continued this experimentation while directing their political anger more directly at the Baʿath regime itself. The realist tendencies of these films, informed by a documentary impulse in the case of Amiralay, were combined with a modernist method of montage and the attempt to defamiliarize the relation between space and the human subject all in the service of a different kind of political and cultural self-expression. Smihi's *The East Wind* can be situated within this broader moment of Third Cinema modernism even if (like the Syrian examples cited) it did not consciously adopt the manifestos or rhetorics of Third Cinema's practitioners. Yet in its desire to tell a story at a historical moment of nationalism and postcolonial independence, it shares some of the formal energy and tactics of these other films.

For example, after a scene in which we see the face of Mohammed V, the Moroccan king exiled by the French in 1953, in the face of the moon (a reference to a popular nationalist mythology that was current in Tangier during the fight against the French), we encounter a sequence of eight shots that resemble archival still images. In the first, we see a truck whose deck is filled to overflowing with men under attack by soldiers and a crowd lining the street on either side of it. As the shots appear on-screen, a chant is audible that the English subtitles translate as, "Sultan Mohammed V back from exile; the puppet Arafat to the grave!" As the shots continue, we are barely aware that in fact the camera's frame is isolating particular areas of a single still photograph that documents a revolutionary nationalist moment. Cutting to a medium shot—another still—of a man in sunglasses next to an overturned jeep, the camera jumps back, then pans around to reveal the rest of the photographic image of burned-out cars and Moroccan men who face the photographer. Smihi extracts eight cinematic shots from these two still photographs, mixing the stillness of the photographic image with the uncanny movement of a camera moving around within that frame—an effect that is reminiscent of the optical zoom in the final shot of *The 400 Blows* (Les quatre cents coups, dir. François Truffaut, 1959). The irruption of a different photographic real into the diegesis of the film serves to locate us instantly in a historical moment: 1956, when most of Morocco gained independence from the French protectorate. It serves to halt the flow of the images of the fiction film with seemingly still moments of an earlier historical time, and gives way to an uncanny sequence of streets devoid of people except for a lone soldier on patrol, further destabilizing our understanding of the place of the fictional within the real, or the real within the fictional.

It is not the first time that Smihi breaks the flow of moving images with stills: recall the images from *Si Moh* invoked at the very beginning of this chapter. Toward the end of that film, its discourse undergoes a marked shift as the viewer encounters a series of still photographic images in which the film's title character is suddenly frozen in time and space, looking, thinking, and sleeping in the empty carriage of a metro train. In this sequence of still images, reminiscent of the visual narration of Chris Marker's *The Jetty* (La jetée, 1963) or of certain moments in the work of Arab and North African peers like Ahmed Bouanani (*6 and 12* [6 et 12, 1968], *Memory 14* [Mémoire 14, 1970]) or Mohamed Afifi (*Of Flesh and Steel* [De chair et d'acier, 1959], *Return to Agadir* [Retour à Agadir, 1967]), Smihi pushes the viewer back out from any assumption of documentary realism into a more suspended state where realism meets the essayistic use of montage and disruption. The still image, as it used in *Si Moh*, is reminiscent of what Sergei Eisenstein and Roland Barthes referred to as the *photogramme*. Barthes's interest in the still was due precisely to its contrapuntal status in relation to the flow of moving images; the still, he argued, rather than being a "subproduct" or "reduction" of the film was paradoxically what might best enable us to understand the "filmic," which is to say that "inarticulable third meaning" of a sequence, beyond information or obvious signification. Barthes claims that, in its stillness, the still "scorns logical time" and instead demands from us that "a film is not simply to be seen and heard but to be scrutinized and listened to attentively." *Si Moh* plays with this sense of shock and scorn: by interrupting the flow of the narrative, the still images encourage a kind of scrutiny and listening that disrupts pity or sentimentality, qualities Smihi wanted to reject in his immigrant's narrative. Moreover, such a scrutiny constitutes a "veritable mutation of reading and its object," a challenge to how we might approach the cinematic text—a challenge eagerly taken up by a filmmaker concerned to find a new expressive language to represent the conditions of reality that he perceives around him.[52] As we momentarily lose our bearings on Si Moh's lonely journey, the stills provoke the possibility of new perspectives on the figure in the frame as a displaced human within an industrialized space, a figure without belonging in the city and yet intrinsically part of its very fabric, the colonial subject present in the metropolitan center who reminds it that its imperial histories mean that its others are constitutively part of its self.

Timothy Corrigan also picks up on the potential for still images to produce new meanings, as he describes their use in the films of Chris Marker. Drawing upon Gilles Deleuze rather than Barthes, Corrigan shows how the presence of still images and their disjunctive combination within the flow of moving cinematic images "creates neither spectatorial 'identification,' a position of familiar emplacement in the world, nor a version of Brechtian 'alienation,' a position of unfamiliar exclusion from that world represented. Rather this is a suspended position of intellectual opportunity and potential, a position within a spatial gap where the interval offers the 'insight of blindness,' where thought becomes the exteriorization of expression."[53] In this essayistic film, *Si Moh*, and in the essayistic passages of films like *The East Wind*, we are offered that very possibility in the "spatial gap" between still images, and are reminded that the modernist intervention that this strategy represents is here present in the work of Smihi, a Maghribi filmmaker come to the

FIGURE 12. Mohammed Larbi and Sidi Ahmed pose for the camera in *A Muslim Childhood*, 2005.

"center," just as it is with Marker, a French filmmaker working at the so-called peripheries.

Smihi's interest in the relation between movement and stasis within the photographic and cinematic image of reality continues in later films. *A Muslim Childhood* takes up the relationship differently in an early sequence where we are introduced to the main characters, a Tangerian family that we will see again in the next two films of Smihi's Tangier trilogy, *Girls and Swallows* and *The Sorrows of a Young Tangerian*. As an omniscient voice-over narration (voiced by Smihi himself) describes the family members, we see a series of shots resembling tableaux vivants in which characters face the camera, motionless yet present within a shot that has duration and is definitively not a still frame. The effect is that of a photographic portrait (fig. 12). Yet there is an uncanny quality to the lack of movement (in these shots, only the slight shifting of a body in space, or the blink of the actors' eyes). The direct look to the camera, famously forbidden in Hollywood and most narrative film codes, is here combined with the dislocating effect of a voice-over narration that, in its omniscience, seems non-diegetic, outside the world of the characters because of its all-knowingness. And indeed, in its knowledge of the characters' foibles and small histories, the voice-over narration resembles that of the Arab realist novel whose intervention within the history of Arabic fiction was to create individual characters whose actions were described and narrated in omniscient ways. Chapter 3 will further explore Smihi's relationship to the tradition of Arab modernism in the novel, as I discuss the intertextuality of his films. But for now it is worth noting that his development of a register that complicates realism with modernism is not only cinematic in its contexts, nor is it only Euro-American. It is precisely in the experimentation across forms and traditions that Smihi's work takes shape.

In accounting for the ways that Smihi's versions of realism tend toward the modernist expression of the self and its contradictions, MacCabe's analysis of literary and cinematic realisms in "Realism and the Cinema" (1974)—where he treats realism as a question of narration more than content or visual style—is helpful. Discussing Rossellini's cinema, MacCabe shows how it does more than simply represent a subject matter (poverty, despair, the destruction of the war), instead offering multiple perspectives through which to view reality. But MacCabe argues that Rossellini's films do not deal well with contradictions of class or history because "the camera ... is not articulated as part of the productive process of the film," and thus the viewer's position is not addressed in any radical way.[54] MacCabe thinks that a realist-inflected cinema can, in fact, articulate contradiction through strategies learned from modernist fiction: "Much in the way that James Joyce in *Ulysses* and *Finnegans Wake* investigated the contradictory ways of articulating reality through an investigation of the different forms of language, one could imagine a more radical strategy of subversion than that practiced by Rossellini in which the possibilities of the camera would be brought more clearly into play."[55] That call takes MacCabe into the terrain of what we would think of as modernist cinema, as practiced by Brecht in *Kuhle Wampe* (1932) or Jean-Luc Godard in *Tout Va Bien* (1972), where "the emphasis is on the particular scenes and the knowledge that can be gained from them rather than the providing of a knowledge which requires no further activity—which is just there on the screen."[56] In effect, MacCabe shows how realisms differ: classic realist literature and classic realist cinema are compared to subversive realisms, both literary and cinematic. And although his essay is concerned with definitions of realism rather than modernism, the subversive strategies he finally calls for take us into that messy critical overlap between realist and modernist, a domain that has provoked fruitful critical commentary and which is the province of Smihi's cinema.[57] In particular, MacCabe's comments about how Joyce might prepare us for a subversive realist cinema are tantalizingly useful for understanding Smihi's cinema, not only with respect to elements of *The East Wind* and *Si Moh*, but with regard to the radical work of his *44, or Tales of the Night*.

MODERNISM AND THE PRETTY IMAGE

44, or Tales of the Night continues Smihi's project of cinematically narrating the Moroccan self in history through a discourse that is anthropological and informed by diverse traditions of narrative and image. While it offers the viewer the promise of richly historical material, much of it shot in authentic settings and bolstered by a concern for detail, it is also a film whose images are carefully composed so as to stress the beauty and sumptuousness of their mise-en-scène. Smihi juggles the realism of shooting beautiful locations with beautifully composed, lit, and filmed wide-screen images of Morocco. In this sense it departs from his previous work in *The East Wind* and *Si Moh*, where he utilized 16mm black-and-white stock, historically associated with documentary and neorealist filmmaking. For *44* Smihi turned to 35mm color film, invoking not the neorealism of Rossellini but the lush cinematography of a later Italian filmmaker, Luchino Visconti. Visconti, of course, is a significant figure in tracing the outer limits of neorealism and its imbrication with modernism. As Noa Steimatsky argues in *Italian Locations: Reinhabiting the Past in Postwar Cinema* (2008), his *Obsession* (Ossessione, 1943) discloses at once a sense of continuity with realist impulses and the rupture of the modern. Like the work of Pasolini and the other filmmakers Steimatsky studies, Visconti's films offer a "productively recurrent configuration of modernist and realist discourses, in varying ideological shades and depths," which are the focus of her book.[58] While staying with the reconfigurations of modernism and realism, Smihi turns to the beauty of one of Visconti's later films, *The Leopard* (1963). Borrowing its look as well as one of its lead actors, Pierre Clémenti, Smihi created a film whose beautiful images demonstrate the possible articulations of art cinema within the domains of history, global aesthetic traditions, and the real.

44 covers the forty-four years of the French protectorate in Morocco, from 1912 to 1956. It follows the character of Moussa, a young man from a poor family in Chefchaouen, in the northern Rif mountains, who goes to study at the university of al-Qarawiyyin in Fez. There he becomes an assistant and personal tutor to the family of El Hajj, a professor at al-Qarawiyyin and a devout, reformist Muslim and nationalist who is wedded to tradition even as his household dabbles in the trappings of modernity (represented in the arrival of a radio, roller skates, and a telephone into the home). Smihi presents the household, as he does in many other films, as a cross section of Moroccan society. Yaqut, a slave, attends to the family, including El Hajj's first and second wives, until the very end of the film, where we witness her death in the pitiful conditions that the family has imposed on her. Abdelhaq, El Hajj's eldest son, suffers his circumcision and humiliation at his father's second marriage (both presented in flashback) and ends the film as an alienated young postcolonial, French educated but lacking a secure place, either there or in Morocco. Moussa is similarly lost, failing at his studies and his attempts at poetry. By the end of the film he is homeless and begging in the streets; as Smihi puts it, he is "swallowed up by history," just like Ammou or Amine at the end of *Moroccan Chronicles*.[59] But *44* rejects any kind of simple chronology for this story, favoring instead a narrational structure of leaps, flashbacks, and juxtapositions. Its anti-teleological form perfectly represents the structure that MacCabe posits, embracing contradiction and requiring work for the viewer, who must interpret the narrational disjuncture and the beauty of its disparate scenes.

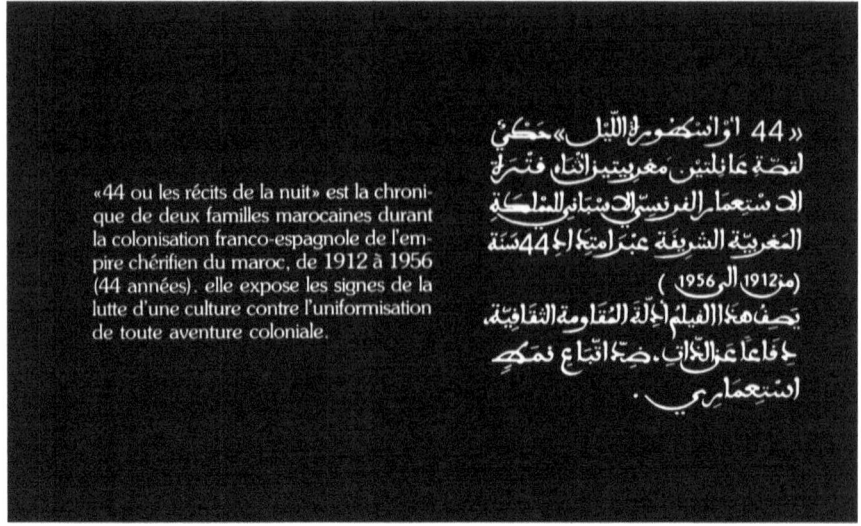

FIGURE 13. Titles like this one in *44, or Tales of the Night*, 1981, utilize the aesthetic qualities of Moroccan calligraphy as graphic elements.

44 thus develops its own version of a modernist realism while embracing beauty and the decorative. In so doing, it pushes away from the dominant trajectories of European realism that have stressed the mundane qualities of the pro-filmic while remaining suspicious of adornment and aestheticism. Rosalind Galt has traced critical skepticism toward beautiful images by revealing what she terms film theory's anti-aesthetic impulse, its scorn for "the pretty." In its suspicion of images that are "colorful, carefully composed, balanced, richly textured, or ornamental" in favor of the monochromatic, uncomposed, urgent, and gritty, film theory and criticism's embrace of realism and neorealism has devalued a whole terrain of filmmaking—one that Smihi's *44* inhabits.[60] While its richly layered use of sound will be considered in the next chapter, here I wish to point to its remarkable use of aesthetic strategies for the image—not in opposition to other realist tendencies we have traced in his films, but as the very means to address history and the real. This film proves that even images that are pretty, decorative, aestheticized, or "anthropological" are vital in rendering a complex, postcolonial Arab realist discourse.

The film opens with an image that is strikingly decorative and demonstrably centered on the rendering of surface. Against a rich blue screen, we see two blocks of text: one, in French, is produced in all lowercase in a stylized Latin font; the other, in Arabic, is written in a highly decorative Moroccan calligraphy (fig. 13). This text introduces us to the film with a literal placement in time: "This is the story of two Moroccan families during the Franco-Spanish colonization of the empire of Morocco, from 1912 to 1956 (44 years). It exposes the signs of one culture's struggle against the uniformity of any colonial adventure." While acting as an informative title (which is followed by others, together occupying the first fifty seconds of the film), the image also suggests a love for the textuality of the title itself and for the beauty of the Moroccan calligraphy in which part of it is set. This is but the first example in the film of a two-dimensional image that stresses the qualities of a decorative surface, and it is significant as both an image of aesthetic note and an example of the strong textual and decorative tradition in Arab-Islamic culture more generally.

Indeed, the titles are neither isolated to this moment in the film nor can they be read as external to the film's style. Smihi uses them throughout *44* as a way to generate some of the multiple perspectives that constitute the narration. Quotations from a range of sources create a multivocality that complements the multivocality of sounds and the juxtaposition of images and scenes, so the very presence of these titles *as text* is important. The tradition of textuality and the decorative in Arab-Islamic culture is well established in part through the importance of the Qur'an as text. While the use of representational images has a complex history and has at times been eschewed, largely on the basis of the *hadith* or sayings of the Prophet Muhammad, textuality and decoration both enjoy a position of heightened aesthetic importance across the history of Arabic culture.[61] Smihi makes frequent use of settings that display the traditions of surface decoration. The Fez interiors with their elaborate tile work, carved wooden doors, and rich fabric upholstery are elements of the culture that are present and ubiquitous in the city, as much so as the rough, palimpsestic walls of the medina alleys where he also shoots.

In this sense, then, Smihi straddles a complex line between realism and what we might call a textually complex aesthetic image—one that remains nonetheless tied to the real. The connection lies in the way that these images render the Moroccan built environment and other material realities as recognizable within an economy attuned to the real. Indeed, we might say they are highly aesthetic and beautiful, but also represent something of the everyday realities of Morocco—material realities that are ever-present but whose qualities of beauty are not fully appreciated. We alternate in the film between these aesthetically beautiful images and those that operate within a more conventional realism. As spectators, we observe the lush, decorative, sometimes shallow space of sequences in Fez or Chefchaouen and are equally exposed to deep-focus, deep-space views of castles, the beach, and the modern city of Casablanca. But to what extent must we take the lush images as antithetical or antagonistic to the real? In her exploration of the decorative image, Galt traces the ways that the pretty image is consistently and negatively counterposed to the realist or political image. The influence of neorealism in the postwar period followed by the politics of the post-1968 era meant the devaluation of the cinematic or aesthetic image in favor of its uncontrived, spontaneous opposite.

Galt writes, "In the wake of Italian neorealism's assertion of uncomposed immediacy as the aesthetic mode ethically appropriate for the postwar world stage, its effects of artless visual contingency were increasingly adopted as signifiers of political radicality and communal self-determination." Similarly, she argues, the pretty image became "a central object of attack" in the post-1968 period.[62] These observations are key for our understanding of where the dominant cinematic discourse developed in the postcolonial North African context. Films like *The Charcoal Maker* (Le charbonnier, dir. Mohamed Bouamari, 1972) or *Wind of the Aurès* (Vent d'Aurès, dir. Mohammed Lakhdar-Hamina, 1966) relied on a gritty neorealist aesthetic for their political impact, just as the Italian-Algerian production *The Battle of Algiers* (dir. Gillo Pontecorvo, 1966) invented a new version of neorealism to represent Algeria.

What Smihi achieves with *44*, however, is more akin to what took shape in Latin America in its rejection of European discourses on cinematic beauty and politics. Smihi's beautiful film is radical in part for its desire to perform a cinematic equivalent to the strategy and slogan its filmmaker saw and admired in the United States in the 1960s: "Black is beautiful." As he has indicated in conversation, Smihi saw this phrase as offering something that he could relate to in a Moroccan context: how to take signifiers of Moroccan-ness, devalued or turned kitsch by the colonial encounter, and allow their beauty to be appreciated by a film audience. Galt's analysis reveals a precedent for such a strategy in the work of Bolivian director and writer Jorge Sanjinés. In an interview published under the title "Political Cinema Must Not Abandon Its Interest in Beauty," Sanjinés argued that a political cinema, "as the cinematic expression of a people without cinema, must be preoccupied with beauty because beauty is an indispensable element. For we are fighting for the beauty of our people, this beauty that imperialism today tries to destroy, to degrade, to overwhelm.... The fight for beauty is the fight for culture, it is the fight for a revolution."[63] Sanjinés's injunction to deploy beauty against the influence of the colonial finds a ready equivalent in Smihi's film, which tends to juxtapose more flatly and typically realist sequences with others marked by different aesthetic qualities.

For example, several sequences of French troops in Fez and Rabat are shot outdoors and sometimes in a realist fashion that reminds us of the documentary images of troops in the streets in *The East Wind*. These sequences, which have a hue of green and gray and blue, exist in stark contrast to the scenes of the two families. There, deep blues, browns, yellows, and white predominate, drawn from the surroundings and location. Smihi's attention to texture and surface is especially notable, and we see it in the treatment of clothing, such as the woven woolen vest worn by Moussa's father, whose fibers are perfectly rendered in a medium close-up, or the beautiful winter jellabas that Moussa wears in Fez. When El Hajj meets the other men for his discussions of religion and politics, they are set before an elaborate interior of blue and white *zellij* (mosaic tiles) that completely encloses

FIGURE 14. The beauty of the decorative image in *44, or Tales of the Night*, 1981.

the conversation on three sides; as the camera cuts in, we can better appreciate the folds of the turban that El Hajj wears as he hosts his guests. And our privileged access to the female interior space of the house later in the film allows us views such as that of El Hajj's wife surrounded by attendants, who pattern her ankle and hands with henna as she reclines on richly brocaded cushions (fig. 14). But Smihi does not use this aesthetic only to show images of richesse. While sumptuous textures and surfaces of Moroccan material culture are celebrated here, they are also contrasted with the extreme poverty and misery that accompanied and subtended them, be it in the streets or in Yaqut's living quarters. The shifts in space and time that the narrative effects enable the juxtaposition, within seconds, of images of despair and poverty with images of great wealth.

The valorization of the objects and textures of Moroccan life was something shared by Smihi's immediate predecessor, near peer, Ahmed Bouanani. Bouanani's own work in the form of documentary fictions like *Tarfaya, or a Poet's Walk* (Tarfaya, ou, la marche d'un poète, 1966) relied upon his extensive research and documentation of oral traditions and folk practices in the south of Morocco, where *Tarfaya* was set. As I have argued elsewhere, the movement of Moroccan modernism sought to redeploy vernacular practices that had been historically devalued by colonialism.[64] Bouanani's work across drawing, poetry, and cinema has constituted, like Smihi's, a response to colonial history and the present that is radical for its embrace of aesthetics, beauty, and the popular. It is a strategy that is also present in the work of Sanjinés and his peers. Returning to the interview that Galt treats so productively, we find Sanjinés arguing that cinema could utilize beauty in the same way Andean villagers did: for them, beautiful objects performed a practical function but also served to bind a people together. Yet Sanjinés asks beauty to signify differently, argues Galt: as a marker of a culture and as resistance to regimes of value that are Eurocentric in origin: "The political film, like the Andean textile, is well made, decorative, and attractive, and the worldview it expresses merges political thought with aesthetic pleasure."[65] Galt's reading of Sanjinés demonstrates that a politics of Third Cinema, contra many assumptions, was at times articulated around questions of aesthetic beauty, not gritty images of reality.

With Galt's work in mind, we can argue that in the case of Smihi's *44, or Tales of the Night* and many of the images in his later color films (especially *A Muslim Childhood*, *Girls and Swallows*, and *The Sorrows of a Young Tangerian*), Smihi's carefully composed and beautiful images are constructed precisely to address questions of history and politics through a representation of cultural specificity and beauty. Yet as they do so, they remain tied to the real through his invocation of an anthropological role for his cinema in the Maghrib. Those same images, however elaborated they may be in a film like *44*, are embedded with the same purposes as *Si Moh*, *The East Wind*, or *Moroccan Chronicles* especially, whose aesthetic is more closely tied to neorealist or documentary precursors. In every case they serve to offer what Smihi has described as a "signs and science" approach to reality. This phrase is one the filmmaker has used to describe his attempt, within the legacy of structuralism, to "de-note, that is, to describe, to work, to unfold, to articulate, and to combine all the signs—historical, cultural, economic, formal, et cetera—which are proper to produce a 'discourse of analysis' of a society and its culture, its contradictions, its ruptures. To produce the image of a society at a critical moment in its history, to allow it to see itself, is to some degree to present what we might call its 'mirror stage.'"[66] Here, then, we can identify the legacy of both structuralism and psychoanalysis in Smihi's thinking, together constituting the impulse I described at the outset of this chapter: to provide a discourse on the self, by the self, for the self and the other. As this chapter has shown, that impulse yields an engagement with the real through strategies that yoke together realist and modernist aesthetics and histories.

In responding to Smihi's particular version of art cinema, this chapter has shown that his films inhabit a position that is much more supple and productive than critical binaries of realism and modernism might suggest. Rather, they generate their emotional and intellectual impact in the way they operate across these categories, using their modernist discursive form to both invoke and exceed realist aesthetics in the service of an argument about encounters with modernity in the Arab world. This chapter has considered how such a strategy operates with respect to the visual images of his films. Yet at every moment Smihi stresses that film is image *and* sound, and the next chapter will show that the interventions we have seen here operate in similarly dynamic ways with respect to the soundtracks of his films.

2

The Voice of the Arabs: Smihi's Soundscapes

In the previous chapter, I argued that Moumen Smihi has created an Arab cinematic modernism that adopts and transforms neorealist and ethnographic histories of cinema to construct a discourse on the Arab and Moroccan self in the world. Smihi's experimentation with the image and its cinematic contexts continues in his use of film sound. As he has stated in many contexts, making films is, for him, a process of research, and sound becomes a plastic element deployed in combination with images to create a new kind of relationship between cinema and the world it represents.[1] In his films, sound works not only to authenticate what we see in the "present" of the image, but also to test and construct other relationships to place—other parts of the Arab world, Africa, Europe—and time (the past, and even possible futures). By forcing us to hear differently, and by drawing on the complex soundscapes of the Arab world, Smihi's films show how the histories of Morocco and the Arab world are inextricably tied, and how they are always emplaced within an even larger set of geopolitical and cultural frames.

While not eschewing direct sound or realistic sound, Smihi has often used his soundtracks as another element in a cinematic *écriture* that is neither constrained by preexisting discourses nor indifferent to them. His combinations of sound and image stress their mutual importance—always speaking of image *and* sound, he refuses to treat cinema as a "visual medium."[2] One can perceive this interest from his earliest moments as a filmmaker and thinker. In 1968, when he was just finishing his studies at L'institut des hautes études cinématographiques (IDHEC), he published an interview with Robert Bresson in a special issue of *Image et son: la revue du cinema*. There he engaged Bresson's views on the soundtrack, which the French filmmaker regarded as having "an importance equal to or greater than the image track." Drawing implicitly on Pierre Schaeffer's idea of a "sound object" (*objet sonore*), Bresson affirmed to Smihi that "there is a sonic reality to objects and they are more dramatic in their sonic reality than in their visual reality."[3] Their dialogue establishes the way that Smihi, even before he shot his first film, was conscious of how sound might convey a sonic reality, as Bresson terms it, but also how it could also push the viewer beyond realism. Watching and hearing Smihi's films, we experience sound as something that unsettles, or contravenes the dynamics of the image, or de-authorizes what we see. Such experimentation challenges how we perceive and conceive of film sound, for Smihi works against the typical tripartite divisions accorded to it: noise, music, voice. The films force our attention to what Michel Chion calls the "sonicness" of all such sources.[4] Influenced by the variegated soundscape of Tangier, but attentive to the sonic environment of other settings, too, Smihi creates soundscapes that signify the depth and complexity of diverse Arab and Moroccan worlds. Smihi's rich sonic spaces destabilize the borders of noise, music, and voice to further a modernist self-expression that evokes local specificities while placing them within trans-Arab and transnational spaces and discourses.

SI MOH AND COMPOSITION IN NOISE

Si Moh, the Unlucky Man (1971) illuminates some of the principles of Smihi's approach to sound as they have developed across many films. The soundtrack is integral to *Si Moh*'s representation of a migrant Moroccan worker in Paris and further radicalizes the combination of images that we see, drawing the Maghrib into the descent toward the "Capital Hell" (as Smihi has termed it) that Si Moh experiences in Paris.[5] As I noted in the previous chapter, *Si Moh* uses only the barest story material, which it subordinates to images that deploy codes of realism in an avant-garde fashion, working across the borders of documentary and fiction. *Si Moh*'s soundtrack is a critical part of the audiovisual combination that Smihi exacts there. It blurs the divisions of music and noise, rarely using voice except as another component of noise. Chion, building on the work of Pierre Schaeffer, has argued that the very distinction between music and noise is one that should be retired. In recognizing the "sonicness" of sound, we learn that the sonic qualities of noise are foundationally no different from those of other types of sound. To mark out certain sounds as "noise," then, is to relegate them to secondary status. Even within the category of nonmusical sounds, "noise," argues Chion, "marks off a deceptive category" of lesser value. As a solution, he proposes not the elevation of noise to positive standing, but the rejection of the noise/sound distinction as "unfounded and segregationist."[6] Such a critical move is already prefigured in Smihi's work, where the noise/sound distinction is actively deconstructed as one element in the sonic modernity. Two types of noise, or sound effects (the more common term in Anglophone criticism), might be identified. Those that strike the viewer as intrusive, harsh, or distracting (due to either loudness or timbre) interact with others that are more naturalistic or real-seeming and that authenticate the mise-en-scène through their sonic presence. Never allowing us to take the latter for granted, however, Smihi experiments with the boundaries of what is expected and unexpected in order to destabilize realisms and create alternative visions of social reality. We see these tendencies taken to their fullest degree in the films *Si Moh, the Unlucky Man* and *The East Wind* (1975).

Listening to *Si Moh*, one becomes aware that the soundtrack is nothing less than a score: all its audible forms of sound are orchestrated so as to effect a singular composition that occupies the entire space of the film. While there are short passages of voice and stretches of music, both "found" and created for the film, much of the soundtrack is noise from natural and built environments; we hear city streets, trains, worksites, apartments, even birds. This "score" can be understood as an iteration of *musique concrète*. The term, originally coined by Schaeffer, who was also its first practitioner, describes music created from recorded sounds arranged as if they were instruments. Found sounds take on the sonic role of instrumentation, and the process of combination with regard to duration and selection—a process that resembles cinematic editing or montage—is critical to the overall "music" produced. In his early composition "Étude aux chemins de fer" (Study for Railroads, 1948), Schaeffer takes the sounds produced by and around a train (such as whistles, wheels on tracks, and engine noises) and arranges them into a sonic composition of approximately three minutes. He mixes what he called "tonal sounds"—those that have a distinct frequency pitch in the Western system, for example an A above middle C—and mixes them with percussive noises that might typically be thought of as unmusical and atonal. A steam whistle offers a hint of melody across an interval of a fourth, a conductor's whistle is heard, and the piece ends with a playful run of whistle tones, but for the most part it consists of the scraping, thumping, crashing, and thudding produced by a train and its interaction with its environment.

Schaeffer's orchestration of trains prepares us for the soundtrack for *Si Moh*, where Smihi produces a soundscape deeply reminiscent of Schaeffer's experiments. The film begins with the strumming of a stringed instrument played with a percussive slap as if on a soundboard or drum, with the sound fixed on one note that harmonizes to itself across an octave. It is urgent, insistent, dramatic, and it gives way, before even the credit slides end, to a series of train noises not unlike Schaeffer's. We hear the sound of the train on tracks, including the distinctive click of the wheels and a reverberating quality that situates the sounds in space and renders them specifically as a metro subway. There is a crescendo of footsteps, voices, an accordion playing a snatch of music. All these sounds take place over a series of images that are unsynchronized: we see nighttime Paris traffic when the train sounds still predominate, then some kind of construction yard detached from those city streets and from the train, and images of people shopping that are never synchronized or even loosely associated with the accordion. This kind of combination, which seldom matches an image to a sound, continues throughout the first few minutes.

Noise continues to stand out over other elements of the soundtrack. An extended sequence of orchestrated sounds takes place during a scene set in the construction yard where Si Moh seeks work. This scene is introduced by the harsh metallic motor whir of a crane moving on tracks, accompanied by rhythmic striking sounds. The attack of the crane noise forms a radical break with the previous scene and, intruding on it as a bridge to the new, the shock and violence of this noise is all the more unrelenting. Sound continues to dominate the entire scene as we follow documentary images of the work site and its surrounding area without the intrusion of voice. It is not until a full two minutes and thirty seconds into the scene that we hear a human voice, as the foreman gives instructions to a group of workers and then begins a short dialogue with Si Moh about the prospect of work. If it is true, as Chion has argued, that most films are *vococentric*, structuring meaning and space around the human voice, then *Si Moh* is profoundly *anti*vococentric, its sonic space constructed fundamentally by noise and occasionally music. In the film's final scene, Si Moh descends into the metro and sits, leafing through postcards from home, surrounded by other homeless men. After a percussive sequence with drum and a humming voice, the mix goes quiet for a period. As the sound comes back up we hear distant car noises, but the sound of numerous chirping birds begins to enter. It grows to a din, to the exclusion of all other sounds, reaching the peak of its crescendo as we witness Si Moh hunched over, his facial expression hidden from us; then it abruptly ceases as the screen goes black and the film ends. The source of the bird chirps remains unseen throughout and, as the mix manipulates its loudness beyond any kind of narrative motivation, we begin to sense that this sound may be subjective for the character—indeed, there is a strong possibility that the birds are the product of imagination or memory. We hear an almost identical cacophony of bird sounds again at the very beginning of Smihi's *Girls and Swallows* (2008), where there is a narrative justification for the sound-off: a title at the start reads, "In Tangier, popular belief has it that the hand that throws stones at swallows will be paralyzed." Those swallows still inhabit the eaves and roofs of the town and are a recognizable part of the city's soundscape. Smihi uses them in *Si Moh* as both abstract noise—a screeching that signifies the psychological pain of the character—and as a quite specific noise that emanates from and occupies the space of memory for this migrant worker, thinking of home.

While *Si Moh* might be the most sustained example of Smihi working in the method of *musique concrète*, it is far from the only instance where he utilizes the complexity of a sound mix to favor noise over music or voice, or to recalibrate the relative importance of those domains by treating them equally rather than vococentrically. In the first few minutes of *The East Wind*, the sound mix contains noise, music, and voice orchestrated in a manner that emphasizes their qualities as sonic domains. As with *Si Moh*, Smihi creates a modernist experimentation with sound that nonetheless offers elements of sonic realism in the way it expresses the aurality of the medina. This kind of "medina ambience," as Smihi has referred to it, furthers his goal of working with image and sound in such a way that they function both in parallel and independently. "We often forget that the cinema is the image *and* the sound, not one more than the other. It seems to me important to research not the redundancy but the complementarity, the recovery, the overlap, such that the sound says what the image lacks and vice versa. We really need to manage to make sound and image signify in parallel and independently."[7] Smihi's proposal is more than a call to pay attention to sound as well as image. It is rather an insistence on research and experimentation, testing how they inform each other dynamically within the same film. Such an experiment animates *The East Wind* and other films that utilize noise in new and inventive ways.

The East Wind constructs the sonic complexity of the medina by refusing the subordination of noise and music to other sound elements. Rather than using noise only to authenticate the visual elaboration of space, Smihi constructs a mix with different instabilities of sound and image. By constructing multiple sound objects that are not so much referential as polysemic, Smihi creates something closer to the *musique concrète* approach of *Si Moh*. The film opens with the solo voice of a woman singing an Amazigh song, followed by the voice of a man singing a different refrain. We alternate between these two for the first few minutes as the space is established through the visual montage described in the previous chapter. As we move out of that sequence, however, the balance radically shifts from a predominance of voice to a predominance of recorded sounds or noises. We see a shot of the beach and then a succession of shots of the medina, first from its exterior, then into its steps and alleyways; over these images, the voices on the soundtrack blur together as the sounds of women and men and children and babies, all unseen, mix with other sounds such as birds and the clanging of a cowbell as a goatherd drives his goats up the steps. All these sounds continue over a shot of a baker preparing bread, but we also hear the slap of his hands against the dough as he punches it down. Shortly after, in shots of Brahim on the beach and in bed, the only audible sound is a loud ticking that is as unexplained and unspecified as are the images; without any referent, the sound seems ominous until, finally, with a shot of a wall clock and its swinging pendulum, the source is specified. As Aïcha's husband performs his ablutions before prayer, we hear a metallic clunking as he pours water from a metal teapot and returns it to the tiled floor; we hear the slop of water and hands against his arms and feet, then the sound of his wooden clogs on the tiles. Most of the scene, then, is dominated by noises as the space of the family is constructed sonically with tension. The brief moments of speech from the grandmother and the husband's prayers function as vocal components of a sound mix dominated by small noises and silence. As a cut sends us back to the street, we hear the goats and their bells again before the mother-in-law speaks to her son about the folly of his plan to take a second spouse.

That brief moment of speech, however, complements rather than breaks with the *musique concrète* of the film's first few minutes. The sounds of chanted prayers, ringing church bells, birds, voices in the streets, and a motor scooter all create a polyphony where voice is but one component in the overall soundscape. *The East Wind* is as interested in the *sound* of its voices as in the specifics of the speech. A similar mixing of voice and noise occurs in the sequence in which a homeless or disturbed man and a young girl interact on the doorstep to a house in the medina. A medium close-up of a girl swinging an iron gate appears suddenly, without explanation, establishment, or context, from the preceding sequence of Aïcha in the market. From this jarring cut, we hear a harsh metallic squeak and, at slightly lesser loudness, the girl's giggly laughter as she pushes the gate back and forth. A wider two-shot reveals the man in a knitted cap seated on the doorstep, also swinging the gate as he laughs, his voice a low baritone to her high-pitched giggle (fig. 15). As Aïcha approaches in a subsequent shot, the gate sound stops but is replaced by his voice in a more pronounced and maniacal laughter. Yet the mix continues to defy realism, for there is more than one track of his laughter, and it is produced so as to double and intensify the sound. Added to this cacophony of voice is the off-screen squawk of the chicken that Aïcha drops and then, suddenly, a siren whose pitch swoops up and holds in a long, extended note over several seconds before decaying at the end of the scene. Smihi thus creates a scene devoid of dialogue where voice becomes just one, nonrealistic element in a sound mix that emphasizes discord and disturbance. We never learn, in any narrative sense, the cause of this man's dementia nor anything of his relationship to the girl behind the gate, and yet the sounds of the gate, the characters' laughter, and even the sacrificial chicken's squawk register sonically as important and disturbing. This sound mix "speaks" where dialogue does not, signifying pain and fracture in the social fabric of Tangier.

In the film's final sequence, analyzed in the previous chapter for its Rouchian documentary qualities, sound continues to signify—over and beyond the power of images—the scale of modernity and its presence as a force in Tangier. Here, sound surpasses the documentary realism that is signaled in the domain of the image, again creating a *musique concrète* that unsettles with contrapuntal force. Two honks of a ship's horn punctuate the relative quiet that begins the scene; yelled voices cry out across the space of the port; and hammers pick up a percussive line that is added to with sounds of electric grinders, machining metal propellers. As the camera cuts away to a brief interlude of medina shots, the sound of the *chergui*, or east wind, increases along with seagull cries before each is drowned out by the

FIGURE 15. The metallic squeak of a gate in an ambiguous scene in *The East Wind*, 1975.

same loud siren heard earlier. As we see Brahim in school, more horns create dissonant chords as we cut back to watch workers move around the port. This composition in noise continues up to the point where a new scene begins in the school. There, voice briefly takes over before the sound and image of a squeaky gate closing, with no human figure in sight, marks an end to the film. Here, as in *Si Moh*, where a cacophony of bird sounds closes the film, Smihi creates sonic worlds that evoke the dissonant modern realities of Paris and Tangier.

While the marketplace in Smihi's *The Medina of Paris: A Square during the Ramadan Market* (1996) pulses with market sounds, one of his other Paris actualities, *The Medina of Paris: Supererogatory Prayer by a Muslim Dignatory—My Father—After Landing at Paris-Orly* (1996), shows a Moroccan man in a jellaba on a prayer mat on a grassy island in the midst of Paris Orly airport, with a terminal and aircraft visible in the background.[8] Its soundtrack juxtaposes airport noises with the solemnity of a prayer and the levity of Josephine Baker's song "J'ai deux amours, mon pays et Paris" (I Have Two Loves, My Country and Paris). Linked together by histories of colonialism and migration, Smihi's two cities are unevenly and unpredictably comprised of noise and voice and music, possibility and despair, beauty and pain. By refusing to hierarchically order sound as subordinate to image, and by creating compositions of music with the sonic objects of noise, Smihi also refuses the dichotomies of "tradition versus modernity" that have long narrated the relationship between Tangier and Paris. Confronting the foreignness of noise and transposing it into musical form, Smihi renders the modernity of Paris as always bound up with its relationship to its colonies, and shows how the intrusion of colonial modernity created fissures and fragmentation within Moroccan society. Sonically and visually exceeding the bounds of realism, *Si Moh*, *The East Wind*, and the *Medina of Paris* films offer a sonic modernism that furthers Smihi's goals of recalibrating the representation of Moroccan and Arab realities.

MUSIC

Smihi's wrangling of noise in the service of a *musique concrète* in *Si Moh* hints at the importance of music to his films more generally. In the terrain of more conventional definitions of music, Smihi also develops a heterogeneity of sources. The films are constantly animated by music, much of it diegetic, and many of them also use non-diegetic music from the European classical tradition. *The Lady from Cairo* (1991) has a non-diegetic score, which makes it unusual among Smihi's films, yet, as we have seen with *Si Moh*, Smihi is adept at using other sources of sound to build the aural equivalent of a musical score. The categories of noise, music, and voice are always questioned as he exploits sound in the broadest possible ways.

While these highly musical films might seem far from the Egyptian tradition of the musical, they work in productive tension rather than outright rejection of its tendencies. Indeed, Smihi's films ooze with love for Egyptian cinema even as they avoid its melodrama and star system. Smihi prefers not to let music telegraph emotions in any straightforward way. The avoidance of score in most of the films (except *44, or Tales of the Night* [1981] and *The Lady from Cairo*) is in keeping with Smihi's invocation of Roland Barthes's distaste for *signalétique* music—"music whose sole effort," says Smihi, "is to try to make evident the *signs* of emotions or feelings and not the emotions or feelings themselves."[9] Smihi's tendency to avoid non-diegetic scores preserves a more critical relationship between images themselves, and between those images and viewers. Where scores do occur, they tend to fulfill a similarly complex function as other areas of the soundtrack, and Smihi occasionally makes them disjunctive with other elements of sound such as noise and voice—and, indeed, with image. *44, or Tales of the Night*, for example, uses an avant-garde score composed by Benjamin Yarmolinsky as well as music by Guido Baggiani, which appears at other moments in the film. In Yarmolinsky's opening sequence, discordant stringed phrases evoke a difficult and distorted historical process. As early as the title sequence and continuing through several shots of the countryside, this non-diegetic music serves as a disconcerting counterpoint to the beauty of the calligraphy and the bucolic possibilities of the landscape. Later, two other non-diegetic themes appear at different moments, this time with sparse instrumentation (piano, or flute and violin) and offering mournful accompaniments to scenes that are generally transitional. These snippets of non-diegetic music weave seamlessly with diegetic on-screen music and move us through moments of abandonment and belonging, across indistinct moments in time.

The Lady from Cairo reveals Smihi's most extensive use of a non-diegetic score. Here his decision is in keeping with the entire experiment of making the film. Living in Cairo, he tried to inhabit the industrial mode of Arab cinema and work with its premises and conventions in his own film while simultaneously creating an internal critique of its suppositions and practices. Non-diegetic scores are crucial to most Egyptian films. While the films are renowned for their sung performances, many of which utilize on-screen orchestras, there are many instances where songs are performed with off-screen music. In these cases, the musical numbers—as with many Hollywood musical numbers—seem to emerge in tension with, or at least in suspension of, the narrative flow. Such is the case, for example, with a famous song like Abdel Halim Hafez's "Bitlumuni lih" from *A Love Story* (Hakayat hub, dir. Helmy Halim, 1959), which pauses the narrative beside a back-projected seashore for more than six minutes of screen time, with an off-screen orchestra accompanying the crooner. In these instances, music becomes detached from the story world and exists outside it—a way of giving space for the performance of musical numbers that themselves are antithetical to realism yet connected to the story world. At other times, non-diegetic scores perform the role they do in many other filmic contexts, that is, to provide emotional weight to the images on-screen.

Smihi works with this convention in *The Lady from Cairo* to great effect. For example, after the credits (where the score creates dramatic swoops of strings to foster a perceived immensity of scale to the narrative and its characters) there is no scored music for the next half hour. But score arrives again, dramatically, when Amina goes to find her cousin Kamal (recently returned from the 1967 war) on the rooftop of her aunt's apartment building. Strings scream in a downward scale accompanied by high-pitched organ sounds, which create a sense of internal anguish and loss of sanity, especially when the mix begins to layer on top of it Amina's frightened screams and Egyptian president Gamal Abdel Nasser's resignation speech (discussed further below). That speech is heard as broadcast radio sound that is diegetic yet has no source in the frame except perhaps Kamal's own thoughts, as if he were an antenna for the doomed president's announcement of defeat. The rest of the score is also reserved for such key moments, most of them involving Amina's encounters with her brother, who has turned toward religious fundamentalism and violence. When she approaches him outside a theater where she has performed, visits or leaves his apartment, or finds him in a shack on the outskirts of Cairo before he is killed, the score telegraphs the danger and impact of these meetings and his transgressive role in her life—and, indeed, in the public life of the city. Finally, at the end of the film, the score deploys a stinger over a headline about the United Nations' declaration of a Palestinian state, then leaves the narrative dangling in an uncomfortable way as the film freeze-frames her face, with the same theme used at the moment of Kamal's retreat to the rooftop. Here, in the film's final moment, the score returns a sense of emotional anguish to the image that refuses any possibility of narrative closure or of a felicitous resolution to Amina's problems.

Non-diegetic, prerecorded music is also used, but sparingly, in the films. In *A Muslim Childhood* (2005), for example, it is well suited to the generic play that Smihi enacts, a kind of dance of intertextuality between filmic and musical references that will be discussed further in the next chapter. A popular French children's song strikes a contrasting note with a montage of Egyptian film posters near the end, and two prerecorded, American popular songs accompany the rolling credits and their brief "flashback" sequences reprising key moments. But other examples of classical music in *A Muslim Childhood* demonstrate a different use of non-diegetic sound.

The first occurs early in the film after Larbi's circumcision. Over a sequence of two shots, both from a low angle in a medina street and tilted toward clouds in the sky, we hear a minor movement from Franz Schubert's piano sonata D959. The spoken narration stops during these shots and the sequence thus exists as a purely meditative or reflective passage between Larbi's circumcision and his recovery. The same piece of music and a similar shot return toward the end of the film, a visual and aural rhyme with the earlier sequence, after we learn from the narrator of the death of Larbi's friend. And a few minutes later, Schubert's theme again accompanies a long shot of waves on the coast, with the voice-over of a poem in Arabic. The effect is pensive and Proustian: Smihi has claimed that the mode of the film owes much to both Charles Dickens and Marcel Proust in that it deals with memory and the past in ways that are deeply personal yet also richly evocative of the details of everyday life.[10] Smihi's quotidian realism mixes with moments of visual beauty and abstraction, and the limited but precise use of the Schubert sonata assists in the construction of mood even as the film adheres mostly to Smihi's love for the diegetic sounds of Moroccan music and culture. An appreciation of Western classical music is also evident in the choice of passages by Schubert, Johann Sebastian Bach, and Franz Liszt in *Moroccan Chronicles* (1999), Baldassare Galuppi in *Girls and Swallows*, and Ludwig van Beethoven in *The Sorrows of a Young Tangerian* (2013). These mostly function non-diegetically, too, tending to be sound-over rather than sound-off for the characters, although we have instances where characters are assumed to hear them, also (Beethoven plays in the apartment of a friend of Larbi's in *The Sorrows of a Young Tangerian*).

More than establishing mood, however, these extracts perform another function in the films: they assist in the construction of a worldliness that exists in both the diegetic and the formal registers. Especially in the Tangier trilogy (*A Muslim Childhood*, *Girls and Swallows*, and *The Sorrows of a Young Tangerian*), classical music is a reminder of the cosmopolitan soundscape of that city of many European influences and residents. In this sense, Schubert belongs in the films as much as do Gnawa musicians (whose musical ancestors were sub-Saharan Africans brought into Morocco from the south) or Amazigh songs. In *Moroccan Chronicles*, when the old man drowns fighting an imaginary whale that turns out to be a trans-Mediterranean ferry, the aftermath of his death is accompanied by the mournful solo violin of Bach's Partita no. 2 in D minor. As a long take reveals the trucks branded with German and Swedish badges rolling off the ferry that killed him and into the port at Tangier, the music we hear conducts a kind of duet with the signs of globalization that fill the images. Similarly, at the end of the framing tale, the young boy's voice-over (as he reads a letter about his decision to run away to Tangier and France) is soon replaced by the same solo violin, connecting Morocco to the world of Europe. Over and over again, non-diegetic prerecorded sound unselfconsciously speaks to Morocco's embeddedness in global discourses of imperial history, trade and migration, and cultural expression.

Despite its prominence in such moments, Smihi's use of sound from outside the filmic world is relatively uncommon. Diegetic music, on the other hand, is everywhere: from beginning to end many of the films are filled with vocal music, local folk music, or radio music. A great deal of it is performed on-screen, but even when it is not, diegetic music is remarkable in its ubiquity. *A Muslim Childhood*, for example, combines the non-diegetic music noted above with lively music from the world of the film. The opening credits, like those of the next two films in the Tangier trilogy, arrive with an explosive use of a fast-paced Moroccan song that combines a principal female voice with a chorus of men and women clapping and drumming. The arresting opening suddenly stops at the first cut, in stark contrast to the meditative Arabic poem described earlier. Then we hear on-screen music in an enigmatic sequence that is connected to Larbi's long-held desire for his family's neighbor, Aouicha, whom we suspect works as a prostitute. As Larbi looks down to the terrace that adjoins his house and has a view to the Tangier bay, and beyond it the Mediterranean, an eyeline match shot reveals the figure of a Gnawa musician (Abdellah El Gourd) standing alone on the rooftop singing a song (credited as "Bambara Bongo") and playing a *sintar* or *guembri* (a three-stringed instrument, fig. 16). There is no audience except for Larbi, unseen, and the song exists in a pure space of musical diversion for the viewer. Later, after another scene in which Larbi reveals his obsession with Aouicha, we hear a musical phrase off-screen with a man's voice and a strummed oud, and after a cut we observe the musician (Ahmed Laamarti) playing the song. Again, no other characters are present, and the song, whose lyrics tell of a man being tortured by his desire for a beautiful pasha's daughter, becomes another kind of local interlude.

FIGURE 16. A Gnawa musician plays on a rooftop near the family's home in *A Muslim Childhood*, 2005.

On-screen music animates sequences in *The East Wind*, too. At the picnic where Aïcha's husband and his friends find frogs in their couscous, there is drumming and dancing. A little later, during an extended sequence at the outdoor market, we hear a wind instrument and drums and then see the musicians playing in very quick shots; the music continues off-screen but is present throughout the scene. And later still, as Aïcha and her friends walk along the beach toward the Hercules Grotto to make her fatal offering to the gods, we hear the *qraqeb*, or castanets, of the Gnawa musician before we see him playing. After the camera picks him up again in a later shot, it holds on him and his movements even as the sound drops out, to be replaced by only the sounds of the sea. On-screen music thus confirms some of the actions and location of the characters, but as the shot of the Gnawa musician reminds us, even the synchronization of heard music to on-screen actions is not guaranteed. Whether they belong to the domains of noise, music, or (as we shall see) voice, all sounds are subject to manipulation in ways that remind us of the materiality and the contingency of the film. Just as Smihi indicated in his interview with Bresson, image and music combine to create different kinds of meanings rather than one confirming the other.

As the presence of the Gnawa musician shows, music is a key aspect of Smihi's embrace of a vernacular Moroccan culture. We *hear* the importance of the everyday Moroccan musical soundscape as the films elevate that music to a level of historical importance. As already mentioned, the opening credits of all three films in the Tangier trilogy create a dynamic play of instruments and voices that plunges the viewer deep into a Tangerian atmosphere before we see a single photographic image. In *44*, *or Tales of the Night*, diegetic music becomes as important as the "pretty" image in Smihi's attempt at presenting a culture to itself cinematographically. In a press dossier for the film Smihi stressed the need, in the wake of the destructive material and ideological presence of colonialism, to develop a representation in image and sound of the elements of a popular culture. To do so meant trying to avoid a simple recuperation or rehabilitation of the culture on-screen while interrogating "by and in the film the forms that belong to a particular culture: the popular representation of the storyteller, the traveling musician, and vernacular chants in dialect; the presence of poetry; and the fragmentation of narrative structure." These investigations, he wrote, necessitate "another kind of writing, for every image is above all the image of the ritual belonging to a society."[11] The previous chapter showed how this strategy worked on the level of the image, but Smihi is adamant that it is also a question of the dynamic of image and sound, so that the culture might *hear* itself as well as see itself. Thus music, including, in his words, "noises, silence, objects, instrumental games," is critical to the process of visualizing and respecting the popular.[12]

RADIO

If *Si Moh* and *The East Wind* force us to attend to sounds that are not usually thought of as elements of music, then the sound of radios in these films further muddies the boundaries between noise, music, and voice while situating such questions in a global sonic domain. The ubiquity of radios and radio broadcasts in these films enables an ongoing discourse about transmission and connectedness across global sites. Actual radios within the mise-en-scène certainly feature here, but the *sound* of radio—even without the visibility of radio devices—is equally important. Within the soundscape of a given environment, radio broadcasts often exist as an involuntary presence. In *The Soundscape: Our Sonic Environment and the Tuning of the World* (1993), R. Murray Schafer alerts us to the multiple sources of sound present in any environment, showing how soundscape is often ignored in favor of visual or material signifiers.[13] Smihi's soundscapes place radio alongside bells, clocks, calls to prayer, or animal noises, such that radio operates as one sound element among many others. But radio also becomes important in its acousmatic qualities: the manner in which it broadcasts voices whose source remains unseen by the listener.[14] In Smihi's films, radio carries acousmatic voices that intervene into the soundscape meaningfully, whether as news bearers or musical presences. Radio thus forms a bridge between those sound elements that would normally be thought of as "noise" and those that more properly function as music or voice. In keeping with the way Smihi's films blur such distinctions to elaborate a new kind of soundscape, radio allows us to better understand the sonic contours of his films while opening our ears to other elements of voice that contribute to the films' modernity.

Radio is important in Smihi's films because it creates a supra-national diegetic space, surpassing the visible local. Radio continually serves as a bridge between the immediacy of a film's setting and the insertion of that setting in larger, regional and global flows. As a historical prop within the mise-en-scène and an aural presence on the soundtrack, radio and radios certainly serve a realist function: radio *was* a critical means of spreading Arab music, culture, and political messages in the moments depicted in Smihi's historical films. But Smihi uses radio for purposes much greater than historical realism. As I have suggested above, sound in these films becomes a means to measure and understand the nature of Arab modernities, and radio, as a modern technology within the region, configures space, politics, and culture in important ways. In the films set in the 1950s and 1960s, like *The East Wind, A Muslim Childhood, The Sorrows of a Young Tangerian*, or *44*, radio organizes the relationship between Moroccan nationalism and pan-Arab discourses while also representing the importance of Arabic musical culture. In the films set at later historical moments, radio continues to mark the shifting geopolitics of the region. *Moroccan Chronicles*, for example, transports the viewer from Nasser's Voice of the Arabs, heard in films like *The East Wind* and *44*, to the Voice of America broadcast and then to the francophone station Medi-FM. *The Medina of Paris: Supererogatory Prayer* presents the song "J'ai deux amours, mon pays et Paris" by African American singer Josephine Baker as a tinny radio reproduction that evokes not only a transatlantic black experience but a Mediterranean one as well. The diegetic sound presence of radio in Smihi's films thus engages complex extra-diegetic historical events while also transmitting a sense of Morocco's place within wider sonic worlds.

An early scene in *The East Wind* shows a group of young boys playing in a medina street, when we hear a crackle and hiss as if from a transistor radio with the words "*Idha ʾat gumhuriyyat misr al-ʿaribiyya min al-Qahira*" (The radio of the Arab Republic of Egypt, from Cairo). The snippet here is from Voice of the Arabs, a radio broadcast established by Nasser in the wake of the 1952 military coup led by himself and Mohammed Naguib that ousted King Faruk and led to the establishment of the republic. Radio had begun much earlier in Egypt, with small-scale amateur stations setting up in the 1920s. And the country had its own radio service starting in 1934, when the government developed a contract with Guglielmo Marconi in the UK for leasing broadcast transmitters; starting in 1947 the broadcasting system became wholly Egyptian owned and operated.[15] Shared listening situations were the norm throughout this period, partly due to the cost of tabletop receivers and the licensing fees charged by the government but also because communal listening in coffee shops suited existing Egyptian social norms. In the 1950s, however, the period in which *The East Wind* is set, the transistor radio revolution was underway. Transistor sets were widely and quickly adopted throughout the Arab world, and their relative cheapness and battery-powered portability meant that they were taken up even in regions without electricity. Building on this development, Nasser recognized that his message of pan-Arabism could be effectively disseminated via radio. Thus Voice of the Arabs was launched in 1953, just one year after the revolt, and it quickly developed into a twenty-four-hour broadcast that, as its signal strength increased, could be heard throughout the Arab world. Occupying both medium-wave and shortwave frequencies, it broadcast with a total power of five hundred watts by 1956, and the CIA reported at the time that, at this level, it could be heard from Morocco to Iraq. As Douglas A. Boyd has detailed, it provided news, commentary, drama, and music, and part of its success relied upon the programming of songs by major singers of the period, including Mohammed Abdel Wahab and Umm Kulthum.[16]

In *The East Wind*, then, this small snippet of voice alerts us to the pervasive influence at that historical moment of Nasser's Voice of the Arabs, and the degree to which the Maghrib was part of the sonic terrain that Nasser wished to build and influence. Indeed, Boyd and others have shown that one of the main ideological characteristics of the Voice of the Arabs in its early years was its support for independence struggles across the Arab world. In particular, its editorial line supported Morocco's King Mohammed V against the French who had exiled him (as shown later in *The East Wind*), and it likewise focused on struggles in Algeria and Tunisia. For example it offered material support to Algerian FLN (Front de Libération Nationale) revolutionaries in Cairo, lending office space and encouraging their broadcasts.[17] Filling a void in local programming (local radio in the Arab countries was much slower to develop) and benefiting from high-power transmission and a seeming immunity to frequency jamming efforts, Voice of the Arabs effectively constructed a pan-Arab space that existed despite the wishes or actions of colonial or local governments.[18]

We see an evocation of this historical moment and Voice of the Arabs' role in it in *44*. The scene takes place in the family's home in Fez immediately after a scene in a Casablanca café where there had been an attack by a nationalist group. It is sound that most clearly narrates the sequence of events: over the plucked guitar score we hear an explosion and the crash of broken glass while the voice of a newspaper seller hawks "*Le Petit Marocain! Paris Match . . . !*" As the guitar score continues across a cut, the camera slowly tracks in toward the doors of a salon that open to reveal a Moroccan family seated around a radio (fig. 17). We hear the whistle of shortwave interference and the tinny voice of an announcer:

> Arab brothers, we'll continue our news from Cairo, the Voice of the Arabs. The news coming from Morocco confirms that a plot is underway against the dignified and legitimate agent of the throne. The feudal chief El Glaoui has sworn to have the head of the King with the support of the colonialist Boniface. After the attack perpetrated yesterday in Casablanca in a European neighborhood, an Army of National Liberation has just been born.

FIGURE 17. A family listens to a Voice of the Arabs radio broadcast in *44, or Tales of the Night*, 1981.

Even before the announcer is finished, the film begins to cut to other locations: al-Qarawiyyin, the medina streets, a Casablanca garage. As it moves across these spaces, we begin to hear the equally thin and staticky voice of King Mohammed V, who was at the time about to be sent into exile by the French. He continues (the first part of the speech is inaudible), " ... our faith constitutes the solidity of the Arab Nation. Our unity will be consecrated by the foundation of the Arab League ... " As he finishes speaking, we cut again to the café we saw previously, where a new voice takes over: this time, Smihi's voice provides the external diegetic sound of a young man reading aloud from the newspaper.

Across these spaces, then, radio plays a critical role in the dissemination of news of anti-colonial politics. For example, in *Girls and Swallows*, Sidi Ahmed is often seen next to a valve radio prominently placed in a living area of the home, where he receives news of the nationalist struggles and, eventually, the momentous news of Moroccan independence, as a radio broadcast. Yet, as structured by the radio, these politics are not simply nationalist but yoked to the rest of the Arab world: the family in Fez learns of the latest news in Casablanca from a radio station in Cairo. This incident in the film, then, like the one in *The East Wind* already mentioned, dramatizes the reach of Voice of the Arabs both technologically and ideologically. By evoking the voice of Ahmed Said (the longtime Voice of the Arabs announcer who, for millions of listeners, became indistinguishable from the program itself), Smihi ties his Fez and Tangier families and Casablanca political events to the sonic space of the wider Arab world.[19]

Indeed, it is not only Smihi's films that evoke and represent the historical place of radio in the Middle East and North Africa; we find it popping up in films from other parts of the region. In Mohamed Bouamari's *The Charcoal Maker* (Le charbonnier, 1972), which is largely devoid of dialogue, radio plays a key role. It is present first during a lengthy broadcast devoted to Algerian and Arab politics, to which the impoverished family listens after eating; the mise-en-scène of the moment is thus similarly structured to that of *44*. It is present again later, when the father sets down a transistor radio that begins to emit the sound of Umm Kulthum. In *The Silences of the Palace* (Samt al-qusur, 1994), Moufida Tlatli's film set in Tunisia in the 1950s, the young protagonist and the servants around her listen to Umm Kulthum via radio broadcasts that track the growing nationalism of the moment. As Kay Dickinson notes in her discussion of Syrian films, radios broadcast political speeches in Mohammad Malas's *Dreams of the City* (Ahlam al-madina, 1985) and Oussama Mohammad's *Step by Step* (Khutwa khutwa, 1978) and feature prominently in ʿAbdullatif ʿAbdulhamid's *Listener's Choice* (Ma yatlubuhu al-mustamiʿun, 2003), where the inhabitants of a village gather as the collective audience for a musical request show. ʿAbdulhamid's *Nights of the Jackal* (Layali ibn awa, 1988), Dickinson argues, makes radio "complementary . . . to rural life," as the programming reflects the work of its listening community, and a stolen radio in Oussama Mohammad's *Sacrifices* (Sunduq al-dunya, 2002) audibly signals the ideological affiliations of Baʿathist politics.[20] As it does in Smihi's films, radio in the Syrian films that Dickinson analyzes works to create a sense of collective identity through nationalist sentiment and existential threat. In the Syrian examples, broadcast alerts about the threat of Israeli invasion create collectivity; in *44* and *The East Wind*, radio solidifies anti-colonial resistance to French occupation.

Further afield, there are still more radios: in an essay devoted to Frantz Fanon's exploration of radio in the Algerian context, Ian Baucom remarks that the "novels, films, plays, and histories of the postcolonial are littered with radios." Noting that radio appears as a critical device in texts as diverse as James Joyce's *Finnegans Wake* (1939), Salman Rushdie's *Midnight's Children* (1981), or Isaac Julien's film of black diaspora, *Young Soul Rebels* (1991), Baucom considers the ways that, for Fanon, "literal acts of radio-listening could contribute to a collective politics of anti-imperial nationalism."[21] In his own text "This Is the Voice of Algeria" (1965), Fanon detailed how radio was first institutionalized in Algeria in the form of Radio-Alger, a French-language station intended for France's settler population in Algeria and inextricably colonial in its address and its consumption. "Radio-Alger," he wrote, "sustains the occupant's culture, marks it off from the non-culture, from the nature of the occupied." As he put it later in the piece, "The Algerian, with his own brand of humor, had defined Radio-Alger as 'Frenchmen speaking to Frenchmen.'" At this moment before the war of liberation, Fanon argued that radio was essentially irrelevant to the native population of Algeria, "a technique in the hands of the occupier which, within the framework of colonial domination, corresponds to no vital need insofar as 'the native' is concerned." To listen to the radio was "the mark of Europeanization in progress, of vulnerability. It was the conscious opening to the influence of the dominator, to his pressure."[22] The cleavage between Radio-Alger and the later FLN radio was, for Fanon, complete and binaristic, the latter being the only means by which Algerians had access to something politically or culturally productive.

Yet, as Rebecca Scales has argued, radio in Algeria worked in ways that were more complex than Fanon allowed. Scales shows that in Algeria, starting in the 1930s, radio was transnational and included broadcasts originating on the opposite side of the Mediterranean that engaged local listeners with Arabic-language news and music. Examples include Radio Bari, a fascist shortwave station in Benito Mussolini's Italy that broadcast in support of nationalist movements in Arab states; and Spanish nationalist stations that broadcast in Arabic from Seville with a relay station in Tetouan, Morocco, and from Ceuta, the Spanish-ruled enclave at the top of Morocco. "During the 1930s," she writes, "transnational radio broadcasting fueled fears within Algeria's colonial administration, France's security services, and in metropolitan political circles about the conjoined threats of foreign subversion and domestic political instability in the colony." "Far from becoming an oppressive instrument of colonial domination, radio and recorded sound, particularly when traveling from outside Algerian borders, consistently eluded the grasp of the colonial state."[23] Scales complicates Fanon's binaristic account of colonial versus anti-colonial radio by showing that Algerians did not begin listening to radio in 1954 simply because of the sudden relevance of the FLN's "Voice of Fighting Algeria," but had indeed practiced their listening through exposure to other radio broadcasts and the circulation of gramophone records. That they took up radio enthusiastically was due not only to the FLN but also to the explosion of transistor sets, as occurred in other Arab countries during the early 1950s and as is demonstrated in Smihi's own films.

Radio in Smihi's films, while tied to anti-imperialism in ways I've noted, always fosters more than straightforwardly nationalist sentiments. Smihi's films dramatize and propose that the anti-colonial movement in Morocco was closely yoked to Arab anti-imperialist sentiments and that it took shape in ways that exceeded the bounds of the nation-state. The anti-imperialism of Voice of the Arabs and the anti-colonialism referenced in Smihi's films created a space of *Arab*, rather than solely Moroccan, nationalism. Smihi's films show how resistance to French colonialism took shape within an Arab anti-imperialism ushered in by Nasser's rule and within a structure of feeling nourished by a broader sense of Arab culture. The patriotism depicted in a film like *44* or in his later trilogy set in Tangier is linked to an expansive sense of nation that Nasser's pan-Arab nationalism and Voice of the Arabs jointly fostered. The Voice of the Arabs in these films offers a sense of a wider Arab political and cultural solidarity within the quest for a modern, postcolonial

Moroccan nation—a solidarity that was fostered sonically by music and especially by the broadcasts of a handful of singers who were to become towering figures in Arab cinema and music, led by Umm Kulthum.[24]

The ubiquity of Umm Kulthum and other singers on the already-ubiquitous radios of Arab cinema is key to an audible discourse on Arab social, cultural, and political life in the 1950s and 1960s. In *The Charcoal Maker* and *The Silences of the Palace*, Umm Kulthum's voice serves to suggest a broader community of social and political life, a horizon of possibility that the protagonists yearn to access. Across many of Smihi's films, broadcast music and song suggest the possibility of a vital Arab culture that might mitigate the oppressive characteristics of colonial rule for the characters and further enable anti-colonial resistance. In this respect, one could compare Smihi's work to Youssef Chahine's, especially as it is positioned by Malek Khouri, who argues that Chahine's films were strong proponents of "the concept of the Arab nation and Arab national identity as heterogeneous and integral to a long-term modernist project for national self-determination as well as economic, social, and cultural renovation and progress."[25] Smihi shares Chahine's sense that the long history of Arab culture, especially expressed through the experiments of the Nahda (explained in the introduction), is vitally connected to the possibility of modernist transformation. While radio is not the only source of such an audible Arab lifeworld in Smihi's films, its broadcast within the films allows the live-ness of a wider Arab world to register. Radio and its historical representation articulate the promise of a pan-Arab politics in a period of anti-colonial struggle, as well as express the ongoing legacy of that project in musical and cultural forms.

But broadcast music and song in Smihi's films also suggest resistance to Moroccan nationalist oppressions in the *post*colonial period. If Nasserite broadcasts feed the anti-colonialism of *44*'s characters, Mohammed Abdel Wahab's Arab nationalist song "Watani al-kabir" (My Great Nation), sung by Abdel Halim Hafez and heard as a radio broadcast at the end of *The Sorrows of a Young Tangerian*, offers the later film's characters an escape from the repressions of *les années de plomb*, or years of lead, when Moroccans were imprisoned and tortured under the government of King Hassan II. Moreover, in the more contemporary moment of the films' production, cultural reference points like Hafez's song might also be read as Smihi's way of reaching beyond the restrictive, insular nationalist politics that have characterized the Arab states in the aftermath of the 1967 defeat, or *naksa*, and the 2011 Arab uprisings. In all these cases, signifying more than nostalgia for a pan-Arabist political project that ultimately withered and failed, the presence of a pan-Arab *culture* in the form of music, song, poetry, and literature expresses Smihi's continued yearning for the possibilities of an expanded sense of Arab cultural and political life.[26]

So far, this account of radio has focused on films set between the 1950s and the 1970s, a moment of struggle against various imperialisms in the region and a moment linked to the expressions of Arab nationalism. What does radio allow us to see in the period since? The soundtracks to Smihi's films also track the globalized mediascapes that have emerged across the postcolonial period, and here too radio becomes a cinematic device that does more than authenticate a particular moment. In *Moroccan Chronicles*, set in the same moment of its production, 1999, radio makes plain the competing voices of the US international mission and Moroccan national broadcasting in both its francophone and (modern standard) arabophone forms. In this film, whose framing tale is based on the *One Thousand and One Nights*, a young boy in Fez listens to Moroccan radio broadcasts on a transistor radio he keeps with him (fig. 18). One such broadcast, which comes near the end of the film as the boy and his mother walk around the Merinid Tombs overlooking Fez, begins with news from Algeria and Palestine, then moves to items from the local courts. Announcers recount the names and cases of women who have filed for divorce following the departures of husbands and fathers (like the boy's own) for France:

> *Male announcer*: "Welcome to our airwaves, here are the headlines. An official meeting in Algeria with the outlawed FIS [Islamic Salvation Front].... Israeli and Palestinian negotiators prepare for the withdrawal for Gaza and Jericho.... This is Rabat, The Radio of Morocco."
>
> *Female announcer*: "Ladies and Gentlemen, now, the news from the courts. The president of the Casablanca court announces that Mme. Rakia has brought suit against her husband, Sabri Brahim. The president of the Kourigba court announces that Madame Chaboune has brought suit against her husband, Mohammed Driouche. The president of the Jerrada court—"

Here the boy abruptly switches off the radio before turning to his mother. The phenomenon of massive migration in the 1980s and 1990s is told predominantly through the broadcast and, rather than offering a sense of unity, radio instead places the boy within an audible landscape of fragmentation and loss. Indeed, by the end, he takes a train bound for Tangier, from where, like thousands of others, he will try to stow away to France. There, the broadcast voice, located in the transistor radio that the boy carries, gives way to an internal diegetic voice-over as the boy reads from a letter he left for his mother, explaining his decision.

In the Tangier sequence in the same film, an old fisherman reclines while listening to the news of events in Pakistan and Tajikistan. The newsreader, speaking Arabic, reveals that we are listening to "*Sawt al-Amrika, fi* Washington" (the Voice of America, in Washington). And earlier, we hear the French of a Moroccan announcer on the Moroccan francophone station Medi-1, "*la radio pour tout le Maghreb*," as we watch transnational shipping and freight pass through the contemporary Tangier port. From the sense of a greater Arab nationalism evoked by Voice of the Arabs in the other films, we move to a globalized postcolonial

THE VOICE OF THE ARABS   93

FIGURE 18. Amine listens to a Moroccan station on his transistor radio, hearing stories of migration and loss, in *Moroccan Chronicles*, 1999.

Morocco, subject to new and different economic and cultural flows that are signaled by competing radio broadcasts in different languages. Across all these examples, Smihi's use of radio signals that these films, like the events and settings they represent, exist within geopolitical and cultural frames that stretch beyond Morocco and beyond the Maghrib. Smihi's sonic modernism, of which radio forms a key element, shows us the relation between the world of the medina and the world at large.

VOICE

The acousmatic, heard-but-not-seen qualities of voice, foundational as they are to the medium of radio, also open up larger questions of voice in these films—both the acousmatic voice-over, which Smihi deploys frequently, and the question of the voice more generally, whether sung or spoken, on-screen or off.[27] Considering the acousmatic voice first allows us to connect the question of radio and its transnational qualities to other aspects of voice and sound. Smihi has always been adept at using voice within complex sound mixes to relay subtleties of meaning to

FIGURE 19. Murmured voices off-screen create an ironic counterpoint to images of colonial oppression in *44, or Tales of the Night*, 1981.

the viewer. For example, early in *44* we see a group of well-dressed French people disembarking from boats on the shore, helped by the French soldiers who are subduing the country and by Moroccans who carry some of the colonists to shore on their backs. A subsequent scene shows a town square full of Europeans and employs a complex mix of voices, some of which we see produced but many of which exist as "voice-off" from characters who pass by the camera: one exclaims about the beauty of Morocco while clarinet music sets up a festive air. As the scene ends, the camera shows a group of soldiers in long shot surrounding a black captive. As a pair of French women in long white dresses, one with a parasol, pass by the group, the camera cuts in to a medium close-up of the black prisoner, who stares directly at the camera as we hear almost inaudible female voices off-screen speaking in French of gardens and flowers (fig. 19). Freed from on-screen dialogue, voice here underpins the image to create a devastatingly ironic juxtaposition of gaiety and oppression. Among the many varieties of acousmatic voices that we hear are non-diegetic voices that seem to be outside the world of the film. An example is the voice-over in *A Muslim Childhood*, which approaches the role of an omniscient narrator who seems to know everything about the characters and their world yet speaks from outside it. But more prominent, perhaps, are other moments of voice-over that are internal diegetic or, in Christian Metz's terminology, "semi-diegetic" in nature—that is, they seem to emanate from somewhere in the story world and yet they are not produced externally in the scene and thus seem subjective to a character or an unseen subject who is somehow connected to the film.

One example is the voice in the second sequence of *Moroccan Chronicles*, which follows a young woman, Shams, and her romantic encounters in the town of Essaouira, which I will discuss further below. Another, more extensive use occurs in *44*, a film whose elliptical structure spirals around the character of Moussa, a young man from the country who is studying at al-Qarawiyyin University in Fez. Moussa straddles the worlds of Qur'anic education and the domestic sphere of El Hajj's home, where he acts as a tutor for El Hajj's children. Seldom heard in dialogue, his thoughts are rendered almost always in internal diegetic voice-over. Even when we see him writing and editing poetry, we hear it as semi-diegetic rather than external (his mouth does not move). His poetry thus remains tentative or incomplete, revealed only as the subjective thoughts of a character who seems unable to find an audible voice, much less one that functions to advance him in the world. The question of the voice and its efficacy in Moussa's case, however, is rendered even more pertinent because of the materialities of the sound itself. Smihi choose the actor Pierre Clémenti for the role of Moussa, impressed with the actor's work for Luchino Visconti especially. But Clémenti's speech, like that of the other characters, is dubbed throughout. Thus the effect of the semi-diegetic voice (spoken by a Moroccan actor) is made all the more uncanny as we hear it applied over shots of the Italian actor. This lack of connection, far from being solely specific to *44*, is something that Michel Chion has observed in sound cinema more generally.

Chion writes that with the advent of the talkies, a dualism entered the relationship of sound and image on-screen. Whereas a silent film leaves voice to the imagination of the spectator, unifying the diegesis with an actor's bodily movements as a mode of expression, in the talking film "the physical nature of film necessarily makes an incision or cut between the body and the voice. Then the cinema does its best to restitch the two together at the seam." Yet, Chion continues, "If the talking cinema has shown anything by restoring voices to bodies, it's precisely that it doesn't hang together; it's decidedly not a seamless match."[28] For Chion, this imperfect match leaves a "scar" that is structurally endemic to the sound film itself. In certain circumstances, then, we can envisage a film that plays with the appearance of that scar and that exploits the dualism and the uncanniness of the relation of voice to body. Mary Anne Doane, for example, in her exploration of the voice in space (which preceded the appearance of Chion's book) cites modernists like René Clair, Fritz Lang, Jean Vigo, Jean-Luc Godard, Jean-Marie Straub, and Marguerite Duras as experimenters with nonsynchronous dialogue. Chion cites them, too, along with Robert Bresson and Jacques Tati, to argue that French cinema is unique in its experimentation with voice.[29] Yet Smihi was engaged in such experimentation as early as 1971 with *Si Moh*, and his tradition continues with the later films.

FIGURE 20. The French *lycée* schoolmaster trains his Moroccan students in French pronunciation in *The East Wind*, 1975.

In *The East Wind*, for example, the final sequence, driven by the noises at the port, also ends with a classroom scene in which Brahim and the young *lycée* students must recite the words *feu-flamme-fou* (fire-flame-mad) in the direction of the master (fig. 20). These words, however, are heard as voice several minutes after we have seen them produced by the bodies of the actors in a short, unmotivated take that has the boys moving their mouths to produce *feu*, but with no sound audible except the noises of the port. When we do see the boys again, in a scene that cuts between them and their teacher, there is a temporal lag between the instruction they are given and the vocal response they produce. This time, the issue is not that the voice is out of sync with the body, but that the screen time represents a gap: body and voice *together* are out of sync with a typical diegetic duration, and things seem just off. Furthermore, after the first reply, the camera moves outside and the remainder of their responses are heard as off-screen sound as the camera instead fixes on the mysterious, unmotivated movement of the two large steel gates, which close on their own to mark the end of the film. The boys' voices float in unison through the space of Tangier, barely moored to their bodies on-screen and operating more as signifiers of a regimented French instruction that is awkwardly, belatedly adopted by its young Moroccan subjects. These voices, mimicking their French models, return in the same tenor but completely unvisualized in *44*. There we overhear them at the school: off-screen, diegetic, as if from another film and another world—that of Tangier. Smihi's acousmatic voices here evince a capacity to travel through related diegetic worlds and to thematically connect different films.

Returning to Moussa in *44*, we see Smihi further exploit the power of his acousmatic presence (or *acousmêtre*, as Chion names it) by the choice of words that his character recites.[30] Moussa's evocative verse in these sequences is drawn from the Fez tradition of women's poetry. Discussed in terms of their textuality in the next chapter, these examples of popular song and poetry emerge in ways that loosely move the narrative (since they evoke Moussa's internal struggles, as a poet and theologian, with words and meaning) but they also exist as reflective interjections that seem disconnected from his silent body. By rendering the poetry through acousmatic voices rather than external ones, and by attaching it to the image of a male character, Smihi allows it to leave its traditional historical reference points and inflect other situations and historical moments, simultaneously complicating the gendered dimensions of Moussa's character. Some of Chion's reflections on the acousmatic voice are perfectly apt here and Smihi's film even complicates them further. As Chion puts it, the acousmatic voice is one that has difficulty finding a home: "It's as if the voice were wandering along the surface, *at once inside and outside*, seeking a place to settle. Especially when a film hasn't yet shown what body this voice normally inhabits. Neither inside nor outside: such is the *acousmêtre*'s fate in the cinema."[31] The poetry of the Fez women is particularly dispersed, heard in a masculine voice associated with a male character, yet a voice that literally does not belong to the actor on-screen. While we might see him as a body, something that can render a *acousmêtre* less powerful in cinema, argues Chion, Moussa is never fully de-acoustamatized since he is never seen to speak the poetry and thus never loses his uncanny acousmatic status.[32] Indeed, Moussa's voice—the words of Fez women in the voice of a Moroccan actor and the on-screen body of an Italian—exemplifies the lack of concrete embodiment that is the fate of the *acousmêtre*. Like its character, this voice belongs to no specific place and is left outside all social structures by the end of the film.

The beginning of *A Muslim Childhood* sets a different pattern for the use of the acousmatic voice, a pattern that it continues through the Tangier trilogy. Immediately after the credit sequence (with lively songs in Moroccan Arabic), a woman's voice recites a poem in classical Arabic over the sound of wind and an extreme long shot of a beach, subtitled as: "Beyond the ramparts, summer is dying away. Silence is getting deeper. Behind the doors, walls, and eyes . . . there are recollections. Pains. Illusions. Dreams. He who remembers is able to master time." Her voice, soft and slowly paced, pronounces the Arabic with attention to both the long and short vowels.³³ The effect is pensive, putting at the beginning of the film a kind of recollection of time that frames the narrative to come (an "autobiographical fiction," or simply "autofiction," as Smihi has termed it) and setting the scene for other narrators whose voices will be heard throughout.³⁴ A short time later, the masculine voice of an omniscient narrator introduces viewers to the story over a three-minute sequence. Connecting us to the intervening scene in the heart of a Moroccan family's house, the narrator begins in French: "The children of the medina were scared stiff by the European city. It was the 'Forbidden Town.' . . . Cosmopolitan, polyglot, with many religions." Moving around the *ville nouvelle*, the camera lingers on different aspects, especially the buildings and areas that illustrate the city's cosmopolitan nature. In the latter half of the sequence, the voice highlights the presence in the medina of the Spanish immigrants who live alongside the Moroccans in preference to the *ville nouvelle*, and the voice-over concludes:

> Ebb and flow of history: after the Arabs had enriched Spain and Europe for centuries, it was the Spaniards' turn to pour the fruity bouquet of their wines and the scent of their ham into the Muslim streets. Those in the colonized medina lived a traditional life but were definitively fascinated by the new world brought by the Boulevard. This is the story of a family from the medina of Tangier in the 1950s.

The narration is voiced by Smihi himself, and here the timbre of his voice is a soft and velvety baritone, recorded close to the microphone for a sense of intimate presence. Thus not only the delivery but the narrator's use of French creates a contrast to the animated *darija* (Moroccan Arabic) of the previous scene of the family.

Within the first seven minutes of the film, then, we move from sung *darija* to spoken formal Arabic in voice-over, back to conversational *darija*, and then to voice-over French. The progression enacts exactly the polyglot atmosphere that Smihi's voice-over relates, not only in the emergence of different languages, but also in their different registers (poetry, spoken vernacular, formal and almost literary narration) and vocal qualities. In fact, the sequence does not end here, but continues for several more shots that are accompanied by no fewer than four separate tracks of off-screen voice: a small child crying, a baby wailing, and two separate strains of singing. At this critical juncture, voice as an element of film form and *voices* as elements of the Tangier soundscape establish their mutual importance to the diegesis and to the discourse.

A Muslim Childhood contains numerous instances of voice-over. Smihi's narrator returns at many junctures to intervene in the movement of the narrative, offering us more information than we learn from the characters or on-screen events. In addition, we hear a narration voiced by a woman that relates a long story recounted to Larbi by his grandmother about the hardships suffered by Moroccans in the war of the Rif, one of the most brutal battles in the extended history of French and

Spanish domination of the country.[35] The film closes with a framing voice-over by the same narrator's voice that opens the film: a woman's voice reciting again from the same poem that tells of the passing of time and especially the season. As the opening voice-over stressed acts of recollection as the summer waned, this verse tends toward a melancholy of mortality, one year after, with spring still not in sight. In *A Muslim Childhood*, then, narratorial voice enacts the polyglot nature of the city while also framing the story in terms that are novelistic, evocative of Smihi's conscious debts to novelists like Proust and Dickens.

This is not the only time that Smihi gives the power of the voice-over to a woman. *The Lady from Cairo* follows Amina as she moves from her rural village to Cairo into the Egyptian media and entertainment industry, and it is aurally structured around her interior subjectivity at many significant moments. As a rare example of a female voice-over in Arab cinema (one thinks also of Selma in *Omar Gatlato* [dir. Merzak Allouache, 1976], or Alia in *The Silences of the Palace*), Amina's narration performs a radical function: that of propelling a woman's consciousness to the very center of the film. Her semi-diegetic voice comments not just on the action that we see around her, especially her protracted search for her brother, who has become politically radicalized, but on her own desires and her difficulties in seeking freedom: "Freedom is not an easy thing. I had to wrench it out. History, my country, my background presented me with quite a challenge. But also the requisite to be myself and only myself." Amina's is the last voice we hear in *The Lady from Cairo*, and her semi-diegetic voice-over suggests a certain authority over the text that she narrates even as the film leaves her future uncertain.

How might we place such experimentation with voice in relation to other Arab films? Viola Shafik has argued that Arab cinema was historically linguistically driven, indebted not only to Egyptian theatrical traditions of the 1920s but typically borrowing linguistic metaphors as the basis for visual images.[36] Few films have made voice itself, more than speech and dialogue, central to their engagement with their story material, but critics have noted the presence and importance of the human voice qua voice in particular contexts. Salah Ezzedine, for example, also cited by Shafik, has argued that the context of Arab popular culture meant that Arab audiences were constituted as "a listening public before ever they became a viewing public." Ezzedine suggest that this is due to the fact that Arabic-speaking culture "concentrates on the oral origin of things whether in respect of legends, tales, communication or entertainment."[37] Further afield from cinema, Adonis stresses that orality underscores the history of Arab poetics: "Pre-Islamic poetry was born as song; it developed as something heard and not read, sung and not written," and it was a form that was collective in that it spoke of known events and histories.[38] Well aware of such histories, Smihi foregrounds the role of the voice in Arab culture and Arab cinema in a way few other filmmakers have done. *The Silences of the Palace* uses voice-over to develop Alia's traumatic flashbacks, as her voice frames the events of the past and addresses their unresolved status in the present. Moreover, voice is central to her acts of resistance by singing, and (as we've noted) to the development of nationalist community. *Omar Gatlato* develops a use of first-person speech directed to the viewer, simultaneously breaking two conventions of narrative cinema: the prohibition against an actor looking directly at the camera, and the breaking of the diegesis by a first-person voice that is simultaneously inside and outside the film. Omar's narration sometimes describes events that are about to take place, separating actions from voice (whereas just minutes earlier, his voice was synchronized with movements and actions on-screen). At one point, as an off-screen voice calls out his name, we see Omar turn and hear in voice-over, "That's Kacem, the butcher. You'll see, I'm going to lose five minutes and he's going to bum some chewing tobacco off me. He's going to complain about me then he's going to yell at his apprentice to show he's the boss."

Omar's voice is prominent in the narrative, but in the society depicted by the film, he is marginal and almost invisible. Yet the film's use of voice elevates his story for a viewer and brings to light the impoverished lives of Omar and his family and friends. Indeed, voice is central to the whole film. Omar's most prized possession is his cassette player on which he listens to *sha'abi* (popular) music and Bollywood soundtracks, some of which he records himself while at the movies. While checking what he thinks is a blank cassette, he discovers that it contains the voice of a woman who somewhat self-consciously describes her attempt at recording: "Are you hearing me? You must hear me ... I'm the only one speaking ..." Omar falls in love with this *acousmêtre* and her intimate, confessional voice, and is determined to find her. Selma is a rare *acousmêtre* in Arab cinema, a role usually reserved for the voice of a singer.

Where *Omar Gatlato* broke with the conventions of the Egyptian musical melodrama tradition from an Algerian auteurist perspective, Shadi Abdel Salam's radical 1969 film *The Night of Counting the Years* (sometimes known as "The Mummy," a translation of its Arabic title, *al-Momia*) constituted an even earlier rupture, and one made within Egypt's cinema. While appearing around the same time as some of the realist films discussed in the previous chapter, Abdel Salam's film is more overtly modernist and has been a profound influence on Smihi. The narrative of a clash between scientific modernity and local custom is expressed through a radical use of sound and image in which voice is paramount. The film narrates the conflict between a group of archaeologists from Cairo and the southern Egyptian tribe they encounter whose home is also the site of pharaonic tombs and mummies. The tribe's illegal trade in artifacts from the tombs puts them in conflict with the Cairene archaeologists who attempt to preserve the remains for science, history, and progress. From the moment the credits begin, Mario Nascimbene's orchestral score builds low and discordant droning sequences with strings and percussion and, as the credits end, the leader of the council of archaeologists begins to speak in classical Arabic. The actor's voice is recorded and mixed with high levels of reverb, and the subsequent combination of deep pitch, reverberative timbre, and solemn, performative Arabic gives his and other characters' speech a portentous and distantiated quality that is felt even in the outdoor sequences. There, in windswept and barren locations in the desert and against all codes of fidelity, we hear characters speak with similar depth and timbre as in the opening sequence. Classical Arabic itself is almost never heard as dialogue in Arabic-language cinema: Shafik cites the film *Dananir* (dir. Ahmed Badrakhan, 1940) as perhaps the only other extensive example of such a practice. Abdel Salam's decision to deploy it in his film bespeaks an interest in using voice—like music and image—to push the viewer back from the ease of identification and pleasure found within the mainstream Egyptian tradition. It thus stands as a film whose inventive and modernist style of sound was continued in Smihi's cinema.

The self-conscious use of voice in *The Night of Counting the Years* should remind us of the lofty and omnipresent voices of singers like Umm Kulthum, Mohammed Abdel Wahab, and Abdel Halim Hafez, and even the widely broadcast voice of Gamal Abdel Nasser. All these voices are found in Smihi's cinema, and all of them continue to associate Smihi's diegetic worlds with a wider Arab cultural and political life that was advanced through orality. In *The Ethical Soundscape* (2006), Charles Hirschkind associates the cassette sermons that proliferated in Cairo from the 1970s onward with a longer tradition of voice and listening within Arabic speaking culture, a history that is linked to the orality of forms like poetry and song. For Hirschkind, the recorded sermons have immediate predecessors in two specific media practices already mentioned in this chapter: "the radio broadcasts of Gamel Abd al-Nasser's speeches during the 1950s and 1960s, and the weekly concerns of the singer Umm Kulthum during the same period." According to Hirschkind, Nasser's broadcast speeches enabled a kind of collective listening experience for Egyptians, just as Umm Kulthum's radio performances on the first Thursday of the month—after 1952, harnessed to the Nasserite political program—also provided "a collective national audition."[39] Hirschkind proposes that Umm Kulthum had the same vocal presence as Nasser: powerful, authoritative, and with a wide reach thanks to the technology of radio. Smihi's films thus develop an existing domain of orality in Arab cinema and culture more generally while continuing the experimentations with sound in the work of filmmakers like Abdel Salam.

Smihi directly references the audible legacy of Arab culture and the role of Nasser's voice—not just his political importance—in *The Lady from Cairo*, where we hear Nasser's voice at the very moment of his political demise. Smihi presents the event as Amina finds her cousin, distraught and traumatized after the 1967 defeat of Arab forces by Israel. The scene combines a traumatic image (the young man cowering in a henhouse, blank-eyed, hunched over his weapon), dramatic music (the orchestral score provides a phrase of descending notes in a minor key),

FIGURE 21. Gamal Abdel Nasser's resignation speech and the trauma of the 1967 defeat register in the soundtrack of *The Lady from Cairo*, 1991.

and the acousmatic voice of Nasser announcing his resignation (fig. 21). Here the intimacy of Nasser's appeal is at its most psychologically unnerving: the announcement was as shocking to the Arab world as the defeat itself, neither of which were expected after Ahmed Said's triumphalist reports over Egyptian radio during the first days of the conflict.[40] Superbly attentive to the voice tradition of Egypt, Smihi later presents us with a short clip of Anwar Sadat's famous speech at the Israeli Knesset, yoking together a televisual documentary history with the vocal legacy of Arab leaders.[41]

Turning to the realm of singers rather than politicians and preachers, the Nasserian tradition was continued not so much by Umm Kulthum, whose appeal relied in part upon the sheer power of her voice and her ability to invoke *tarab*, or enchantment,[42] but rather by Abdel Halim Hafez, who like Nasser relied on the microphone to convey his special vocal qualities of intimacy and softness, utilizing a kind of "crooning" generally regarded as sentimental and feminine. Hafez features prominently in Smihi's films, especially *Girls and Swallows*, where he is invoked in a scene between Larbi and Rabea: Larbi asks her if she's ever heard of Hafez, and she replies by singing snatches of "Bitlumuni lih" and "Asmar Ya Asmarani," two songs that featured prominently in his filmic oeuvre (the first one he made famous in *A Love Story*, the second was sung *to* him by Faeza Ahmed in *The Empty Pillow* (al-Wisada al-khalia, dir. Salah Abu Seif, 1957). Hafez is also one of the voices heard at the end of *The Sorrows of a Young Tangerian* as the young radicals march through the forested Perdicaris Park in Tangier: the sound we hear is a radio's squeal as it tunes in and out of the song "Watani al-kabir," composed by Mohammed Abdel Wahab and sung by a cluster of famous artists, including Hafez. Smihi uses Hafez as a figure signifying a sense of Arab unity and political commitment but also as a voice associated with a softer masculinity that befits the lead character in the Tangier trilogy: someone attempting to find his way through the maze of sexual desire, political commitment, and culture. Chapter 5 will have more to say about Smihi's development of a critique of gender, but for now it is worth noting not only that Hafez's voice provides Smihi with a wider Arab vocal legacy that his films actively engage, but that voice here also serves to push the bounds of gender representation in his films.

For example, in *The Lady from Cairo*, the character of Amina possesses a semi-diegetic voice-over and the film presents her search for identity through vocal experimentation and expression. We see her develop a number of stage routines, trying out the styles of jazz, cabaret, disco, and more, and the film turns on the manner in which her voice is constantly stymied by the men around her within an industry that wants only its next marketable star. Her search for personal freedom begins in the first minutes of the film as we hear her singing in the fields, and even when not performing on stage, she sings at key narrative moments (for example at a restaurant in Alexandria as she drunkenly romances a soccer star). Indeed, *The Lady from Cairo* continues the interest in women's voices that Smihi began in *The East Wind*. In that film, as we have noted, soundtrack is used to accentuate the soundscape of Tangier and in particular its found qualities of noise. But the film is also about Aïcha's voice: while her character is almost silent, in a film with little dialogue (its subtitle is "the violent silence"), the rarity of her voice when it is heard (alone, or with a neighbor in an everyday exchange) makes it stand out. In *Moroccan Chronicles*, Shams's character becomes a modern Desdemona, avenging the injustices done to the character in Shakespeare's *Othello*. We first see her singing the song "Stormy Weather" in the courtyard of her home as she scrubs the floor, and later hear her in English, French, and Arabic as she teases Tewfik, her suitor. But the most prominent use of her voice comes in the final moments of the second part of the film as she recites lines from Shakespeare's play, dramatizing Iago and Othello's dialogue about female deception over a succession of shots of the ramparts at Essaouira, where Orson Welles shot his film version of the tragedy.

If Smihi's voice-overs by female characters have few precedents in Arab cinema, the use of a sung female voices is more familiar. One of them is particularly prominent across his and Arab cinema more generally: Umm Kulthum, or the "Voice of Egypt," as Virginia Danielson refers to her, whose voice was instantly recognizable throughout the Arab world and central to Egypt's radio broadcasts, as noted above. Umm Kulthum herself recognized the immense significance of radio in the development of her popularity, once declaring, "We are in the transistor age.... Everyone is able to listen to radio anywhere."[43] But it was the quality of her voice itself that drew listeners in from the 1920s through the height of her popularity in the 1940s and even through periods depicted in Smihi's films, namely Tangier of the 1950s and 1960s. As Danielson recounts, Umm Kulthum had established herself as the preeminent singer in Egypt by the late 1930s, rivaled only by Mohammed Abdel Wahab: "Using her native abilities as a foundation, she cultivated what the cognoscenti of Cairo taught as historically Arab aesthetics of singing and joined them to the style of the *mashayikh* [religious singers]. She applied that sound to new compositions, and it became one of her signal accomplishments. The basis of her idiom was meticulously controlled vocal power."[44] Umm Kulthum's vocal power gave her the ability to sing and project her voice effectively over long periods of time; concerts of up to six hours were not uncommon, and during these she deployed a range of different styles or "colors," including *bahha* (hoarseness) and *ghunna* (nasality), the latter being a particular signifier of what most people regarded as authentic, traditional Arab singing.[45] Thus by the 1940s, not only had Umm Kulthum become a national phenomenon (from working-class beginnings in the Nile Delta, she became wealthy and famous for her music) but also a regional one, beloved across the Arab world thanks to her "first Thursday" radio broadcasts. Moreover, and importantly in the context of Smihi's films, after the Egyptian coup of 1952 she became more prominent as a public figure within a nationalist and Nasserite politics.[46]

Her vocal appearance in Smihi's films (even her physical appearance as an image at a few different moments) thus functions on multiple levels. As a voice, hers joins the many others in the films that compete for our attention in a soundscape that is attuned to accent, language, space, and tone. Her vocal tone, her distinctive delivery, and the sheer power of her voice exist in a mix with radically different contrasting voices. As well as marking space within the films, her voice connects Smihi's locales to a wider Arab soundscape that (in the historical moment represented in some of the films) was Nasserian and pan-Arab. Moreover, her voice offers a kind of benchmark for qualities of properness, authenticity, and respectability: Umm Kulthum was praised for her perfect pronunciation of Qur'anic Arabic, the pureness of sentiment of her religious songs, and her respectability.[47] A café scene in *A Muslim Childhood* references this status. A sound bridge of stringed music connects a scene in the streets of the medina to a new scene inside a café, which Larbi enters with a friend. The strings belong to the diegetic sound of Umm Kulthum's orchestra, and as the cut takes us to the new scene (beginning with a shot of two portraits, one of King Mohammed V), the loudness of the music markedly increases as Umm Kulthum's voice arrives. The next shot cements our understanding of her voice by alighting on a photographic portrait of her on the wall of the café, under a large valve radio on a shelf (fig. 22). But what is remarkable on the level of voice is the contrast between the voices heard in the streets and the café and that of Umm Kulthum herself. Larbi and his friends have

FIGURE 22. A photograph of Umm Kulthum shares space with a valve radio and a portrait of the exiled king Mohammed V in *A Muslim Childhood*, 2005.

been roughly reciting a rhyme in Moroccan *darija* that is about circumcision, syphilis, and anal infection; Ta'iz, a local in the café, is loudly describing how he used to shit while in prison. The café owner, dressed in a *tarbouche* (fez) and a waistcoat, attempts to silence him, saying he's had enough of such obscenity, especially with the "son of a preacher" (Larbi) listening in. Yet the conversation and the argument about it continue as the café owner tries to kick Larbi out and silence his friend. All the while, we hear Umm Kulthum singing in her recognizable and deeply proper voice. Hers is one of the many overlapping voices in the multifaceted, polyphonic soundspace of the medina, but it also represents a contrast between the loftier elements of Arab musical culture and the rough vernacular of the Tangier medina. Crucially, Smihi's film does not favor one discourse over the other, but it does allow their difference to manifest through sound.

Importantly, then, Smihi's use of voice marks his cinematic world as multifaceted and polyphonic. This is as true for the sound of spoken dialogue as it is for the acousmatic or sung voice. No matter the language and speech of the films, the diversity of voices and their qualities construct a world that is theatrical, poetic, musical, radiophonic, political, formal, and vernacular. With his characters, Smihi mediates between the two poles observed by Chion: the experimentation of the "voice-obsessive" directors like the French modernists, who give their characters "colorless, drab voices with dull diction" and "for whom saying one word is a dramatic and complicated affair," and the Fellini-esque tradition of riotous collective, overlapping voice.[48] One can, for example, identify the first tendency in *The Sorrows of a Young Tangerian*, where characters often speak in what seem like overly stilted tones: Larbi has a somewhat wooden delivery throughout, especially as he renounces religion in the uncomfortably long take that Smihi shoots from a high angle, looking down at his parents, or in his declarations to his teacher, Muriel, which he makes awkwardly in self-conscious French. The same might be said of the character of Malika, one of his young friends. Yet within the same film we have a radically different model in the dynamic performance of voice, offered for example by the two merchants who bicker over their produce until Sidi Ahmed adjudicates. Like the first dinner in *A Muslim Childhood*, where Lalla Alia berates her husband for his failure to adequately provide for the family, this scene is animated by argumentative *darija*, whose fricative properties are utilized to great effect as Smihi layers voices and exclamations. Such scenes are reminiscent of Chion's reading of Italian cinema:

> When someone begins to speak, everyone joins in; it's all right to leave behind your own individual vocal contours, then return to them. No one makes a big deal out of it. Fellini . . . plays to the hilt the freedom cinema gives him to mix together voices and accents. At the same time that he succeeds in giving each a very particular silhouette, as Tati does, he also manages to turn them loose together, let them drift and overlap, make voice-balloons in space. He throws them all into a great cauldron of voices, shouts, snickers, sighs, and murmurings in various languages. . . . In Fellini the voice is not something to be mastered or contained, like the Devil. It is mixed and collective, a sort of overall poly-voice each of whose component voices is an individualized emanation.[49]

Not only does such a model describe the multilayered voices of the medina in the Tangier trilogy, it aptly describes *44*, too, in particular Smihi's practice of presenting his characters' voices, all of which were dubbed during postproduction in Casablanca. Smihi worked in a manner he called Viscontian (recall that Pierre Clémenti had acted in Visconti's *The Leopard* [1963], an intertext of Smihi's own film), thus invoking Visconti's daring casting of Alain Delon, the French actor, or Burt Lancaster's stunning performance as an Italian prince, also dubbed in Italian. Of course, non-sync voice recording was the standard Italian practice for sound films, and Smihi's use of the technique thus had a long precedent in world cinema. Smihi has noted that he was scared of the practice until he saw Pier Paolo Pasolini's *Arabian Nights* (1974), which freely dubbed voices to nonprofessional actors from a range of countries.[50] His use of it in *44* is but one more example of how voice is critical in the complex modernist soundscapes of his films, and of the filmmaker's deep embeddedness in wider traditions. Whether in the domains of noise and its sculpting, the diversity of diegetic and non-diegetic music, the mediating role of radio, or the complex registers of voice, these films actively participate in the traditions and discourses of Arab and non-Arab societies and in global cinema history. Tracing the intertextual pathways of such participation is the task of the next chapter.

3

Kan ya makan

Intertextuality and Arab Modernism

The previous chapter, and the one before it, emphasized the domain of cinematic language as I considered how Moumen Smihi's uses of image and sound constitute an Arab cinematic modernism. That modernism, as a form of *écriture*, or writing, is deeply concerned with textuality: how images and sounds render a world visually and aurally so that viewers might read, feel, and decipher it. This chapter builds on those arguments about language and form to address the realm of intertextuality in relation to Arab modernism and world cinema. As with many experiments of Arab modernity, Moroccan and Arab cinema have often been treated as reactive and beholden to other, foreign traditions: derivative of Euro-American forms and genres, or self-Orientalizing if they adopt a perspective that critiques religion or social practices. Maghribi cinema in particular, when its practitioners have veered away from more overtly commercial forms, has often been critiqued as overly Francophile, as if any deviation from popular forms must indicate a sullying of local authenticity by French influence; Smihi's work has often attracted such a charge.[1] Yet such perspectives overlook the degree to which an Arab cinematic modernism actively embraces intertextuality—not from an inferiority complex, but in critical and artistic engagement with other texts—and how, exceeding even intentional citation, the intertextuality of films like Smihi's places them within the broader corpus of a modernist world cinema. Thus released from the demands to be read solely in nationally or regionally specific ways, these films show that many of cinematic modernism's genealogies are wanting to the extent that they do not take into account Smihi's cinema and the films of those around him.

Smihi's intertextuality is intimately related to the spirit of the Nahda that his work inhabits. As a movement of regeneration or awakening, Nahda always involved an enthusiastic and multidirectional process of reading, writing, and translation. In his introduction to a recent collection of Nahda texts, Tarek El-Ariss argues that, while the narrative of the "rediscovery of Europe" described by Ibrahim Abu-Lughod, Albert Hourani, and others has predominated in English-language accounts, the Nahda's trajectories were never simply Arab-European but involved the incorporation and translation of ideas and texts that linked the Arab world to Russia, India, and other sites.[2] Similarly, Robyn Creswell considers the Beiruti modernism he studies "a movement of multiple translations: European and American poetry, first of all, but also of the classical past."[3] Elizabeth Suzanne Kassab shows how the Syrian journal *Qadaya wa-shahadat* published major texts by Arab authors alongside *tarjamat* (translations) that "included pieces by Marshall Berman, Fredric Jameson, Jean Baudrillard, Walter Benjamin, Frantz Fanon and Edward Said."[4] It is this generous sense of a Nahda with multiple points of translation and citation that I wish to invoke with respect to Smihi's work and to Arab cinematic modernism more generally.

In its desire to create a new, modern Arab subjectivity, Smihi's cinema relies on an intertextuality that is worldly and multidirectional, linking Arab and Islamic literary sources to European, US, Latin American, Asian, and Arab cinemas. In discussing his engagements with various kinds of realism or sound practice, for example, I have already shown how Smihi's films resonate with the work of others, like Roberto Rossellini, Michelangelo Antonioni, Luchino Visconti, Salah Abu Seif, or Jean Rouch in cinema, Pierre Schaeffer or Gnawa singers in sound, or Naguib Mahfouz or Leo Tolstoy in the novel. When the character of Amine's mother in *Moroccan Chronicles* begins all of her Maghribi stories with the words "*Kan ya makan*," or "Once upon a time," she too invokes the intertextuality of the *Arabian Nights* in a film built—like those stories, and like Pasolini's version of them in his *Arabian Nights* (1974)—from a host of other texts. My chapter title, with its nod to the film and its intertextual sources, explores those affinities and citations in an even wider frame to show that intertextuality is central to the way Smihi's films create a modern Arab subjectivity in the spirit of a new Nahda. Moreover, in so doing, I argue that accounts of world cinema that stress the qualities of the global and transnational might look, as seldom before, toward Arab cinematic modernism as a key site in which to understand the interplay of geopolitical histories, textuality, and aesthetics. Taking seriously these Arab discourses and histories of intertextuality and modernism, oriented as they are to sites outside the Arab world as well as within it, offers a way through the impasses that set Arab cinema and European cinemas in a relation of dependence and hegemony or that create separate spheres of belonging. As I will show, the deep engagement with Arabic sources—both cinematic and pre-cinematic—that Smihi's films display is matched only by the affinity and love that his films show for other, non-Arab cinemas and sources. Such a relation, akin to what Laura Marks has termed *hanan al-cinema*, or affection for cinema and its moving images, is not only central to understanding Smihi's work, but rather makes his films and their Arab modernism critically important to any full account of world cinema and its interventions.[5]

As I established in the introduction, as well as being embedded in the histories and lived experience of Tangier and his knowledge of Arab and Islamic culture, Smihi's creative practice also owes much to his time in Paris as a student of Roland Barthes, Jacques Lacan, and Henri Langlois. It is thus instructive to examine how Smihi's thinking draws upon the cinematic and literary theories of writing and intertextuality as they emerged from the European structuralist and poststructuralist projects, while also dwelling in more expansive contexts; European theory, along with the cinema and culture of the Arab world, Africa, and the Americas, is part of the intellectual conversation of his films. As I have suggested already, Smihi elaborates a *ciné-écriture* (or *cinécriture*) that we might trace to Alexandre Astruc, one of the first filmmakers or critics to make the analogy between writing and the creative process of cinema through the concept of the *caméra-stylo*, or camerapen. For Astruc, the comparison between writing and cinema is partly compensatory, treating cinematic expression as on par with other forms of writing (the essay or the novel, specifically).[6] But as the notion of *cinécriture* has been developed through the work of other filmmakers and theorists, it has taken on a more expansive sense. For Agnès Varda, for example, the term is not indicative of cinema's indebtedness to other written forms but rather evokes cinematic specificity and the medium's capacity to generate thought and sensation.[7]

Such formulations are important for Smihi's own thinking on writing, cinema, authorship, and intertextuality. His 1973 essay on Sergei Eisenstein's *cinécriture* develops the multiple puns that the French language generates for this word, and plays with the notion of *cinécrit*, to denote what is cinematically written, and *cinécritique*, for the practice of cinema criticism or the criticism of what has been written.[8] Further, *cinécrit* is also *ci (n')écrit*, a "this here" that has been written or not written. In the very practice of his Eisenstein essay, then, as in his cinema, Smihi is alert to the ways that *écriture* has functioned in French thought to expand the possibilities of language beyond its spoken forms and into the terrain of textuality. Indeed, in the tradition of Barthes and the literary magazine *Tel Quel*, Smihi positions textuality as the possibility of openness in language. What is at stake in all cinematic research, he argues, is "the establishment of a system that is at once open and multiple in its possibility, not of a closed or hermetic system to which one seeks to apply laws. The 'this here' that is written or not written [*le ci (n') écrit*] is constituted in a perpetual critical relation to itself. But *cinécritique* is also a relation to a social terrain: critique and subversion of the social law, the law of knowledge and of the Other."[9]

Smihi here opens the possibility of intertextuality as more than deliberate citation but rather a condition of textuality itself. Such an approach is in keeping with the destabilization of the discourse of the author that occurred in structuralist and poststructuralist thought that came in the wake of the *politique des auteurs*, especially with respect to the work of Barthes. For Barthes, authorship could not function as a viable or self-evident concept when faced with the malleability of language, reading, and writing: the author, like the "I," was no more than the effect of discourse. The film author "tended to shift from being the generating source of the text to becoming merely a term in the process of reading and spectating, a space where discourses intersect, a shifting configuration produced by the intersection of a group of films with historically constituted ways of reading and viewing."[10] As an avid reader and former student of Barthes, Smihi is well aware of the generative potential of this Barthesian vision of intertextuality in particular, and he juggles both senses of intertextuality: as authorial practice and as a constitutive part of cinema's discourse.

Indeed, Smihi's lengthy account of the work of Claude Lévi-Strauss in his essay "L'aventure structuraliste" (The Structuralist Adventure, 1970) makes clear that the filmmaker understands textuality as something that exceeds the idea of origins or authorship:

> We know that discourses and texts, currents and thoughts, perpetuate themselves and pass back and forth to each other in the same flow. Discourse and text become entangled, amalgamate each other, imbricate and nourish each other, and pass continually back and forth in a sort of ritual, solemn, and majestic *ronde*. It is through their meeting in a site of convergence, a chamber of multiple cross-references, that lines, tendencies, shared preoccupations (more than divergences), common researches, and paths leading to the same horizons trace, in the calligraphic sense of the term, their own contours.[11]

Here Smihi demonstrates knowledge of the conditions under which textuality operates and discourses emerge and evinces a recognition of Lévi-Strauss's concern with the narration of culture. In fact, reading further in the essay, one sees that what Smihi finds liberating in Lévi-Strauss is the anthropologist's interest in escaping a deterministic and hierarchical mode of thought whereby civilization is only the province of the West. As Smihi outlines the idea of the *pensée sauvage*, whereby Lévi-Strauss considers the Native American system of flower classification as every bit as scientific as Europe's, we understand how he finds in the French anthropologist a generosity of thought that might help to elucidate the popular practices, thinking, and culture of the Maghrib and the Arab world.[12]

In this way, the qualities of generosity, reciprocity, and exchange that Smihi finds in the work of Lévi-Strauss are also conditions of the worldly cinematic intertextuality of his films. The relativism key to Lévi-Strauss's structuralist anthropology, where discourses are dependent on each other for meaning, is foundational for the cinematic modernism of Smihi's films, which develop their relationships with other traditions in the quest for a new, modern subjectivity in the manner of the Nahda texts alluded to earlier. In another essay, "Libé" (1982), Smihi further articulates that relation between the heterogeneity of an intertextual practice with the desire for *cinécriture* that derives from his particular placement as an Arab and Moroccan filmmaker. His intention, he writes, is to create images and sounds that are

> of my culture, of my cultural sites: Morocco, Arab-ness, Islam, colonization, the birth of modernity, the rereading of the cultural heritage, terrors and demands of underdevelopment. I film, and I want to film [in order] to realize a desire that is urgent and multiple. It's the desire for an autobiographical discourse (a subject, a country, a city, a sociocultural group). It is an aesthetic desire: to work on and practice a writing with image and sound, all the while nourishing it by the contributions of the history of the Arab-Muslim aesthetic.[13]

Here, then, Smihi harnesses the ideas of writing, intertextuality, and discursive play generated in his reading of Lévi-Strauss to a concern for a discourse of the self that he draws from Sigmund Freud and Jacques Lacan. It is that discourse on the self that turns intertextuality from something merely academic or ludic to a practice with high stakes for the identity and expression of a culture. The *cinécriture* that Smihi embraces is a process of writing-as-speech in which "as spectator or filmmaker, I release my images, I unfold them, I project them, in an unending autobiography, circular, *en abyme*, a dance of lives and of discourses, a *ronde* of stories without end."[14] Cinematic *écriture* thus becomes a vital way to engage popular and oral forms along with all manner of written and technologically mediated texts. The spaces of "the image-sound discourse," as he puts it, are "the sites of joining and fertilization" in which orality, literature, technology, music, and other forms are jointly articulated. For Smihi, "Arab society's access to modernity is rightly conditioned by this long and deep work of synthesis, of phagocytosis, of the interception and transformation of structures."[15] Arab modernity, then, is by necessity based on a process of intertextual and intercultural traffic of the type that the Nahda thinkers re-invoked: a relationship to Europe, certainly, but also to other elements within Arab history that had been buried or forgotten. *Cinécriture* is the practice that can, through its intertextual and synthetic character, establish a modernity built in difference and not self-sameness.

The biological metaphor of phagocytosis, or *phagocytage* in French, is one that Smihi uses more than once to describe such an intertextual practice. Phagocytosis is the process by which a cell devours nutrients or incorporates bacteria around it to sustain itself, and Smihi uses it as a way to animate his understanding of intertextuality as a practice by which cinema turns to and incorporates other preexisting discourses in a movement that effaces origins or hierarchies in a practice of radical plurality and endless incorporation. *Cinécriture* for a Maghribi and Arab filmmaker, he suggests, requires phagocytosic intertextuality. The work of cinema that he has in mind is both self-consciously and unconsciously—one might say uncontrollably—comprised of, intertwined with, and even consuming of other discourses. How else can the postcolonial Moroccan or Arab subject speak? For Smihi, and indeed for an Arab cinematic modernism more generally, cinema as a practice of research on culture, identity, and the self energizes cinematic form and language and shapes it in ways that are diverse and hybrid, raiding everything while creating something distinctive: cinema links orality to literature, technologies, music, and other cultural forms.

Seen in this light, intertextuality in Smihi's films reveals an operation that exceeds the terms of European theories or of writing as literature. Attending to the intertextuality of Smihi's *cinécriture* leads us by necessity to an Arab modernism that continues the project of the Nahda and forces us to acknowledge the worldliness of many of Arab cinema's experiments, beyond the expected trajectories of postcolonial influence or debt. While one can trace a set of self-conscious cinematic and literary references in Smihi's films—as one might expect given his personal erudition and breadth of knowledge—the intertextuality of his films finally exceeds his authorial grasp. For this chapter, treating these films seriously means assessing the roles played by, respectively, the history of Arabo-Islamic philosophy; popular memory and culture in the Maghrib; Arabic music and poetry; and, finally, other experiments with Arab modernism and cinema as they have taken shape in literature and other art forms. For it is in this expanded sense of intertextual affiliation and history that we find Arab cinema in its most radical and modernist form, speaking linguistic, cultural, and local specificities while claiming its place within world cinema.

ARAB-ISLAMIC ART, ARCHITECTURE, AND PHILOSOPHY

In *Art and Architecture in the Islamic Tradition* (2011), Mohammed Hamdouni Alami relates a history of ornamentation and decoration in architecture from a perspective that stresses its intertextuality. Considering the love of the decorative in Morocco and the Arab world, Alami argues that "what has been called 'Islamic architecture' has little if any religious content. The elaboration of the architectural types at hand appears to have been a complex synthesis of different legacies, and cultural and political statements as well."[16] Alami traces a history that is dominated by Islamic influence but not proper only to Islam; rather, art in the Arab-Islamic tradition is shared by all the inhabitants of the region by virtue of its ubiquity and beauty. His contention thus opens the aesthetics of the Arab built environment to a textuality that exceeds the religious. Smihi's films evoke this understanding of Arab-Islamic architecture as a system of signs, language, aesthetics, and style. Such a legacy is sometimes addressed diegetically in the films in their characters'

FIGURE 23. The beauty of the *zellij* in El Hajj's Fez home in *44, or Tales of the Night*, 1981.

engagements with religion; in the next chapter I will turn to the ways that the religious dimension unfurls. But art and architecture here are important in ways that are not at all devotional. Instead, Smihi's films utilize architecture as an active and semantically productive element of mise-en-scène rather than simply as decor or backdrop. For example, when Smihi frames his characters in *44, or Tales of the Night* (1981) before the tiled and decorative surfaces of the Qarawiyyin mosque, madrasa, or caravanserai, it is in large part to engage the visual history of that architecture, which will be contrasted in the film with other forms that evoke different traditions, for instance the modern architecture built by the French in Rabat or Casablanca.

These locations, then—the images of actual places—are granted a textuality in the films. Sometimes that textuality is quite literal, in the form of the elaborate calligraphy embedded in the walls. Other times the textual is constituted in the swirl of a pattern—in the colors and layout of tiles, or the form of an arch. In *44*, El Hajj's house is first seen in a composition that frames its occupant, wearing a white jellaba that covers his body and head (it has the distinctive Moroccan hood), from behind. The white of the garment matches the white in the patterned floor tiles of the house's patio surrounding the central fountain. To his left are huge paneled cedar doors, walls covered in *zellij* (mosaic tiles), and windows covered with lattice frames. Later, in another striking composition, we see two intersecting tiled walls as El Hajj stands in a cedar doorway (fig. 23). In the beauty of this mise-en-scène we can also read a textual history that is Islamic and Arab, and that interacts with other forms deriving from other histories. What we might call "Islamic aesthetics" in these films is a domain of textuality that exists beyond the purview of religious observance and practice.

By engaging with the aesthetics of Arab antiquity, then, Smihi is also engaging the philosophical currents (some in the domains of science and philosophy, rather than theology per se) that circulated around them. For example, in *44* when we see Moussa, the young student, in a window of a madrasa in Fez, the shot highlights the sculpted stucco walls with their elaborate ornamental decoration as well as the cedar lintels and window surrounds. This patterning was typical of the Fez *madaris*, which according to Naïma Boujibar and Mohamed Mezzine were all "built along the same architectural principles. . . . The patio walls, and the walls of the galleries and of certain corridors, are richly decorated with mosaic tiles known as *zellij*. The tops of the walls consist of chiselled plaster which protrudes out over sculpted and painted wood panels, whilst in the prayer hall, ornamentation is concentrated around the *mihrab* and the ceiling."[17] Moussa is a *talib* (university student), or seeker of knowledge (the word *talib* comes from the Arabic verb *talaba*, to seek or demand). The *madaris* (plural of madrasa) in Fez were a product of the Merinid period (from the thirteenth to the fifteenth century) and a constitutive part of the education that students received there. Mezzine explains: "The system of teaching particular to the Islamic civilisation was based on a multidisciplinary approach, which, with the exclusion of theology, considered to be the pillar of all knowledge, consisted of disciplines (termed secular) such as astrology, mathematics or medicine. . . . A metropolis of humanities, sciences and arts, Merinid Fez . . . lay at the pinnacle of this teaching system due mostly to the encouragement of sultans, themselves men of science and culture."[18] Indeed, Mezzine's imagined itinerary of a young student from the mountains of the Rif to the town of Fez, hoping to be admitted to al-Qarawiyyin University (detailed in a chapter called "A Day in the Life of a Taleb in Fez"), is the story of Moussa. What Smihi's character enters into, therefore, is not simply a mise-en-scène that exactly captures the Fez of the protectorate period (UNESCO protection has ensured that some of the *madaris* and *fun-adiq* [hotels or inns, plural of *funduq*] remain as they have for centuries) but a textuality of architecture and surface that embodies the philosophical discourses of the time. Such a textuality is the visual counterpart to the seminars that we see him join, settings that were both theological and secular, covering (as Mezzine explains) "jurisprudence, Qur'anic exegesis, and the prophetic tradition, *hadith*" as well as "rational sciences such as logic, mathematics, philosophy, medicine and astronomy."[19] Smihi's use of the madrasa thus evokes a scientific and intellectual world that surpasses religion.

Laura Marks has also discussed the implications of surface decoration in Islamic architecture, and her thesis about the affinities between Islamic art and new media art demonstrates how the textuality and materiality of Islamic aesthetics embodied discourses on the world that, while religious in nature, were also implicated in other rationalist philosophies being advanced at the time. The type of decoration visible in the stucco forms of the madrasa walls or lintels is characterized by what Marks calls "the abstract line and haptic space." Drawing on Gilles Deleuze and Félix Guattari, Marks argues that "when line and shape are freed from depiction, lines become abstract, sculptural form dissolves into haptic space, and meaning is deferred to the subjective discovery of the viewer. These may not be religious ideas, but they thrived in a religious culture that sought alternatives to figurative depiction."[20] The patterns that became known as arabesques drew on earlier examples from Greek and Roman art but developed in directions that led away from botanical fidelity and toward pure abstraction. The arabesques, in their avoidance of figuration, encouraged the eye to roam about the surface and find pleasure in the complexity and abstraction. Such abstraction in form certainly suited religious tendencies toward aniconism, but it also offered new modes of vision organized around subjective perception. Marks notes that "a number of early medieval Islamic thinkers developed theories of aesthetic response as simultaneously rational and subjective," and points in particular to the theories of the tenth- and eleventh-century philosopher Ibn al-Haytham (usually referred to in Anglophone contexts as Alhazen).[21] Comparing his thinking with that of his contemporaries like Ibn Sina (or Avicenna) or the later Ibn Rushd (or Averroes, twelfth century), Marks argues that these rationalist philosophers sought to explain the role played by subjectivity in Islamic aesthetics, which relied on a beholder to perceive what was offered by the artwork or surface.

Al-Haytham addressed this question through his theories of optics. Overturning the prevailing wisdom that light traveled out from the eye to land on objects, he showed that the eye was in fact receptive, taking in light rays that move toward it from the objects of one's gaze. Following Gülrü Necipoglu, Marks suggests that al-Haytham's theories of perception were in all likelihood based on his own experience of arabesques and the abstract, haptic images of Islamic art in Cairo, where he spent some years working. Ibn Sina similarly argued for the brain's organization of sense perceptions that the body receives, and Ibn Rushd, a century later, maintained that Islamic aesthetics require an active, discriminating presence, a beholder, to make sense of what is available in the artwork. Marks concludes that these thinkers "abundantly demonstrate the importance for Islamic aesthetics of subjectivity in completing the work of art (or any other perceived thing)."[22] The surface decoration of the *zellij* and stucco patterning that Smihi presents in Moussa's Fez, along with the architecture of the *madaris*, are therefore embodiments of centuries of Islamic aesthetic experimentation and of a rich array of Islamic discourses on the world, both religiously and scientifically oriented.

Indeed, Smihi's engagement with al-Haytham is not limited to the thinker's ideas on perception as they pertain to the visual culture of Islamic architecture; he is also indebted to al-Haytham's early work as part of the prehistory of cinema, a prehistory that extends beyond the usual Western reference points of Renaissance perspective and theories of space. In a 1974 issue of the Moroccan modernist journal *Intégral* Smihi published a kind of experimental, essayistic scenario on al-Haytham. Set in two columns marked "images" and "sons/commentaires," it juxtaposes the various tendrils of European and Arab discourses on the eye, optics, light, and phenomena relevant to cinema. He positions al-Haytham and Islamic philosophy within the trajectory of experimentation that led to the camera obscura and the Lumière brothers, arguing that as we broach this history we enter also the history of Islamic philosophy. "Encyclopedic knowledge," he telegraphs. "Islam: heterogeneous thought: the meeting and fusing of plural discourses. The route that leads from astronomy . . . to optics . . . isn't out of sync. Islamic knowledge is scattered. The 'contemporaneity' of Ibn al-Haytham demonstrates this dispersal."[23] The revelation here, for those unaccustomed to the scientific aspect of Islamic knowledge, is that al-Haytham's theories might be part of a genealogy of vision and cinema. Smihi recaptures the possibilities inherent in the Islamic tradition for the most modern of inventions, the cinema, and thus reestablishes a claim for cinema as a mode of Arab cultural expression.

That al-Haytham might help theorize both cinema itself as a modern invention and the experience of the beholder of Islamic art and architecture is an idea deeply embedded in the images Smihi uses in *44*. Reaffirming the circularity and nonexclusivity of all such sources, Smihi affirms again that "all knowledge is the perpetual production (not the product) of great formations of discourse which reproduce themselves, represent themselves, and disseminate themselves: such is the chain-spiral of knowledge (not cyclical or closed)."[24] Smihi's position, then, is to claim the entirety of an Islamic past—a past that is also scientific, not only theological or devotional. His films treat these histories of aesthetics and ideas not as sacred and confined to a religious history but as elements of the total thought and self-conception of a culture, in which purely Islamic elements mix with elements that are Christian and Jewish. In other words, what might be theologically rendered becomes a matter of culture and practice and textuality that is interwoven with adjacent systems of thought and related forms of cultural expression.

Crucially, however, such referentiality is always more than a matter of simple depiction. As I showed in chapter 1, *44* self-consciously utilizes a pretty discourse of visually sumptuous images to convey a cultural identity to the viewer. In the Fez scenes, Smihi utilizes a mise-en-scène marked by rich colors and flat compositions that stress texture over depth. In his use of wide-screen images that are themselves decorative and organized by their complex surfaces—images whose beauty is haptic in the sense that Marks describes (encouraging the eye to roam over their contours)—Smihi conveys the very principles of the artisanal creations that his film represents. Boujibar and Mezzine's commentary about these Merinid forms might have been written about *44*. Smihi's images, like the Merinid creations, in which surface decoration is glorified, seduce the viewer through the confidence of their composition, the delicacy of their coloring, and the finesse of their execution.[25]

Staying with *44*, one can observe in the film an intertextual reference to Islamic scholarship and antiquity on other diegetic levels. The narrative structure is complex, even serpentine, drawing on Arabic and modern European models alike. The film creates leaps across diegetic time to cover the forty-four years of the protectorate, and the narration never overtly signals these leaps. Sometimes a jump is hinted at by one of the film's elaborate title cards, which draw on the decorative textual qualities of the Moroccan calligraphic tradition to introduce new narrative chapters while visually inserting themselves in the broader intertextuality of *44*. The film opens with a title card that quotes James Joyce scholar Frank Budgen, a reference I will discuss further below, and extracts from the writings of Louis Hubert Lyautey (administrator of the French protectorate in its early years) are incorporated in other cards for their explanatory quality (they situate us in time and space for some key scenes) and for the irony of their juxtaposition. But such European citations are less important than the thoroughgoing way that the film engages with premodern Islamic writing.

Not overtly cited in the film, yet nonetheless influencing its form, are the writings of al-Jahiz, a Baghdad writer and bibliophile who was prominent in the ninth century during the Abbasid Caliphate. Smihi signaled his importance in an interview conducted a few years before *44*, while discussing the narrative form of *The East Wind* (1975). Having quickly cited the influence of Dziga Vertov and Robert Flaherty, with their play of documentary and fiction, Smihi cautioned that the very division of documentary versus fiction is embedded in Western classifications of genre and form (which might also include comedy, melodrama, et cetera). He argued that instead one might understand the digressive play and movement of a film like *The East Wind* as a "Jahiz-ian structure of *istitrad*," or digression, which avoids divisions of subject matter and content in favor of a structure of argumentation resembling a dance.[26] Al-Jahiz develops the idea of *istitrad* in his book *Kitab al-bayan wa-l-tabiyyin* (Book of Exposition and Demonstration, 1313), but his emphasis on *al-bayan* (loosely, exposition or rhetoric) occurs throughout many of his works, and his own practice of intertextuality resonates throughout his texts. For example, his *Kitab al-hayawan* (The Book of Animals) is enamored with writing and with other books. James E. Montgomery describes it as a "sprawling composition" that is indebted to other texts by the author himself and by those around him, drawing on "quotations of poetry, from folktales and stories, from earlier lexographic treatises devoted to the animal kingdom, from lecture courses which al-Jahiz had presumably attended and possibly delivered himself, from current debates in science, philosophy and theology, especially from the recently translated version of Aristotle's *Historia Animalium*, and from personal observation."[27] The result is a work that is prolifically intertextual and marked by a structure of complexity.

The influence of al-Jahiz's thought is palpable throughout Smihi's work. Indeed, one can find in al-Jahiz a figure complementary to that of Roland Barthes in terms of his contributions to an understanding of language and the role of meaning. In *Kitab al-hayawan*, the notion of *al-bayan* allows the author to account for the meanings produced by all the living objects in the world as they interact with one another and with inanimate forms, which al-Jahiz catalogs extensively. *Al-bayan* is thus a means for al-Jahiz to account for the potentially infinite possibilities of language and signification in the world. Indeed, Alami, cited above, invokes al-Jahiz when theorizing the multisemic possibilities of Islamic architecture beyond the realm of the religious. Referring to al-Jahiz, he notes that *al-bayan* describes "the process of the production of meaning. It is the collection of all the means by which signification is produced. And if the utterance, *al-alfat*, the sum of all existing words is limited, the meanings it produces are boundless."[28] Smihi's own fascination with the work of Barthes—particularly *S/Z* (1970), with its embrace of the polysemic nature of textuality and its invocation of a plural, writerly text whose meanings are unfinished—is thus complementary to his recognition of al-Jahiz. This fact is important to us in two ways: it reveals that this global modernist filmmaker is consciously indebted to Arab-Islamic sources as well as to the more easily identifiable (for an Anglo-American-European critic) French reference points; and it demonstrates that one cannot continue to infer that Arab modernists like Smihi are bound only to frames of reference emanating from Europe, their former colonizer. But beyond the conscious intellectual references that a learned filmmaker like Smihi might reveal, it is our duty as critics to better acknowledge that world cinema and modernism are not built only from a restricted European or US canon. The radical structure and experimentation of Smihi's films is as much due to their roots in Arab traditions as to anything that came after; their modernism is built from intertextual affiliations whose directions are multiple. As is the case throughout Smihi's films, these intertextual engagements with writers and thinkers coexist in a spirit of nonhierarchical, pluralistic, and worldly discourse.

The East Wind and *44* resonate with the pluralistic, expansive, semiotically rich influence of al-Jahiz and the long history of art and architecture in the Islamic tradition. These might seem a long way from the picaresque narratives of *A Muslim Childhood* (2005), *Girls and Swallows* (2008), and *The Sorrows of a Young Tangerian* (2013), with their tales of Mohammed Larbi's journey through boyhood to adulthood. While their domestic settings often evince the same love for the architectural traditions of *zellij* within the space of the home as do the Fez settings of *44*, the more obvious reference points might be the contemporary currents of Egyptian and Hollywood cinema, for example, or the traditions of French literature (Marcel Proust) or the English novel (Charles Dickens). Yet these films, like the framing tale of *Moroccan Chronicles* (1999), also draw heavily on the legacy of the twelfth-century Andalusian philosopher Ibn Tufayl. A contemporary of Andalusian Spain's other famous scientist and philosopher, Ibn Rushd, Ibn Tufayl was trained as a physician and spent two decades in the court of Sultan Abu Yaʿqub Yusuf. But it is as author of *Hayy Ibn Yaqzan* that Ibn Tufayl is most significant.[29] This novel tells the story of a boy raised on a remote island without human contact. He identifies himself as different from the animals around him, yet is also able to observe and learn from them and, as he grows older, develops his faculties of reason. Samar Attar writes, "Not only did Hayy discover how to kindle fire, or to build a hut, or to domesticate animals, or to invent tools, but he also learnt how to become a physician, a biologist, an astronomer, a physicist, a psychologist and a philosopher. No one helped him reach his goal except his reason and scientific experimentation."[30]

As Attar and others have argued, not only is Ibn Tufayl's text the likely influence for Daniel Defoe's *Robinson Crusoe* (1719), but it underlies much of the European Enlightenment's stress on the need to question authority and religious doctrine through individual reason.[31] While working under the authoritarian Almohad dynasty, whose leaders were aggressive in their literalist interpretation of Islam, Ibn Tufayl himself was allowed relative latitude to make his philosophical inquiries under Abu Yaqʿub Yusuf. Ibn Rushd fared much worse under Yusuf's successor, Abu Yusuf Yaqʿub al-Mansur, and was imprisoned for a period. For Smihi, Ibn Tufayl's work poses a challenge to doctrinaire religious thought—even to that of the Almohads themselves—and, in the spirit of his other intellectual heroes like Ibn Rushd and Ibn Sina, continues to provide a model for the development of an Arab philosophical tradition that is informed and shaped by the history of Islam and that privileges concepts like learning, reason, and tolerance. In this sense, Smihi is exactly in concert with Attar's argument that these three thinkers "heralded the modern age in Europe.... Indeed, Kant's term '*Sapere aude!*' Have the courage to use your own reason, is the summation of what Ibn Tufayl and other Moslem philosophers have taught Europe."[32] Smihi is as passionate as Attar in his affirmations that the roots of the Enlightenment project are found in Arab thought, and that these roots must be reignited and used as precedent for a renewed project of Arab reason: a *tanwir* or Arab Enlightenment. To build a project of Arab modernity, for Smihi, is not to impose a European modernity over a reticent or retarded Arab culture but rather a project of recognizing a modernity whose traces are immanent in Arab thinking and writing. Such a perspective places him in the company of the many other Nahda proponents who saw *tanwir* as a critical goal of Nahda thought.[33]

The presence of a young boy at the center of many of Smihi's feature films is evocative of the central premise of Ibn Tufayl's novel. Brahim in *The East Wind*, Mohammed Larbi in the Tangier trilogy, and al-Hajj's son in *44* are all boys who are to varying degrees cut off from their society and learn to fend for themselves through a degree of autodidacticism driven by experimentation. Brahim's schooling at the *lycée* places him within an atmosphere diametrically opposed to that of his father (with his prayers) or the marabout (with his magical practices). As we see him at the end of the film, orphaned, we think of him as one who will by necessity negotiate the world of education in the French Enlightenment tradition, a tradition that we now know has roots in the period in which Tangier itself was formed—part of the Andalusian-Mediterranean environment that nurtured Ibn Tufayl and Ibn Rushd. El Hajj's son in *44* is similarly caught between the Islamic discourses that his father and Moussa inhabit with great devotion and the scientific discourses that he has learned while studying in France. Neither Brahim nor El Hajj's son are able to perform the reconciliation that Hayy manages, however. Hayy's encounter with the character of Absal (who represents the civilized and religious tradition, or *manqul*, of the text) eventually results in him making peace with himself as he discovers the possibilities of coexistence between his own independent thinking and the religious devotion of those who do not share his proclivities for reason and experimentation. *The East Wind* and *44*, however, close on the trauma of these tendencies remaining unreconciled for their young characters.

In the Tangier trilogy, however, there is further evidence of Smihi engaging with the textuality of Ibn Tufayl's novel, and we might see these films as proto-texts for the filmmaker's more definitive adaptation of *Hayy Ibn Yaqzan* that is still to come.[34] While Ibn Tufayl's challenge to religious *doxa* sits within the more general critique of religion that Smihi enacts (a critique explored more fully in the next chapter), *A Muslim Childhood* and *Girls and Swallows* already reveal the young protagonist as one who strives for the same level of self-knowledge exhibited by Hayy. In the first interior scene of *A Muslim Childhood*, where the family eats dinner together, Larbi asks his father for money to go to the movies; he wants to see a film called *The Birth of Islam* and stresses that he'll learn from it while improving his French through his reading of subtitles. Encountering the Jansenism of his French education, which stresses punishments and deprivation, he seeks further experience in cinema and in the novels that he reads, translated into Arabic, by writers like Honoré de Balzac (fig. 24) as well as the popular Arabic press that he finds. Indeed, the cinema becomes a realm of experience and experimentation for Larbi. He gravitates to it after he rebels against the pedagogical models he is offered by both the *lycée* and the Qur'anic school he attends, where he only escapes a beating by virtue of his father's role as a magistrate in the community. We see Larbi run away from his family, who do not seem to notice his absence. The voice-over tells us: "He took to the streets. He went his way free and easy like the wind. 'I ran away on the very day of my birth,' Peter Pan used to say." The scene continues, showing Larbi in the *hawma* (the *quartier* or hood), which the narrator tells us is full of madness, violence, and emotional instability (fig. 25).

Larbi and his friends also seek other places to hide. In the subsequent scene we see Larbi and a friend at the top of the casbah in Tangier, smoking cigarettes, singing, and playing, the friend with a flower in his hair and then both boys with cowboy bandannas. From here they encounter prostitutes on the steps of a medina street and the camera lingers on the flirtations, arguments, and transactions that

FIGURE 24 (Top). Larbi's autodidacticism includes reading an Arabic translation of Honoré de Balzac, anthologized in this issue of *Kitabi* (My Book), in *A Muslim Childhood*, 2005.

FIGURE 25 (Bottom). Larbi experiences the intense and sometimes rough corners of the medina in *A Muslim Childhood*, 2005.

occur around them. Then we see them in a café full of men drinking and telling bawdy stories (it's here that they encounter the music of Umm Kulthum, explored in the previous chapter). All these encounters testify to an adolescence of experience and experimentation that is outside the learned environments of school and official knowledge. Even more crucially, the narrator tells us (over a montage of theater marquees and sounds of an Egyptian musical) that cinema was what allowed

Larbi a sense of self, more than his immediate environment or any preordained sense of religion: "Neither family, school, or piety, were of any help to Larbi Salmi. To feel all alone in the world at the cinema was what gave him hope." Whether it be sexuality, death, or love, Larbi seems to choose the kind of autodidacticism (assisted by cinema and literature) that is developed in Ibn Tufayl's work.

The tension between the desire for self-knowledge and self-education and the constraints imposed by social structures—whether of family, religion, or even political affiliations—continues in the other films of the trilogy. Never as isolated in the second film as in the first, Larbi nonetheless explores his environment by feel and by test: reading the tenth-century writer Abu al-Faraj al-Isfahani's *Kitab al-aghani* (Book of Songs) or Taha Hussein's *The Call of the Curlew* (1934, English translation 1980), spying on Rabea as she works in her nightclothes, or investigating a soiled napkin she leaves outside her room. Smihi presents him as an individual trying to make sense of a world that is insufficiently explained by the dominant narratives surrounding him, principally those of religion, school, and political upheaval. *The Sorrows of a Young Tangerian* continues this exploration of Larbi's independence, culminating in the lengthy scene, shot in a single long take, where he renounces religion before his parents. In claiming that he has lost his faith, Larbi cites Jean-Jacques Rousseau and Voltaire to declare that god is a human invention, and evokes the Encyclopedists to affirm his support instead for the republic (in an earlier moment, he mentions that he is sympathetic to the ideas of Denis Diderot, founder and editor of the *Encyclopédie*, published from 1751). Yet this explicit recognition of French Enlightenment thought by writers who stressed the necessity of separating religion from reason is a continuation of the trajectory that his films also trace back to Ibn Tufayl, Ibn Rushd, and the thinkers of the golden age of Islamic culture. Smihi counts the Baghdadi writers, poets, architects, and musicians (among them al-Isfahani) as proto-Encyclopedists, wanting to develop their own *tanwir* within the Islamic culture of their time.[35]

ARABIC LANGUAGE, LITERARY MODERNISM, AND WORLD LITERATURE

In his engagement with Ibn Tufayl's work, Smihi also addresses an issue of language that animates all his films. Interwoven with the modernity of thinking that can be found in Ibn Tufayl's oeuvre is Smihi's use of Arabic. While Islamic theology places great emphasis on the holiness of the Qur'an and treats Qur'anic Arabic as the language's highest form, writers like Ibn Tufayl and the eleventh-century Syrian poet Abu al-ʿAlaʾ al-Maʿarri also used the language in a manner that was not religious or devotional. This creative use of Arabic toward purposes other than the sacred is immensely important to Smihi, and the different histories and potentials of formal Arabic and spoken dialectical Arabics are audible and palpable in his films. In this respect, al-Maʿarri is of keen interest. This poet, who has variously been described as a skeptic, an atheist, a heretic, and a misanthrope, was also inventive and obsessive about his use of Arabic. Drawing it away from the mysticism or devotional tendencies of poets like the twelfth- to thirteenth-century writer Ibn al-ʿArabi, al-Maʿarri exploited the humor and iconoclasm that was possible with the language. One of his best-known works, *Risalat al-ghufran* (Epistle of Forgiveness), has been described by its English translators as a "lengthy, mocking reply by a cantankerous maverick, obsessed with lexicography and grammar, to a rambling, groveling, and self-righteous letter by an obscure grammarian and mediocre stylist."[36] Al-Maʿarri experimented with Arabic, exploiting its capacity for puns and using it as a vehicle with which to challenge religious orthodoxy. In this way he was, as another of his translators agrees, "a pioneer of the *Aufklärung* [Enlightenment]" whose "open-minded and independent way of looking at things led him to conclusions which often agree with those of modern thought."[37] For example, one of his many skeptical admonishments of religion (not only Islam, but also other religions he saw around him in Syria), went as follows:

> They all err—Moslems, Christians,
> Jews, and Magians:
> Two makes Humanity's universal sect:
> One man intelligent without religion,
> And one religious without intellect.[38]

It is a sentiment that directly underlies Larbi's rejection of religious belief in *The Sorrows of a Young Tangerian*, and although much European thought has long forgotten the fact, it is an element of Arab literary tradition that rivals the skepticism of Ibn Rushd or Ibn Tufayl.

Not only does Smihi's work evoke the spirit of al-Maʿarri, but *44* integrates his poetry seamlessly into the very textuality of the film. Moussa's voice-over and voice-offs are structured around the poems of the Fez women's poetry school, as we saw in the previous chapter, but at one key moment, Moussa recites verses from al-Maʿarri's collection *Saqt al-zand*:

> Friends, here are the tombs of our contemporaries,
> but where are those of times past?
> May your footsteps be gentle, don't apply too much pressure on this old soil,
> made entirely of corpses.
> Move forward carefully if you can,
> and don't trample on the remains of old skeletons.
> Ask the two stars of the Little Bear constellation about the tribes . . .
> and nations that they have forgotten.
> The entirety of life is but suffering,
> I am astonished that we desire eternity![39]

In its placement in Smihi's film, al-Maʿarri's poetry constitutes a reflection on the pain and suffering that Moussa has observed around him and that, in the next scene, afflicts Yaqut, the family's servant confined to the boiler room.

Al-Maʿarri's poetry thus signifies in two ways in the film: its content contributes to a mood of elegy and mournfulness, and its form enables Smihi to continue to mine the same vein of intertextuality that he does with the Fez decorative art. That is, just as the art of the surface has been associated with Islamic aesthetics and yet also embodies a nonreligious, even proto-modernist meaning, so does al-Maʿarri's classical Arabic point away from the Qurʾanic recitation that we also hear in the film toward a flexible, supple, Arabic that is the vehicle of the profane, the skeptical, the scientific, and the rational. In this way, Smihi draws al-Maʿarri and Ibn Rushd into the terrain of his beloved critic Taha Hussein. Hussein was part of the movement in Egypt to modernize the classical Arabic language in order to render it available to an Arab nationalist project and facilitate communication across the many Arabic-speaking countries. In an attempt to relax some of the formal rules of Qurʾanic Arabic, rules that writers like al-Maʿarri and al-Jahiz were apt to explore, the movement to create a *fusha*, or eloquent form of modern Arabic, sought to imbue some of the flexibility of the *ʿamiyyat*, or dialects, into the language. While a certain amount of cultural policy was involved in this history (Hussein was not only an advisor to the education ministry but later served as minister for education in Egypt), the language was also modernized by the practice of writers like Naguib Mahfouz, whose novels not only developed a kind of modernist realism described in chapter 1, but also worked to situate Arabic as a language of contemporary relevance. While the debates around the place of *fusha* (or formal, Modern Standard Arabic [MSA]) continue, we encounter in Smihi's work a love and appreciation of its possibilities as a language of modern thinking and expression. As he argues in his interviews and writing as passionately as in his films, modern Arabic has produced, in addition to the Arabic novel, a rich literature of theater (the work of Tawfiq al-Hakim, for example) and an elaborate tradition of calligraphy.

The work of Arab modernist writers like al-Hakim, Mahfouz, and Hussein is thus of critical importance not only to Smihi's intellectual and artistic development but as a textual presence in the films themselves. These texts demand that we recognize the existence and importance of the writers' artistic production, but also that we understand the importance and modernity of *fusha* as a language of modern thought and expression beyond the history and institutionalization of classical Arabic as the language of the Qurʾan. For example Hussein's first book, *Fi al-shiʿr al-jahili* (On Jahili Poetry, 1926), decoupled the Arab language from its privileged relationship to Islam by using methods of literary criticism to analyze poetry. In so doing, Hussein claimed that the category of a distinct type of poetry belonging to a pre-Islamic period of *jahiliyya* (ignorance) was constructed arbitrarily so as to privilege what came after it: Islam and Qur'anic Arabic. While Hussein did not set out to criticize the Qur'an, his method of literary analysis, which he saw as scientific in the European tradition of literary criticism he had encountered in Paris, scandalized the religious establishment in Egypt and the book was quickly banned and its author dismissed from his academic position at Cairo University.[40] Hussein's books are visualized more than once in the Tangier trilogy. Most memorably they are seen near the beginning of *Girls and Swallows*, where *The Call of the Curlew* and *'Adib* (A Man of Letters, 1935) share a table with al-Isfahani's *Kitab al-aghani* (Book of Songs) and a poetry collection called *Endless Kisses*. After we are shown *The Call of the Curlew* in close-up, Larbi reads from its text.

The films also explicitly cite the Egyptian writer Tawfiq al-Hakim, who radicalized Egyptian theater by moving it beyond its previous dichotomies (comedic farce or translations of Western works). In plays like *Ahl al-kahf* (People of the Cave, 1933) and *Shahrazad* (1934), al-Hakim tried to integrate the experimentation he had observed in the Western dramatic tradition into a modern, indigenous form of drama.[41] In *The Sorrows of a Young Tangerian*, Smihi stages a sequence from al-Hakim's *Shahrazad* within his own film. It is set up in a black-and-white intertitle written in the style of a poster or program ("The Missionaries of Art present *Shahrazad*, a play by the great writer Tawfiq al-Hakim, at the Cervantes Theater, Tangier, Saturday, November 7, 1962"), and while Larbi and his friends discuss working together on a theater performance with the barber (and police informant) Daoudi, in the previous scene the theatrical performance is never placed in the narrative diegetically (we see no audience, although we hear some canned off-screen applause at the end, and the camera stays within the proscenium throughout). The scene from *Shahrazad*, in which Smihi's characters (like Larbi and Daoudi) play the parts of al-Hakim's characters, is completely integrated into *The Sorrows of a Young Tangerian* as a scene in its own right, lasting at least five minutes in screen duration and staged in a rich monochrome of scarlet, white, and black (Daoudi has blackened his skin for the role of 'Abd, a black slave). Here, then, al-Hakim's drama of infidelity, suspicion, and oppressive punishment offers a complement to the film's narrative of surveillance, betrayal, and torture during *les années du plomb*, or "years of lead," the repressive period under the rule of King Hassan II (1961–99).

Egyptian literary realism and modernism were influential on Egyptian cinema of the 1950s and 1960s, as Viola Shafik has noted.[42] Many of Naguib Mahfouz's novels were adapted for the screen during that period, and even though some of these were made with little or no input from Mahfouz himself and differed from his originals in key ways, they built upon recognition of his name and praise for his method.[43] Tawfik Saleh's *Diary of a Country Prosecutor* (1968) was adapted from a 1933 novel by al-Hakim, and writers like 'Abd al-Rahman al-Sharqawi and Taha Hussein also saw their work adapted for the screen. Mahfouz made his own contribution as screenwriter of more than twenty films between 1947 and 1959. He wrote exclusively for the cinema for the eight years between 1952 and 1959, collaborated with Salah Abu Seif on twelve of the latter's films, and saw cinema as a way to create a new Arab citizen after a period of cinematic *jahiliyya* or ignorance.[44] The literary legacy is important for Smihi, who recognizes it as formative in the development of Arab modernism even if, by his estimation, very little of that spirit was transferable into cinema, at least not by adaptation: a scene in *The Lady from Cairo* (1991) satirizes the idea that a director might simply adapt Mahfouz's Cairo trilogy in the most banal way possible. Rather, what we can perceive in Smihi's work is a recognition of the contributions of realist and modernist literature and the need to find analogous means of representation in the cinema. As recently as 2017, while praising the impact of writers like Gustave Flaubert, Tolstoy, Mahfouz, and Hussein on his work, he rejected the idea of literary adaptations of "great works," citing instead filmmakers like Alfred Hitchcock, Luis Buñuel, Satyajit Ray, or François Truffaut, all of whom worked with lesser-known story material.

The literary texts that Smihi cites go well beyond the domain of Arabic literature and cross French, European, Irish, British, and US texts—a worldly referentiality befitting of Smihi's Tangerian origins. The younger Larbi in *A Muslim Childhood* reads Honoré de Balzac, and his older counterpart in *Girls and Swallows* is enamored with Johann Wolfgang von Goethe. In *44*, the nationalist group that Moussa joins stages a production of William Shakespeare's *Othello*, the performance of which turns into a moment of anti-colonial solidarity (fig. 26). Nor was this the last time that Smihi would use Shakespeare's radical tragedy. *Moroccan Chronicles* relies heavily on the film, as Shams, in voice-over, quotes Othello's speech to Iago: "Lie with her? Lie on her? We say 'lie on her' when they belie her! Lie with her—that's fulsome. Handkerchief—confessions—handkerchief!" Placing the speech in the voice of Shams reverses the suspicion and hostility directed at Desdemona while animating Shakespeare's drama in a Moroccan setting, as Shams confuses one potential suitor by failing to meet with him, choosing another instead. Before she cites Shakespeare, Shams, in *Moroccan Chronicles*, is seen reading Virginia Woolf's *A Room of One's Own* (1929). Similar to his interest in the autodidact of Ibn Tufayl's *Hayy Ibn Yaqzan*, Smihi gives equal weight here to a young woman bucking tradition and family and dedicating herself to her desires and aspirations and experiments, activities articulated by the literary citations voiced or visualized in the film.

Such a sentiment of modernist dissent is in keeping with the influence of other writers whom Smihi experienced as a youth in Tangier and who pepper the films. Aside from Paul Bowles (whom Smihi knew as a young man—he collaborated with him on *Caftan of Love* [1989] and Bowles actually appears in that film), writers like Jack Kerouac, Tennessee Williams, and Allen Ginsberg all left their mark on his practice, as did James Joyce. I have mentioned in passing that the titles of *44* make reference to Frank Budgen's reading of Joyce. In a remarkably cinematic pas-

FIGURE 26. A performance of William Shakespeare's *Othello* becomes the occasion for a nationalist solidarity song in defiance of the French elites in the audience in *44, or Tales of the Night*, 1981.

sage that aptly describes the narration of Smihi's film, Budgen describes *Ulysses*'s point of view in the following terms:

> The viewpoint changes from one sentence to another so that the reader must be continually on the alert to follow the variations of scale and angle. The view constantly changes from a close-up to a bird's eye view. A character is introduced to us at close-up range, and suddenly, without warning, the movement of another character a mile distant is described. [The scale suddenly changes.] Bodies become small in relation to the vast space around them. The persons look like moving specks. It is a town seen from the top of a tower.[45]

As much as the film follows the digressive structure of *istitrad* discussed above, then, and even as it also resembles the digressive, sequential structure of *One Thousand and One Nights*, the film is also Joycean in its scope. Finally, while perhaps not within the definition of the strictly literary, the long sequence from Freud's *A General Introduction to Psychoanalysis* (1920) read by the schoolteacher in *The Sorrows of a Young Tangerian* also demonstrates the relevance of the textuality of psychoanalysis for the contemporary world of Tangier that the film depicts. Further in the terrain of the theoretical and the philosophical, Smihi's Arabic and French subtitle for *The East Wind*— '*anif al-samt* or *le silence violent* (the violent silence)—evokes the work of Georges Bataille as well as invoking a more general polysemy.[46]

VERNACULAR MODERNISM AND WORLD CINEMA

A Muslim Childhood's citations of Balzac place the French realist's book in the same shot as the French adventure comic series *Blek*. Taha Hussein's texts appear alongside the comic series *Kiwi*.[47] Larbi's fondness for postcards and posters of Hollywood movie stars like Gary Cooper is matched only by his appreciation of Egyptian popular film idols like Abdel Halim Hafez. And the beauty of Qur'anic *hada'ith*, or classical Arabic songs, is counterposed with vulgar street rhymes. Such instances should give clues to a larger context of intertextuality: while Smihi's films demonstrate the depth of the Arabic literary heritage, the beauty and modernity of Arabic as a language, and the region's modernist experimentation with literature and theater, they are simultaneously passionate about and wedded to iterations of popular culture, language, and local custom. They constantly mix high art with vernacular practices, foreign influences with national and local ideas. All of these combine to create a form of vernacular modernism, drawing on what is local but fusing it in a relation of newness with influences from other traditions. I have already shown the intertextuality of these films' literary references, both Arab and non-Arab. In the remainder of the chapter, I want to suggest how we might recognize the interrelationship of local non-cinematic practices within a textuality that is also comprised of, and an active participant in, world cinema. Understanding that relationship has stakes for how we think of Arab modernism outside of a relationship of domination or colonial influence and in terms more complex than those offered by discourses of nationalism and cultural authenticity. And it will put the local and the everyday on an equal footing with the foreign, creating a worldliness that is both radical in how it understands the politics and realities of the present and hopeful in how it gestures to the future.

Alongside their love of modern and classical forms of Arabic, the films demonstrate an intense appreciation for the variety of *'amiyyat* (dialects) that are spoken across the region—like Egyptian Arabic and the Moroccan vernacular referred to in the Maghrib as *darija*. Moroccan *darija* is a syncretic language that transforms the sound of classical Arabic by eliding vowels and stressing the interaction of consonants. Its lexicon and pronunciation differ from place to place around the country, incorporating different words from Tamazight, Tariffit, and Tashilhit languages (spoken widely, especially in rural areas) as well as from French. As such, it has a historical particularity that can be juxtaposed with the many instances of classical or modern Arabic that are also invoked in the films. Language and its deployment, along with other popular practices, thus become an aspect of intertextuality. Smihi's love for what he has termed "ideolects" is reflected in this interaction between language and popular custom.

One of the earliest and most illustrative examples of Smihi's engagement with such an intertextuality is evident in *The East Wind*. Smihi takes the ubiquity and sound of the *chergui* to signal something dramatically conflictual in the multilayered spaces of the city. The montage of local languages and popular customs exists on the level of both sound and image. The film opens with a juxtaposition of two Amazigh songs and moves through several sequences that, as I established in chapter 1, are documentary-like in their focus on the practices of medina residents. The choreography of greetings between the women doing laundry on the rooftop is remarkable in its attention to the sounds and rhythm of their voices, but here it is the customary formula of the interaction that is of interest. The frequent visual references to marabout-ism and popular religious custom are also evident in the sequence in which Aïcha's family sees the face of the exiled king Mohammed V in the moon. During the years of the French protectorate, this popular belief was one aspect of an anti-colonial structure of feeling: nationalists often reported seeing Mohammed V's face in the moon during the years of his exile, sustaining nationalist dreams of a future in which the French would be expelled and the king reinstated. Smihi's actors in *The East Wind* were largely nonprofessional and thus performed their own social roles, backgrounds, and languages. Even those who were actors by training were encouraged to lose their technique and speak in their respective dialects (Fassi from Fez, Tanjawi from Tangier, Rifian from the rural areas of the Rif mountains, and so on). His method of direction and his actors' method of performance was thus, by his description, sociological or anthropological rather than industrial or professional. Crucially, however, just as one might find reference points for such practices in European cinema practices (Michelangelo Antonioni's constructions of city spaces, Robert Bresson's use of actors as models, or Roberto Rossellini's belief in the possibility of nonprofessional actors and real locations), Smihi has likewise always responded to elements within Arab or Moroccan thought or practice. In a 1978 interview in Arabic he stated his interest in representing the specificities of the Moroccan mise-en-scène, since every culture, he argued, has its own relationship between bodies and space.[48]

Lest these references to other films, to different languages, and to varied social practices appear simply as a matter of citation, however, we might rather see them in the terms of the heteroglossia and polyphony that Mikhail Bakhtin evoked in his discussions of intertextuality. For example, Bakhtin's notion of heteroglossia evokes the sense of conflicting official and unofficial languages that I have observed as germane to the Arabic context, which is marked by divergent strains of Arabic. More particularly, though, the multivocal qualities of polyphony as Bakhtin defines them in *Problems of Dostoevsky's Poetics* (1963) can also account for the radical openness of Smihi's films. Bakhtin claims that rather than offering different voices controlled by a singular point of view or authorial position, Fyodor Dostoevsky's polyphony grants them their own social worlds—worlds that are not pulled into unity by the author. Dostoevsky's polyphonic worlds exist dialogically and are suggestive of different and conflicting subjective positions; any unity is only the unity of multiplicity.[49] Smihi's Tangerian films offer a quite literal sense of Bakhtin's polyphony. As I indicated in the last chapter, the overlapping, Fellini-esque character of the film's vocal sound constructs Tangier as a space of juxtaposed cultures and languages, but such a polyphony is not limited to voice alone; it is just as true of the intertextuality of languages and customs.

Such notions of multivocality and polyphony are of key significance to Smihi's invocation of popular practices in *Moroccan Chronicles*. From the outset, the film does more than combine the intertextuality of Smihi's obvious Western literary, filmic, and musical citations (in addition to the Virginia Woolf reference, already cited, Shams sings "Stormy Weather" and the soundtrack includes Johann Sebastian Bach, Franz Schubert, and Franz Liszt). Rather, it also mobilizes innumerable local oral and popular traditions, such as the storytelling of the *hakawati*, or ambulatory storyteller; the tradition of the gymnasts in the square, coming from the long line of Sufi followers of Sidi Ahmed ou Moussa; the music and chant of the Gnawa musicians; the wearing of the white *haik*, or traditional white women's garment that is typical of Essaouira, and so on. Smihi described his intense interest in and commitment to these elements in an interview about *The East Wind*. In response to the question, "This film depends on popular heritage in its language, is that so?" he replied:

> I, too, think that a lot of the elements of this language in the movie stem from the Moroccan popular folklore.... What I am interested in personally is to trace the *pensée sauvage* [Smihi here uses Lévi-Strauss's term, but translates it into Arabic as *al-fikr al-washi*] within Arab culture; to find it all you need is to listen to popular culture. Moroccan popular thought manifested itself throughout centuries and generations in many fields, some that are in my practice as synthetic forms: the art and technique of building cities, architectural art, abstract art forms that appear in the ornamentation of weaving and the art form of patterns in painting and metals, as well as in popular imagination in the form of story-telling, legends, proverbs, jubilant cries . . . in narrative forms as mentioned before, as well as in the beauty and the genius of Arabic traditional popular paintings, or Persian paintings or miniatures, which offer to us, as *cinéastes*, a visual reference we cannot ignore in our own practice.[50]

Here we have evidence of Smihi's intention to elevate the popular to the same level of importance as other forms of textuality and to refuse any kind of hierarchization of European high culture over the local and the popular. All are accorded equal weight in his vernacular modernist practice.

Such a concern for the revaluation of the popular is also evident in *44*, a film he has described as being inspired by the American slogan "Black is beautiful."[51] *44* is Smihi's attempt at a kind of radical narcissism in which he takes elements of the culture and shows them back to itself while simultaneously tracing the indignities suffered through the forty-four years of the French protectorate. The film's actual narration, which as we have seen can be tied to the Arab philosophies of al-Jahiz and the modernist narration of James Joyce, is equally organized by the perspective of a *hakawati*, or storyteller, who relates the battles against the French in the Rif mountains. It is in such a context—a small, rural village visited by the *hakawati*—that we see the figure of Smihi himself as discussed in the opening paragraph of my introduction. The film's narration responds to the *halqa* tradition of public storytelling (represented in key scenes in this film as well as in *Moroccan Chronicles* in the sequences that show public storytellers in the famous Jemaa el-Fnaa square) along with its Joycean and Jahiz-ian elements. As I noted in chapter 2, much of the poetry recited and used as Moussa's interior monologue in the film is from a long tradition of Fez oral verse whose female authors are anonymous. According to Mohammed El-Fasi, who collected and translated many of these poems as *Chants anciens des femmes de Fes* (Ancient Songs of the Women of Fez), the poetry was spoken and sung by women in garden settings around Fez: "These poems were destined to be sung in pleasurable events organized by the families in the gardens that surround the city of Fez. The young women, balanced on swings, devoted themselves to their movements and each one struck up an *aroubi* either of her composition or from a communal repertoire which was transmitted orally from generation to generation without knowing who was the true author."[52] These poems, writes El-Fasi, were exclusively romantic in nature and often speak longingly of a lover but always in the context of strong expressions of Muslim faith and the ability of God to alleviate the suffering imposed by distance or loss. El-Fasi, however, also points out that whereas classical poetry employed an exclusively masculine voice and gendered the object of affection as always feminine, "here we are in the presence of the opposite phenomenon; it is the women who speak of their loves using the feminine."[53] While I will comment further on the gendered dimensions of the poetic verse in a later chapter, I want to signal here the way that Smihi's adoption of this and other popular practices works against their colonial appropriation and/or denigration. In contrast to the loss or appropriation of Moroccan custom, then, Smihi redeploys all these elements, allowing them to structure his narratives and inflect his representations of history.

Here we might compare Smihi's work to some of his Moroccan cinema contemporaries, or those who just preceded him. I have elsewhere discussed what I called the "vernacular modernism" of the 1950s and 1960s *courts-métrages* and documentaries produced under the auspices of the Centre cinématographique marocain. Mohamed Afifi and Ahmed Bouanani in particular were notable for their conjoining of experimentations in documentary representation with an interest in popular practices and global modernisms. The intertextuality of those films is comprised of US culture, European avant-gardes, and local elements. Bouanani, for example, filled the soundtrack of his radical film on Casablanca, *6 and 12* (6 et 12, 1968), with bebop jazz and American rock 'n' roll even as his films like *Tarfaya, or a Poet's Walk* (Tarfaya, ou, la marche d'un poète, 1966) continued a long-standing documentation and visualization of Moroccan folk traditions that one can trace across the Moroccan modernism of the time.[54] Such an intertextuality reveals that the recovery and valorization of the local might be conjoined to the influence of international modernism in productive, vernacular ways. Rather than seal the local within a kind of reclaimed nationalist authenticity, to be always resistant to the foreign, such a modernism embraces a critical worldliness. Smihi's films offer a way to recognize how cinema, as a product of colonization, might still function in relation to other preexisting elements of culture in Morocco, North Africa, and the Arab world more broadly. In particular Smihi's own interest in the potential for cinema to be a kind of anthropology—his expressed debt to Jean Rouch and Robert Flaherty, one might say—emerges from his desire for cinema to reflect a culture to itself and yet at once be engaged in a world. This, he argues, is the task of a cinema that can engage with the oral and written history of a given culture while also accessing modernity—not simply as modernization, but as a modernity of ideas and images and sounds.

If I have so far used the term "vernacular modernism" to address the use of popular and quotidian practices in the context of Moroccan experiments with modernism, I also intend to invoke it with respect to a local cinema's negotiation of foreign influences, as in Miriam Hansen's formulation of Shanghai cinema with respect to Hollywood.[55] Smihi's films, in their intertextuality, demonstrate how a Moroccan and Arab modernism is comprised of an engagement not only with local customs, voices, and discourses but also with a world cinema that influences it and to which, in turn, it must be seen as integral. Such influences are multidirectional, spanning the proximate or ubiquitous (Egyptian and Arab, Hollywood, and European cinema) and the more distant (Asian and Latin American film), and popular and art traditions. For example, despite the fact that their aesthetic and mode of production stand in opposition to the factory system of Egyptian commercial cinema, Smihi's films also demonstrate his deep love for its popular traditions, stars, and influence. As I argued in chapter 2, Smihi's invocation of Egyptian popular cinema often manifests as the inclusion of songs by singers like Umm Kulthum, Abdel Halim Hafez, and Asmahan. But the integration of Egyptian popular cinema into the films operates on the visual level also.

In *A Muslim Childhood*, Larbi and his friend Ouahrani are transfixed by the sight of Hind Rostom dancing seductively in a bikini for Farid al-Atrash in Youssef Chahine's film *You Are My Love* (Inta habibi, 1957). Smihi includes footage of the Chahine film playing in the theater in a moment of intertextual homage to Egyptian cinema and its place in Tangerian life. The posters that grace the theater there (and the walls of Larbi's room in *Girls and Swallows*) are another explicit sign of the ubiquity of Egyptian cinema in the Tangerian and Moroccan landscape. Toward the end of *A Muslim Childhood* the camera lovingly pans in extreme close-up over details of posters for films like *Rendezvous with a Stranger* (Mawaʻid maʻ al-majul, dir. Atef

Salem, 1959), starring Samia Gamal and Omar Sharif; *Among the Ruins* (Bain al-atlal, dir. Ezzel Dine Zulficar, 1959), starring Faten Hamama; *I Am Free* (Ana hurra, dir. Salah Abu Seif, 1958), starring Lubna Abdel Aziz; or *A Day in My Life* (Yawm min 'umri, dir. Atef Salem, 1961), starring Abdel Halim Hafez. In an earlier scene Larbi pointed all of these out to Ouahrani, making him his apprentice in the appreciation of these Egyptian stars: "Look, Faten Hamama ... another star! Isn't she beautiful?" In *The Lady from Cairo*, soon after her arrival in Cairo, Amina attends a screening of *Love and Revenge* (Gharam wa intiqam, 1944), directed by Youssef Wahby and with songs written by Asmahan's brother, Farid al-Atrash, and watches Asmahan perform the song "Merry Nights in Vienna." As in *A Muslim Childhood*, Smihi includes this footage on the big screen of his own fictional diegesis, as he intercuts Amina and the audience watching and listening attentively. The enthusiastic endorsement of the film by Amina and her friend as they exit the theater complements the wide shots of the theater's lobby and poster art, presaging the similar scene in *A Muslim Childhood*; taken together, these scenes cement the idea of the cinema, as an institution and a physical site, as a kind of (secular) sacred space.

Yet if the stars and musical numbers of these films are instrumental in the popular landscape of Smihi's films, Egyptian cinema's realist experiments, referred to in chapter 1, also constitute an important intertextual presence. Near the end of *The Lady from Cairo*, a scene takes place in which Amina's brother, Yahia, is killed in front of the pyramids (fig. 27), evoking the many Egyptian films that end with a scene set in Giza with the pyramids as a backdrop; the closest to Smihi's in its visual and narrative terms is Atef al-Tayeb's *The Bus Driver* (Suwaq al-atubus, 1983).[56] And Yahia's funeral, in the southern Nile region, not far from Luxor, offers many intertextual references to Shadi Abdel Salam's film *The Night of Counting the Years* (al-Momia [The Mummy], 1969) in the sound of the wind on the soundtrack, the visually striking scenery of the valley, which recalls the opening of the earlier film, and even the visual presence of a character who strikingly resembles that of Abdel Salam's principal character of al-Wannus. Indeed, Smihi's own writing about cinema offers evidence of the kind of conscious citation and influence he has sometimes engaged in his work. Within a realist tradition that he traces to filmmakers like Kamal Selim (*The Will* [1939]), Youssef Chahine (*Cairo Station* [1958]), and Hussein Kamal (*The Postman* [1968]), Smihi reserves particular praise for Tawfik Saleh's film *Diary of a Country Prosecutor*, which, he argues, unites literary models (it was based, as I have mentioned, on a novel by Tawfiq al-Hakim), the modern narrative form of the diary, and the traditional elements of *One Thousand and One Nights* and other popular tales. Saleh's film inscribes popular discourses into a style that is also modern and international, narrating the encounter between an urban lawyer and the population of an impoverished village in the Nile valley. Smihi's admiration for Saleh's mixing of elements and registers gives a further context for his methods in *44*, as he relies intensively on Moroccan popular customs while

134   CHAPTER THREE

FIGURE 27. The pyramids at Giza as the intertextual backdrop for a murder in *The Lady from Cairo*, 1991.

also invoking the literary models that I signaled earlier in this chapter (including al-Maʿarri, Mahfouz, Joyce, and others).

Smihi was to investigate this period and its practitioners intensively in his film *Egyptian Cinema: Defense and Illustration* (1989). The film begins with Youssef Chahine seated in his billiard room next to a huge world globe that, sitting on the billiard table, dwarfs the film director, who smokes and speaks animatedly to the camera about the role of the film producer in Egypt versus the rest of the world. Soon after comes a sequence of traveling shots around Cairo and its environs over which Smihi's voice narrates, in Arabic (with a French voice translating, as it does throughout the film), the role of Egypt in the history of Arab cinema and the Nahda, and the history of ideas in the world. The film includes interviews with many of the directors whose work he cites in his own films and writing, such as Salah Abu Seif (who features prominently, often speaking from Chahine's house in front of a dramatic Egyptian painting), Tawfik Saleh, Mohamed Khan, Bashir al-Dik (who wrote the screenplay for Smihi's *The Lady from Cairo*), Khairy Beshara, and Inas El-Degheidy; the actors Ahmed Zaki, Adel Iman, and Yousra; and the critic Samir Farid. In the film, then, Smihi activates his intertextual energies in critical engagement with the thinking and the images that these individuals produced. More than an homage to other films or figures, the film itself produces an intertextual flow of images of Cairo as a cinematic space, creating mobile montage sequences of movie posters and billboards intercut with traveling shots of Cairene streets and stills from films.

FIGURE 28. Alfred Hitchcock's *The Man Who Knew Too Much*, 1956, fictionalizes the space of the Jemaa el-Fnaa; Moumen Smihi would reprise this scene in *Moroccan Chronicles*, 1999.

Just as Smihi's films navigate the influence and legacy of Egypt, the hegemonic cinema in the region, so have they profited from critical engagement with both the dominant representational force of Hollywood and US cinema's auteur-driven, more marginal currents. The imagined geography of Michael Curtiz's *Casablanca* (1942) or Josef von Sternberg's *Morocco* (1930) are but two examples of a long history of exoticized and Orientalist Hollywood representations of Morocco.[57] Yet the fact that *Casablanca* was not made in Casablanca nor *Morocco* in Morocco has not prevented Moroccans from taking up its representations and others like it, as Brian T. Edwards has documented.[58] To narrate the cinematic relationship of Hollywood and Morocco (in terms of both representation and production) only as a story of cultural hegemony obscures a longer history of Moroccan engagements with US cinema, one that includes the films of the eccentric Moroccan cinema pioneer Mohamed Osfour, who drew on Tarzan and Douglas Fairbanks when shooting with homemade equipment around his home city of Casablanca, and the postcolonial Moroccan modernists mentioned above.[59] Smihi's intertextual engagements with Hollywood reformulate the relationship between Hollywood, European imaginaries, and Morocco. Hitchcock's *The Man Who Knew Too Much* (1956) uses Marrakesh's famous Jemaa el-Fnaa square as the site of the midwestern couple's fascination with an Orient that is strange, enchanting, and, as they will find, dangerous (fig. 28). But in reprising Hitchcock's scene—replete with snake charmers, acrobats, and storytellers—Smihi's *Moroccan Chronicles* reclaims the longevity and vivacity of performances and practices that have long been part of the popular culture of the square. The film both acknowledges the terms of Morocco's entry

FIGURE 29. A scene shot at the Essaouira ramparts for *Moroccan Chronicles*, 1999, recalls Orson Welles's *Othello*, 1951.

into the circulation of Hollywood cinema—standing for an otherness that might be exoticized within an economy of sameness—and yet manages to claim from Hitchcock's movie an irreducible quality to those same practices, a quality that might be useful for a representation of Moroccan custom back to itself.

A similar kind of doubling operates in the second part of the same film, which Smihi shot on the ramparts of Essaouira (fig. 29). Built in the eighteenth century by Genoese engineers at the command of the Moroccan king Mohammed III, after two centuries of Portuguese control of the coast, the ramparts were used by Orson Welles for his 1951 film of Shakespeare's *Othello*; he also shot footage at al-Jadida, farther up the coast. As I noted above, Shakespeare's text itself becomes an intertextual reference, in that Smihi extracts from its already-charged racial narrative (of the Moor and the Jew) another potential story about the suppression of Desdemona's desire. Smihi takes the dramatic cinematic spaces of Welles's film and repurposes them to offer further evidence of how Morocco itself is worlded by its cinematic past. Within the intertextual world of Smihi's Essaouira, one that includes Welles's *Othello* (1951), Shakespeare's *Othello*, and Virginia Woolf's *A Room of One's Own*, the filmmaker creates a polyphony of Moroccan and non-

Moroccan voices. Such a polyphony allows the film to address multiple planes of meaning simultaneously, evoking for example the determining limitations of foreign visions of Morocco but also the possibilities those visions might offer for thinking back against colonialism or against the patriarchal elements of Moroccan society.

While the names of Hollywood filmmakers like John Ford appear in Smihi's credits (the Tangier trilogy films list literary, musical, and filmic citations in the end credits, making explicit some of his intertextual leanings) and others crop up regularly in interviews, his interest in auteurs extends (as Hitchcock and Welles would suggest) to those on the edges of the studio system, like Nicholas Ray, or who worked as émigrés, including Fritz Lang and Sternberg, especially the latter's work with Marlene Dietrich on *Morocco*; in this way, he inherited something of the auteurist sensibilities of his Paris peers at the Cinémathèque *française*.[60] His own mode of production and control over his work resembles the approach of a filmmaker like John Cassavetes: he was suspicious of his peers who returned from France to take jobs in the Centre cinématographique marocain, referring to them as "functionaries," and has preferred to retain complete creative control by raising his own budgets and retaining rights to all his films. He continually expresses fondness for the work of Woody Allen, and the next chapter will further explore what he takes from Allen's cinematic world in terms of religion and identity. And, while eschewing cars and freeways, the itinerant trajectory of *Moroccan Chronicles* owes a considerable debt to maverick films like Terrence Malick's *Badlands* (1973) or Monte Hellman's *Two-Lane Blacktop* (1971), as Smihi takes the viewer through the Moroccan locations of Fez, Marrakesh, Essaouira, and Tangier, finally launching his young protagonist on a journey *illa Fransa* (to France) by the end.

The case of Hitchcock, Welles, and Sternberg, where the citations to Hollywood actually involve imaginary or material engagements with Morocco, is extended by other cinematic intertexts. Whereas Pier Paolo Pasolini's visions of sacrilege and joyful perversity in films like his "trilogy of life"—*The Decameron* (1971), *The Canterbury Tales* (1972), and especially *Arabian Nights* (1974)—partly structure Smihi's own representations of religion and social relations, the Italian filmmaker's use of Morocco as a location for *Oedipus Rex* (1967) was something Smihi found especially compelling; again, one can turn to *44* to find a Pasolinian landscape.[61] Implicit in the traces of these other films that have engaged with Morocco is the sense that they wrote *through* and not simply *about* the discourses of Morocco and its social structure and can thus be productively reengaged in a modern discourse on Morocco's place in the world. In *With Matisse in Tangier* (1993), a documentary on the painter's Tangier sojourn, Smihi's narration—which he wrote and voices himself throughout—makes the claim that the European visitor was able, through his outsider status, to capture subtleties and contradictions of Moroccan society that were scarcely talked about, for instance the role of the black, sub-Saharan

FIGURE 30. A close-up of a Moroccan woman's face forms part of Moumen Smihi's restaging of Matisse's 1912 painting *Fatma, the Mulatto Woman* in *With Matisse in Tangier*, 1993.

African slave within the Moroccan household, or the double-faceted status of a Moroccan woman, often cloistered within a private space over which she is nonetheless in control. The film thus restages paintings by Henri Matisse like *Moroccan Cafe* (1913), *Zohra Standing* (1912), or *Fatma, the Mulatto Woman* (1912) in a new, live mise-en-scène of tableaux vivants (fig. 30). Rather than suspect representations anchored in European authorial control, texts like Matisse's paintings, Welles's *Othello*, and Hitchcock's *The Man Who Knew Too Much* signify beyond the limits of Orientalism in that they also include voices and intertexts of the social worlds in which they were formed: European and Moroccan. The consistent presence in his films of traces of other work (be it American, European, Japanese, or from elsewhere) and the films' overt engagement with Occidental ideas along with Moroccan, Arabic, and Islamic ones means that one must take seriously the extent to which the films' intertexts become generative of self-knowledge and self-representation within Morocco rather than pointing back to something outside it. In other words, Smihi's intertextuality is not a relationship of debt or derivation, and it performs a different kind of work than standing in for colonial discourses that the film must reject.

The intertextual engagement with world cinema goes beyond the cadre of films that either represent Morocco or that were shot there on location. One can identify many moments in which histories of world cinema and individual films and filmmakers assist these films in constructing an argument about history, modernity, and the relationships between the local and the foreign or between the popular and high culture. In 44, Smihi consciously turned to European as well as other cinematic examples. His use of wide exterior shots and composition in deep space to further a historical depiction of war and opposing armies is particularly reminiscent of Miklós Jansco's work. He presents the bands of horsemen in the Rif and Atlas mountains with the same grandiose swoop of movement that Jansco deploys in *The Red and the White* (1967). In both films, the wide-screen, wide-angle shot allows for a mise-en-scène that accentuates the historical forces at work (for Jansco's film, Hungarians against Russians; for Smihi, Moroccans against the French). Of a similar historical moment and marked, like Jansco's work, by the encounter with the Soviet Union, Armenian Soviet director Sergei Parajanov's film *The Color of Pomegranates* (1969) offers a riotous combination of color, costume, and theatricality that has visible traces in the way 44 presents the sumptuousness of Moroccan interiors and the bourgeois family, even if lacking the former film's more surreal elements.

In a somewhat more sober approach to history and in the search for a form that might reconcile elements of popular culture with cinema's modernity, Smihi evokes the exquisitely shot historical films of Japanese filmmaker Kenji Mizoguchi. The influence of a film like *Ugetsu* (1953), with its ghost story and attention to female beauty and suffering, is apparent in Smihi's *Caftan of Love*, whose characters negotiate ambiguous doublings and a sometimes violent dreamlike mise-en-scène (fig. 31); *Caftan of Love*, in its interest in the doubled female figure, also owes much to Hitchcock's *Vertigo* (1958), as Smihi has pointed out.[62] While lacking the means of Mizoguchi's sweeping crane shots, Smihi's film nonetheless retains the Japanese director's use of the long take and concentration on an elaborate, highly controlled, historical mise-en-scène. Indeed, the films of Mizoguchi, Akira Kurosawa, and Yasujiro Ozu, in their very different modes and in the interplay between those modes, form a conscious set of intertexts for Smihi. In a 1984 roundtable on Arab cinema in Milan, Smihi commented on the distinction drawn in Japanese cinema history between the *jidai-geki* (historical film) and the *gendai-deki* (film about modern Japan), suggesting that it could offer for Moroccan and Arab cinema a comparable project of *taqlidi* (traditional) or *'asri* (modern) films. Understanding those differences, he proposed, might help Arab cinema address not only questions of history and the suppression of cultural patrimony under colonialism, but also the challenges of modernity.[63]

As early as *The East Wind* and as recently as *The Sorrows of a Young Tangerian*, one sees the profound influence of Yasujiro Ozu's reorganization of cinematic space with respect to Japanese society and modernity. For Ozu, placing the camera at the level of a person seated on a tatami mat and the use of deep focus made the visual field more adequately correspond to the way that space was practiced by the subjects of his films and facilitated the use of architecture as a kind of theatrical

FIGURE 31. The poster for *Caftan of Love*, 1989, enacts a doubling of languages (Arabic and French) and of subjects: Rachida's violent other resides in the "big mirror" that evokes Mohammed Mrabet's original story.

FIGURE 32. With a nod to Yasujiro Ozu, Moumen Smihi uses a wide shot from a low vantage point in *Girls and Swallows*, 2008.

stage.[64] While profoundly influenced by US cinema, Ozu also shot Japanese architecture in a way that exploited its particularity and opened it to performance. As Donald Richie notes, he "used rooms as a proscenium . . . and since his fixed camera position precluded his following his characters about, their entrances and exits are often as theatrical looking as they are in real Japanese life."[65] Smihi adopts a similar approach in presenting the interiors of the Moroccan homes where he sets his narratives. For example, in *Girls and Swallows* the camera often deploys wide shots of the family seated on low divans. The composition in depth accentuates the perspective across an expanse of tiled floor, breaking the space with walls and doorways (fig. 32). The comedy of Larbi's relationships to other family members in *A Muslim Childhood* often turns on his entrances and exits into the frame, around doors and walls and staircases. Turning an economical style of shooting—in part due to limited budgets—to an advantage, the fixed camera positions that characterize Smihi's Tangier films allow for an interaction between characters and space that resonates with the kind of modernism we have seen thus far: at once recognizing the beauty and particularity of Moroccan vernacular architecture and aesthetic style while simultaneously placing the film into circuits of worldliness. Such techniques, then, rather than functioning simply as citations of a filmmaker he admires, are key to Smihi's films' functioning with respect to cinema, Morocco, and the world.

If the low angles and fixed camera positions of many of Smihi's films resonate with Ozu, their accompanying use of the long take places them in relation to other directors who deploy duration as an aesthetic style. Examples abound. Early in *A*

Muslim Childhood, where the narrator describes how Sidi Ahmed would organize family photos, the accompanying shots show the family standing in the courtyard of their home, facing the camera in a static pose. The mise-en-scène has an uncanny effect: the characters appear as if in a still image, yet are in fact posing for the camera and moving slightly, and the tableaux vivants that result resemble those that Raúl Ruiz creates in *Hypothesis of the Stolen Painting* (L'Hypothèse du tableau volé, 1987), where the static arrangement of groups of people reconstituting a painting is disturbed by the perception of movement in the frame. Smihi himself has cited the director Manoel de Oliveira, whose seven-minute take of the wheel of a horse-drawn carriage in *Day of Despair* (1992) made an impression on him for its simplicity of means and daring effect. Hou Hsiao-Hsien is another long-take director whom Smihi discovered after shooting the long takes of *Girls and Swallows* and *The Sorrows of a Young Tangerian*.[66]

Yet it is another Taiwanese director, Tsai Ming-liang, whose extreme long takes resonate most compellingly with Smihi's. The cinephilia of a film like *What Time Is It There?* (2001), with its Paris encounter with Jean-Pierre Léaud, Truffaut's actor from *The 400 Blows* (1959), has an easily recognizable counterpart in Smihi's work, where Larbi's city experiences in *A Muslim Childhood* continue in the spirit of Léaud's character in Truffaut's landmark film. But Tsai's restaging of cinematic genealogies in *Goodbye, Dragon Inn* (2003), with its extended incorporation of his intertext, the *wuxia* (martial arts) film *Dragon Inn* (dir. King Hu, 1967), into a scene set in a theater, has visible affinities in the many moments that Smihi shows us films in cinemas, such as the examples already cited from *The Lady from Cairo* and *A Muslim Childhood*. In *The Sorrows of a Young Tangerian* Smihi integrates the minute-long final scene from a film by Jean Renoir, *The Elusive Corporal* (Le Caporal epinglé, 1962), into his own film, showing his characters entering and exiting the theater in which it is playing. The excruciatingly long take that Tsai deploys as we contemplate the cleaning of an empty theater has a charge that some sequences of *The Sorrows of a Young Tangerian* also emulate, and the uncomfortably long take where Larbi renounces religion recalls the (arguably greater) shock value of the rendezvous between a father and son in a gay bathhouse that Tsai creates in *The River* (1997). The use of the long take, then, while allowing Smihi's films to focalize the intensity of familial and social relationships, also places them within a global cinema of cinephilia and modernist experimentation.

I have already mentioned Satyajit Ray's work in the context of realism and the ways it has been theorized with respect to world cinema. It is important to note, however, the thematic and visual referentiality that Smihi's films share with his, also. Ray's daring opening shot atop a moving streetcar in *The Big City* (Mahanagar, 1963), where we see the end of the trolley pole moving along an electrical wire, sparking as it goes, renders the technological arrival of modernity in the manner of sensation, as Keya Ganguly points out.[67] *Pather Panchali* (1955) dramatizes a character's (as well as the viewer's) perception of this kind of shock as Apu encounters power lines and a train in the midst of a grassy field. Smihi's films create versions of both kinds of encounter. *Si Moh, the Unlucky Man* (1971), as noted in earlier chapters, introduces the sensational and shocking aspects of the big modern city as visual and sonic elements that the character Si Moh must navigate. *The East Wind* includes a scene that virtually reprises *Pather Panchali*, when Brahim comes across a moving train in the countryside. And *44* places considerable visual and sonic attention on the arrival of the radio, telephone, and roller skate. As Ray is concerned with integrating the technologies of modernity and colonization into the Indian setting, so is Smihi attentive to the historical relationships between Morocco, its past, and the interplay between technological modernization and cultural modernity.

When discussing Ray's cinema, Moinak Biswas suggests that neorealism offered a way for Indian filmmakers to enter world cinema.[68] This chapter has shown that the intertextuality of Smihi's films performs a related function. While conscious citation on Smihi's part is a mark of the director's cinephilia and active embrace of an auteurist model of filmmaking, the larger intertexuality of his films—elements of which are beyond his authorial concern or conceit—speak to the ways that I want to situate the works within Arab modernism and world cinema more generally. Ignoring the intertexts of these films or attributing them to a relationship of colonial debt or cinematic imperialism (from Hollywood, or Europe, or even Egypt's industries) is to overlook the complexity, genealogy, and originality of his work, which as I have shown draws on many sources beyond the expected Eurocentric domains. Smihi's cinema affirms the long history of Arab experimentation with ideas and forms, the rich legacy of architecture, philosophy, and literature, and the more recent confluence of cinematic visions from within the region and far beyond it. This, I argue, is the kind of Nahda that the work demands: a worldly engagement with ideas, images, and sounds from wherever they might be useful in the service of new narratives of Arab and Moroccan subjectivity. Such a new Nahda is nowhere more visibly and publicly fought than in debates around religion, gender, and sexuality, and it is to these topics that the next two chapters turn.

4

Religion, Secularism, Modernity

Here and in the next chapter, I use the observations about cinematic language and intertextuality generated in the previous three chapters to inform my exploration of two contemporary Arab cultural debates in which Moumen Smihi's cinema participates: the place of religion in society, and the role of gender and sexuality. This chapter shows how Smihi's cinema offers a vision of a multi-confessional, tolerant, and secular Moroccan and Arab world—one that embodies the spirit of a new Nahda. In one sense, Smihi's films are an answer to Islamophobic discourses in the West that conflate all Arabs with Islam and all Muslims with religious radicalism. The films disaggregate religion from the language and culture of the Arab world, showing it to be one discourse amid a diverse terrain of cultural practices and ideas. Of even greater importance, however, is the films' internal critique, which is not primarily focused on the West. Smihi's films treat the status of religion and the secular as urgent issues within Morocco and across the region, and they do so by offering a sometimes radical perspective from inside Moroccan and Arab thought and experience. Thus Smihi's cinema embodies the spirit of Arab thinkers of the liberal age—Muslim, Christian, and Jewish—who developed visions of Arab life in which freedom of expression and respect for diverse values and beliefs would be nurtured and protected.

Here, then, Smihi's cinematic modernism works to articulate an Arab conception of modernity, one that draws upon Islamic and non-Islamic discussions of reason and its possible coexistence with religious ideas and faith. This modernism is indeed turned toward a secular form of modernity, but one in which the term "secular" is multivalent, open, and noncoercive. Recent work in the humanities and social sciences, particularly in the domain of anthropology, has rigorously questioned the category of the secular and practices of secularism. For example, Talal Asad has extensively interrogated the very categories of "secular" and "religious" so as to argue for their mutual constitution. His work has contributed to a radical questioning of the ideas of a liberal Enlightenment and universal humanism and their political expression in the form of liberal democracies.[1] Focused in part on the political applications of secularism in the increasingly diverse societies of Europe and the United States (for example, by challenging contemporary formations of the laïcité [secularism] of the French Republic), work following Asad's has also been invested in reassessing Islamist movements within the Arab world. In particular it has resisted any tendencies to read them as some kind of deviation or regression from the aims of the Enlightenment, which is thereby understood as a Western and sometimes imperializing project.[2] One criticism of this kind of "post-secular" thinking, however, has been that it treats the secular practices of the West as subject to critique while too quickly equating Islam with "tradition" or assigning to it a character of cultural authenticity.[3] Some critics of the post-secular turn see in it a resistance to universalism, risking (in Aziz al-Azmeh's view) an essentialism by which Arabs exist outside of history and where any critique of religious life is assumed to be a sign of Western interference that must be relativized and fought.[4]

To engage with the full breadth and complexity of the debates around the secular and secularism is well beyond the scope and purpose of this chapter. Instead, my aim is to understand how Smihi's films portray the historical diversity of religious practice and adherence within the Arab world, and to better understand the contexts by which some of them call for ways of life in which religion is not the predominant form of social or political organization. Second, and relatedly, I try to show how such positions might be linked to long-standing debates within the Arab world rather than seen a priori as a sign of Westernization or neo-imperial influence in the immediate present. For an Arab artist to question the status of religion in society, as many Arab (and non-Arab) artists have done, should be seen as an example of dissent and political argument within a given social context, not simply as a sign of complicity with a foreign agenda. Third, and importantly, the chapter understands these films as creative expressions within a terrain of film and culture that occupies the local and the transnational. As this book argues throughout, Smihi's films unabashedly straddle the intensely local and the global by dint of their representations and their participation in global cinema flows. In thus tracing the intellectual routes that Smihi's films (and writings) have followed with respect to religion, I understand them always in relation to the cinematic.

Taken together, the films never advocate a prescriptive form of secularism as a political doctrine, nor even a rigid narration of what the secular might be, and they have no truck with secularism as a coercive project of the state.[5] As Mayanthi L. Fernando has argued with respect to France, secularism has often been practiced as a form of racialized exclusion that justifies itself through a presumptively settled definition of secularity that is in fact always contradictory.[6] Here I acknowledge the unsettled nature of secularity while retaining the term "secular" to signal how these films use Nahda debates to search for alternatives to the status quo in Morocco, where religion is thoroughly imbricated in the state and occupies a privileged status in public life. Rather than embrace a rigidly exclusionist logic, Smihi's films exert a call to renegotiate the relationships between religion, reason, and personal freedoms as they are experienced within the Arab world. Such a call is wholly in keeping with the films' sense that the Arab world is dynamic, not static, and that religion is not the only measure of Arab identities. What is most important, then, is the film's representation of religion as a phenomenon in the world that might be treated like any other social, political, or cultural discourse: subject to question, open to critique, and able to be represented in terms that exceed the sacred. The films develop this position in relation to both Arab and Islamic history and world cinema; both are foundational to Smihi's desire for a society built on freedom of expression.

This chapter isolates four strands in the way that the films address questions about religion. The first stresses the diversity of religious tradition within the Maghrib: Smihi's films, especially the Tangier trilogy, make plain the historical coexistence of the three monotheistic, Abrahamic religions of Judaism, Christianity, and Islam. Refusing to conflate the terms "Arab" and "Islam," Smihi references the long Andalusian and Maghribi history that constructed multiple crossing points and overlapping histories among the religious groups present in the region. Second, I show how Smihi's films stress the social dimensions of religion as a matter of ritual and practice. Some films complicate assumptions about religious conformity or orthodoxy: for example the kinds of practices conducted in *The East Wind* (1975) are anathema to Sunni Islam yet were long present in the Maghrib, and some, such as the worship of marabouts (saints or holy men) continue as a kind of syncretic fusion of pre-Islamic and Islamic practices. The influence of anthropology is felt here, too: rather than accepting at face value the nature of certain customs as religious, Smihi's films indicate that practices like circumcision or the wearing of various kinds of head coverings are, beyond their religious codings, *practices* that are historical, cultural, and customary in form. Third, I demonstrate how Smihi's films produce a new discourse on the relation of the sacred and the sacrilegious in the Arab world. Whether through the use of profanity in the films' popular vernacular or by a refusal to mystify practices presented as cultural, Smihi both represents religion and allows us to look askew at it in the manner of well-known, non-Arab filmmakers; those he cites include Luis Buñuel, Federico Fellini, Pier Paolo Pasolini, and Woody Allen. Drawing on such examples of world cinema for their secular understandings of sacredness and profanity enables me to posit a broader consideration of the relation between Islam and modernity in the final section of the chapter. Here I demonstrate that an internal critique of the role of religion has existed within Arab societies for centuries and show how Smihi's films suggest that such a history might still be available and necessary in the present. In this way, I argue, his cinema thus brings Ibn Tufayl (the author of *Hayy Ibn Yaqzan* discussed in chapter 3), poets like Abu al-ʿAlaʾ al-Maʿarri (also discussed in chapter 3), and the eighth- and ninth-century heretic Abu Nuwas together with European Enlightenment thinkers and global cinematic modernism to constitute a new kind of *tanwiri* (Arab Enlightenment) film project.

RELIGIOUS DIVERSITY

Smihi grew up in a Tangier that was religiously diverse. This milieu contributed to the ecumenism of his films, and those set in Tangier offer particularly vivid examples of the mixture of religious faiths in the city.[7] In *The East Wind*, an early scene shows Brahim praying with a class of other young boys in a Qurʾanic school, all of them chanting in unison. We see Brahim and other boys in medium shots and close-ups that alternate with wide shots of the entire class seated before their teacher. But as the scene ends, church bells signal a cut to a wide shot of the medina as the sound of the prayer continues. Then, after another cut, we see the spire of a Spanish church in the medina and the mix of Qurʾanic prayer and church bells lingers for another second before the prayer fades out and the bells predominate. In successive shots we see Catholic women in headscarves and dark clothing speaking Spanish, a man walking a dog, and a young woman with a skirt above the knee holding the hand of a girl dressed in an equally fashionable short skirt, all of them associated with the sound of the church bells. Some of the same characters are seen a little later, again speaking Spanish. And, in a later moment that I described in chapter 2, we hear the voice of an announcer from Radio Cairo. Over his announcement, we also perceive the sound of a muezzin calling the prayer for Muslims and another clock chime associated with a Christian, particularly English, church. This dense layering of sounds and images signifies the religious diversity of the place and the moment, while also offering a sense of Tangier within the soundscape of Arab nationalism.

Smihi develops this sense of religious coexistence further in *A Muslim Childhood* (2005), *Girls and Swallows* (2008), and *The Sorrows of a Young Tangerian* (2013), where we see Muslim, Christian, and Jewish inhabitants of the city. Coexistence, the films suggest, does not always mean complete harmony, and here Smihi offers a nuanced portrait of a time when Morocco and Tangier were religiously more heterogeneous than today. As Susan Gilson Miller notes, Tangier was once home to a significant native Jewish population, and in the time Smihi's trilogy begins, the 1950s, this community was still very much present.[8] It was not until the 1960s and 1970s that most Moroccan Jews emigrated to Israel (the subject of at least two documentary films, *Tinghir-Jerusalem: Echoes of the Mellah* [dir. Kamal

FIGURE 33. Sidi Ahmed sits with his Jewish neighbor Señora Sultana, who has sought his help, in *A Muslim Childhood*, 2005.

Hachkar, 2012] and *They Were Promised the Sea* [Pour une nouvelle Seville, dir. Kathy Wazana, 2012]). The narrator's voice-over in *A Muslim Childhood* describes the city as "polyglot" and "multi-confessional," and we are shown this in a montage of shots of the city already described in chapter 1. But as well as creating a mise-en-scène that reflects the built environment and its multi-confessional presence—with mosques and churches and buildings belonging to French, Spanish, English, and other international powers—Smihi makes the religious diversity of Tangier into a narrative issue.

In one short scene, for example, Sidi Ahmed—the theologian and *fqih* (Islamic legal expert) with the soft heart—is seated with his neighbor, Señora Sultana, who speaks a mixture of *darija* (Moroccan Arabic) and Spanish (fig. 33). Sultana, who earlier in the film tailored some new pants for Larbi, has come to inform the father that one of the local boys, Abdelwahed, throws rocks into her yard because she is Jewish. Sidi Ahmed reflects on the problem and says he fears that if he tells the teacher at the Qur'anic school, he will inflict too severe a punishment on the boy (beating his feet till they bleed, he surmises). Consequently, Sidi Ahmed asks himself out loud what is to be done and the scene closes with his indecision. The next two films in the Tangier trilogy offer other examples of the Jewish life of Tangier but, as with Señora Sultana, suggest that such a multi-confessional environment is not free of conflict. Indeed, *Girls and Swallows*, the second film of the trilogy, continues the plot element introduced in *A Muslim Childhood* in which Sultana is pestered by her neighbors. In an early scene, Larbi and his friend Abdelwahed, now teenagers, are loitering in a narrow medina street when Abdelwahed sees a

Jewish boy approaching, wearing a yarmulke and tzitzit. He prods Larbi with the challenge, "It's Elie, the Jew; you attack him, I'll finish him off!" As Elie approaches, Larbi taunts him—"You should stay in the mellah!"—and shoves him.[9] Elie, however, quickly overpowers Larbi in a headlock and pushes him to the ground, saying, "This time you get off lightly; the next time, watch out!" Abdelwahed laughs at Larbi, "You're the Jew now," and a few minutes later harasses Señora Sultana as she sits outside her house on a chair. Abdelwahed kicks a babouche (pointed slipper) away from her feet and treats it like a soccer ball, but Larbi protests and Sultana follows them, crying out in Spanish, "Can't we live peacefully? What are you doing? Get out of here!"

The scene and others like it that feature Jewish families or individuals thus remind us of the long-standing historical presence of Jews in the Maghrib and firmly demonstrate that the idea of Moroccan or Arab Jews is not oxymoronic but rather a critical part of the region's history.[10] Recent studies by a number of scholars have reconsidered the history of Jewish life in Morocco, compensating for years of relative scarcity in the historical study of Moroccan Jewish history.[11] Part of the historical turn to Moroccan Jewish history has involved—as with many other aspects of Moroccan society—the reconsideration of the painful years of *les années du plomb* or "years of lead," the repressive period under the rule of King Hassan II, which lasted from 1961 to 1999. This period coincided with the migration of most of Morocco's Jewish citizens to Israel, and by some accounts Hassan II was actively complicit in this exodus.[12] As Oren Kosansky and Aomar Boum suggest, the increased prominence of "the Jewish question" in Moroccan cinema and public discourse more generally is connected to a recent recuperation of Moroccan Jewish history into nationalist discourses of pluralism and tolerance under the present king, Mohammed VI. Yet the reception of *Marock* (dir. Leila Marrakchi, 2006) still provoked controversy because of its depiction of a relationship between a young Muslim and her Jewish boyfriend.[13] And the films that Kosansky and Boum discuss avoid reconstructing the Moroccan Jewish past as utopian; *Where Are You Going, Moshe?* (dir. Hassan Benjelloun, 2007) and *Goodbye Mothers* (Adieu mères, dir. Mohamed Ismaïl, 2007) also present instances of prejudice against or suspicion of Moroccan Jews. Similarly, Smihi's trilogy is concerned to remind us that the history of coexistence was not without discrimination. Whereas the visit of Sultana to tailor Larbi's trousers or her entreaty with Sidi Ahmed show the friendly relationship she has with Sidi Ahmed and his wife Lalla Alia, the harassment that she and Elie experience also suggest that tensions were present between Jewish and non-Jewish families at the time.[14]

Smihi's films also include numerous allusions to the Christian presence in Tangier and in Morocco more generally, sometimes as evidence of religious diversity, at other moments in order to stress that Christianity was tied up with colonialism. In *44, or Tales of the Night* (1981), Christianity is inextricably linked to the occupying presence of the French and Spanish in the country. In its first few minutes, 44 shows the initial arrival of the French in Fez as residents hurry indoors, warning, "The Christians are coming!" Later, a group of Moroccans who were to be recruited as collaborators into the French army with promises of rations throw down their backpacks and shout, "Down with the pork-eaters!" The *hakawati* (ambulatory storyteller) in the Rif town tells the assembled children a story about the famous figure of the resistance, the Amazigh girl Itto, who saved her tribe from an attack by lighting fires to warn them of the approaching French. To disguise herself she dressed "in the clothing of the Christians." In these instances, French attacks on Moroccans are articulated in terms of a war of Christians against Muslims.

In the Tangier films, however, the presence of Christians is associated less with colonial force and more with the religious diversity of the city. By inserting hints of prejudice or mockery in his narratives, Smihi indexes the petty conflicts and rhetorical constructions of religious difference during the period. At the same time, however, his films also affirm the constitutive presence of Jews and Christians in the fabric of Tangerian life. In *The East Wind* and *A Muslim Childhood*, for example, images of Christianity are developed mostly through the built environment of the town, with its English church near the Grand Socco and the Catholic church in the medina. Indeed, the voice-over in *A Muslim Childhood* explains that the Spanish were the only Europeans who lived inside the medina, a fact we see reflected in the interactions between a store owner and his Spanish customer in *The East Wind*; the shopkeeper shifts between Spanish and *darija* depending on whether he is speaking with the Señora or with Aïcha's husband. Catholic Spanish, then, are seen as integral to the medina in the 1950s, just as Jews were (in fact, the synagogue in the medina is located just meters from the Christian church). Toward the end of *A Muslim Childhood*, Larbi and his friend sit on the ramparts of the casbah playing a game of poker while pretending to be pirates. As they argue over the amount of money to put down, Larbi announces, "This is part of the loot I took from the Christian women!" In *Girls and Swallows*, Aïcha is insulted by one of her would-be Moroccan lovers who protests that she is going to "go to America with a Christian." Abdelwahed, whose prejudices toward Jews are already clear, chimes in to say that Muslims should not consort with Christians. And in *The Sorrows of a Young Tangerian*, the French schoolteacher, Muriel, on whom Larbi develops a crush, is dumped by her Moroccan boyfriend, Abdel, whose parents objected to his marrying a Christian and instead arrange a marriage with a rich Moroccan cousin. In all these examples, the films perform two important functions with respect to religion: they affirm the historical presence of all three monotheistic faiths, recognizing that Moroccan history is more diverse than might be assumed. And second, while not erasing the political or religious tensions that accompanied the presence of Christians, Jews, and Muslims in the social fabric of Morocco and the Arab world, they do suggest that such an atmosphere of coexistence is indeed possible and necessary in the present. In no small part, this is because they are willing to treat religion not as something sacred but as social fact.

RELIGION AS PRACTICE AND RITUAL

Many of the films treat religion not through constructions of sacredness or piety but as ritual, custom, or practice. This is in keeping with the anthropological sense of culture that we have seen Smihi develop in other ways across his films. For example, he presents circumcision ceremonies in three different films: *44, Moroccan Chronicles,* and *A Muslim Childhood.* Despite the strong associations of circumcisions with Islam, the films show them primarily as social practices that are connected to the transmission of culture and patriarchy. As customs, they fulfill the function of organizing social relations, and the films strip them of any organic or lasting relationship with the sacred. One way in which this desacralization is achieved is by presenting the events with black humor while also suggesting the trauma that they present for the male characters. Near the beginning of *A Muslim Childhood,* after a long sequence of voice-over in which the narrator explains the family's status and Sidi Ahmed's approach to religion and the world, the next scene opens with preparations for Larbi and his brother Khalil's circumcision.[15] As one of the family members approaches Larbi to unbutton his trousers, the boy pushes him away and runs up the stairs and out of frame. Arriving on the rooftop, where his mother and other women are preparing food for the circumcision celebrations, he yells in alarm and asks what is happening, clinging to his mother in fright.[16]

While the narrative actions are traumatic for Larbi and Khalil, Smihi directs the scene with the absurdity of a chase sequence: we cut back to the lower level of the house to see two men head up the stairs, then cut back to the rooftop as Larbi kicks over baskets and trays of couscous and ducks into a doorway. The two men have now been joined by two others, and when all four break down the door to chase after Larbi, the shot holds the same framing until they return in the opposite direction, this time with Larbi held aloft as they hustle him out of the shot and away from the roof. The next shot shows a close-up of a bottle of iodine, some cotton wool, and a robed hand picking up a pair of scissors. As the scissors are held aloft, we hear a cry before the cut, which here takes a cinematic, not literal, form and leads to the next shot of Larbi and Khalil recovering in bed, surrounded by gifts and family.[17] As the boys continue to look blank and traumatized, the camera frames the spectacle of the women rejoicing over what they say will make the boys into men, while Lalla Alia jokes that Sidi Ahmed, too, was afraid, and ran off to the mosque as the circumcision procedure was about to take place.

Throughout this scene, then, the religious aspects of the practice are deemphasized.[18] A circumcision also opens an earlier film, *Moroccan Chronicles,* and here too the ceremony is represented in a mixture of drama and farce. Amine, like

Larbi, runs from his circumcisers, but this time, unlike in *A Muslim Childhood*, his mother is also worried due to her husband's absence and the consequently untraditional nature of the ceremony. Amine, like Larbi, is carried to the circumciser kicking and screaming, and his treatment, as one Moroccan viewer suggested to me, more resembles the taking of a sheep to the sacrifice of ʿid al-kabir than the solemnity of a circumcision.[19] In both of these films, the representation of circumcisions stresses conformity and the overdetermined patriarchal display of authority and submission that organizes and even supersedes the religious dimensions of the practice.[20] A more solemn presentation of circumcision takes place in *44*, as a flashback motivated by the adult son's pensive stare out the window of his father's house after his death. As the film presents that circumcision, it stresses the insistent noise of the musicians in the street and, with handheld camera, the hurried transfer of the young boy into the house to meet his circumciser. The raucous sounds of the women beginning their party, also discussed in chapter 2, show that the ritualized violence of this rite is both radically transformative and even traumatic for the boy while being taken up as a community celebration by those around him: the solemn "*bismillah*" (in God's name) as we see the boy undergoing the procedure is contrasted to the dance and partying among the women. And yet here, too, as in *A Muslim Childhood*, the father (El Hajj) is too soft to be present for the event; we see him pacing on the rooftop as his son is prepared for the knife.

Smihi, then, performs a mix of satire and critique. That satire is evident in the way *A Muslim Childhood*'s circumcision scene tends toward the absurd, undermining the idea of it as a solemn covenant willingly undergone by the family and even the boy. Similarly, in *Moroccan Chronicles*, the religious element of the practice disappears; we see it primarily as a kind of duty to which the mother is subjected even as she is criticized for failing to perform it correctly. And in *44*, the event is presented in retrospect as part of the young man's alienation from the father (who, the film suggests, abandoned him at this moment of initiation) and from the societies he feels detached from: Moroccan and European, both.

Other films mix conventional signifiers of Islam, like circumcision, with practices that complicate or fall outside of it. In *The East Wind*, Aïcha's initial response to the threat of her husband marrying another woman is to listen to the suggestions of her neighbor, who prescribes various folk remedies to stall the husband's plans. First she is instructed to receive a massage with the oil of a fish. After that she is to make offerings to the "men of the sea" at Hercules Grotto and submit to being immersed in the waves there seven times. The neighbor herself volunteers for the last task. The film shows us the massage and the first trip to the Grotto, where Aïcha offers up a tagine as supplication. Later, her mother suggests that she visit a local marabout, for "his hand is blessed, his writing magical and very effective." In a subsequent scene, they do so. He first mixes something for Aïcha to drink, then gives her two amulets, one of which she must slide under her husband's pillow; the other she must wear. He also instructs her to buy a black chicken and sacrifice it, and then, on the festival of Sidi Kacem, bathe seven times in the water. All of this, he promises, will result in her husband remaining well attached to her. Each of these instructions is followed in turn (culminating in the fatal trip to Hercules Grotto, where Aïcha either lets go or is washed away), and the film devotes considerable attention to showing us each ritual: the amulet is placed under the pillow and, in a following shot, we see the husband somehow perturbed by its presence. Aïcha buys the chicken and carries it through the city in a sequence already discussed, and brings it to the festival of Sidi Kacem for its throat to be slit. Indeed, Smihi even shows the sacrifice and the chicken's final moments writhing on the ground.

The role of the marabout in these instances is indicative of how Moroccan Islam continues to include heterodox practices that are outside the strictures of Sunni Islam. Some can be traced to Amazigh (Berber) pre-Islamic rituals; others are connected to Sufi practice, which is widespread in other parts of Africa as well as in Morocco (and is growing in visibility due to Mohammed VI's embrace of it as a politically "safer" alternative to Saudi Wahhabism, whose influence in Morocco dates to the eighteenth century).[21] In *The East Wind*, then, Aïcha engages with a long tradition of spiritual practice that is nonetheless one of sacrilege and resistance to the more official form of Islam that her husband conducts with his daily prayers. The differences between activities marked as magical, ritualistic, or religious are complex. Here we see Smihi adopting an approach we might call Durkheimian: treating all religious practice as a matter of what Émile Durkheim called "social fact," thus relativizing whatever distinctions might be made between religion and ritual.[22] Without taking on the entirety of Durkheim's functionalist approach here, his notion of social fact is useful in thinking about how the films represent social life in the Maghrib. The place and importance of saints in Moroccan popular practice is not shared in all varieties of Islam and especially in the eastern versions of the Sunna faith. Edward Westermarck, in his two-volume study of ritual and belief in Morocco, distinguishes between magic—those practices oriented around the desire to control impersonal forces or spirits—and religion, oriented around pleasing a higher power or deity.[23] Other writers, too, as Catherine Bell describes, use various methods to distinguish magical rituals from religious rituals or practices: "Rites deemed to be truly non utilitarian, a matter of 'pure worship' so to speak, were categorized as religious, while those nonrational acts that appeared to seek a very practical result, such as healing or rainfall, were deemed to be magic." Yet more recent accounts of ritual tend to treat it as a spectrum of possibility that might include everything from the customs of sporting teams and the social elements of church life to "the swearing in of the president" or "school graduation ceremonies."[24] Bell hastens to note that this sense of equivalence does not mean that all such rituals are the same or equivalent, but simply that they are more connected than they are different.

This construction of equivalence between varied practices of the sacred is a productive way in which to consider the role of ritual in Smihi's films. Rather than think about magic, ritual, or religion as discrete practices in films like *The East Wind* or *44*, we might instead focus on the films' depiction of *all* such practices as versions of ritual. What characterizes these films is an understanding that ritual may be either sacred or profane, with the distinction corresponding not to some kind of divinely ordained hierarchy but rather to the social functions of ritual itself. Durkheim's distinction between the sacred and the profane is useful here; he recognized it as fundamental to the ways that religious practice is conceived of as organized. But the process of attributing qualities of the sacred to certain domains is fundamentally social, in his view. Bell notes, "As a social phenomenon, [Durkheim] concluded, religion is a set of ideas and practices by which people sacralize the social structure and bonds of the community."[25] In this sense, then, the social and communal identifications and practices that we see in the ritualistic or magical practices of *The East Wind*—instigated by the marabout or by the community of women around Aïcha—are neither "just" magical nor ritualistic and are no less important or world-defining than the Qur'anic prayers recited by the young men in the Islamic school in Tangier. Whether seen as syncretic, unorthodox, or pagan, the massages with fish and the amulets under the pillow are as important to the sacred world of the film as the husband's diligent prayers and ablutions.

The East Wind's visual construction of Aïcha's veil also participates in a similar strategy of desacralization. Smihi treats the veil not as a sacred object but as a prop within a cinematic discourse that might signify differently depending on its context. Maintaining a cinematic relationship to realism, *The East Wind* shows Moroccan women who do not wear the veil, and also those who do, like Aïcha, in domestic situations among family where a head covering is not required. Moreover, Smihi utilizes Aïcha's face and head coverings as a dynamic element of his mise-en-scène, decoupling those costume elements from their religious and sacred function and instead re-signifying them as both signifiers of her confinement (also suggested by the numerous gates and grilles behind which we see her) and at the same time devices she can deploy to control her interactions with her environment. In this way, we might note that his use of the veil as an element of the film's mise-en-scène is completely different from its appearance in a Moroccan film like Farida Benlyazid's *A Door to the Sky* (1989), where its adoption works to signify the protagonist's passage from the status of a secular, Westernized woman to a newly initiated Sufi Muslim; the film itself creates a discourse of the sacred.[26] In Smihi's film, on the other hand, the veil becomes a mutable object within the film's discourse. When Aïcha confronts the mentally ill man in the medina, she removes her face covering, revealing her stare. As she observes the colonial garden party in the *ville nouvelle*, she again shows her face in an exchange of glances with one of the Moroccan servants at the party.

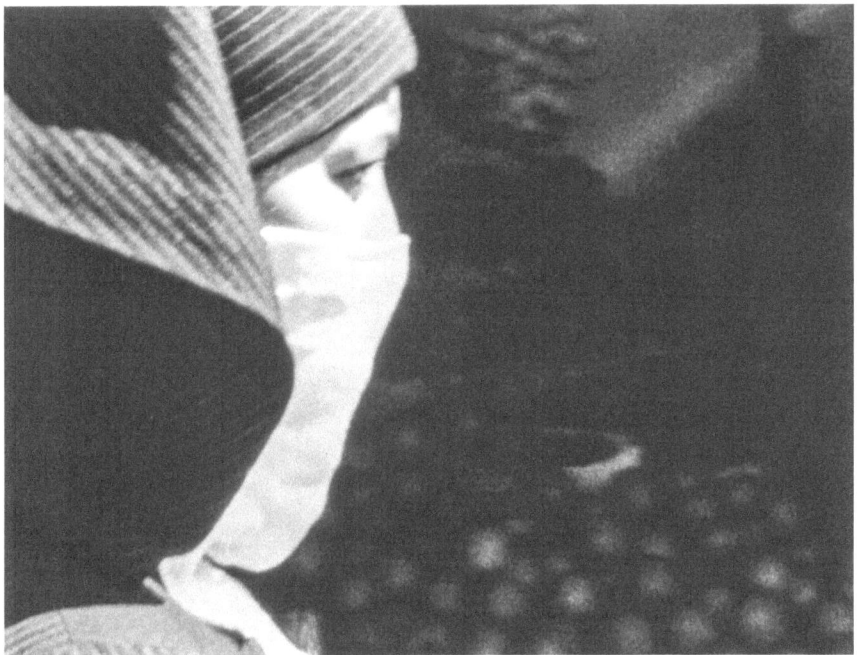

FIGURE 34. The jellaba and veil are dynamic elements of the mise-en-scène in *The East Wind*, 1975.

In fact, her face covering is but one element of an ensemble that includes her long black jellaba, which has a hood. Aïcha's head is sometimes wrapped in a scarf that leaves some of her hair showing, and when she leaves the house she first covers her face with a white scarf, which she ties at the back of her head like a bandanna (the first time we see her do this, she ties a scarf around the tagine she takes as an offering to the sea, an action that links the two practices as ritual). She then pulls her jellaba over her head and flips the hem back to create a kind of pointed hat. When she wishes, she can pull the scarf down to hang around her neck and reveal her face, as she does while walking through the *ville nouvelle*. Her clothing is thus integral to her character's practiced relationship to the city and its environs, and its visual qualities are utilized to create an Eisensteinian dynamism in the frame (one recalls the compositions of the hammock sequence in *Battleship Potemkin* [1926] or the tonal montage of sails, fog, sea, and docks in the port sequence of that film). Such a dynamism of composition is noticeable in many scenes, but one example is when Aïcha moves through the crowded marketplace in the medina in successive close-ups (fig. 34). In chapter 1, I analyzed a shot from the same scene with an almost identical framing in which Smihi utilizes different image planes to place Aïcha within the flow of the medina (see fig. 6). But in this

FIGURE 35. Shadi Abdel Salam's *The Night of Counting the Years*, 1969, with its strong modernist compositions and use of conflicting volumes in the frame, is an important precedent for Moumen Smihi's mise-en-scène.

moment, later in the same take, her body is isolated from the fore- and background planes such that we can pay more attention to Smihi's use of body and costume (the tendency continues in several later shots whose framing moves from close-up into medium close-up while continuing to isolate her). Here, Smihi's use of the fabric and the "volumes" it creates might also remind us of the shapes that Egyptian filmmaker Shadi Abdel Salam creates from the long black garments of the Nile villagers in *The Night of Counting the Years* (al-Momia [The Mummy], 1969), garments that become integral to his modernist visual compositions (fig. 35). In both cases, these films point beyond a realist function for the image and beyond a meaning that signifies "religion" or "tradition"; instead, the materiality of costumes and the body are shapes within a defamiliarized space.

Similarly, if we return to the circumcisions of *44, Moroccan Chronicles*, and *A Muslim Childhood*, we can understand better how these supposedly sacred religious ceremonies are in fact coequal to the other ritualistic practices we observe, such as the smoking of kif and music-induced trancelike state of the troubadour figure in *44*, or the chanting and dancing to the Gnawa musicians in the Jemaa el-Fnaa in *Moroccan Chronicles*, or the charming of snakes with pipe music that is also found in that film's celebration of the popular. All of these things exist on a continuum of social practice and should not be hierarchized. However, if we go further than the social functionalist approach and take into account the more psychoanalytic accounts of circumcision offered by Vincent Crapanzano, we understand another aspect of Smihi's representation of these moments in the lives of the boys and men. Crapanzano, while understanding that a practice deemed sacred is as much a ritual as any other, nonetheless refuses to account for that ritual in the terms that its society dictates; instead, he sees it as metaphor. That is, notwithstanding any religious overtones, Moroccan society, he writes, tends to regard the custom as an act that precipitates the passage of a boy into manhood. Yet by refusing to accept that the physical act itself does what the metaphor describes, Crapanzano instead *reads* the act psychoanalytically for what it does to the boy and how it functions within an economy of gender and violence. For Crapanzano, the ritual cannot mark a passage between boyhood and manhood for "there is in both ritual and everyday life no passage whatsoever—only the mark of passage, the mutilation that is itself an absence, a negation."[27] It is not incidental but foundational to the practice that the boy feels anxiety and pain and is repositioned to fear the violence of the father (who is usually absent for the ceremony, Crapanzano notes) and his representatives. This is indeed the impact of the circumcisions in Smihi's films. The procedure that is introduced with such anticipation and excitement by the women of *44* and *A Muslim Childhood* is one in which the father exacts a violence on the son even as he is physically absent. In *Moroccan Chronicles*, the absence is redoubled since the father is missing altogether, having emigrated to France. Smihi's presentation of the ritual of the circumcision participates in a critique that Crapanzano's analysis makes plain. In these films, circumcision is a ritualized act of patriarchal authority in the form of violence against the masculine body and it is intimately connected to the manner in which Moroccan society is structured in terms of submission to authority.

In these examples, we are reminded of Smihi's desire to "present a culture to itself," the imperative that has structured many aspects of his films, from their engagement with realism to their use of sound to their intertextuality and their presentation of the range of practices that might be in some way sacred or religious. This engagement with the totality of cultural practices, however, is not dispassionate or objective. Underpinning the representation of the rituals of Moroccan and Arab society is a strong sense of critique—a simultaneous appreciation and love of the popular and quotidian ways of life with a strong incentive toward a different mode of social engagement. In the next part of this chapter, we will consider how the films suggest the limits of religion as a form of social practice, with ritual appearing as a form of activity that embraces the profane as well as the religious. As these films present the many elements of Moroccan life that are engaged with ideas of sacredness, they simultaneously celebrate the possibilities of sacrilege and its place within the world.

SACREDNESS AND SACRILEGE

A Muslim Childhood first broaches the difference between the sacred and the sacrilegious early on, when the family eats a modest meal of soup and bread. As I noted in chapter 2, the scene develops a humorous play of voices and conflicting arguments around the idea of Mohammed Larbi attending the cinema, where he will be exposed to ideas that, in the view of his father, Sidi Ahmed, may contradict Islam. Crucially, however, the film presents this conversation less as an invective or prohibition on the part of Sidi Ahmed and more as an exploration and discussion: Doesn't the film make fun of Islam? No, replies Larbi. Does it not represent the prophet, he asks? No, again, promises Larbi, it shows only the shadow of the prophet's camel! Sidi Ahmed changes the subject to reassure his wife about the family's fortunes and the sufficiency of the meal, and the scene ends. At this early point in the film, then, Smihi presents Islam as a matter for discussion and debate in the household, managing it with a gently irreverent tone: the father discusses the prophet with a mouthful of bread, and the mention of the camel's shadow is humorous.

A little later, Larbi is concerned to again ask whether cinema is a sin and his father reaffirms his "no." Larbi then asks, "Is attending the French school a sin?" and here his father replies at length. He calls the boy's suggestion "stupid," saying, "Science is light and ignorance a disgrace!" before affirming that it is a Muslim's duty to seek the scientific truth and, since the French promise truth in their curriculum, it behooves him to go and pursue it. I will return to this scene's suggestion of an intimate relationship between Islam and science, since the father's model of a moderate Islam, open to Western science and art, has deep significance for Smihi's practice (as it did for the filmmaker personally). The scenes with the father prepare us for the many other instances in the Tangier trilogy where moments of religiosity are undermined or their sacredness questioned or interrupted by the sacrilegious or the secular. Such moments are often at one with the popular and quotidian.

For example, the montage of shots that introduces Tangier and its residents shows us the ham and wine sold and enjoyed by the city's Spanish residents; the voice-over mentions that after receiving civilization and culture from the Arabs for centuries, it was the Europeans' turn to "pour the fruity bouquet of their wines and the scent of their ham into the Muslim streets." Since the film is also quick to point out the presence of the Spanish church inside the medina, this fact introduces a dichotomy between the sacred activities of the Spanish and their attachment to the supposedly sacrilegious qualities of alcohol. Moroccans, too, consume wine (and beer) in all the films of the trilogy: Larbi is invited for beers with his friends and teacher in *The Sorrows of a Young Tangerian*, and Aouicha visits Dean's

FIGURE 36. "A pipe of kif for one fuck" is the agreement reached between prostitute and client in *A Muslim Childhood*, 2005.

Bar with a client in *Girls and Swallows*. Alcohol and cigarettes figure in *A Muslim Childhood* in a prominent series of jump cuts of a table cluttered with drinks. Appearing immediately after a scene where a man and a prostitute, both Moroccan, reach an agreement on "a pipe of kif for one fuck" (fig. 36) accompanied by a song whose lyrics sing of a "marvelous night followed by a beautiful sunrise," the scene suggests that Moroccans enjoy illicit sex along with the haram (forbidden by Islamic law) pleasures of alcohol, tobacco, and kif.

Indeed, the presence of wine in the Arab and Muslim world has a long history and its evocation in art could be traced in many directions. Its role as a sacrilegious element even within a culture of the sacred has a precedent in the eighth- and ninth-century Baghdadi poetry of Abu Nuwas. Abu Nuwas is famed for both his exuberant wine poetry and his odes to male lovers, making his work seem doubly scandalous by the standards of contemporary conservative Islam. That Abu Nuwas could have been a central figure in the classical Arabic poetry tradition (as Philip F. Kennedy would place him) speaks to the long history of sacrilege within Islamic culture.[28] Abu Nuwas's disdain for the hypocrisy of religious individuals who would pray and drink while condemning other drinkers is part of his consistent fight against the taboos instituted by religion to the detriment, he thought, of true social understanding. As Adonis argues, Abu Nuwas "advocates urban life and values, and calls for the dogma to be transcended and taboos disregarded." He looks forward to what Adonis describes as "the advent of a culture in which there will be no repression and no restrictions," and his love of wine exemplifies the possibilities of such a life. His poetry "turns drunkenness, which frees bodies from the control of logic and traditions, into a symbol of total liberation."[29] In a very real sense, Abu Nuwas was a precursor to the libertine European moderns with whom we might be more familiar, like Charles Baudelaire. Indeed, as we may remember from the introduction, Adonis himself found in Baudelaire a way back to the radical modernity of Abu Nuwas, Abu Tammam (eighth to ninth century), and al-Maʿarri.[30] Al-Maʿarri had his own moments of profanity, such as when he is imagining the qualities of the women he finds in Paradise, all more shapely and available than those on Earth, and the rivers of wine that might be found there. Such sensibilities, then, are present in the many evocations of wine and drinking in the Tangier trilogy, especially.

While evoking the history of sacrilege in the Arab literary tradition, Smihi is also turning to earlier embodiments of profanity and irreligious feeling within European and other cinemas. In the context of Abu Nuwas and al-Maʿarri's bawdy poetry of drinking and sex, we might think of Pasolini's carnivalesque film *Arabian Nights* (1974), based on the tales of *One Thousand and One Nights*, whose characters revel in drinking and bodily pleasures. Pasolini, like Smihi, returns to a different kind of past to intervene in the politics and social mores of the present; the Italian film, the third part in his "trilogy of life," furthers Pasolini's interest in depicting non-European and precapitalist environments. His *Arabian Nights* offers an alternative to the bourgeois Catholic morality of Italy that he so despised, stressing the pleasures that were available in a different moment and a different culture. Pasolini's characters laugh and drink and fuck their way through an environment in which Islam was predominant, but his construction of that historical moment allows for religion, sex, and pleasure to coexist. Such an approach also characterized his *The Decameron* (1971), where it is Christianity that is brought into the world of the carnal. There, Masetto, who has pretended to be deaf-mute in order to enter a convent, enjoys a series of sexual encounters with a group of nuns who, one by one, drag him into a shed and wear him out with the urgency of their desires. The instigator of the sex justifies her plan (which involves hitting Masetto's genitals with a stick to get his attention) by saying to a sister, who worries that it will break their vow of chastity, "We make promises to God that we don't keep all the time!" Can we imagine such scenes transposed to Moroccan cinema? Smihi understands that, for the most part, we cannot, but his films, less radically than Pasolini on their face, nonetheless attempt to countenance such possibilities through the precedents and intertextuality of Arabic poetry and European cinema alike.[31]

In this context, the work of the Spanish director Luis Buñuel is especially noteworthy. In Buñuel, Smihi finds another Mediterranean director whose culture is marked by its overwhelmingly religious character. Like Pasolini, Buñuel embraced sacrilege and social critique while adopting the aesthetic legacy and icons of Catholicism. *Viridiana* (1961) begins in a convent, where the young Viridiana (Silvia Pinal) is about to take her vows but is unwillingly caught in a web of lust and violence. She visits her uncle on a farm, where she prays with a crucifix and a life-size crown of thorns at her side. Obsessed with her resemblance to his dead wife, her uncle drugs her, lays her out on his bed, and places a lace tiara on her head. Buñuel positions her with her hands at her sides, choral music playing on the gramophone, to resemble paintings of the dead Christ. Her uncle then exposes her breasts and molests her while she sleeps. Much later, after the uncle has killed himself and she and her cousin have established the farm as a refuge for the homeless, the paupers hold a boozy banquet. The film, which has maintained a seductively mobile camera throughout, creates a freeze-frame that replicates the iconography of Christ's Last Supper, before a woman exposes herself and a man dons Viridiana's veil and corsetry and dances to George Frideric Handel's Messiah. On Viridiana's return, one of them attempts to rape her. In starkly beautiful cinematography with all the iconography of Catholicism, the film daringly cuts from a burning crown of thorns to a rock 'n' roll record on the gramophone as, in the final scene, Buñuel insinuates a ménage à trois among Viridiana, her cousin, and their housekeeper. Returning to Pasolini, we remember that the first scene of his *Mamma Roma* (1962) constructs its own drunken "last supper" animated by a trio of pigs that Mamma Roma (Anna Magnani) chases with a broom while making raucous jokes about prostitution and singing loudly about love and sex. That film, too, has its own version of a dead Christ as, much later, Mamma Roma's son lies dying in a hospital bed in a shot whose foreshortening and eroticized male body resembles Andrea Mantegna's famous painting *Lamentation over the Dead Christ* (c. 1480). Another of Pasolini's films, *La ricotta* (1963), includes a hilariously blasphemous scene in which Christ's followers, deposing him from the cross, drop their dead savior in fits of laughter.

For Smihi, the examples of Buñuel and Pasolini's films are evidence of cinema's ability to embody a religious aesthetic and address a religious culture while, themselves, adopting elements of satire and sacrilege. Indeed, as in the case of Pasolini, such satire and critique does not even come with an assumption of atheism; Pasolini's films demonstrate a deep engagement with Christianity even as they mock its institutions. The ability to create films with such a nuanced vision of culture, history, and religion has been deeply influential on Smihi and has prompted his claim that one cannot make films in the Maghrib without being cognizant of the legacy of filmmakers like Buñuel and Pasolini.[32] In other words, by recognizing that religion might influence a culture but that the cinema of that culture is not bound solely to the sacred, these Mediterranean filmmakers offer Smihi a model for negotiating the long influence of Islam on the culture of the Maghrib and Arab world. With Buñuel and Pasolini, sacrilege and disrespect for religious hypocrisy can sit side by side with an appreciation of and reliance on the aesthetics and history of Catholicism. Faith can be represented diegetically, or religious aesthetics incorporated, without the discourse of the film being constrained to the sacred.

Such a position helps us understand Smihi's wonderfully playful and enigmatic one-minute Lumière-style film whose full title is *The Medina of Paris: Supererogatory Prayer by a Muslim Dignatory—My Father—After Landing at Paris-Orly* (1996). A supererogatory prayer (*salat al-nafl*) is one that is optional, perhaps performed to compensate for any deficiencies in one's obligatory prayers, or for extra benefits to the one praying. The prayer in this film is performed outside at Paris-Orly, the hub for many flights to North Africa, on an island of grass with automobile traffic circulating around it, and its practitioner is barely audible above the din of the aircraft coming and going in the background. As described in chapter 2, a third element of the film's soundtrack, along with airport noise and the voice of the Moroccan father, is a radio recording of Josephine Baker, the African American singer who migrated from the United States to France and became a naturalized French citizen, singing of her "two loves, my country and Paris." The film thus teases us with a multitude of possible interpretations: the visual juxtaposition of a pious expression of faith with the overwhelming technology might support a reductive reading of a "clash of tradition and modernity," yet the film is too complex for such clichés. Instead, by avoiding a straightforwardly devotional presentation through its combination of disparate elements, it places religious observation in a worlded frame of migration, diaspora, multi-confessionalism, secularity, and religion, the messy interplay of these elements making up the "medina of Paris" of the film's title. In its mode of presentation, then, it seems to respond to some of the intertextual reference points that Smihi cites in his own thinking about the cinematic depiction of religion and everyday life.

Smihi writes in "Cinema Arabiyya" (1993) that "the relationship with religion is much more a relationship of culture and history than a relation of exercise and practice," citing Woody Allen as one of the artists with whom that relationship is expressed in a contemporary urban setting. He continues, "My work inscribes itself in Arab-Muslim culture in the same way that Woody Allen in New York (or a director in Italy or Paris) inscribes his work in the Judeo-Christian culture."[33] If Arab popular culture has forgotten the contributions of its sacrilegious writers like al-Ma'arri and Abu Nuwas, then it might, Smihi argues, at least remember the more recent and widely disseminated work of directors like Allen or, more radically, Pasolini or Buñuel. While the rebellion against religious doctrine of the latter two still retains some power to shock, the heretical connotations of their work are permissible in Western contexts. In Smihi's view, such examples are critical for the future of Arab cinema and its relationship to modernity.

ISLAM AND MODERNITY

The struggle that these films index concerns more than just the place of sacrilege within a religious culture. Rather, Smihi's work constructs a discourse on a broader struggle about Islam and modernity. Ultimately, the films suggest, the Arab world will continue to falter without its own *tanwir* project; Islam and modernity cannot be reconciled without a renewed engagement with the rationalism of the Arab and Muslim scholars, poets, and intellectuals who span many generations. Smihi's films and writing invoke Ibn Rushd, Ibn Tufayl, Ibn Sina, Abu Nuwas, and al-Ma'arri, from an earlier age. They reference, sometimes explicitly, sometimes not, Nahda reformers like Rifa'a Rafi' al-Tahtawi, Taha Hussein, Huda Sha'arawi, or Butrus al-Bustani. And they also evoke those whose voices in recent times have continued to argue for some version of secularism and openness, such as Samir Kassir, Fatima al-Mernissi, Mohammed Tibi, Aziz al-Azmeh, and others. Across the films, one can perceive the yearning for a way of life that does not condemn Islam but understands the limits of any religion as a way of organizing social structures and thought, considering it a matter of personal conscience, social belonging, or private belief rather than state or public prerogative. Smihi, in other words, takes up Abu Nuwas's edict: "You have your religion, I have mine." Yet, as I will continue to show, the secular outlook of these films is never dogmatic or authoritarian. Rather, Smihi dares to represent the means by which Moroccans and Arabs have engaged ideas (from the West as well as from within the Muslim world) that, by admitting science and reason, make complex Islam's role in explaining the world. Ultimately, the modernity that the films prepare us for is one that serves the same generous, egalitarian humanism that we have seen throughout Smihi's work—one in which freedom of thought, freedom of belief, freedom of sexual and gendered expression, and political justice are all welcome. In this sense, the critique of religion and the embrace of the secular here are part and parcel of what we will see in the next chapter: a cinema that looks forward to a time when desire and sexuality are present and open, in a society in which Arab and non-Arab subjects of all faiths or no faith enjoy freedom and respect.

Crucially, such a call for modernity in Smihi's films is not a capitulation to ideas assumed to be Western (as I have stressed throughout this book), but rather a call for respect for history. As with many other secular critics (al-Azmeh, Tibi, Aamir R. Mufti, and many others), Smihi believes that suppositions of an essential link between Arabs, Arabic language, and Islam should be refuted. In the spirit of other Nahdawi figures, he hails the way that the Nahda modernized the language so as to make it available for intellectual and practical purposes of all kinds; indeed, he argues that Arabic has always had this history, even before it became enshrined as the language of the Qur'an.[34] In this sense he rejects the Orientalist presupposition that Arabic represents something intrinsically theological or that it has some essential link to the "Arab mind."[35] Smihi's films historicize the language in ways that acknowledge its deep connections to the history of Islam while refusing to essentialize either language or religion. While Islam's predominance in the region has inflected Arab art, culture, and politics, to reduce Arab culture to Islamic culture, he argues, is ahistorical and dangerous, tantamount to seeing all European culture through the lens of Protestantism or Catholicism.[36] For Smihi, as for the kinds of thinkers that his films overtly and covertly cite, history can provide what Elizabeth Suzanne Kassab has called a "reservoir of experiences and events from which one can and ought to learn in order to deal with the pressing moral and political questions of the present. For the secularists, the recognition of the reality of history aids in staying in touch with reality and in preserving a modicum of agency in shaping history, instead of being passively subjected to its alleged essences."[37] Like other secular thinkers, including those that Kassab cites, Smihi wants to engage the entirety of history across the Arab world, not only the elements that pertain to Islam, thus enabling a society that can recognize the historical role of religion while not being bound to its practice as prerequisite for identity or subjectivity.

Across his films, Smihi dramatizes different versions of the encounter between Islam and modernity. His most recent (at the time of this writing) feature film, *The Sorrows of a Young Tangerian*, provides the most radical solution to the problem in the young Larbi's rejection of religion. But other films, too, survey the different prospects for that encounter. In their presentation of the ways religion might feature within Morocco and the Arab world, we see the scope of Smihi's vision for a culture that might be engaged with its history, sensible to its present, and integrated into the wider world.

One such way that Islam is addressed in the films is by showing its capacity for tolerance. Many of the films represent a spirit of moderation in the teachings and practice of Islam, especially in the development of the character of Sidi Ahmed across the Tangier trilogy. It is Sidi Ahmed's nature to preach a moderate version of Islam, and the trilogy presents his tendencies toward tolerance, kindness, and empathy as he interprets the teachings of the Qur'an to his family. In *A Muslim Childhood*, when Lalla Alia's brother comes to the home to harass their mother (Larbi's grandmother), Sidi Ahmed appears conflicted and sits uncomfortably at the edge of the frame. The grandmother, whose husband has begun to insult her now that he has taken a second wife, is nonetheless distraught at the conflict that has ensued between her husband and son, who have come to blows. Sidi Ahmed responds to this news with verses from the Qur'an warning of the potential for a father to alienate his wives and children, and the sacrilege of a son raising his hand against his father. As Lalla Alia's brother berates their mother for allegedly cowing to the patriarch, Sidi Ahmed opines: "Allah allows every man four wives provided he is fair to them. But Allah adds: 'You won't be able to be fair by treating them equally. Whatever you do, you're bound to tip the scales.'" While not condemning polygamy, then, he notes that the Prophet urges caution in practice. A little later in the same film, Sidi Ahmed relates to Larbi a story drawn from a collection of

Friday sermons (edited, we learn in the credits, by 'Abdallah Gannun, a respected Tangier theologian and author who was also Smihi's uncle).[38] The story concerns a prostitute who finds a stray and thirsty dog and offers water, held in her veil, for the dog to drink. Seeing her act of kindness, Allah forgives her sins as a prostitute.

Both stories, like the one in *Girls and Swallows* where Sidi Ahmed speaks of Islam's respect for women (which I will discuss in the next chapter), turn on questions of gender and the place of women in Islam. In the present context, however, we can also see them as part of Sidi Ahmed's tendency toward a moderate and gentle form of Islam that has humanistic ends. Speaking with Uncle Hilal in *Girls and Swallows* (whom the film suggests may have slept with Rabea, much to Larbi's dismay), Sidi Ahmed notes that while fornication is forbidden, the Qur'an suggests that punishment for drinking wine is received only in the afterlife. I have already noted his reluctance to see his children punished at the Islamic school. He is also loving and nonjudgmental when Larbi, curled up in his father's arm for a nap, asks a supposedly hypothetical question about what kind of ablutions Islam requires after "Satan hits him" in the form of a wet dream; Sidi Ahmed caresses the boy's stomach affectionately while calmly advising that one must go to the hammam after such an experience. His moderation is seen, too, in *Girls and Swallows*, when he is asked his thoughts regarding a girl in the extended family who does not wear a headscarf. In a circuitous response to the question, Sidi Ahmed tells the story of a saint, Maïmouna, who, after never knowing how to pray in any elaborate way, was schooled by a theologian. But she soon forgot everything she'd been taught and, as Sidi Ahmed's story goes, ran after the theologian as he left by boat, racing across the sea as her feet touched the waves, seeking his advice again. The theologian replies that her faith itself is bigger than any ritual and that her everyday, simple way of professing it is not a weakness. In all these examples, we perceive a discourse on Islam as a moderate and peaceful religion offering a system of values that serves the community generally, as well as a structure of belief that puts the individual in touch with the sacred.

Here, as in so many other moments, Smihi invokes wider intellectual and cultural currents in the Arab world. Sidi Ahmed's parable about the headscarf resonates with the arguments against the veil that circulated during the Nahda, including those that called not for a break with Islam but rather a reform in its practice. Such is the opinion articulated by the writer Nazira Zeineddine, a Lebanese Druze woman who published a four-hundred-page treatise that advocated women's unveiling, excerpts of which were recently translated in Tarek El-Ariss's bilingual edition of Nahda texts. As Leyla Dakhli has shown, Zeineddine wrote her work in the form of a *tafsir*, or theological treatise, taking that classically organized form and rendering it "modernist in the way it mobilized critical thought and called for action to defend women's rights."[39] Zeineddine's language echoes the call for the freedom in Smihi's films, but retains a discourse of faith:

> Welcome, sacred freedom, freedom of thought and freedom of will, for you are the essence of faith, the foundation of all Renaissance [*Nahda*], and the deliverer of truth through inquiry. Welcome, freedom that grants us the right to preserve our honor and to rise in ways that strengthen our honor and bring us closer to the true faith and that benefit us and our children and our nation.[40]

Zeineddine's call might have been voiced by many of Smihi's characters, even by Sidi Ahmed himself, the gentle reformer and family patriarch.

Sidi Ahmed's moderate way of dealing with his family, however, is also seen to have certain limits, which tend to challenge his humanism and confound him into inaction; indeed, these dilemmas become narrative issues in every film and, at their most extreme, construct his character as somewhat impotent. Such an impasse is signaled in *Girls and Swallows* after the nationalist forces fighting the French decree that the festival of *'id al-kabir* should not be celebrated that year with the sacrifice of a sheep out of respect to those who sacrificed their lives for the independence struggle. Sidi Ahmed confides to his wife that a faithful Muslim cannot ignore a divine commandment to honor the festival with a sacrifice. The dilemma seems to immobilize him until he realizes that Lalla Alia's father could sacrifice a sheep on his farm, in privacy, and we cut to a sequence of shots in which we see him and some others carrying a sheep up from the farm; in the next scene he divides the carcass and sends his family on errands to discreetly deliver shares of meat to those who deserve them: the poor and those who are less able.

While he overcomes this problem decisively, at other moments we are left with the impression that the path of moderation that he embodies and strives for cannot withstand the pressures of the world that surrounds the family, a world that sometimes rejects sacredness or faith. Such a conflict is signaled in a scene from *A Muslim Childhood*, shot from a noticeably high angle looking down onto a courtyard (an angle that Smihi retains for the difficult conversation between Larbi and his father in *The Sorrows of a Young Tangerian*). Larbi's mother is furious at the discovery that Larbi, goaded by a gang of boys on the beach, hit his brother with a brick, making his head bleed. "That's what lenient education leads to!" she yells, insisting, "He must be taught a lesson!" "A lesson!" agrees Sidi Ahmed. "I will teach him one. . . . He would deserve it! But first, he must understand that Allah knows everything! I am going to deal with him ruthlessly!" He removes his belt and doubles it, as if preparing to flog Larbi, but Lalla Alia retorts, "As usual, you pretend you are!" Sidi Ahmed is seemingly stuck between the desire to mete out a punishment and a desire to build the principle of belief that should, supposedly, drive his son's conduct: that Allah is all-seeing, that he knows even the smallest of acts, that nothing escapes him. "'A wicked person is hateful,'" he quotes from the Qur'an. "'Only goodness can ensure our salvation.' Do you understand what I mean?" Faced with such a discrepancy between the virtue that should, in his mind, come with faith and the real conditions of human action, Sidi Ahmed suffers from indecision. Indeed, this is the last scene in *A Muslim Childhood* in which we even see him; there is no closure to the problem that he faces with his son's behavior, and the film allows his conflicted authority to remain unresolved.

The idea of Islamic tolerance has often been mobilized to attack an Islamophobia that treats the religion as irreducibly connected to violence or hatred of the West. These films solidly reject such prejudices, and their vision of a tolerant Islam contributes to such a rejection. But while Sidi Ahmed's role makes visible the discourse on tolerance, these films go to still more radical ends by engaging a much larger discourse on Islam in relation to Western modernity, science, and thought. Here, too, Smihi draws on the legacy of Nahda thinkers as well as those who have come before and after them; yet his call for a new kind of modernity is thoroughly articulated with and through cinema. While the Nahda gives him literary and intellectual examples, filmmakers like Buñuel and Pasolini offer a way to, as Smihi puts it, "exit from theology" when accounting for the world.[41] In what follows, I will consider the challenges that the Nahda posed for Islamic reform so as to better contextualize how Smihi's films hint at the possibilities of a secular modernity for Morocco and the Arab world.

Sidi Ahmed's character in the Tangier trilogy again provides a way of tracking the extent to which these various discourses of religion and modernity might be reconciled; Sidi Ahmed, in his tolerance, also appears to offer the possibility of a *rencontre* between Islam and new ideas associated with Europe. His insistence to Larbi that Islam is in favor of science and learning and that it is, consequently, no sin for Larbi to attend French school does more than respect the diversity of cultures present in Tangier. It is also a reminder of what occurred across the Arab world in the nineteenth and twentieth centuries as European ideas began to circulate widely and Islamic thinkers engaged with them. As I suggested in the introduction, we might trace different histories of that encounter. For Albert Hourani, whose account has become dominant, the late eighteenth century saw the Ottoman empire in decline and, as it lost its military prowess and watched Europe grow in power, a new generation of reformers, well versed in European languages and cultures, decided to modernize. The Ottoman army was reformed by the sultans Selim III and Mahumud II, and after the formative moment of Napoleon's arrival in Egypt in 1798 the new Ottoman governor of Egypt, Muhammad ʿAli Pasha, continued their modernizing impulses while also dispatching delegations to Europe, such as Rifaʿa Rafiʿ al-Tahtawi's, in order to learn from Europe.[42] As I have noted, such an account tends to unnecessarily center Europe as the instigator of all change, whereas other narratives, attuned to developments beyond political and military history, can accommodate a more fluid interplay between Europe, the Arab world, and other sites, as El-Ariss has argued.[43] Indeed, while recognizing some of the practices of modern Europe as potential models, many Muslim thinkers denied that there should be a contradiction between such practices and Islam and, indeed, believed that "modern reform was not only a legitimate but a necessary implication of the social teaching of Islam."[44] In situating the question of Islam in Smihi's films or even in relation to twentieth-century modernity more generally, then, we should recognize the ways in which such interactions with European practices were part of a Nahda in which diverse areas of learning and religious, political, and social expressions were tested and put in play.

Smihi's Tangier trilogy, in its depiction of Islam, takes for granted such histories of reform and encounter. In particular, the films ascribe to the character of Sidi Ahmed some of the characteristics of the nineteenth-century cleric Muhammad 'Abduh, an Egyptian reformer who advocated a kind of reconciliatory path for Islam in the debates around how to deal with European modernity. As Kassab and Hourani have argued, 'Abduh was convinced that Muslims could not reverse the changes they saw taking place around them, nor could they ignore the reach and power of modern ideas and practices. Europe was already in the consciousness of the Arab world through the reforms and encounters just described. The challenge for Muslims, argued 'Abduh, was to show how the principles of Islam were in fact compatible with science and reason and how, indeed, many of the developments of European modernity were in fact immanent in the Islamic system of values. The true Muslim, he argued, was one who engaged rational inquiry, accepted scientific truths, and used Islam as a system of values by which to organize the world so understood. In this sense, argues Hourani, 'Abduh developed a distinction introduced earlier by the Islamic scholar Ibn Tamiyya, who distinguished between acts related to revelation and divine worship and those with more worldly and social aspects. Hourani characterizes the distinction thus: "Qur'an and *hadith* [the words of the Prophet Muhammad] laid down specific rules about worship; about relations with other men, they laid down for the most part only general principles, leaving it to men to apply them to all the circumstances of life. This was the legitimate sphere of *ijtihad*, of human judgment exercised responsibly and in accordance with certain principles."[45] In light of such a description, we can observe that Sidi Ahmed struggles with the sphere of *ijtihad*, of how to best exercise the faith in application to everyday challenges related to living with one's neighbors, being politically responsive to colonialism's oppressions, or choosing an education and language system for one's children. Such challenges could only be met through the dynamic interaction of Islamic principles with the kinds of learning emanating from Europe during that time, and in that sense Sidi Ahmed's openness to French education for his son is a symptom of his attempts to reconcile his faith with the new phenomena appearing all around him in Tangier and that his son, Larbi, is rushing toward.

In his role as a *fqih*, Sidi Ahmed appears in the films as almost an embodiment of 'Abduh. Devout and serious in his faith, gentle in his disposition, attempting to turn all situations to a confirmation of the rightness of Islam and its capacity for understanding the world, he attempts to incorporate the new modern world into his Islamic worldview.[46] According to Hourani, bridging the gulf between science and religion in Muslim society could not, for 'Abduh, be effected through denial or regression:

> It could not be done by a return to the past, by stopping the process of change begun by Muhammad Ali. It could only be done by accepting the need for change, and by linking that change to the principles of Islam: by showing that the changes which were taking place were not only permitted by Islam, but were indeed its necessary implications if it was rightly understood, and that Islam could serve both as a principle of change and a salutary control over it.[47]

Smihi continues to mark Sidi Ahmed with this spirit of necessary reform throughout *A Muslim Childhood* and *Girls and Swallows*, where we see him struggle to integrate new ideas into a devout Muslim lifestyle. His strength of conviction never seems in doubt, yet that does not mask the contradictions that drive his son to a quite different conclusion in *The Sorrows of a Young Tangerian*.

While 'Abduh's thought and philosophy are implicitly present in the character of Sidi Ahmed and his attempts to further a tolerant Islam reconciled with an Arab modernity, Taha Hussein, another Nahda reformer, is literally present in the diegesis of the films. Hussein, who was educated at al-Azhar University in Cairo and then at the Sorbonne in Paris, disrupted the Egyptian political establishment upon his return to Egypt from France. As mentioned in chapter 3, his book *Fi al-shi'r al-jahili* (On Jahili Poetry, 1926) argued that Islamic discourses had created an opposition between a pre-Islamic period of chaos and disorder and an Islamic period rendered in contrast as moral, righteous, and more significant. Moreover, he suggested that some of the pre-Islamic poetry was in fact written after Islam.[48] Hussein's "crime" had been to use methods of literary criticism and skepticism to analyze *jahili* poetry and to challenge the status of the Qur'an as a sacred object. Hourani further explains that Hussein's scholarship "aroused opposition both because it suggested a critical method which, if applied to the texts of religion, might cast doubt on their authenticity, and because it struck at the roots of the traditional structure of Arabic learning by which the faith was buttressed."[49] Yet he was also clear that he was not challenging structures of belief, and he remained a Muslim. He did, however, call for science and democracy based on what he had experienced in Europe, and he tried to show (in his 1938 book *The Future of Culture in Egypt*) that since Egypt had always been connected to Europe via the Mediterranean, it was thus predisposed to such creative developments.[50]

As I've already noted, Hussein's thinking has been instrumental for Smihi, who frequently cites it as foundational to the manner in which his films seek to engage questions of religion and the world. Hussein is an example of someone who, without wishing to destroy the Islamic system of faith, saw it as necessarily a personal domain that did not have to structure the realms of political representation or intellectual inquiry; such inquiry could still proceed in relation to, but not subordinated to, Islamic thought. Hussein's work appears visibly in the films, and his name is invoked by both Larbi and his father. In *A Muslim Childhood*, after Larbi has set off firecrackers in his pants in a fit of jealous pique, he sits in bed with Sidi Ahmed at his side. Larbi describes what he sees as the importance of Taha Hussein's legacy of struggle against the obscurantists who criticized him for his book on the poetry of the *jahiliyya* (literally, ignorance; but here pre-Islamic period). Sidi Ahmed, in turn, refers to Hussein as "the founder of modern Arab thought" and "the master of Arab literature." He is thus another example of a Muslim intellectual unafraid to engage both Arab and European traditions in pursuit of an Arab modernity.

While precedents for an encounter between science and Islam—an encounter that marks *A Muslim Childhood* and *Girls and Swallows* in particular—can be identified in the work of ʿAbduh and his predecessors, the dream of reconciliation between Islam and modernity is called into question in other films. Moussa, in *44*, seemingly cannot access even the trappings of the modernity that El Hajj's family partially embraces. He moves between the enclosed university world of al-Qarawiyyin, the isolation of the village in Chefchaouen, and the world that El Hajj's family tries to inhabit—modern in their relationship to the European school that the son and second wife attend, dressed in their French school uniforms and learning math, excited for the European technologies of the telephone and roller skates but deeply traditional in their fealty to El Hajj's domain. Moussa cannot reconcile these differences for himself, nor can he remain in the semi-modern world that the family experiences.[51] Framing him more and more in isolation, the camera shows his increasingly solitary situation. By the end of the film, he seems, as Smihi puts it, "swallowed up by history," left to play mournful music and beg in the streets outside the family's Fez home (fig. 37).[52] Whereas Abdelhaq, El Hajj's son, is shown leaving the home for France. Having completed an education in the French *lycée*, he is destined for studies in the heart of the modern colonial power. Yet the film does not regard this as any kind of triumphal or teleological move and, as we see the son in the closing shots, trying to master his economics textbook, his future remains unclear.

This kind of suspended state—ambiguously postcolonial by the end of the story, but also reflective of the moment in which the film was made (1981)—corresponds to what Bassam Tibi and other writers have characterized as the state of despair or stasis in the wake of the breakdown of the Ottoman empire, the violent encounter with European colonialism, and the failure of Arab nationalism.[53] What is left is an unreconciled relationship with the kind of secular modernity that Europe has claimed for itself but whose history in many Arab societies has been fragmented or short-circuited. El Hajj's son is thus caught in the predicament that

FIGURE 37. Moussa, "swallowed up by history," plays his violin and begs in the alleys of Fez in *44, or Tales of the Night*, 1981.

al-Azmeh describes thus: "Arab societies have been dragged into world history by unbreakable bonds characterized by domination, dependency, political and cultural satellization, dislocation; but they have not been able to forge a new and durable articulation of their own internal economic, social and cultural bonds. The consequence is a sort of historical purgatory, belonging neither to their own past nor to anyone's present."[54] I have already suggested, then, that the films pose a kind of impossible contradiction between attempts at Islamic reform that would seek to reestablish and reaffirm Islamic reason as a cultural alternative to the reason of the European Enlightenment tradition, and the possibilities of a secular tradition organized around Arab Enlightenment principles—a *tanwir*—by which religion and state might be separated. As we have already seen, the films are at pains to represent the multivocality, multi-confessionality, and diversity of Tangier and the historical role of Judaism and Christianity in the Arab countries. But in *The Sorrows of a Young Tangerian*, Smihi goes further to stage what the rupture between religion and secular life might look like.

This rupture is most dramatically present in the long scene in the family home where Larbi and his mother sit on either side of Sidi Ahmed. The conversation begins as a complaint from Lalla Alia about the family's financial struggles: she can make only the most meager meals, and the children are poorly dressed. Sidi Ahmed's response is that Allah preaches patience, contentment, and complacency—that she should, essentially, be happy with her lot. Larbi, stretched

FIGURE 38. A radically long take from an unusually high angle signals rupture in the home as Larbi renounces religion in *The Sorrows of a Young Tangerian*, 2013.

out on the divan, mocks his father's recourse to what he calls "submission" and "defeatism." Sidi Ahmed relates a long parable, evidently not for the first time, and afterward turns to his son and suggests that after he completes high school his income as a civil servant would be useful for the family, but Larbi reacts by saying that he intends to go to university and study literature and philosophy and that marriage and kids are not for him. His father is unhappy, comparing philosophy to the work of Satan, but Larbi turns up the heat, avowing a revolutionary politics of justice and criticizing Sidi Ahmed for sticking with the Islamic system of timekeeping and calling non-Arabic speakers strangers. After Sidi Ahmed again protests, Larbi continues: "Papa, I have lost my faith. For Rousseau and Voltaire there was a supreme being. But man doesn't need religion. In fact, God is a human invention. And also, like the Encyclopedists, I'm for the republic."

Larbi's declaration radically disturbs the space of the home. The camera position, recall from chapter 1, is high and angled down on the three family members, but shortly before Larbi's bombshell it moves back even farther from a long shot to a more extreme, even wider long shot (fig. 38). A prayer rug—shortly to be used by Sidi Ahmed as salve to his shock—is centered at the foot of the frame and the layout of the space is more prominent than the expressions on the character's faces. Smihi has staged something shocking and even unique in Moroccan cinema or Arab cinema more broadly: a Muslim character declaring atheism within the narrative of a film.[55] The effect is momentous: after a moment of uncomfortable silence Sidi Ahmed reacts, saying that he had feared this moment and asking Allah for forgiveness, then, "If you ever repeat that . . . ! Allah says that atheism is sacrilege.

Allah must be obeyed. His servants must be obeyed. If you ever repeat that, you are no longer my son!" He curses Larbi as a "dog" and orders him out of the house before falling to the ground to pray with Lalla Alia. The scene ends with a cut to an exterior shot as Larbi leaves the house, followed by another as he arrives at the home of his teacher, over which his own voice reads from Friedrich Nietzsche: "'God is dead. God remains dead. And we have killed him. How shall we console ourselves, the murderers of murderers?'"

The shock of Larbi's declaration of atheism reverberates through the film, but more than that, through all the films. In a sense it is the culmination of what all have hinted at in their presentation of the contradictions and strains of Islam in the context of modernity. While thinkers like 'Abduh and the Islamic reformists had certain solutions for this dilemma, they always involved recovering what they saw as the Islamic roots of reason, and Smihi here seems to move us in another direction: What if the Islamic world were instead to demand or to countenance a break between religion and public life? What if it allowed for the freedom of thought and belief that could let atheists declare their lack of faith?

The Sorrows of a Young Tangerian signals these possibilities in a manner that combines a contemporary political critique of the period with a broader plea for freedom of speech, of thought, of ideas. In short, it is a plea for a *tanwir*, an Enlightenment comparable to the one that took place in Europe but which, the film shows, must be conceived and practiced within the Arab and Moroccan worlds. While the film gestures toward this possibility in almost every respect, a particularly vital succession of scenes demonstrates some of the precursors to Larbi's affirmation of atheism to his father. The young characters are all enrolled in the Tangier *lycée* and their activism outside the classroom is depicted as intimately connected to what takes place within it. Early on, we see their French teacher, Florence, begin a lecture on Darwinism to the main characters—Larbi, Malika, Fouad, Othman, Mjidou. The scene opens with a close-up of a portrait of Hassan II, who ruled Morocco from 1961 until his death in 1999, and the voice of the teacher is heard over it as the film cuts to a wide shot of the classroom and the students listening intently. On the board is written in French the title of Darwin's *On the Origin of Species*: "Charles Darwin, L'origine des espèces, 1859." The juxtaposition is alarming (fig. 39) and occurs a second time as the teacher is explaining the fundamental principles and implications of Darwin's discoveries. Hassan II's rule was marked by his consolidation of the power of his 'Alawite dynasty and the severe repression he exerted on his subjects, a strategy that seems anathema to the kind of breakthrough the teacher is describing. The portrait, however, also serves as a kind of panoptic figure, as the film apparently jumps ahead in time from the discussion of Darwin to a discussion of Socrates and the Greeks. Here, the teacher states, "One could say that the thoughts of Socrates, the works of the tragedians, the poets, constitute a veritable spiritual protest against the cruelty and the atrocities of the Greek civil

FIGURE 39. Larbi's teacher moves from Darwinism to Socrates and the Greek tradition, while a portrait of King Hassan II hovers over the discussion, in *The Sorrows of a Young Tangerian*, 2013.

war during the time of Pericles. It's really a denunciation of the madness of imperial domination." A student replies, "In a way, that's why Sartre and [Francis] Jeanson supported the Algerians against the French in Algeria."[56] The teacher brushes off the comment—"Perhaps . . ."—and points the students to a bookcase she has set up at the back of the room. The next shot shows a collection of books as varied as Fyodor Dostoevsky's *Demons* (1871), Simone de Beauvoir's *The Long March: An Account of Modern China* (1957), both in French, and a collection of other novels and philosophical and political texts in Arabic and French.

A collection of books is a regular motif in the Tangier trilogy; we see similar shots in each film covering a range of modern Arab, European, and US authors. The films lead toward a liberal thought that characterizes their vision of modernity. In the next shot, then, it is no surprise to see the same teacher leading a different class, walking among her students as she begins to introduce the work of key Enlightenment thinkers: "My personal convictions are not important. Voltaire and Rousseau were great thinkers, who gave so much to humanity. I'm here to familiarize you, my students, with their philosophy. Is that clear?" Then there is a cut across an evident temporal ellipsis, and the teacher sits at her desk and reads this long passage:

> "In the course of centuries the naive self-love of men has had to submit to two major blows at the hands of science. The first was when they learned that the Earth, far from being the center of the universe, only formed a tiny fragment of a cosmic system, whose vastness was impossible to imagine. This first demonstration is associated in

our mind with the name of Copernicus, though something similar had already been asserted by Alexandrian science. The second blow fell when biological research destroyed man's supposedly privileged place in creation and proved his descent from the animal kingdom and his ineradicable animal nature. This last revolution has been accomplished in our own time by Charles Darwin, Wallace, and their predecessors, though not without provoking the most violent contemporary opposition. But human megalomania will have suffered its third and most wounding blow from the psychological research of our own time which seeks to prove to the ego that it is not even master of its own house but must content itself with scanty information of what is going on unconsciously in its mind. We psychoanalysts are only the first and not the only ones to utter this call to introspection but it seems to be our fate to give it its most forcible expression and to support it with empirical material which affects every individual. Hence arises the general revolt against our science, the disregard of all considerations of academic civility and the releasing of the opposition from every restraint of impartial logic." That was Freud. *Introduction to Psychoanalysis*, 1916.[57]

The extraordinary length and somber tone of her reading, a foundational introduction to Freud's thought by the psychoanalyst himself, is rendered dramatic in her loving inflection and by the fact that she is emotionally moved to tears by the words. Beginning with "We psychoanalysts . . . ," Florence's voice trembles and tears come to her eyes. She regains her composure well enough to finish the passage, but whimpers a little throughout and sobs again at the end as she reads the name "Freud." Cuts within the scene to the faces of her students show them rapt and silent with attention. That a dramatic reading of Freud has a teacher in tears and a class captivated signals the manner in which this Jewish secular thinker figures in the fabric of the film as revolutionary, not only in his own time and place, as the passage recounts, but in the situation of the Maghrib as the students are experiencing it. Together with Voltaire and Darwin and Jean-Jacques Rousseau, Freud registers in the film as a signifier of the dangerously modern ideas that provoked controversy in Europe (leading to the opposition and attacks so poignantly described by him, that moved Florence so much) and that would be invoked to perilous ends in the activism carried out by the young friends in Tangier, whose activities are closely monitored and recorded by the secret police, leading eventually to the detainment and torture of some of them.

If this scene introduces the intellectual underpinning of European secular modernity, the next short scene introduces its popular equivalent, as another teacher, Madame Desars (played by Claude Pomme) introduces the students to the popular tradition of the *café-concert* or *caf'-conc'*, as it was colloquially known. She cites the Larousse dictionary to explain that the *café-concert* was a place where one paid for the entertainment through drinking, and that it "signaled the emergence of a popular culture from which came the rich tradition of the *chanson française* [French song], the music hall, and the cinema—all forms of expression

FIGURE 40. Madame Desars (Claude Pomme), costumed as Marlene Dietrich, presents the history of the *café-concert* in *The Sorrows of a Young Tangerian*, 2013.

that are spaces of laughter, satire, freedom and excess." She then snaps open a top hat to complete an outfit reminiscent of Marlene Dietrich's Amy Jolly in *Morocco* (dir. Josef von Sternberg, 1930) and sings the students a *chanson* that evokes a *flânerie* around the boulevards of Paris (fig. 40). The scene thus eulogizes an early form of popular entertainment culture that was crucial in the development of cinema. Kelley Conway, in a chapter subtitled "The Rise of the Unruly Woman," explains that the *café-concert*

> was a boisterous entertainment space whose roots can be traced to Café des Aveugles, which opened in 1731 in the basement of the Café Italian at the Palais-Royal.... The *café-chantant* [as it was also called] proliferated in the aftermath of the Revolution, when the monopoly enjoyed by *théâtres de privilèges* (officially patronized theaters) ended. [The *café-concerts*] were clustered around the *barrières d'octroi* (tax collection points at the city gates), the Palais-Royal, the Tuileries, the main faubourgs [slums], and the large boulevards of the city: Temple, Strasbourg, Ménilmontant, and Saint-Denis. The café-chantant was most often a modest affair.... Most significantly, the cafés-chantants were accessible to those of all social categories.[58]

This meant, of course, that the *café-concerts* were associated with working-class women, prostitutes, and public drinking. Conway's history thus reminds us of a space in which women had a kind of autonomy and where boisterous profanity was available to those who chose it.

Such accessibility to the profane and freedom of expression is part of the fabric of critique that *The Sorrows of a Young Tangerian* creates. What is found in the *caf'-*

conc' example is far from nostalgic Francophilia. It is rather an appreciation of the kind of public culture that might be produced in a society that has demoted religion and the monarchy from their role as dominant forces. One sees such an energy in the consistency of the calls for liberty throughout *The Sorrows of a Young Tangerian*, a liberty figured as freedom from compulsory religion but also tied strongly to resistance to authoritarian state powers. In an adjacent scene, two young lovers, the very white and blond Malika (played by Astrid Roos) and her boyfriend, Fouad (Hamza Elbardai), are in a modernist house whose lobby is adorned with friezes of Greek and Roman scenes. Before even seeing them, we hear Malika and her friend singing, over a sequence of static establishing shots around the building, the following verse (in French, but translated here):

> They were a hundred and twenty, they were in the thousands
> Naked and thin, trembling, in sealed train cars
> Who tore at the night with their fingernails
> They were thousands, they were a hundred and twenty

The verse is from the French song "Nuit et brouillard" (Night and Fog) by Jean Ferrat, released in 1963, and while it carries clear references to the Holocaust in both its name and the images it evokes here, it becomes a more generalized plea for freedom as it continues (still in French):

> They were named Jean-Pierre, Natacha, or Samuel
> Some of them prayed to Jesus, Jehovah, or Vishnu
> Others didn't pray at all, but no matter the sky
> They simply wanted to not live on their knees.[59]

Interpolated between the verses is a conversation between Malika and Fouad in which she bewails the "sacrosanct tradition" to which they must "bow down" in order to conceal their love. He replies that his mother does not understand their mentality or their times, and kisses her tenderly; she admits that her parents do not know she is with him, either. It remains unclear whether the issue involves different religions or simply their age, but the romantic problem is articulated together with a much larger one that has to do with freedom of expression and political agency.

This group of young political activists, then, ties its desires for a liberated Morocco to the twinned discourses of the European Enlightenment and Arab nationalism. This is heard dramatically at the end of the film: Madame Desars leads them in a classroom rendition of "In Paris," made famous by Yves Montand, a song that memorializes the Paris of every kind of person—students and drinkers and drifters and lovers who dance hand in hand in the streets in a world made possible by the storming of the Bastille. But the song is juxtaposed immediately in the next and final scene with the band of outsiders walking in unison through

Perdicaris Park as Abdel Halim Hafez's voice sings, "Oh beloved homeland, homeland of the Arab people!" As the film leaves both songs ringing in the ears of its viewers, it allows two horizons of change and possibility. In its gentle satirizing of both Larbi's intense love for European thought and its lockstep revolutionary vanguard, it is far from prescriptive or naive in its conclusions: we might be tempted to recall, on the one hand, that the other side of enlightened and free Paris is the hellish world that Si Moh experiences, and on the other, that the project of Arab nationalism had its own coercive application of secularism that led to the rise of Islamism and further suppressions.

The film is not, then, utopian in its impulses. Despite these conditions, however, in its dramatic call for freedoms of all sorts, it does not shy from suggesting that a kind of Arab Enlightenment is urgently needed, one that relegates religion to a role where it functions without the power of compulsion. Freud, Darwin, Voltaire, Rousseau, and others are cited as the hopes for the building of a new Morocco or Arab world that might yet come. There is a project of secular thinking that proceeds from that tradition, but it is not confined to Europe, nor do its proponents in the Arab world believe that it is only through Europe that it should be thought. As this chapter has shown, Smihi's films offer the roots of a secular critique through Islam's many engagements with the rationalist tradition. While the break with religious authority over public life is associated with the European Enlightenment, such an association should not limit the applicability of some Enlightenment ideals for the contemporary Arab world, nor the development of an Arab *tanwir*. Paraphrasing the Egyptian philosopher Fouad Zakariyya, Elizabeth Suzanne Kassab writes that "Islamic heritage contains significant manifestations of rationalist, independent critique. This critique is thus not the exclusive property of some trends of Western culture. It is part and parcel of Islamic culture, and reviving it is the most urgent cultural imperative in the Arab world."[60] Other thinkers, like Bassam Tibi and Aziz al-Azmeh, have continued Zakariyya's call by developing positions that acknowledge European and US colonialism without a wholesale rejection of modernity's principles. As al-Azmeh argues, European history and thought cannot be reduced only to their worst manifestations. Films like *The East Wind* and *44*, and by extension Smihi's entire oeuvre, demonstrate that it is possible to develop a critique of colonial history while recognizing the existence and usefulness of aspects of European modernity.

The Moroccan feminist sociologist Fatima Mernissi pursued a trenchant critique of those who would deny the usefulness of freedom of expression, democracy, and other Enlightenment concepts to the Muslim world on the basis of some supposition that the latter must be guarded at all costs from the taint of Europe and the United States. To argue for such a cultural relativism, Mernissi claimed, is to condemn the Arab world to backwardness and dependency—to ask it to take the weapons and technologies that have made the West dominant, yet without the principles of governance or liberty that underpin a cultural modernity and that might challenge that very Western dominance.[61] Such an attitude, she argues, while occasionally found in the guise of allowing for Muslim or Arab difference, further removes the Arab world from history and denies it the same prospects of freedom as the West. Similarly, al-Azmeh has argued forcefully that the project of Islam as cultural authenticity creates a complicity with the most neo-Orientalist of ideas about the Arab world (its fixed, unchanging nature; the Muslim propensity for despotism) while accepting the fiat by which the Islamist language of a "return" to Islamic tradition conceals the very invention of that tradition for political purposes in the present.[62]

The aim for Arab thinkers like Mernissi and Tibi and al-Azmeh, then, is not to destroy religion but to find for it a place conducive to the needs of a modernity that assures subjecthood and freedoms for all. Taken in tandem with Smihi's critical writing, we can see this as the central project of the Tangier trilogy, too. At the same time, the films resist utopian or simplistic readings, and hasten to show their characters' flaws. Larbi, for all his intensity, does not escape complicity with the world that he rejects. At the end of *Sorrows of a Young Tangerian*, his father succeeds in getting Larbi to pray with him in the car on the way to the airport, seeking a safe passage for him; then, over Larbi's protests at his subservience to the system, he intercedes on his son's behalf, using his personal connections to safeguard Larbi's passport and exit from the country. Indeed, Larbi himself escapes from the revolutionary project he has called for by voluntarily migrating to France, leaving the political activism to the others in favor of his intellectual and literary pursuits. But the urgency of the film's cry for a different world resonates throughout. The characters, in the intensity of their passion for critique and for freedoms of thought, expression, and desire, articulate their yearning for a promise whose seeds are everywhere in history yet which still remains unfulfilled.

5

For a New Nahda: Gender, Sexuality, and Freedom

Moumen Smihi's critique of patriarchy spans his entire career. His first feature, *The East Wind* (1975), is remarkable for its consideration of Moroccan social relations, especially those pertaining to gender. Through the dramatic formal means already discussed in earlier chapters, it makes plain the stakes for women in a polygamous and patriarchal family structure. But *The East Wind* is not unique for its focus on a central female character; Smihi also structured a later film, *The Lady from Cairo* (1991), around the perspective of a woman, and other films devote considerable attention to the place of their female characters, as I will show. Such a focus, however, comprises only one part of Smihi's critique of gendered relations in a patriarchal society: along with their analysis of the role of women, his films are simultaneously invested in a critique of masculinity. This nuanced attention to the working of gender runs through all the films and intersects with their investigations of sexuality. Across the entire arc of Smihi's career, questions of gender are a key terrain on which social relations are measured and contested. The ongoing work of skepticism and critique in which the films engage—their call for a renewed Nahda—often manifests through investigations of familial and kinship relations and by reckoning with sexual desire.

This chapter will argue, then, that the domain of gender and sexuality is a site through which Smihi's films continue their radical critique of the status quo, both of Moroccan society and of the wider Arab world. At the same time, they offer the viewer a nuanced and rich picture of the traces of other pasts and possibilities that might be recovered and nourished toward the pursuit of a better world. In this way, the films' representations of gender intersect with the extensive critique that we have seen Smihi bring to the question of religion. As always, these traces and possibilities are not hermetically enclosed within Arab or Moroccan society; Smihi is neither an essentialist nor a proponent of a fixed or culturalist identity. Nor are the films' critiques dependent only on Europe or the West for their provenance. Their challenge to the status quo is a worldly one, indebted equally to the heretical, libertine poet Abu Nuwas and to the discoveries of Sigmund Freud, resonant with the critiques of Arab feminists like Fatima Mernissi while entranced with the free sexuality of the French New Wave or the pansexual world of Pier Paolo Pasolini's *Arabian Nights* (1974). They are also in dialogue with those of other Arab filmmakers like Nouri Bouzid, who depicts the traumas of Arab masculinities in the post-1967 political climate.

This chapter will address these questions in three parts. First, I will consider how Smihi's films construct space as a gendered and contested phenomenon. Their keen attention to architecture and spatiality enables a thoroughgoing examination of gender in the context of Moroccan life. Second, I will address the question of gender in the public sphere of Moroccan society. Here I will illuminate Smihi's critique of the constraints that a patriarchal society places on women but also show the ways that women in these films adapt and occupy public space, contradicting Western stereotypes about women in Arab and Muslim contexts. Third, the chapter considers the question of sexuality and sexual desire, an area that the films address directly. In this section, the focus is on the many ways the films critique the assumption that Moroccan or Arab societies are intrinsically inimical to homosexuality or to female desire, while at the same time mounting a scathing critique of homophobia and the severely restricted domain of sexual expression for both women and men.

GENDER AND SPACE

The construction of gendered critique through spatial representation is established in *The East Wind* in ways that also animate *44, or Tales of the Night* (1981), *A Muslim Childhood* (2005), *Girls and Swallows* (2008), and *The Sorrows of a Young Tangerian* (2013). In all of these films, Smihi works with the spatial particularities of domestic and urban architecture to provide a historicized critique of patriarchy and gender roles. *The East Wind* dramatically advances this strategy across the entire duration of the narrative. It opens with a sequence of shots around the city of Tangier, beginning with the *ville nouvelle* but moving into the medina, too, a sequence addressed in chapter 1. When the camera begins to show the inner space of the house in the medina, the shots are predominantly populated by Aïcha, her mother, and the children. It is they who dominate the salon space and kitchen to which we repeatedly return. When the husband is shown in the house, he is typically confined to the courtyard (where he occupies himself with praying) or in his own bed, where we see him attempting to sleep, first while receiving the mother's admonishments and later while lying on the amulet that Aïcha has placed under

FIGURE 41. Aïcha's husband, sitting outside the house, grooms his beard while interviewing a potential second wife in *The East Wind*, 1975.

the pillow to retain his affections over any other possible spouse. Other than in these scenes, he is mostly seen in the street or other extra-domestic spaces. He joins his friend, the shopkeeper, to organize his second marriage, and later they sit outside to interview a potential wife (fig. 41); he visits a prostitute, collects rents from around town, and ventures out of the confines of the city with an all-male group to enjoy a meal of couscous. We rarely see him in the home interacting with his family; his prayers and Qur'anic study keep him separate from the others. Aïcha, on the other hand, is more often associated with other family members and is almost always seen with them when at home. Interiors, then, are spaces of domesticity and familial responsibility where women are often together while men have mobility outside.

Smihi departs from this pattern, however, in ways that upset the binary association of women with interior space and men with exterior space. Mediating the interior-exterior dichotomy is the conversation that takes place on the rooftop between Aïcha and her neighbor. Their discussion is enabled by the responsibility of laundry—they hang clothes while speaking about Aïcha's family and the husband's plan for a second spouse. As Mernissi points out, men were typically not allowed on the terraces of the medina houses; the potential for moving from house to house meant that they could potentially disrupt the privacy of the harem.[1] By setting his scene on these terraces, Smihi gives primacy to those female-centric spaces as socially and narratively important. Even more dramatically, however, he plays with relations of mobility and space when he stages Aïcha's walk through the souk and out into the *ville nouvelle*, an itinerary that is ordained for her by the marabout, who suggests that she sacrifice a black chicken to help foil her husband's plan. There, Smihi grants her not just movement but the power of a curious, investigative, and even scornful gaze, as I discussed in chapter 1.

Her independence, however, is somewhat deceptive. Smihi both presents the possibilities for a woman who is able to negotiate the space of the city for herself, yet simultaneously shows that such independence is, in her case, a symptom of the oppressive atmosphere she suffers at home. There, Aïcha is destined to be the second-class spouse of a man who shows little interest in her, but in her attempt to move outside the domestic and into public space, she is beaten back by the demands and exigencies of religion and societal expectations. The vicissitudes of these negotiations of femininity and space were recognized in an insightful contemporaneous essay in *Cahiers du cinéma*, in which Abdelwahab Meddeb draws attention to the many ways in which *The East Wind*'s women constitute their own spaces of feminine power and solidarity, yet are ultimately stymied by the patriarchal systems they must grapple with.[2] Ultimately, then, Aïcha's renegotiation of and departure from domestic gendered space is a fraught one that culminates in her death under the waves at Hercules Grotto (fig. 42).

44, or Tales of the Night likewise plays with the inversion of gendered spatial dichotomies. For the most part this tension is exercised through El Hajj's two wives, and the question of femininity and domestic space becomes tied up with the film's representation of polygamy, religious conformism, and racism. One of the primary settings is the home of a religious family in Fez. In keeping with the spatial organization of Fez architecture, the film privileges interior space over exterior. Moroccan domestic architecture in general, and Fez homes in particular, reserve decorative elements for their interiors; from the outside a home may look stark and plain. We see this home first from the street, but only the door (heavy, with decorative iron hinges and some detailing of the wood, as is typical) and the flat, unremarkable wall around it are visible. A cut to the interior, however, shows us the intricate patterning of the tiles on the walls, the wrought-iron window lattices, and the beautiful cedar panels that surround them. In subsequent scenes the family is placed within this home in a variety of locations and moments. We see El Hajj's wife for the first time seated with another female family member, doing needlework. And it is also within the home that we see her having the conversation with El Hajj about his desire to marry a second spouse. As he guarantees her place as head of the household, she demands that he conduct the marriage without

FIGURE 42. Aïcha is sucked under the waves at Hercules Grotto in a death rendered ambiguous through astonishing images and montage in *The East Wind*, 1975.

fanfare or celebration. At this point Smihi introduces one of his digressive cutaways, a frequent strategy in this film composed of multiple digressions. As the wife's voice-over anchors the viewer back to this conversation, the film moves outside to the rooftop where Yaqut, the slave, hangs laundry while El Hajj's son, seated at a wall, takes a pair of scissors and clips the wings of a dove. As it flaps out of his grasp, we cut back to the tense scene between El Hajj and his wife, then back again to the dove, which now tries unsuccessfully to fly, bumping uselessly into the wall. The sequence of shots associates domesticity, femininity, and confinement.

This equivalence is complicated, then, after the arrival of the second spouse (played by Marie-France Pisier), who, true to El Hajj's promise, arrives in the dead of night and is ushered quietly into the house. Shortly after, one of the low, wide-angle shots that Smihi frequently favors shows the family seated at the divan before a round table, with El Hajj's wives next to each other. The first wife throws the second a piece of bread; the second unceremoniously tosses it back at her with a look of disdain (fig. 43). The domestic scene, then, is a space of tension between the two women, and El Hajj's polygamy becomes subject to the film's scrutiny, especially given the accompanying sequence where his son runs distraught across

FIGURE 43. El Hajj's first and second wives eye each other with disdain in *44, or Tales of the Night*, 1981.

the Fez hills, balling his fists and screaming at the iniquity of the second marriage. Yet the tension between the two wives and their sharing of domestic space is only one part of the critique of patriarchal relationships of domesticity and polygamy—relationships that are contested within Islamic feminism and Arab feminism more broadly.[3] Even more striking, perhaps, is how the character of Yaqut, the slave, serves to address the interrelationship of race and gender at a moment in Morocco's history.

We first see Yaqut in a beautiful Moroccan garden at the center of an ornately tiled building. Yet the beauty of the setting belies the violence of what takes place there: Yaqut (whose actual name is Fatma) is brought before El Hajj, who, after ascertaining that she is as described, and "at the agreed-upon price," pronounces: "From now on, you'll be known as Yaqut." In a brilliantly acted shot-reverse-shot that fully implicates El Hajj in the slave trade, Yaqut stares at him, her head bowed but her eyes raised in a seeming challenge to his presumption. He looks unnerved but defiant, and Yaqut is seen in subsequent scenes as the family's servant. Here, then, the film is clear that while a spatial division may allow men greater access to an external social space than women, it is not a neat binary that "simply" condemns some general category of women to domestic space. Rather, we see that class and racial divisions radically change how women occupy that space. El Hajj's first and second spouses, in all their privilege, have more in common with each other than with Yaqut, who is bossed around by all the family and lives in a

FIGURE 44. Yaqut's quarters in the basement of the house, where she dies alone in *44, or Tales of the Night*, 1981.

basement room next to the furnace, which she must stoke to keep the hammam at temperature. Her living quarters are cramped, dirty, and damp, and she suffers a miserable death there at the end of the film (fig. 44). The role of Yaqut breaks the near-absence of black women in the visual history of Moroccan cinema and simultaneously records the racism that has been a part of the country's history.[4]

Smihi later signaled the taboo role of race and slavery in Morocco in his film about the painter Henri Matisse, *With Matisse in Tangier* (1993). There he presents Matisse's paintings of mixed-race Moroccan women ("mulattos" in the titles of the paintings) and comments in his narration that Matisse's representations make them deliberately hard to read. While they might perform weakness or humiliation, he notes, at the same time they are present as proud figures who were in many cases matrons of the harem or heads of the household staff. Smihi, in conversation, has said that to him, Matisse's images evoke a perceptive understanding of the humiliation that the slave in Morocco had to endure, forced to dissemble a kind of submissive status that was inconsistent with the efficacy of their labor and their importance in the household. Far from recapitulating the domination and oppression of the black slave in his own mise-en-scène, then, Smihi's presentation of Yaqut offers the power of critique of a system of slavery that Morocco has been slow to acknowledge.[5] This critique is intensively spatialized within the domestic environment.

In the Tangier trilogy, the question of gender and space becomes particularly charged, as was the case in *The East Wind*. Across all three films, Smihi presents evidence of how a domestic and patriarchal hierarchy of space delimits the range of possibilities for women while ensuring the mobility and independence of men. In keeping with their mode of critique throughout, however, the films also bear witness to the extraordinary possibilities for subversion of such gendered hierarchies through both the engagement of European practices of modernity and, importantly, the invocation of alternative horizons within the history of the Arab and Islamic worlds. The films' refusal to privilege one such domain of experience over the other is what makes their commitment to thinking through gender and sexuality so incisive. In *A Muslim Childhood*, the family first appears seated around a low table, eating the modest meal that Lalla Alia has prepared for them. She is unveiled, wearing her hair braided in a bun. Her look is fashionable despite the everyday typicality of the meal, and it is significant that Smihi shows her with no head covering whatsoever in the scene. It stresses the fact that in a family setting, Muslim women have no obligation to cover their heads, but it also begins to introduce Lalla Alia's character as quite consciously seeking a liberal self-fashioning, concentrating on hair and dress, that reflects a modern sensibility at odds with many of those around her. The narrator comments on her and the family's customs in the subsequent scene when they pose for a Spanish photographer in a series of shots that Smihi frames as tableaux vivants. As Lalla Alia poses for the camera in a gray jellaba, her head covered but her face uncovered (the white covering sits at her jaw and covers her neck, but not her face), the narrator informs us: "Lalla Alia could show her face to a Jewish or Christian photographer but she could not go out without wearing a veil. As a descendent of the Prophet, Sidi Ahmed had made a point of marrying a daughter of the religious nobility. He had to give his children a Cherifian [noble, descended from the Prophet] mother. Her childhood had been awful: illiterate, rough, terrorized by an angry father. This young woman from a very strict milieu admired the modern ways of the Boulevard [Pasteur, in the *ville nouvelle*], but she never went there."

Lalla Alia's subjectivity is thus constituted through the domestic and familial relationships within which she is situated: her marriage to Sidi Ahmed is conditioned by her noble lineage, but her experience of life is equally structured by the violence of her father and her confinement as a married woman within the terrain of the home and the medina. While the film never indicates that Sidi Ahmed is violent or repressive, the narrator's voice-over does suggest that Lalla Alia was likely subject to the same customs of the Moroccan domestic harem that Mernissi describes in her memoir, *Dreams of Trespass* (1994). Such harems (Mernissi grew up in one) were different from the kind of Ottoman imperial harem "that has fascinated the West almost to the point of obsession." Rather, she explains, they were defined more by seclusion than polygamy and functioned to maintain an extended family household in which generations lived together.[6] This does not mean that they were innocent of gendered meanings, of course; as Irvin Cemil Schick points out, the harem was a "technology of gender" (Teresa de Lauretis's term), and its spatial arrangements functioned to produce and encode gender difference within asymmetries of power.[7] Although we see her in the home preening with a new bob haircut and a long, Spanish-style dress, for Lalla Alia such enjoyment of modern, European accoutrements only ever occurs behind the closed doors of the family house (for other women in the film, this is not so, as a late scene in the theater proves). This is equally the case for the other films in the trilogy, *Girls and Swallows* and *The Sorrows of a Young Tangerian*, where Lalla Alia certainly takes a prominent role, but only within the space of the home.

Indeed, the very issue of her seclusion and the social role of women becomes a narrative question in *Girls and Swallows*. Seated in Larbi's bedroom, Lalla Alia asks her son to visit his grandfather, which precipitates a dyspeptic rant from the son about how his paternal grandfather rejects him and his uncle hides from him. Larbi's humiliation, which he says that his father shares, stems from the fact that his father's family sees him as the son of a mere girl, the daughter of a *fqih* (theologian and Islamic scholar) married to another *fqih*—the fact of her age marks her as contemptible in the eyes of Sidi Ahmed's family. The conversation reveals the extent of the patriarchal constructions of polygamy that undergird this social stratum of Morocco, but in the passionate narration by Lalla Alia, we see also the strength and force of the social critique mounted by the women. Larbi insults her by asking why she puts up with the contempt shown her, and he even accuses her of being backward in her thinking. Lalla Alia's reply forcefully articulates the stakes for a young woman like herself: never sent to school, illiterate, and subject to the strict rule of the father, a religious man who left his daughters and wives alone by day, confined in their house, and then condemned them to silence during the evenings, when he would clear his throat and read from the Qur'an. Her father, she says, would have "slit her throat" if she'd gone to the French store she liked, Les Galeries Lafayette (on the Rue Siaghine, a medina street that leads from the Petit Socco to the Grand Socco and that also houses the Spanish Catholic Church of the Immaculate Conception and, a few short blocks away, the Jewish synagogue).[8]

Larbi brags that his own father, Sidi Ahmed, would never forbid such a thing, and that his (paternal) aunt, Aïcha, is able to leave the house any time she wishes. Lalla Alia retorts that Aïcha's relative freedom is due to the fact that her father allowed her to go to school and thus fostered her independence; she even, Lalla Alia claims, goes to a Spanish teahouse on her own. Lalla Alia clearly understands that the decisions of a patriarch can have life-altering effects on the women in his household. Their fortunes are entirely bound up with the whims of the men. Here, the film indexes debates and differences of opinion about how seclusion is to be practiced, with the harem and the veil being two modes of sequestration that had to be renegotiated in the context of a postcolonial state. Marilyn Booth's analysis of the "fallen woman" genre of Egyptian fiction focuses on how modernization created anxieties about the borders of seclusion as women adopted new forms of mobility through schooling and thus negotiated new norms of visibility as the female body became "disconnected from its anchoring in domestic space."[9] Booth's argument about how young women in these Egyptian narratives transgress spatial boundaries and patriarchal expectations is beautifully illustrated in the second sequence of *Moroccan Chronicles*, as Shams navigates paternal expectations, Western education, and sexual desire. Her appearances unveiled and flirtatiously soliciting Tewfik's attention alternate with her adoption of the white *haik* that completely encloses her body but for the eyes.

Returning to *A Muslim Childhood*, however, Larbi's criticism there is directed not at masculine control over women, but at the women themselves: insulting his mother for her supposed backwardness, he asks why his grandmother put up with his grandfather's polygamy, suggesting that the grandfather even had sex with his servants. Lalla Alia answers his teenage lack of respect and presumption with an impassioned account of what it was like to actually be a mother or a daughter in the house, an account that begins forcefully with the words "As if she had a choice!" But her story ends with a statement of independence and self-worth, one that seems like a cry for recognition. "Oh, I know that I'm illiterate," she says, "but I'm flesh and blood! I can feel the world and understand it. Why do some men want to bury their wives alive?" After a brief pause, the force of a contradiction asserts itself as she adds, "Allah, forgive me for speaking ill of my parents."

In this sequence Smihi makes a verbal intertextual reference back to *The East Wind*, one that explicitly links the situation of Lalla Alia and others like her to the narrative of Aïcha. In the middle of her account of her suffering in the home of her father, Lalla Alia recalls a grandfather clock that her father had brought from Spain. She describes to Larbi its sound, the "tick-tock" remembered from her childhood. The memory seems disconnected from the rest of her story, except to the extent that it enables her to articulate her sense that she is a thinking, feeling person like anyone else. But it also prompts us, the viewers, to recall the wall clock in *The East Wind*, whose ticking is part of that film's soundscape. In both instances, the clock's sound, while it marks time, perhaps marks the contradictions of that world, which had to straddle the *tarikh* (Islamic calendar) and a Western one. Mernissi has written about the complexities of that relationship in *Islam and Democracy* (1992), and Smihi has also recalled that his own family measured time by the cycle of prayers, not by Greenwich.[10] Yet, as Lalla Alia's recollection seems to suggest, the clock itself, ticking away day and night, reminds them of and connects them to a wider world outside the domestic space in which they are, in her words, entombed.

Complicating such a picture, Smihi shows the dominating force of the fathers and husbands who control the very futures of these women, and simultaneously the extraordinary power that Moroccan women constitute within their domestic space. The film that most clearly demonstrates that power is *Girls and Swallows*.

Indeed, while the protagonist is Larbi, the teenage boy, the narrative center is most definitely the female-centric space of the home and the women who inhabit it. As many scenes make clear, Larbi cannot control or even understand the world of his mother and her friends. The wide, low shots that Smihi uses extensively—a gesture to Yasujiro Ozu—accentuate the number of women who frequent the house and the importance of their circle. Larbi and Sidi Ahmed frequently appear to the side of this circle, and when they are enclosed within it (on the three-sided divan that fills a corner of the salon) they are outnumbered and seem overwhelmed by the women surrounding them. Through such representations Smihi offers both a critique of the conditions the women inhabit and a celebration of their world, one that recontextualizes their role away from Orientalist presumptions that stress only victimhood.

An early scene demonstrates this combination of critique and recontextualization. Five women are seated around the divan, with Larbi to one side. They are Lalla Alia, Sidi Ahmed's wife and Larbi's mother; Lalla Alia's sister, Aïcha; Aïcha's friend, known as Mtougia (the name of her husband, who has many wives); Mtougia's daughter, Rabea; and a neighbor. Aïcha tells of the mistreatment of the black servant Yaqut, who was thrown out and left on the street until Sidi Ahmed saved her and Aïcha's family took her in. Mtougia reports that she and her fellow wives feel oppressed by their husband and seek Sidi Ahmed's support. She even relates that her husband beats her "dizzy and lazy" daughter, Rabea, who is sitting with them. Later in the film, Mtougia listens to Aïcha reading lines from a poem by the twentieth-century Lebanese American poet Iliya Abu Madi ("The Evening" [al-Masa']) which addresses the narrator's friend, Salma.[11] Mtougia is touched by the beauty of the poetry and bemoans the fact that she, like all of Mtougia's wives, is illiterate and did not have the opportunity to attend school that Aïcha and Lalla Alia's father gave them. In a scene with Fatema, Sidi Ahmed and Lalla Alia's housekeeper, Rabea again references her pitiful conditions at home: the family's two black slaves hit her with a stick, and she is forced to do excessive amounts of housework. Moments later, with Larbi, Rabea again discusses the beatings she receives from her father, joking that at least the house is big and she has plenty of places to hide.

In stark contrast to Mtougia and Rabea's domestic situation, Sidi Ahmed takes a gentle and kind hand: he would never countenance the treatment that Mtougia and Rabea receive, and the women praise his kindness toward Yaqut. Moreover, the women effectively control and administer the domestic space despite his titular authority. Fatema invites Rabea to stay as often as she wishes so as to avoid the beatings and work at home, and that scene ends with Fatema, Rabea, and Batoul (another young female friend of the family) singing together. Second, and even more strikingly, the film closes with a credit sequence showing all the women who share this domestic space together in a static long shot of the tiled parlor, where many of the earlier conversations between the assembled women and Sidi Ahmed

FIGURE 45. Larbi is pushed to the edge of the frame in *Girls and Swallows*, 2008.

took place. They take turns dancing at the center of the floor while the rest of their group sings and claps exuberantly in a celebration of movement and female bodies. In a single take of more than three and a half minutes, broken only by a brief cutaway to a shot of the skylight and a scarf flying into the air below it, this wide-angle shot emplaces a community of women at the heart of the home and claims it as a feminist space. As the dances continue, Larbi, whose sexual advances (as we'll see) are rebuffed throughout by Rabea, Aouicha, and Batoul, crosses the floor briefly to speak to Lalla Alia, at the farthest right edge of the frame (fig. 45). But he barely reaches her when he is summarily ejected from the scene, shooed away by his mother with a push at his hip followed by a backhanded slap to his arse. The scene is in some ways the culmination of the rejection he has consistently encountered from women, but here, rather than a repudiation of his sexual desires, the mise-en-scène stresses the question of who controls space. The harem might signify subservience to a Western viewer, but Smihi demonstrates it also as a space of female desire and power.

GENDER AND THE PUBLIC SPHERE

While women's role in and association with domestic space is multivalent in the Tangier trilogy, Smihi also shows the ways in which Moroccan women were increasingly reshaping the public sphere. His images of 1950s and 1960s Tangier in the first two films demonstrate how women occupied public space in shifting and varied modes. During the conversation between the assembled women and Sidi Ahmed referred to above, the conversation shifts from the treatment of Mtougia's wives and daughter, Rabea, to the latter's style of dress. Lalla Alia volunteers enthusiastically that Rabea dresses "in a European way, like their Royal Highnesses the Princesses." Mtougia adds that, like Rabea, the princesses don't wear the veil in photos. Sidi Ahmed's sister opines that "the Moroccan woman has to emancipate herself!" and they joke that things would be easier if dressing in a European way wasn't so expensive. Sidi Ahmed suggests that, in the wake of King Mohammed V's speech in Tangier, everything about Moroccan society has begun to change.

The reference to Mohammed V's daughters is a historically accurate one: photos of two of them, Lalla Fatima Zohra and Lalla Aïcha, often showed them without a headscarf, and one photo of Fatima Zohra in particular shows her with a ponytail, a fashionable tightly fitting dress, and jewelry and other accessories. The characters of Smihi's film, far from objecting to her self-fashioning, approve and are impressed by the movement toward emancipation embedded in many nationalist political practices of the time, as Mernissi points out. By Mernissi's account, the Moroccan nationalists, who were working against the French presence and in favor of the king, Mohammed V, had a politics of gender equality that became influential with many women in the cities. Her own mother was influenced, Mernissi recalls, by the climate instigated by the nationalists in Fez, whose daughters "began appearing in the streets with bare faces and bare legs, in Western dresses with the distinctive Western handbags on their shoulders." On the eve of independence in 1956, her mother came home from a nationalist march and "her hair was uncovered and her face was bare. From then on, there were no more black *litham* [a triangular piece of silk covering the nose] to be seen covering young women's faces in Fez Medina; only old ladies and young, newly migrant peasants kept the veil."[12]

Smihi's characters thus reflect accurately and provocatively the changing social mores of the time and the kinds of feminist impulses of the nationalist period. Those impulses, however, predated the nationalist period and spread beyond Morocco; they were important to the Nahda more generally. Nazira Zeineddine's treatise *Unveiling and Veiling* (al-Sufur wa-l-hijab, 1928) asserted the right of women to unveil as a measure of a wider freedom of thought and expression that she associated with Muhammad 'Abduh's reformist Islam. Introducing her argument, she wrote: "I am among those women who have favored unveiling over the wearing of the veil. In accordance with freedom of thought and under the banner of sovereign scientific authority, I hereby present to you my views and reflections in favor of unveiling and the liberation of women.... As some wise men have said, 'Free thought is the foundation of all Renaissance. We ought to pave the way for it to flourish.'"[13] Smihi's film thus references the historical conditions of the moment in which it is set, and the longer tradition of feminism within the Nahda movement.

Beyond the domestic space of the family, the character of Aouicha clearly represents, over two films, the changing possibilities and perils of being a Moroccan woman in public space. Her character appears in both *A Muslim Childhood* and

Girls and Swallows as a woman of independence and sexual freedom. She acts kindly toward Larbi in *A Muslim Childhood*, and it is clear in a couple of scenes that he is smitten with her even though she is older, more sophisticated, and thus beyond his reach. In *Girls and Swallows*, however, she has an outspoken dialogue with Larbi about the role of women in society, and even though Larbi still responds to her as the object of his affections, the film represents her as something much more than that. Like Mtougia's wives and daughter, she is the victim of domestic abuse at home: "My father beat me for reading comics. 'Books corrupt,' he'd say. Then, one day, I left his house. I worked as a maid in Jewish homes; they pay better than Muslims! And then I met Sordi and his Christian, Spanish, English friends. I dreamed of becoming a modern woman." But Sordi, we learn in a later scene, is possessive and aggressive, verbally abusing her for allegedly wishing to go to the United States with another man. Complaining that he saved her from misery, he insults her and calls her a dirty wife, but she retorts: "I didn't run away from my father just to put up with you! Hands off! It's independence now! I'm a free woman!" However antagonistic her father and Sordi might be, she resists clearly in terms that are also articulated by other, less independent women like Aïcha, Lalla Alia, and Mtougia. Aouicha is always unveiled, wearing fashionable dresses and looking elegant and refined, and it is this elegance and independence (at least in part) that seems to render her so attractive to Larbi, who is twice seen, in *Girls and Swallows*, entreating her from below her balcony while she laughs at his persistence.

Aouicha represents a woman who is able to freely move around the city and has a degree of independence. In *A Muslim Childhood* she is married to a redheaded man whom she refers to as "crazy" (a description that rhymes with her situation in the later *Girls and Swallows*, in the scene with Sordi described above), and the possibility that she sees other men, either for money or for pleasure, is strongly hinted at in both films. To be sure, both films show the way that she is stigmatized for her sexual liberty, but in so doing they dare to side with her in a strong declaration of her independence. Other women complement these assertions of independence. A character named Shams-Doha appears as a family friend in *A Muslim Childhood*, and we encounter her in a lengthy single-take scene on the rooftop patio of the family's home. She sits down, leather purse at her side, with a fashionable haircut and without a headscarf, and lights a cigarette. Sidi Ahmed immediately asks their servant to bring an ashtray for their guest, and after she praises his openness and generosity, he explains his tolerance for such a haram activity (one forbidden by Islamic law): "A man of god once listened to a street musician and interrupted his prayers to dance with him. We all have cravings deep down. . . . Do as you like, and make yourself at home." The scene continues from there as a discussion of women's freedom in particular: Shams-Doha remarks that Khadija, another young woman befriended by the family and sitting next to her, is being pressured by her parents to marry a police officer. Questioned as to whether this is appropriate under Islam, Sidi Ahmed replies that it is not and that the young woman's wishes must also be taken into consideration for any marriage. Shams-Doha exclaims in agreement that Islam is the best religion but that Muslims do not practice as they should. "Times have changed," she says. "A woman must be mistress of her own fate. We're going backward." Shams-Doha seems to reference both the changed possibilities for women in the modern era but also the emergence of conservative tendencies that would seek to re-sequester women as subject to male control. As Sidi Ahmed incants a line from the Qur'an in support of these sentiments, Shams-Doha teases him lovingly, pronouncing with mock gravitas, "Ah, if only all men were like Sidi Ahmed!"

This scene gives context to a later one in the lobby of the theater where this younger generation of liberated Moroccans gathers. The cinema is a space of liberty and freedom of expression for Larbi, Khadija, Shams-Doha, and Aouicha, who come together after a screening. This scene, too, turns on the importance of women's freedom and contribution to society. Larbi descends from the balcony with his friend Ouahrani and, as I described in chapter 3, they pause to look at the Egyptian film posters lining the walls. They then move from the stairs to a conversation with Khadija, who works at the theater and recounts a short story of being kidnapped as a child and adopted into a Tangier family. Khadija later meets Shams-Doha and the two discuss the latest fashions and the stockings that Shams-Doha has brought back from Paris, before they're joined by Aouicha to discuss her problems with her husband. Unlike Lalla Alia, these women pride themselves on their fashionableness and enjoy their freedom of movement and expression.

In these scenes, Smihi visualizes some of the real debates and movements around the status of women in Morocco at that time. The nationalists influenced not only the practice of veiling and women's clothing, but women's education, too. Mernissi's memoir attributes the arc of her life to the possibility of a secular education for girls, something the nationalists made possible. In this they were supported by two religious authorities of the al-Qarawiyyin Mosque, Mohammed al-Fassi and Moulay Belarbi Alaoui. Mernissi thus moved from a Qur'anic school to a secular one "where girls learned mathematics, foreign languages, and geography, often were taught by male teachers, and played gymnastics in shorts."[14] This is the kind of world that Shams-Doha envisages on the rooftop, and the kind that Sidi Ahmed's gentle ways seem to also allow for. The younger women in Mernissi's memoir longed to be like Mrs. Bennis, who wore a jellaba in the medina but rode in an Oldsmobile unveiled when in the *ville nouvelle*. And her mother wanted her to be like the princess Lalla Aïcha who, as *Girls and Swallows* recounts, was a role model for young women who saw the possibility of dressing in modern clothes, dispensing with the veil, and accessing a kind of bilingual and bicultural existence, both European and Moroccan. While some, like Mernissi's own father, saw things like cigarettes and chewing gum as accoutrements of US culture brought by the Americans in Casablanca, others, like Sidi Ahmed in the trilogy, model tolerance and the ability of women to find their own place in the world.[15]

Smihi's films thus visualize many locations and flash points for these debates: the movie theater, the bodies and clothing of women, schools, the home. Such debates were not occurring only in Morocco, of course. The Nahda reformers had much to say about the subject of women, and contemporary Arab feminists have produced compelling analyses of the Nahda debates and the place of women's liberation within them. Whereas Qasim Amin's *Tahrir al-mara'a* (Liberation of Women, 1899) is often cited as a key text of the Nahda period, his book contributed to an already lively debate about women's rights, as Marilyn Booth has pointed out. By the time of Amin's book, Booth writes, "female intellectuals like 'A'isha Taymur, Zaynab Fawwaz, and Maryam Makariyus were already writing on these topics, as were women in Turkey, while leading male intellectuals and bureaucrats such as Butrus al-Bustani in Ottoman Syria, Namik Kemal in the Ottoman capital, and Rifa'a Rafi' al-Tahtawi and 'Ali Mubarak in Egypt had been publicly encouraging the formal, institutional schooling of female children since the 1840s."[16] Other feminist authors like Hoda Elsadda have produced nuanced critiques of Amin while also highlighting previously overlooked contributions by women of the Nahda.[17] Elsadda and others have thus illuminated how discourses of nationalism, modernization, and Westernization intersected with Islamic and non-Islamic positions furthered by Arab women.[18] Smihi's films thus reference debates with significant precedents in Morocco and across the region, and recognize the longevity of feminist issues there.

The trilogy again picks up the question of women's liberation in its third installment. In *The Sorrows of a Young Tangerian*, the younger generation of women, Larbi's peers at the age of high school and university, are leftist activists. One of the film's most passionate speeches in favor of dissent and revolution comes from Malika, one of Larbi's high school friends. As they all meet at the abandoned house in Perdicaris Park in the hills above Tangier, the young men of the group discuss revolutionary strategy on one side of the house. On the other, Malika discusses her activism with her French teacher, Florence. Florence—fulfilling the role that Smihi recalls his own, leftist teachers in Tangier playing—encourages her nascent activism, saying she should never give up her fight even though Malika, upset and despondent at the magnitude of the task, seems to waver.[19] In the next scene, the young men debate Jean-Paul Sartre, Naguib Mahfouz, and Paris before discussing the arrest of their colleagues in the large Moroccan cities, but shortly after, we find Malika arguing with her cousin. While her cousin appears to call for a slow and methodical approach to political change in the country ("a little patience, a little organization"), Malika cries out angrily, "Tradition, feudalism, averting eyes, kissing hands: it's over! We're getting rid of it all to start over.... We're here to fight, not just to get our university bursaries. . . . What we want is freedom of expression! To think, to think! Do you know what that means?" She ends by telling her cousin that it's too late for delay; a general strike has been called. The film gently mocks the militancy of Malika's group as they walk in lockstep to and from the house at the beginning and end of the scene. Yet at the same time it shows a generation of young women in the period evoked (the 1960s, after independence but during the time of the repressive postcolonial government) organizing and leading the leftist cause, unveiled, undaunted, determined.[20]

Smihi's interest in the position of women in public life is not unique to the Tangier trilogy. *The Lady from Cairo* (1991) is built around a central female character, Amina, who gives up her rural lifestyle to become a star in Cairo's film and entertainment industry. The title pays homage to Orson Welles's *The Lady from Shanghai* (1947) and, if the plots have little in common, Rita Hayworth's fame and abilities as a star who danced and was effectively created in Hollywood (with a changed name and a new hairline) are taken up in Smihi's narrative. Amina is played by Yousra, herself an Egyptian star who has appeared in many films, including those of Youssef Chahine (*Alexandria Again and Forever* [1990]; *The Emigrant* [1994]), Yousry Nasrallah (*Mercedes* [1993]), and Marwan Hamed (*The Yacoubian Building* [2006]). Smihi frames Amina's story as the narrative of a young woman enchanted by dreams of fame, determined to escape her provincial past but running headlong into the prejudices and obstacles of a patriarchal society and an oppressive industry. We first see Amina in her Nile village surroundings, working in the fields and carrying a sheaf of sugarcane on her head, and then with a blind old *sheikh* (respected village elder) who knew her father (a singer and fighter in the 1956 campaign for the Suez Canal) and encourages her singing ambitions. Telling him that she wants to be a star like Shadia or Leila Mourad, Amina gets a glimpse of her future lifestyle when she observes, from the sidelines, a garden party held in Luxor (close to her village). Entranced by the city and the elegant party with its many staff and well-dressed guests, she meets a producer who will later become her manager and lover in Cairo. After her brother, Yahia, a political poet and intending revolutionary, goes to Cairo without her, Amina decides to follow her own path while searching for him.

Smihi transitions from the village to Cairo in a classical manner, with a shot of a train and a montage of Cairene scenes, anchored by a voice-over in which Amina presents her journey as "the adventure of a single woman who sought to spread the voice of her *sheikh* and his far-off village, attracted by some dream that guided her way . . . the dream of freedom." Her journey is framed as one of independence and promise. Her story as the film tells it, however, is one of constant sexism and exploitation: from the revolutionaries she encounters, including her brother, and from the many men around the industry whom she meets in her quest for stardom. Smihi manages to maintain a doubled perspective: on the one hand, the film demonstrates the price Amina pays as a woman in Egypt's entertainment industry, yet the film maintains her story at its center and never insinuates that she is fallen or immoral, or should be ashamed of her sexual desires. Back in her village, her brother had already scoffed that there is no role for women in his revolution and dismisses her aspirations as "women's nonsense." And once she reaches Cairo, she finds herself prey to the sexual advances and ulterior motives of those around her. While sitting with a female friend by the river, for example, Amina encounters Abdessatar, the *pasha* (as she refers to him) or upper-class gentleman whom she met briefly in Luxor in an earlier scene (where he was taken with her humble origins and beauty). She expresses her love of music and her desire to learn to sing and act in movies, and Abdessatar suggests that he has connections and can help her, but only if she comes to his mansion to audition. Despite the hour, and against the advice of her friend, the naive and intrigued Amina agrees. When they arrive, he quickly pours her a stiff drink, beckons her to sit with him, and suggests the audition can wait. Despite her sheltered background, however, Amina is clever in handling his advances. Turning down his suggestion of a song by Shadia or Leila Mourad, she instead sings him a verse by her beloved village *sheikh* and resists his subsequent sexual advances. When he promises to make her a star, she holds out the possibility of sex only if he marries her and agrees to help her locate her brother and find him a job.

The theme of seduction is common to many Egyptian films; Viola Shafik cites one account that more than 50 percent of films in 1942 and 1943 included a female character who was either raped or seduced. Some of these roles were played by Amina's idols like Leila Mourad, and according to Shafik many films represented seduction and sexual exploitation as a classed phenomenon in which working-class characters like Mourad's were sexually abused by upper-class characters, as in *Fate's Stroke* (Darbit al-qadar, dir. Youssef Wahby, 1947).[21] Thus the theme of a young woman fighting off a sexually predatory older, richer man (like the *pasha*, later her husband) was common, and Smihi references this phenomenon quite explicitly in his narrative.

Moreover, in continuing to show the degree to which Amina is manipulated by the men around her, *The Lady from Cairo* also references the many narratives that feature women who become or are assumed to be prostitutes. Such was the case with many of the starring roles played by Hind Rostom, who was often, as Jean Said Makdisi comments, portrayed as "a victim of her own sexuality."[22] As Nargis in *Struggle on the Nile* (dir. ʿAtef Salem, 1959) she works for a gang of criminals to seduce and dupe the gullible Musahib (played by Omar Sharif) while falling in love with Mujahed (Rushdy Abaza). She is portrayed as sexually aggressive, provocative, and deceptive, and is killed at the end of the film, in a long fight sequence, by a blow to the head meant for Mujahed. The narrative thus punishes her for her infidelity, while the wronged Mujahed survives and the innocent Musahib gets to go home to his family with the money she was sent to steal. In *Beginning and End* (dir. Salah Abu Seif, 1960) Rostom is a prostitute who has come from poverty, and in *Shafiqa the Copt* (Shafiqa al-qibtiyya, dir. Hasan al-Imam, 1963) a fallen woman with a drug habit. Whether symbolically punished in death or suicide (the latter is the fate of Rostom's character in *Beginning and End*) or redeemed from prostitution with a slap (as with Soad Hosni's titular character in *Take Care of Zuzu* [dir. Hasan al-Imam, 1972]), characters like Hosni's and Rostom's often fall into what Shafik has termed the "virgin-whore dichotomy, visualized through fallen women, prostitutes, or belly dancers."[23] While at times their sexualized performances (like Rostom's first appearance as a provocative folk dancer in *Struggle on the Nile* or Samia Gamal's belly dance in *A Glass and a Cigarette* [1955]) could be read against the grain as celebrations of female sexuality, their characters are nonetheless punished in the narrative.

Smihi's film, then, places Amina within this legacy of exploitation and presumed sexual degeneracy, but it changes the terms by refusing to punish its heroine for her sexuality. In one scene she is taken for a prostitute; having begged her husband for the chance to work, he suggests she perform at Hamdoune's, a cabaret club in Cairo. She is taken aback at the connotations of cabaret, but he angrily replies that Zsa Zsa Gabor got her start at clubs in Paris, and in the next scene we see her there, waiting her turn to sing as a popular older singer dances and flirts with her and Abdessatar smokes and gambles with his friends at a nearby table, oblivious to her discomfort. One patron mistakes her for a prostitute and asks her to his table, a suggestion that provokes her husband's ire. At the end of the film, her brother also insults her as "a prostitute who should be stoned." But while these characters make such sexual insinuations, the film presents her as sexually independent and Smihi's narrative does not punish its character for her desires. Rather, it presents her sexuality as integral to the story of her attempt to succeed and survive in the industry. Having achieved some success later in the film, we see her eye up a soccer player in a televised match she's watching from her bed after an argument with Abdessatar. In the very next shot, the player is riding with her in a sports car along the corniche in Alexandria; the film puts her in the driver's seat of a sexual affair with a famous soccer star. Laughing about the private detective who follows them, Amina suggests that, seeing that she is now a "big star," there is little Abdessatar can do to prevent her pursuing her own desires, and the film is explicit about the sexual freedom and independence of this new relationship. In the next scene she flirts with her bare-chested star on the beach, allowing him to embrace her. The film continues to present her as in control of her sexual desire even as the relationship sours. Later, she and the soccer player eat and drink together at a restaurant as patrons recognize her from television. They sing and dance drunkenly and passionately, but she becomes frustrated at his arrogance, and when he probes and insists that he has a right to know all her secrets, she calls him an animal and leaves in a display of disgust.

The film's presentation of her as an assertive sexual being, and its refusal to cast her in the terms that its male characters do, signifies a break with the representational patterns of the Egyptian cinema whose conventions Smihi references. Amina's independence and commitment to personal freedom makes her an unusual female character in Egyptian cinema. In keeping with the bifocal critique of Smihi's films—critiquing masculinity while also offering new possibilities for the representation of femininity—the film builds a picture of the consistent obstacles to that freedom. Abdessatar treats her as chattel, and his low opinion of her talents ("Darling, you are a star just by being my wife!") is evident. Omar, the journalist-cum-promoter whom she befriends, also becomes part of the industrial machine that the film critiques. In one early scene, during her apprenticeship, Smihi places Amina at the center of a wide shot in which Omar and Abdessatar talk across her about her progress and her name, which her husband says reminds him of "a housemaid, a bread oven, kitchen, dishrags." They assign her a new stage name and place her under the supervision of Omar, who creates publicity for her, insisting (against her protests) that "stars have to have an extraordinary life" and that he will be "enhancing" and "packaging" her image.

In a final scene of resistance to such manipulation, Smihi situates Amina in defiant relation to all the men in her life who have oppressed her. Yahia, Amina's brother, is dead by this point, attacked by his fundamentalist associates, but somewhat comically, the others (Abdessatar, Omar, the detective, and the soccer player) arrive too late to stop Amina from boarding a plane and are left to fume jealously at one another in the departures lobby. As we cut back to her, on the plane and waiting to take off, she muses in another voice-over, "I'll need some distance.... Conquering freedom is not easy." The film then constructs a series of sound flashbacks as she retrieves the castanets from her bag and we hear her, first, back in the village with her old *sheikh*, then being renamed Gouhara by Omar and Abdessatar. As we hear her protest, "Why don't you like the name Amina?" Smihi freezes the frame on her face (fig. 46). The film thus ends (in the manner of François Truffaut's *The 400 Blows* [Les quatre cents coups, 1959]) on an ambiguous note that intimates that the "Lady from Cairo" may not ever fully achieve the independence she seeks. On the one hand, it seems clear-eyed about the inability of a woman like Amina ever to achieve freedom in a patriarchal industry that wishes to exploit her and in a patriarchal society in which men devalue her. Yet on the other hand, despite this seemingly negative ending, the film presents its own compelling portrait of a woman who refuses to acquiesce to these conditions. In presenting her freedom as

FIGURE 46. *The Lady from Cairo*, 1991, ends with a freeze-frame recalling François Truffaut's *The 400 Blows*, 1959, before fading to black.

nonnegotiable, Smihi issues a call not just for the kind of public role that women might play in the world, but also for the sexual freedom that Amina attempts to retain for herself.

SEXUALITY AND DESIRE

Smihi's filmic investigations of gendered subjectivities are always engaged with matters of sex, sexuality, and sexual desire. In this respect, his work resembles more the films of his peers in Tunisia where, as Robert Lang points out, questions of sexuality have often been addressed explicitly in feature-length narrative fictions. Lang argues that "some of the Tunisian cinema's singularity can be found in its willingness—unusual in contemporary Arab societies—to present the allegory of the embattled situation of the public third-world culture and society in the private, individual terms of sexuality."[24] Smihi tends to avoid allegory, but his films do offer an exceptionally focused critique of gender and sexuality. His dedication to these issues throughout his career has not thus far provoked the public controversies in Morocco that films like *Much Loved* (dir. Nabil Ayouch, 2015) or *Marock* (dir. Leila Marrakchi, 2006) have. But I argue that we cannot understand the roots of these more commercially oriented films, which use melodrama to make visible such issues in their narratives, without Smihi's more modernist approach. His films historicize and investigate the issues that occupy the more recent films by associating them with broader histories of Arab thought and modernity.

In *After the American Century* (2016), Brian T. Edwards offers a compelling account of the ways that sexuality has entered the public cultural sphere in Morocco, focusing in particular on the controversies surrounding *Marock* and the literary work of Abdellah Taïa, and recent scholarly writing on cinema and literature has paid increasing attention to questions of nonnormative sexualities in the Maghrib.[25] Such developments are helpful in disaggregating gender from an exclusive focus on the relationship between women, Islam, and nation, something that has tended to preoccupy most criticism on Moroccan cinema to the exclusion of comprehensive debate on sexuality. Whether in extensive treatments like Florence Martin's book on Maghribi women filmmakers, *Screens and Veils* (2011), or in chapters within larger works like Valérie Orlando's focus on "feminine lenses" in *Screening Morocco* (2011), many writers have focused more on the (welcome) fact of Moroccan women's active participation in the sphere of filmmaking, or on their representations of Maghribi women's histories, than on sex and sexuality.[26] Suzanne Gauch, for example, is the only critic to discuss the butch lesbian coding of the character of Bahia in Farida Benlyazid's *Door to the Sky* (1989), a film that has attracted considerable critical attention. Gauch's observation complicates the film's portrayal of difference between French and Moroccan identities. She also focuses part of her discussion of *Bedwin Hacker* (dir. Nadia El Fani, 2003) around the bisexuality of the film's lead character.[27] Here I join with Gauch and Lang to demonstrate the value in also attending to sexuality in the discussion of Maghribi cinema, and I show how Smihi's work is critical to that enterprise.

Smihi's films pose questions of sexuality and sexual desire insistently, demonstrating not only that those questions are intertwined with gender but also that they have long histories in the contexts of Arab and North African politics and public and private life. The Tangier trilogy quite consciously positions sex and sexual desire at the heart of everyday life in Tangier and, following the characters of Larbi and those around him, addresses the queer qualities of childhood and teenage sexuality and desire across masculinity and femininity. Larbi's desires are often inchoate, unformed, and sometimes not easily assimilated into stable or normative adult models. In what follows, then, I read the ambiguities of childhood, along with the registers of teen and adult sexualities, as part of a queer representation of Tangerian and Arab life. This queer reading does not turn only on overt expressions of same-sex desire; it also attends to sexual and gendered expressions that are often freer and more utopian than compulsory heterosexuality would allow. As the films show the institutional and political restraints that such regimes of heterosexuality impose, they also advocate for desires and possibilities that might make new, freer, queerer worlds.

Several scenes in *A Muslim Childhood* evoke an intense mixture of queer experimentation and intimacy, interwoven with the threat or experience of violence. Larbi often plays and jousts with a group of boys from the *hawma* (roughly, the hood), a part of the medina the voice-over describes as "closed," marked by everyday violence and the tragedy of poverty. On one occasion, Larbi and another friend leave those

FIGURE 47. Larbi's friend sits queerly on a wall in the Tangier casbah in *A Muslim Childhood*, 2005.

mean streets and walk out to an overlook at the casbah, the highest point of the medina (a casbah is usually the site of a defensive fortress). As the boys sit together, the voice-over intimates that amid the "violence and obscenity" of their lives, Larbi and his friends sought out spaces of tranquility and privacy around the city and that this garden, overlooking the straits of Gibraltar, was one such sanctuary. We are told as well that it was marked by "guilty loves." As they walk together, Larbi's friend touches and teases him and Larbi pushes him away, and we see the two of them in long shot approaching the garden and its wall. After a cut, we see the friend seated on the wall in a performatively feminine way, his legs crossed and a flower behind one ear, while he flamboyantly smokes and sings like a female Egyptian star (fig. 47). Cutting to Larbi, the camera shows him blowing petals from a thistle and singing a love song; in the next shot, the two wear bandannas over their faces like bank robbers and play a game, trading insults. Walking back the way they came, they continue the game of touching and shoving, and in a subsequent shot, as they begin to mount the steps of a street filled with prostitutes, Larbi's friend grabs him and kisses his ear. This kind of flirtation, bound up with Larbi's simultaneous disavowal and solicitation of such intimacy, pushing and shoving his friend, continues through the scene. Smihi makes it clear, then, that Larbi's experience of sexuality in this film is dispersed across multiple objects and sentiments. It is sensory, concerned with scents and with touch (as we will see further below), and it is foundationally, thoroughly queer.

A scene in *Girls and Swallows* continues the interest in gender performativity. On the rooftop of the family's home in the medina, Rabea and her friend Batoul, dressed in stylish European clothes—Rabea in a knee-length skirt with a white blouse and red

FIGURE 48. Larbi, wearing Rabea's scarf and lipstick, dances to Paul Anka on a Tangier rooftop in *Girls and Swallows*, 2008.

scarf, Batoul in a red polka-dot blouse, both with hair exposed and a little cleavage visible—pore over a fashion magazine together. We see close-ups of the page they look at and attentively trace with their fingers: a bra and a slip by a French brand. Soon after Larbi arrives, Batoul leaves and Rabea and Larbi talk. He asks to borrow her scarf, which he knots around his neck, and she offers to put lipstick on him. Nervous at first, Larbi assents to the makeup, and Rabea paints his lips bright red as the two laugh and dance together to a Paul Anka song, "You Are My Destiny," which is mixed up loud in the soundtrack. The scene has a delightfully campy quality, and its performance of a slippery kind of gender identification as part of Larbi's flirtation with Rabea feminizes him here, as it does his friend in *A Muslim Childhood* (fig. 48).

We might be tempted, in these scenes of nascent queer childhood, just as in the scenes of hammams or all-female spaces in *44, or Tales of the Night*, to detect the influence of an Orientalism that ascribes to its "Orient" the qualities of polymorphous perversity, sensuality, or same-sex eroticism that Smihi's scenes construct. Edward Said's *Orientalism* (1978) described the kind of sexualized vision of the Arab world that European and US writers from Gustave Flaubert to Richard Francis Burton to André Gide and many others pursued in their writing; the French tradition of Orientalist tableaux, including the one that graced the cover of the Vintage paperback edition of Said's book (Jean-Léon Gérôme's *The Snake Charmer* [c. 1879]), continued that fantasy.[28] The French *cinéma colonial* constructed fantasies of feminine licentiousness and homoeroticism with films like *Atlantis* (*L'Atlantide*, dir. Jacques Feyder, 1921) and *Pépé le Moko* (dir. Julien Duvivier, 1937), and in Hollywood Josef von Sternberg cited this kind of fetishized aesthetic in *Morocco* (1930). Yet just as postcolonial scholars have pointed to the ways in which such visions lend themselves also to oppositional readings,[29] queer theorists of non-Western locations have also shown how such visions paradoxically offer insights into non-Western constructions of sexuality that resist the identity categories so easily utilized in the West. Jarrod Hayes writes, "The production of the Orient as queer marked it as a site of sexual resistance to the institution of heterosexuality as a compulsory regime in the West."[30] We might also add "and of homonormativity," since Joseph A. Massad and others have shown that same-sex sexual practices in the Arab or Muslim worlds cannot be assumed to neatly follow the identity categories of Euro-American modernity.[31] Visions of a queer Orient, then, serve multiple possibilities: first, they may in fact capture something that the Orientalists, often disillusioned with the West's own strictures, got "right," something outside normative models of sexual identity. We have already sensed Smihi's appreciation of that seemingly paradoxical possibility in his citation of films like *Morocco* or *The Man Who Knew Too Much* (1956), or his reading of Henri Matisse's paintings. But second, there is the possibility that Orientalist visions might also be available for deployment by artists concerned to affirm queer possibility in the face of the aggressive heterosexualized discourses, often sanctioned by official religion and state, that would wish to eradicate them.[32]

What this means, then, is that Smihi's depiction of some of the queer aspects of Moroccan life emerges from a complex layering of his own experience and his intellectual sensibilities. Growing up in a "queer Tangier," he saw the neighborhood's Spanish drag queens, the *mariquitas*, coming and going with complete freedom from a hammam run by a Sephardic Jewish woman, Rica, just a stone's throw from Smihi's family home.[33] As Brian T. Edwards has argued, queer writers like Jean Genet and Paul Bowles also profited from and extended Tangier's cosmopolitan queer reputation.[34] But far from mere personal reminiscence, Smihi's films demonstrate his respect for the way that polymorphous perversity (in his terms, drawing on Freud) or queerness (in mine) exists to unsettle the repressively heterosexual discourse of religion and the state. The films represent the existence of such desires in Maghribi male subjects who might simultaneously desire the practices or identifications they so violently repress. The nascent queer desire between the boys of *A Muslim Childhood*, however natural and unremarkable it might seem, is always entangled with the threat of violence. After a scene at the beach in which Larbi hits his own brother for annoying him and refusing to leave, the group of boys turns on another of its members (one whom Larbi harassed earlier), pushing him to the ground and beating him. A series of title cards spells out the dangerous mix of homoeroticism and homophobic violence that underpins all such encounters: "The kids of the neighborhood were terrorized at the idea of being raped, penetrated, or soiled. There was no insult more serious, more degrading, than being called *zamel*. Queer. Pansy. Faggot. A kid who took it up the arse was considered to be humiliated, a submissive, a weakling that from now on anyone could humiliate. It was an attack. The children of the neighborhood fought to the death to be rid of that suspicion." The scene is strikingly similar to the environment that Moroccan writer Abdellah Taïa has described of his own boyhood in Salé. Taïa's call in 2012 for sexual freedom to be part of the then-hopeful uprisings of the "Arab Spring" stems from his recollection of being the effeminate *zamel* preyed upon by other men, who disavowed their interest in boys but were happy to use him for their pleasure.[35] Such violence between men also emerges in Hamid Benani's film *Traces* (1970), as an all-male group turns on one of its own, tying him to a tree, stripping him to the waist, and flogging him while threatening him with a snake; earlier, they swam together in a river after having sex with a masked woman.[36] The homoerotics of the flogging scene are not particularly emphasized, but the narrative builds on the possibility that these acts of shared male bonding (sex with a woman, swimming, violence toward others) exist on a continuum with a kind of sexualized violence toward one another. These scenarios, of course, register the existence of the recognizably violent line between homosociality and homosexuality analyzed so incisively by Eve Kosofsky Sedgwick, among others, along with its concomitant prohibitions against passive anal sex.[37] To be fucked in *A Muslim Childhood* is the ultimate crime and signifies the ultimate loss of manhood; the film shows a world in which it could never yet be pleasurable.

Indeed, rape by another man is what tortures Farfat, the young protagonist of Nouri Bouzid's *Man of Ashes* (L'homme des cendres, 1986), who internalizes the violence of his abuse as a child at the hands of Ameur, the carpenter to whom he was apprenticed and who raped him. Farfat scrawls his own self-directed homophobic graffiti ("Farfat is not a man") around the walls of the neighborhood, and it is not until he kills Ameur in a rage at the end, before killing himself, that he is freed of his past and its implications for his masculinity. The violence to which he is subjected is wholly transformed into guilt and shame but, as Robert Lang's incisive reading points out, it is not the only kind of violence he experiences. Lang, drawing on the filmmaker's extensive commentary on this issue, argues that Bouzid is the preeminent Tunisian chronicler of the logic by which Arab Muslim masculinities are formed, one in which the threat of castration, enacted in the violence of circumcision, is redoubled in the threat of anal rape but also in the necessity to ascend to normative heterosexuality expressed in marriage and fatherhood (thus enacting the same traumas on a son).[38] *Man of Ashes* dramatizes all of these social imperatives while showing the subjective cost of the prohibition against homosexuality. Larbi, too, is positioned in close proximity to these violent possibilities, and in the scene above it is the threat of being identified as a *zamel* that animates his actions. While this time it is the other boy who is beaten, the scene ends with Larbi taunted and isolated from the group, walking alone on the beach. Thus the film situates him in a sexual terrain that is mapped onto the city of Tangier itself: his neighbors like Aouicha and the prostitutes in the street situate him within heterosexual relations while, simultaneously, his own desires also exist within the homosociality and repressed queer desire of the *hawma* and his male friends.

This same alternation between the possibilities of queer sex and the prohibition against it subtends one of the final scenes in *A Muslim Childhood*. Larbi and his sickly friend, Ouahrani, have gone to the theater to see an Egyptian film playing there. The scene opens in the dark of the cinema, with Khadija ushering in a middle-aged man wearing a fez. The voice-over coincides with him taking his seat: "The cinema was also a place of danger, and one day Larbi encountered [*a rencontré*] death there." The scene, as we shall see, plays with the twofold sense of the verb *rencontrer*: literally, it can mean both "to meet" or "to encounter." The film playing is *Fatma* (dir. Ahmed Badrakhan, 1947), in which Umm Kulthum sings "Ha aqablu bukra" (I Will Meet Him Tomorrow). As she sings, off-screen for us, we see this man continually glancing to his right and we cut to Larbi, in medium close-up, who is seated alone in the direction of the eyeline. The man moves to sit next to him and then, as the camera reframes with a tilt down Larbi's body, stretches out his hand to place it on Larbi's bare knee, which is exposed by his short pants. Larbi's reaction is instant: in a fraction of a second he slaps at him, knocking off his fez, and exits the frame. The camera holds on the man sitting still as if nothing has happened.

Clearly, with the narrator's comment about "meeting death" in the theater, the voice-over extends the possibility that this expression of sexual desire is tantamount to death for Larbi. Such an equation is not espoused by the film itself, however, which rather expresses the logic of Moroccan society of the time—one similar to that which Lang described with respect to Bouzid and Tunisian cinema and society. For Larbi, whose own desires seem queerly flexible, to be recognized as the *zamel* (or to be taken advantage of by an adult) was, as we've already seen, a scenario tantamount to death. Nevertheless, in *listening* to the sequence, we recognize that the combination of voice-over and song makes a more literal association, too. The voice-over recounts that this was the last time Larbi was to see Ouahrani and Khadija, and that Ouahrani died the next day from tuberculosis. Umm Kulthum's song suggests that the meeting that will take place *bukra* (tomorrow) is, indeed, with (Ouahrani's) death. Even in this fantastic and sacred space of the theater, then, crucible of illicit desires both on- and off-screen, Larbi is never far from illness and mortality.

Continuing the trilogy's depiction of the omnipresent yet covert existence of queer sex, *Girls and Swallows* hints that Larbi may have had sex with the Spanish tailor whom he visits for a suit fitting. In the first of two scenes, the tailor offers to measure Larbi, then closes the window shutters, one after the other. As he turns toward Larbi, there is a long and awkward silence as the two stand motionless, looking at each other, before the film cuts to Larbi at the overlook on the Boulevard Pasteur, facing the Tangier medina, the Mediterranean, and Spain beyond. The ellipsis is ambiguous but suggestive, containing the possibility of sex that the narrative cannot make explicit. After the interlude overlooking the port, the film cuts back to the tailor's rooms again, as Larbi returns (after an unspecified time) to try on the suit. Promising that he will come to see Juan again (the tailor replies, "with pleasure"), Larbi then asks him a favor: he'd like to come with his neighbor, Aouicha. Juan quickly rejects his suggestion: "I want no women here . . . no-one but us two . . . don't ask me that!" Larbi protests that Juan's house is large and keeps repeating his question, but Juan is insistent.

Leaving aside Larbi's overinflated sense of his chances with Aouicha (who, as on many other occasions, laughingly sends him packing in the next scene), it is clear that Larbi here manages to confuse sexual encounters with Juan with the prospect of a larger domain of pleasure: if Juan is evidently a queer libertine, then why not bring a woman, too! For the Larbi of *Girls and Swallows*, it appears, desire is not limited to a particular gender but is rather something more untethered, where the accessibility of homosexual sex might signal the prospect of more and other possibilities. Such is not the case for Juan: while his sexual desire is not stigmatized by the film, it is contained within an adult homosocial world to which women do not have access. But for Larbi (especially the younger Larbi of *A Muslim Childhood*), the queer or polymorphous pleasures of childhood extend into the realm of fetishism. *A Muslim Childhood*, for example, makes Larbi's fascination with Aouicha into an important part of the narrative of sexuality that the film constructs. Aouicha is first shown on the roof of her house, adjoining Larbi's, painting her toenails. Climbing to the terraces, which as we know were female spaces, Larbi watches her in a widely framed point-of-view shot from a high angle before the camera cuts closer into a medium shot, and finally a close-up of Aouicha's pedicured toes. Larbi's transgressive gaze here should remind us of the Freudian account of fetishism: disavowing the fact of the mother's castration while arresting his attention onto a proximate substitute.[39] This fetishism is further developed, too: having cleared away the boys who hang around her doorway and entered her house with an anonymous man, Aouicha later emerges on her own. She sits on the step with the doe-eyed Larbi and asks him to take her stiletto-heeled shoes to be mended (fig. 49). He at first refuses, but after she insists and gives him a kiss on the head, he agrees. In the next scene, the camera pans around an elevated lookout at the casbah (where he previously sat with his flower-adorned friend) and finds Larbi in a medium long shot, sitting on a wall, holding Aouicha's shoes to his face and smelling them. There is a cut to a close-up, and we see him slowly and deliberately sniff and kiss one and then the other, moving back and forth between them as if to drink in their scent.

Such instances are not isolated to *A Muslim Childhood*. An even bolder example occurs in the third film of the trilogy. In *The Sorrows of a Young Tangerian*, we follow Larbi's unrequited love for his French teacher, Muriel, whom he invites to his home and who is in love with a Moroccan man who eventually leaves her (because he can't marry a Christian). Muriel makes plans to leave, but first asks Larbi (in a scene in which he stammeringly tries to confess his love for her) to look after a

FIGURE 49. Aouicha asks Larbi to take her shoes to be mended in *A Muslim Childhood*, 2005.

suitcase that she can't immediately take along. Subsequently, an extremely long take set in a bedroom (Muriel's, we assume) begins with non-diegetic classical piano music in an allegro movement that stops dramatically as Larbi snaps the clasps on Muriel's valise. The scene continues in an awkward silence, without music, for two minutes, the only sounds being the rustle of Muriel's clothing as Larbi takes it, piece by piece, out of the suitcase. Bringing each item to his face, he sensuously moves it around and inhales its scent—a pair of gloves, then a shirt, a slip or nightgown, and finally stockings—before lying down to let his entire head fall into the assembled clothes in the suitcase (fig. 50). In all these scenes, Smihi boldly presents elements of sexual desire that are intensely private, even perverse, and makes them part of a queerly felt childhood and adolescence. It is significant that they attach to the films' protagonist, since even though the films also depict the promise of sexual liberation as political liberation, they remain skeptical of heroic male figures.

The Tangier trilogy certainly suggests that sexual desire and pleasure of all kinds might be necessary as part of a wider movement of liberation: liberation of women, national liberation from colonial rule, liberation from the repressions of a postcolonial state. Such prospects are developed at many moments *Girls and Swallows*, where desire is linked to prospects for political change and personal pleasure. The character of Uncle Hilal, Lalla Alia's brother, is important in this respect. With his arrival in the home, the erotic charge between Larbi and Rabea, established through the film, is complicated by her fascination with this man, an intellectual and a poet who speaks of love and liberation in the same breath. After a series of comic jealous encounters around the sleeping arrangements for his visit (Larbi

FIGURE 50. Left alone with Muriel's intimate apparel, Larbi drinks in her scent in a fetishistic moment in *The Sorrows of a Young Tangerian*, 2013.

doesn't want to share a room with Hilal, and Rabea is clearly infatuated with the visitor), Hilal ends up on the divan in the main parlor. Larbi gingerly creeps downstairs in his underwear to spy on him as he sleeps, only to find Rabea asleep on an intersecting side of the divan, their heads almost touching. As with the scene in Juan's tailor shop, the film leaves ambiguous whether they had sex or simply spent the night flirtatiously close, but Larbi is furious. The film links the erotic dynamic between Hilal and Rabea to his charisma as an intellectual and a political activist; in a later scene with Larbi, Hilal discusses nationalism, the Arabic language, and the work of Taha Hussein. Embodying the feminism of a Nahda reformer like Qasim Amin, Hilal suggests that Rabea will likely become stuck in an arranged marriage but that, with modernization and the work of leftists like him, the liberation of women will surely come.

The Sorrows of a Young Tangerian goes further in linking sexual pleasure and liberation with political liberation. It suggests that Larbi is somewhat left behind in his idealistic longing for a literary kind of love, the kind that manifests in his reading but that he is too shy to access in everyday life. His French teacher Florence is the one who most challenges him. Shortly after the key scene in which he renounces religion before his father, Larbi visits Florence's apartment. In her airy, light-filled salon is a messy divan strewn with cushions and side chairs draped with men's and women's clothing. As Larbi sits uncomfortably to the side in a suit jacket, his friend Othmane reclines on the opposite side of the room, shirt open to the waist, exposing his chest. Florence sits between them. Questioned by Florence regarding his views on love and whether he has a girlfriend, Larbi proclaims a seriousness of purpose that he thinks is lacking in those around him. But Florence insists that "*il y a du plaisir!*" (there's pleasure!) and insists to Larbi that "carnal love," as she calls it, also has a place in the world, while Othmane, for his part, speaks about the advantages of a "marriage of pleasure." The libertine views they express are not some Parisian imposition. They have a precedent in the Arabic literary culture that Smihi's bookish young protagonist so admires. Abu Nuwas's erotic wine poems offer a thoroughly open sexuality that is very often, but not always, homoerotic and always directed to pleasure. In a *qasida* (ode) evoking the poetry of the pre-Islamic period, Abu Nuwas writes of a wine-filled orgy:

> May the light-hearted libertine experience joy
> And an easy life and obtain the good things!
> May it rain upon a gathering of youths with whom I carouse,
> Among whom there is no idiocy!
> This one is for that one just as this one and this other are for that:
> A gathering all in order, its rope of union utterly intact.[40]

Abu Nuwas's orgy of this one with that one and all the others might exceed what Othmane and Florence have in mind, but with their calls for pleasure and their promise to buy beers (to celebrate the Algerian revolution) for this overly serious young philosopher, the libertines of *The Sorrows of a Young Tangerian* evoke a long Arab history of carnal pleasure.

Indeed, the evocation of Abu Nuwas in this context also points us back to Pasolini, whose *Arabian Nights* includes Abu Nuwas as a character who recites his hedonistic poems in the presence of Harun al-Rashid, the eighth-century Baghdadi caliph who is a staple of the stories. In the previous chapter, we saw how Smihi's films search for the kind of blasphemous possibility that characterized the work of Pasolini and Luis Buñuel; here, Pasolini's importance for Smihi derives from his treatment of sex, particularly in *Arabian Nights*, the third in his "trilogy of life" series. *Arabian Nights* celebrates the *jouissance* called for by Florence and Othmane. Throughout, sex is unrestrained, immodest, pansexual, and life affirming, as it was in Abu Nuwas's poetry. Pasolini depicted sexual pleasure as carrying political promise outside of the capitalist relations of property and marriage, and there is something of this utopian quality in Smihi's (more restrained, by necessity) depiction of sexual desire.[41] Whether in the queer gender play of the young Larbi and his friend, the varied sexual possibilities that exist both in the medina and the *ville nouvelle*, or the sense that the young revolutionaries of *The Sorrows of a Young Tangerian* care as much about getting laid as they do about revolution,[42] these films link the sexual to the political. Across the trilogy, Smihi dares not only to show the existence of queer and nonqueer practices and desires—a political act in itself in the current Moroccan environment of prohibition—but also to suggest that they can never be left out of the liberation the films call for.

This chapter has shown how Smihi's work has embedded issues of gender and sexuality within a broader critique of contemporary Arab and Moroccan society and within a longer history of diverse debates and practices in Arab culture. By isolating questions concerning the practice of space, the role of women and men in the public sphere, and the address of sexual desire, I have shown how the films defend against Orientalist and Islamophobic stereotypes of the Arab world while also mounting a staunch critique of the status quo. And in a queer reading of their approach to gender and sexual desire, I have shown how the films sound a cry for gendered and sexual freedoms of all kinds. In many respects, then, Smihi's representation of gender and sexuality complements and extends the critique of religion that I traced in the previous chapter. There, the films develop a secular perspective on the world that is built from a recognition of the Arab-Islamic, Jewish, Christian, and atheistic tendencies found across the region. Showing the possibilities for religious tolerance, the films nonetheless point toward a time when religion is no longer the prime axis of social or political life. In all these ways, the films demonstrate their participation in a continuation of the Nahda project, not as some kind of nostalgic return to discourses of the late nineteenth and early twentieth centuries, but as affirmation that the Nahda project has been an ongoing and compelling one for artists and writers ever since.

Smihi's oeuvre demonstrates precisely the sense that Tarek El-Ariss evokes when he writes: "Though the Nahda is usually associated with the nineteenth century, its legacy persists, as if something in it has not yet been accomplished or settled." El-Ariss's exploration of a "never actualized but always becoming Nahda" captures the way that Smihi's films, across the director's fifty-year career, consciously take up the movement's provocations in a contemporary moment—one in which struggles for freedom of many kinds are as urgent as ever before.[43] Smihi's interventions, I have argued throughout, take shape within a cinematic modernism that uses a complex engagement with realism, a radical approach to film sound, and a heterogeneous intertextuality to place Arab cinema firmly within world cinema. Resolutely tied to the local but actively engaging other horizons, Smihi's films reveal the role that Arab cinema and culture deserves in the histories and theories of modernity and modernism, and they evince a restless desire for cinema to help usher in new, freer ways to live.

NOTES

INTRODUCTION

1. For an account of ʿAbd al-Karim and the Rifian resistance to the Spanish and then the French see Susan Gilson Miller, *A History of Modern Morocco* (New York: Cambridge University Press, 2013), 104–11.

2. Sidi Ahmed ou Moussa, a sixteenth-century marabout, or Sufi saint, is widely associated with the tradition of acrobats and wandering singers and storytellers (his *ouled*, or, literally, boys) who formed part of the popular resistance to colonialism in Morocco. See Ahmed Bouanani, "An Introduction to Popular Moroccan Poetry," trans. Robyn Creswell, in *Souffles-Anfas: A Critical Anthology from the Moroccan Journal of Culture and Politics*, ed. Olivia C. Harrison and Teresa Villa-Ignacio (Stanford, CA: Stanford University Press, 2016), 46–55.

3. Amazigh people, sometimes referred to as Berber, are the indigenous inhabitants of Morocco and North Africa.

4. Jens Hanssen and Max Weiss, eds., *Arabic Thought beyond the Liberal Age: Towards an Intellectual History of the Nahda* (Cambridge, UK: Cambridge University Press, 2016), xvi. They attribute the concept of the Nahda as an archive to Nadia Bou Ali, "Collecting the Nation: Lexicography and National Pedagogy in *al-nahda al-ʿarabiyya*," in *Archives, Museums and Collecting Practices in the Modern Arab World*, ed. Sonja Mejcher-Atassi and John Pedro Schwartz (Surrey, UK: Ashgate, 2012), 33–56.

5. See for example Kamran Rastegar, *Literary Modernity between the Middle East and Europe: Textual Transactions in Nineteenth-Century Arabic, English, and Persian Literatures* (Oxon, UK, and New York: Routledge, 2007); Robyn Creswell, *City of Beginnings: Poetic Modernism in Beirut* (Princeton, NJ: Princeton University Press, 2019); Andrea Flores Khalil, *The Arab Avant-Garde: Experiments in North African Art and Literature*, Studies in African Literature (Westport, CT: Praeger, 2003); Stefan G. Meyer, *The Experimental Arabic Novel: Postcolonial Literary Modernism in the Levant* (Albany: State University of New York

Press, 2001). On modernism and music see Thomas Burkhalter, Kay Dickinson, and Benjamin J. Harbert, eds., *The Arab Avant-Garde: Music, Politics, Modernity* (Middletown, CT: Wesleyan University Press, 2013). On art see Anneka Lenssen, Sarah A. Rogers, and Nada M. Shabout, eds., *Modern Art in the Arab World: Primary Documents* (New York: Museum of Modern Art, 2018).

6. Stephanie Dennison and Song Hwee Lim make the case for a discipline of "world cinema" to do exactly that in their introduction to *Remapping World Cinema: Identity, Culture and Politics in Film* (London: Wallflower, 2006), 6–9.

7. Lúcia Nagib, "Towards a Positive Definition of World Cinema," in *Remapping World Cinema*, 30–37.

8. Dudley Andrew, "An Atlas of World Cinema," in *Remapping World Cinema*, 19.

9. Here and throughout I use the term Maghrib (sometimes spelled Maghreb) to refer to North Africa generally. As a proper noun in Arabic, *al-Maghrib* is the official name for Morocco (and also means both "sunset" and "the West," or the place where the sun goes down). In French usage, the term *le Maghreb* usually refers only to Morocco, Algeria, and Tunisia—all sites of French interest and colonial control.

10. Muʾmin al-Smihi, *Hadith al-sinima* [Conversations about cinema] (Tangier: Siliki Ikhwan, 2005), 1:30.

11. See Miller, *A History of Modern Morocco*, 83–84, 88; Graham H. Stuart, *The International City of Tangier* (Stanford, CA: Stanford University Press, 1931); Rom Landau, *Portrait of Tangier* (London: Robert Hale, 1952).

12. One of the characteristics of the French protectorate in Morocco was that rather than taking over the *mudun* (plural of "medina"), the French built modern cities adjacent to them. For a discussion of these projects, in which French planners often conducted work that "was profoundly modern but also characterized by a deep respect for the traditional Moroccan building arts," see Miller, *A History of Modern Morocco*, 92–94.

13. The word *darija* simply means "dialect" in Arabic; it is used by Moroccans as a specific noun for the Moroccan dialect, which is a mixture of Arabic, French, and Tamazight languages.

14. Taha Hussein, *The Days: His Autobiography in Three Parts*, trans. E. H. Paxon, Hilary Wayment, and Kenneth Crag (Cairo: American University of Cairo Press, 1997).

15. Smihi, interview with the author, July 10, 2010, Tangier, hereafter "Smihi interview."

16. A discussion of these formative influences also appears in an essay Smihi wrote for an Egyptian research center during his Cairo sojourn: Moumen Smihi, "Un cinéaste marocain au Caire," *Égypte/Monde Arabe*, December 31, 1991, 49–62. This was later included as "Mythologies Arabes" [Arab mythologies], in *Écrire sur le cinéma* (Tangier: Slaïki Frères, 2006), 151–64.

17. The films' stories, discussed in more detail in the chapters that follow, are connected. *A Muslim Childhood* follows the experiences of the young Mohammed Larbi, around ten years old, growing up in the medina of Tangier in the early 1950s in a religious family, attending a French school, and gravitating to reading and cinema. *Girls and Swallows* picks up his story as a teenager, still living at home, and negotiating not only his sexual desires but the nationalist currents of the times as the fight against French occupation continues; the film is set across the moment of independence in 1956, which is announced in the film after we are shown the return of the exiled king Mohammed V. *The Sorrows of a Young Tangerian* is set

further into Larbi's teenage years after his family has moved into the *ville nouvelle*. In his final year of high school, Larbi shocks his family by renouncing religion and exploring a world beyond his family. While implicated in the radical politics of his friends, who fight the repressions of the postcolonial state, Larbi is still more fond of books and his teachers, especially his French teacher, Muriel. At the end of the film, he leaves Morocco to study in France.

18. Smihi interview. The relationship between Sartre, existentialism, and the Arab world is explored extensively in Yoav Di-Capua, *No Exit: Arab Existentialism, Jean-Paul Sartre, and Decolonization* (Chicago: University of Chicago Press, 2018).

19. Smihi interview.

20. Smihi describes this conversation in his essay "Paris, notre Mecque" [Paris, our Mecca], *Cinémaction* 56 (1990): 137.

21. Tazi became part of Smihi's intellectual and cultural circle in the Moroccan house whose members included Daniel Dayan, who also studied with Barthes at the l'Ecole Pratique des Hautes Etudes between 1965 and 1973, wrote a thesis on the film *Stagecoach* (dir. John Ford, 1939), and later wrote an influential article on point of view in cinema, "The Tutor Code of Classical Cinema," *Film Quarterly* 28, no. 1 (1974): 22–31, as well as other works on cinema and media; Hamid Berrada, the president-in-exile of UNEM (Union des étudiants du Maroc; the political Union of Moroccan Students) and later a prominent journalist whose daughter, the artist Yto Berrada, founded Cinémathèque de Tanger; and Hassan Hadj Nassar, a Marxist sociologist. Smihi, personal communication with the author, August 8, 2019.

22. Smihi interview. For other production details, including the information about the sum of money lent (approximately US$10,000 in 1975), see "Entretien avec Moumen Smihi. Chergui ou le silence violent" [Interview with Moumen Smihi. The East Wind or the violent silence]. With Amran El-Maleh. *Intégral*, no. 11 (1976): 32.

23. See Moumen Smihi, "Moumen Smihi et la distribution au Maroc: Le refus et le silence" [Moumen Smihi and distribution in Morocco: denial and silence], *Lamalif* 82 (1976): 31–35.

24. Practically speaking, some of these articles also provided him with small sums of money. Smihi had refused the route of most of his Moroccan predecessors, who upon graduation from IDHEC took jobs in the Centre cinématographique marocain. Working as salaried employees, they were allowed occasional license to work on their own films, but for the most part were state employees bound by the strictures that came with that position. In choosing the path of independence, Smihi also made his financial position more precarious.

25. Smihi interview.

26. Europe is most commonly cited as the point of engagement but, as Tarek El-Ariss demonstrates in a newly translated collection of Nahda writings, the traffic was transnational in multiple directions. Tarek El-Ariss, ed., *The Arab Renaissance: A Bilingual Anthology of the Nahda* (New York: Modern Language Association, 2018).

27. Adonis, *Introduction to Arab Poetics*, trans. Catherine Cobham (London: Saqi, 1990), 80, 81.

28. For an extensive treatment of Sartre's significance for Arab intellectuals see Di-Capua, *No Exit*.

29. Olivia C. Harrison and Teresa Villa-Ignacio, "Introduction: *Souffles-Anfas* for the New Millennium," in *Souffles-Anfas*, 1.

30. Harrison and Villa-Ignacio, "Introduction: *Souffles-Anfas* for the New Millennium," 5–6. The Mashriq is the Arabic term for the eastern part of the Arab world, comprising the area from Egypt to Iraq. Deriving from the verb *sharaqa* ("to rise," used for the sun), it refers to the place where the sun rises (i.e., the east), distinct from al-Maghrib, mentioned above, where it sets.

31. Harrison and Villa-Ignacio, "Introduction: *Souffles-Anfas* for the New Millennium," 4; Abdellatif Laâbi, "Realities and Dilemmas of National Culture I," trans. Olivia C. Harrison and Teresa Villa-Ignacio, in *Souffles-Anfas*, 61–73.

32. Abdelkebir Khatibi, "Double Criticism: The Decolonization of Arab Sociology," in *Contemporary North Africa: Issues of Development and Integration*, ed. Halim Barakat (Washington, DC: Center for Contemporary Arab Studies, Georgetown University, 1985), 9–19. See also Abdelkebir Khatibi, *Maghreb Pluriel* (Paris: Editions Denoël, 1983).

33. Smihi interview. See also Moumen Smihi, "Lettre du Maroc," *Cinématograph* 109 (April 1985): 26–27, republished as "Choc de cultures" [Culture shock], in *Écrire sur le cinéma*, 133–36; Smihi, "Paris, notre Mecque," 136–39.

34. Moumen Smihi, notes for a class presentation, University of California, Santa Cruz, 2007.

35. Moumen Smihi, "Deux rives" [Two sides] (1999), in *Écrire sur le cinéma*, 169–70.

36. Peter Limbrick, "Moumen Smihi's Tanjawi/Tangérois/Tangerian Cinema," *Third Text* 26, no. 4 (2012): 443–54.

37. On Tangier's historical role as a link see Daniel Rondeau, *Tanger* (Paris: Quai Voltaire, 1987).

38. Roy Armes, *New Voices in Arab Cinema* (Bloomington: Indiana University Press, 2015), 10.

39. Moumen Smihi, "Image de soi, pour soi et pour l'autre" [Image of the self, for the self and for the other] (1997), in *Écrire sur le cinéma*, 137–45. Lambert began his career as a critic and editor, notably of the British journal *Sight and Sound*, before moving to Hollywood and writing screenplays. He lived in Tangier for a long period and was a friend of Paul Bowles.

40. Smihi, *Écrire sur le cinéma*; Mu'min al-Smihi, *Hadith al-sinima* [Conversations about cinema], 2 vols. (Tangier: Siliki Ikhwan, 2005, 2006); Mu'min al-Smihi, *Fi al-sinima al-'arabiyya* [On Arab cinema] (Tangier: Siliki Ikhwan, 2009); Mu'min al-Smihi, *'Abqariyat sinima'iyya* [Geniuses of cinema] (Tangier: Siliki Ikhwan, 2011); Mu'min al-Smihi, *al-Zul al-dar* [The shadow of the signifier] (Tangier: Siliki Ikhwan, 2013), and the other texts cited in the bibliography under his name. See also Roland Carrée, "Moumen Smihi: Grandir à Tanger," *Répliques* 9 (2017): 112–43; Louis Séguin, "Paris, Tanger: Les deux amours de Moumen Smihi" [Paris, Tangier: Moumen Smihi's two loves], *Cahiers du cinéma* 733 (2017): 70–72.

41. The "other studies" include Sandra Gayle Carter, *What Moroccan Cinema?: A Historical and Critical Study, 1956–2006* (Lanham, MD: Lexington, 2009); Moulay Driss Jaïdi, *Le cinema au Maroc* [Cinema in Morocco] (Rabat: Collection al-Majal, 1991); Kevin Dwyer, *Beyond Casablanca: M. A. Tazi and the Adventure of Moroccan Cinema* (Bloomington: Indiana University Press, 2004); Ahmed Bouanani, "La septième porte" [The seventh gate], unpublished manuscript, n.p., private collection of Touda Bouanani.

42. Bouanani, "La septième porte," n.p. For other contemporary perspectives on the problem see Jamal Eddine Naji, who satirizes the situation in an imagined conversation

between two filmmakers, in "Une problématique à ponctuer" [A problematic to punctuate], *Lamalif* 80 (1976): 36–39; Jean-Pierre Millecam, "Deep Morocco," *Lamalif* 114 (1980): 55–56.

43. Roy Armes devotes a chapter to *The East Wind* in his *Postcolonial Images: Studies in North African Film* (Bloomington: Indiana University Press, 2005), 87–95; and an English translation of Guy Hennebelle's interview with Smihi, "Moroccan Society as Mythology," appears in *Film and Politics in the Third World*, ed. John Downing (New York: Praeger, 1987), 77–87. Carter discusses Smihi briefly in *What Moroccan Cinema?*, 139; Lhoussain Simour has an essay on *The East Wind*, "Narrating Silence and (Re)locating Space: Cinematic Reflexions on Moumen Smihi's *al-Shergui awi* [sic] *al-samt al-anif (al-Shergui or the Violent Silence)*," in the student film journal *Film Matters* 3 (2010): 14–19; and there is a sketchy, sometimes inaccurate discussion of *The East Wind* in Christa Jones, *Cave Culture in Maghrebi Literature: Imagining Self and Nation* (Lanham, MD: Lexington, 2012), 121–25. My first essay on the filmmaker, "Moumen Smihi's Tanjawi/Tangérois/Tangerian Cinema," appeared in *Third Text* in 2012.

44. There are too many to list, but see for example Abdelwahab Meddeb, "L'oeil féminin de la ville: *Chergui*" [The city's female eye: *Chergui*], *Cahiers du cinéma* 262/263 (1976): 103–8; Henry Welsh, "El Chergui," *Jeune Cinéma* 93 (March 1976): 32–33; Jacques Mandelbaum, "Chroniques marocaines: trois contes d'un cinéaste marocain radical" [Moroccan Chronicles: Three tales by a radical Moroccan cinéaste], *Le Monde*, November 17, 1999, 2; Millecam, "Deep Morocco"; Mohamed Jibril, "Silence, on tourne!" [Quiet on the set!] *Lamalif* 117 (1980): 46–47. More recent work includes interviews by Mohammed Bakrim such as "De Matisse à Taha Hussein" [From Matisse to Taha Hussein], *Al Bayane*, May 7, 2015, http://albayane.press.ma/de-matisse-a-taha-hossein.html; and "Du documentaire et de la fiction" [Of documentary and fiction], *Al Bayane*, May 8, 2015, http://albayane.press.ma/du-documentaire-et-de-la-fiction.html; a long interview in Carrée, "Moumen Smihi: Grandir à Tanger," 112–43; and another by Louis Séguin, "Paris, Tanger: Les deux amours de Moumen Smihi," 70–72.

45. In the anthology *Sinima Mu'min al-Smihi. Qalaq al-tajrib wa fa'iliyyat al-ta'sis al-nathri* [The cinema of Moumen Smihi: Passion for experimentation and richness of theoretical foundation], ed. Jumiat al-qabas al-sinima wa-l-thaqafa [Al Qabas association for cinema and culture] (Errachidia, Morocco: Benlefqih, 2010), see: Hamid Itbatu, "al-Qalaq al-nathri wa rihanat al-tajrib fi al-tajriba al-sinima'iyya li Mu'min al-Smihi" [Theoretical passion and the stakes of experimentation in Moumen Smihi's cinematic essay], 1–32; Hamid Itbatu, "Hawar ma'a Mu'min al-Smihi" [Dialogue with Moumen Smihi], 46–98; Nur al-Din Muhaqiq, "Shi'riyyat al-hub wa hawas al-injidab qira'a fi film *al-Sharqi* li Mu'min al-Smihi" [The poetics of love and the madness of fascination: a reading of *The East Wind* by Moumen Smihi], 33–37; Othman Bisani, "al-Antrubuluji wa-l-untuluji fi *al-Sharqi aw al-samt al-'anif* [Anthropology and ontology in *The East Wind or the violent silence*], 38–45. For an earlier Moroccan essay on historical films, including *44, or Tales of the Night*, see Mustafa Mesnaoui, "al-Sinima al-tarikh: *44 aw usturat al-layl* namuthja" [Historical cinema: The *44, or Tales of the Night* model], *Dirassat Sinima'iyya* 12 (October 1990): 40–45.

46. Those programs, at the Berkeley Art Museum and Pacific Film Archive, Walker Art Center (Minneapolis), Block Cinema (Chicago), and Tate Modern (London), have had a noticeable effect on the circulation of Smihi's work and writing about it, just as the recent translations of Bouanani's writings and screenings of his films have created more interest and visibility regarding his work. Brian T. Edwards notes his delight and surprise at seeing

Smihi's *Moroccan Chronicles* for the first time at the Block and reflects on related issues of circulation in *After the American Century: The Ends of U.S. Culture in the Middle East* (New York: Columbia University Press, 2016), xiii–xv. Information on the availability of Smihi's films can be found at https://limbrick.sites.ucsc.edu.

47. Laura U. Marks writes of such networks as an alternative to the "hylomorphic," or top-down, structure of cultural expression, and that Arab experimental cinema often depends upon them for its very existence. Laura U. Marks, *Hanan al-Cinema: Affections for the Moving Image* (Cambridge, MA: MIT Press, 2015), 25.

48. Tom Gunning, *The Films of Fritz Lang: Allegories of Vision and Modernity* (London: BFI, 2000), 5.

49. Gunning, *The Films of Fritz Lang*, 5.

50. Gunning, *The Films of Fritz Lang*, 6.

51. Moumen Smihi, "Cinima arabia" [Arab cinema] (1993), in *Écrire sur le cinéma*, 106. The full quote reads "La potentialité, ce serait que l'image arrive, à l'instar de la littérature, à rendre compte de façon esthétique, spectaculaire, divertissante, des questions de fond qui existent par rapport à la culture, à l'identité, à l'histoire arabe que nous avons évoquées. C'est ce qui justifie que nous sommes quelques uns à vouloir créer un cinéma arabe qui soit intégrable à la totalité de l'Histoire du cinéma" [The potential would be for the image to manage to tackle the profound questions that exist with respect to Arab culture, identity, and identity that we have evoked, and in an aesthetic, spectacular, and entertaining way, just as literature can. That's what explains why some of us want to create an Arab cinema that could be integrated in the entire history of cinema].

52. Bouanani, "La septième porte," n.p.

53. Carter counts at least ten films produced there in *What Moroccan Cinema?*, 47–48; see also Viola Shafik, *Arab Cinema: History and Cultural Identity* (Cairo: American University in Cairo Press, 2016), 17.

54. Smihi, personal communication with the author, August 9, 2019.

55. Bouanani, "La septième porte," n.p.

56. Smihi, "Mythologies Arabes," 152; Pierre Boulanger, *Le cinema colonial: de* l'Atlantide *à* Lawrence d'Arabie [The colonial cinema: from *Atlantis* to *Lawrence of Arabia*] (Paris: Éditions Segher, 1975), 172.

57. Insaf Ouhiba, "Zwoboda, André," in *Dictionnaire des orientalistes de langue française*, ed. François Pouillon (Paris: Karthala, 2008), 988.

58. Smihi, "Mythologies Arabes," 160.

59. Smihi, "Mythologies Arabes," 151. In translating from the French, I have changed the transliterations of the names of writers that Smihi cites.

60. Karl Schoonover and Rosalind Galt, *Queer Cinema in the World* (Durham, NC, and London: Duke University Press, 2016), esp. 33–34.

61. Smihi, "Choc de cultures," 135.

62. Malek Khouri argues that the career of Youssef Chahine also offers a wide-ranging engagement with the principles of the Nahda and its usefulness for Arab nationalism. Malek Khouri, *The Arab National Project in Youssef Chahine's Cinema* (Cairo: University of Cairo Press, 2010).

63. For example Albert Hourani, *Arabic Thought in the Liberal Age, 1798–1939* (1962; repr., Cambridge, UK: Cambridge University Press, 1983), credits Napoleon's invasion as

one of the factors that led to Muhammad ʿAli's attempts to modernize Egypt and his sustained interest in European accomplishments.

64. The book is available in a bilingual four-volume edition and a two-volume English-only translation: Ahmad Faris al-Shidyaq, *Leg over Leg*, ed. and trans. Humphrey Davies, 4 vols. (New York: New York University Press, 2014); Ahmad Faris al-Shidyaq, *Leg over Leg*, trans. Humphrey Davies, 2 vols. (New York: New York University Press, 2015).

65. Rebecca C. Johnson, "Foreword," in al-Shidyaq, *Leg over Leg* (2015 English-only edition), 1:x, 1:xi.

66. Fawwaz Traboulsi, "Ahmad Faris al-Shidyaq (1804–87): The Quest for Another Modernity," in *Arabic Thought beyond the Liberal Age*, 175–86.

67. Tarek El-Ariss, *Trials of Arab Modernity: Literary Affects and the New Political* (New York: Fordham University Press, 2013), 11.

68. Rifaʿa Rafiʿ al-Tahtawi, *An Imam in Paris: Account of a Stay in France by an Egyptian Cleric (1826–1831)*, trans. Daniel L. Newman (London: Saqi, 2011), 17–30.

69. Elizabeth Suzanne Kassab, *Contemporary Arab Thought: Cultural Critique in Comparative Perspective* (New York: Columbia University Press, 2010), 22.

70. Joel Beinin, "Egyptian Workers in the Liberal Age and Beyond," in *Arabic Thought against the Authoritarian Age: Towards an Intellectual History of the Present*, ed. Jens Hanssen and Max Weiss (Cambridge, UK: Cambridge University Press, 2018), 239.

71. Hourani, *Arabic Thought in the Liberal Age*, 254.

72. Leyla Dakhli, "The Autumn of the Nahda in Light of the Arab Spring: Some Figures in the Carpet," in *Arabic Thought beyond the Liberal Age*, 354, 352–53.

73. Hanssen and Weiss, *Arabic Thought beyond the Liberal Age*, xvi; Bou Ali, "Collecting the Nation," 33–56.

74. Elias Khoury, "For a Third Nahda," trans. Max Weiss with Jens Hanssen, in *Arabic Thought against the Authoritarian Age*, 357–69.

75. On this point see Orit Bashkin, who argues that the focus on genealogies of Islamic thought has had the effect of "obscuring the importance of secular, Marxist, and nationalist thinkers of the 1940s and 1950s." Orit Bashkin, "Arabic Thought in the Radical Age: Emile Habibi, the Israeli Communist Party, and the Production of Arab Jewish Radicalism, 1946–1961," in *Arabic Thought against the Authoritarian Age*, 64.

76. In particular see El-Ariss, *Trials of Arab Modernity*; El-Ariss, *The Arab Renaissance*; and the essays collected in Hanssen and Weiss's two volumes, *Arabic Thought beyond the Liberal Age* and *Arabic Thought against the Authoritarian Age*, discussed further here. On Arab modernity more generally see Rastegar, *Literary Modernity between the Middle East and Europe*; Jeffrey Sacks, *Iterations of Loss: Mutilation and Aesthetic Form, al-Shidyaq to Darwish* (New York: Fordham University Press, 2015); Stephen Sheehi, *Foundations of Modern Arab Identity* (Gainesville: University of Florida Press, 2004).

77. Max Weiss and Jens Hanssen, "Introduction: Arabic Intellectual History between the Postwar and the Postcolonial," in *Arabic Thought against the Authoritarian Age*, 2.

78. Traboulsi, "Ahmad Faris al-Shidyaq (1804–87)"; Elizabeth Suzanne Kassab, "Summoning the Spirit of Enlightenment: On the Nahda Revival in *Qadaya wa-shahadat*," in *Arabic Thought against the Authoritarian Age*, 311–35; Khoury, "For a Third Nahda," 357–69; Dakhli, "The Autumn of the Nahda in Light of the Arab Spring," 351–71; Marilyn Booth, "Liberal Thought and the 'Problem' of Women: Cairo, 1890s," in *Arabic Thought beyond the*

Liberal Age, 187–213; Bashkin, "Arabic Thought in the Radical Age," 62–85; Robyn Creswell, "Modernism in Translation: Poetry and Intellectual History in Beirut," in *Arabic Thought against the Authoritarian Age*, 113–42; Yoav Di-Capua, "Changing the Arab Intellectual Guard: On the Fall of the *udaba'*, 1940–1960," in *Arabic Thought against the Authoritarian Age*, 41–61; and others in *Arabic Thought beyond the Liberal Age* and *Arabic Thought against the Authoritarian Age*. See also El-Ariss, *Trials of Arab Modernity*; Sheehi, *Foundations of Modern Arab Identity*; Sacks, *Iterations of Loss*.

79. Weiss and Hanssen, "Introduction: Arabic Intellectual History between the Postwar and the Postcolonial," 21.

80. Weiss and Hanssen, "Introduction: Arabic Intellectual History between the Postwar and the Postcolonial," 21.

81. El-Ariss, *Trials of Arab Modernity*, 176.

82. Marshall Berman, *All That Is Solid Melts into Air: The Experience of Modernity* (New York: Simon and Schuster, 1982), 16–17.

83. For various accounts of modernity, modernism, and their relation see Berman, *All That Is Solid Melts into Air*; Fredric Jameson, *Postmodernism, or, The Logic of Late Capitalism* (Durham, NC: Duke University Press, 1999), esp. 302–13; Jürgen Habermas, "Modernity—an Incomplete Project," trans. Seyla Ben-Habib, in *The Anti-Aesthetic: Essays on Postmodern Culture*, ed. Hal Foster (Port Townsend, WA: Bay Press, 1983), 3–15; Dilip Parameshwar Gaonkar, "On Alternative Modernities," in *Alternative Modernities*, ed. Dilip Parameshwar Gaonkar (Durham, NC: Duke University Press, 2001), 1–23.

84. Fredric Jameson makes this point forcefully in *A Singular Modernity* (London: Verso, 2002), esp. 12–13.

85. See Gayatri Chakravorty Spivak, "Can the Subaltern Speak?," in *The Post-Colonial Studies Reader*, ed. Bill Ashcroft, Gareth Griffiths, and Helen Tiffin (Oxford: Routledge, 1995), 28–37; Gayatri Chakravorty Spivak, *A Critique of Postcolonial Reason: Toward a History of the Vanishing Present* (Cambridge, MA: Harvard University Press, 1999); Edward Said, *Orientalism* (New York: Vintage, 1979).

86. Dipesh Chakrabarty, *Provincializing Europe: Postcolonial Thought and Historical Difference* (2000; repr., Princeton, NJ: Princeton University Press, 2008), 43.

87. Hanssen and Weiss, "Preface," in *Arabic Thought beyond the Liberal Age*, 16. See also Kassab, *Contemporary Arab Thought*.

88. Dipesh Chakrabarty, "Introduction," in *Habitations of Modernity: Essays in the Wake of Subaltern Studies* (Chicago: University of Chicago Press, 2002), xxi.

89. Kassab, "Summoning the Spirit of Enlightenment," 335. See also Elizabeth Suzanne Kassab, *Enlightenment on the Eve of Revolution: The Egyptian and Syrian Debates* (New York: Columbia University Press, 2019). Because the latter work was published just as my own book went into production, I have not been able to engage with it here. But Kassab's arguments about the contemporary relevance of *tanwir* debates resonate deeply with what I argue with respect to Smihi's work.

90. Gaonkar, "On Alternative Modernities," 18; Jameson, *A Singular Modernity*.

91. Gaonkar, "On Alternative Modernities," 14–15.

92. Keya Ganguly, *Cinema, Emergence, and the Films of Satyajit Ray* (Berkeley: University of California Press, 2010), 214.

93. Gaonkar, "On Alternative Modernities," 18.

94. Miriam Hansen, "Fallen Women, Rising Stars, New Horizons: Shanghai Silent Film as Vernacular Modernism," *Film Quarterly* 54, no. 1 (2000): 13.

95. Here Hansen builds on an argument she made earlier in Miriam Hansen, "The Mass Production of the Senses: Classical Cinema as Vernacular Modernism," in *Reinventing Film Studies*, ed. Christine Gledhill and Linda Williams (2000; repr., London: Hodder Arnold, 2007), 332–50.

96. Peter Limbrick, "Vernacular Modernism, Film Culture, and Moroccan Short Film and Documentary," *Framework* 56, no. 2 (2015): 388–413.

97. On this point see Rey Chow, *Primitive Passions: Visuality, Sexuality, Ethnography, and Contemporary Chinese Cinema* (New York: Columbia University Press, 1995), 182–202.

98. The term "Berber" is not commonly used within Morocco itself, where those to whom it refers prefer to be known as Amazigh.

99. On this point see Masha Salazkina, "Introduction: Film Theory in the Age of Neoliberal Globalization," introduction to the dossier "Geopolitics of Film and Media Theory," *Framework* 56, no. 2 (2015): 325–49.

100. Miller, *A History of Modern Morocco*, 3.

101. Kenza Sefrioui, *La revue Souffles 1976–1973: Espoirs de révolution culturelle au Maroc* [The journal Souffles 1976–1973: Hopes of cultural revolution in Morocco] (Casablanca: Éditions de Sirocco, 2013).

102. Harrison and Villa-Ignacio, *Souffles-Anfas*.

103. El-Ariss, *Trials of Arab Modernity*.

104. Creswell, *City of Beginnings*, 19–20.

105. The term *al-halqa* refers to a tradition of theatrical public storytelling usually performed in front of a circle of listeners. Widely practiced in the Maghrib, it can involve a diverse set of practices that, according to Khalid Amine and Marvin Carlson, range "from storytelling to acrobatic dancing, snake charming, fortunetelling, boxing, herbal vending, healing, and singing in different languages. *Al-halqa* still remains today the most significant cadre for performance behavior throughout the Maghrib; an array of other artistic practices are in fact framed within a circle of *al-halqa*." Khalid Amine and Marvin Carlson, *The Theatres of Morocco, Algeria, and Tunisia: Performance Traditions of the Maghreb* (New York: Palgrave, 2012), 29.

106. El-Ariss, *Trials of Arab Modernity*, 9–10; Marks, *Hanan al-Cinema*, 12–13.

CHAPTER ONE

1. On Mahfouz and Egyptian realism see Samir Farid, *Najib Mahfuz wa-l-sinima* [Naguib Mahfouz and the cinema] (Cairo: al-Haya al-'Ama li-Qusur al-Thaqafa, 1990); Samir Farid, *al-Waqi'iyya al-jadida fi al-sinima al-Misriyya* [The new realism in Egyptian cinema] (Cairo: al-Haya al-Misriyya al-'Ama li-l-Kitab, 1992); Nathaniel Greenberg, *The Aesthetic of Revolution in the Film and Literature of Naguib Mahfouz (1952–1967)* (Lanham, MD: Lexington, 2014).

2. See Nouri Bouzid, "New Realism in Arab Cinema: The Defeat-Conscious Cinema," trans. Shereen el-Ezabi, *Alif: Journal of Comparative Poetics* 15 (1995): 242–50.

3. Viola Shafik, *Arab Cinema: History and Cultural Identity* (1998; repr., Cairo: American University in Cairo Press, 2016), 127–43, 184–85; Claude Michel Cluny, *Dictionnaire des*

nouveaux cinemas arabes [Dictionary of the new Arab cinemas] (Paris: Sindbad, 1978); Bouzid, "New Realism in Arab Cinema," 242–50.

4. Moumen Smihi, "Maghrebitude," in *Écrire sur le cinéma* (Tangier: Slaïki Frères, 2006), 44.

5. Shafik, *Arab Cinema*, 138, 141.

6. Rosalind Galt and Karl Schoonover, "Introduction: The Impurity of Art Cinema," in *Global Art Cinema: New Theories and Histories*, ed. Rosalind Galt and Karl Schoonover (London: Oxford University Press, 2010), 3.

7. Galt and Schoonover, "Introduction: The Impurity of Art Cinema," 17.

8. See Ernst Bloch, George Lukács, Bertolt Brecht, Walter Benjamin, and Theodor Adorno, *Aesthetics and Politics* (1977; repr., London: Verso, 1980). In this volume, of particular interest and insight are Fredric Jameson's reflections on the totality of these debates: Fredric Jameson, "Reflections in Conclusion," 196–213.

9. Jameson, "Reflections in Conclusion," 205.

10. Moumen Smihi, "Moroccan Society as Mythology," in *Film and Politics in the Third World*, ed. John Downing (New York: Praeger, 1987), 79.

11. John David Rhodes, "Pasolini's Exquisite Flowers: The 'Cinema of Poetry' as a Theory of Art Cinema," in *Global Art Cinema*, 151.

12. Moumen Smihi, "Anthropologie culturelle" [Cultural anthropology] (1984), in *Écrire sur le cinéma*, 86–87.

13. Smihi has made this point strongly in interviews, such as in an onstage Q&A with this author following a screening of *A Muslim Childhood* at Tate Modern, London, May 17, 2014. For his comments on *44, Moroccan Chronicles*, *A Muslim Childhood*, and *Sorrows of a Young Tangerian*, play the recordings at https://www.tate.org.uk/context-comment/audio/moumen-smihi-poet-tangier-audio-recordings#open298637.

14. Moumen Smihi, "Libé" [Liberation] (1982), in *Écrire sur le cinéma*, 69.

15. A *cité universitaire* is a residential hall for university students. The Cité internationale universitaire in Paris has many houses organized by nationality; Smihi lived in the Moroccan house.

16. Author interview with Sakini, Melbourne, Australia, September 29, 2011.

17. Moumen Smihi, "Antonioni: la ville sans l'homme" [Antonioni: The city without the person] (1983), in *Écrire sur le cinéma*, 74.

18. Karl Schoonover, *Brutal Vision: The Neorealist Body in Postwar Italian Cinema* (Minneapolis: University of Minnesota Press, 2012), 40.

19. Smihi stated in an interview that, while neither a woman nor a sociologist, he wished to show a woman in the context of her quotidian environment. Moumen Smihi, "Riyah sharqiyya wa samt ʿanif" [The East Wind and violent silence] (1978), in Muʾmin al-Smihi, *Hadith al-sinima* [Conversations about cinema] (Tangier: Siliki Ikhwan, 2005), 1:27. The essay title subtly differs from the film's actual subtitle and reverses its idafa construction (*ʿanif al-samt*), which could be translated equivalently as "the violence of silence."

20. André Bazin, *What Is Cinema? Volume II*, trans. Hugh Gray (Berkeley: University of California Press, 1971), 23. Schoonover makes this point in his discussion of the body in neorealism in *Brutal Vision*, 44.

21. She has continued to star in major productions like *Alexandria . . . New York* (dir. Youssef Chahine, 2004) and *The Yacoubian Building* (dir. Marwan Hamed, 2006).

22. Smihi, recording at the Tate, May 18, 2014, https://www.tate.org.uk/context-comment/audio/moumen-smihi-poet-tangier-audio-recordings#open298637.

23. Roland Carrée, "Moumen Smihi: Grandir à Tanger," *Répliques* 9 (2017): 127.

24. As Chouki El Hamel explains, the term Gnawa can refer both to a distinctive style of music and to those who developed it, West Africans who were originally enslaved in Morocco. See Chouki El Hamel, *Black Morocco: A History of Slavery, Race, and Islam* (New York: Cambridge University Press, 2013), esp. 273–96.

25. Moinak Biswas, "In the Mirror of an Alternative Globalism: The Neorealist Encounter in India," in *Italian Neorealism and Global Cinema*, ed. Laura E. Ruberto and Kristi M. Wilson (Detroit: Wayne State University Press, 2007), 81.

26. Biswas, "In the Mirror of an Alternative Globalism," 83.

27. Smihi, "Anthropologie culturelle," 86.

28. Mohamed Khan, *An Introduction to the Egyptian Cinema* (London: Informatics, 1969), 31–32.

29. Ibrahim al-Ariss, "Salah Abu Seif on Salah Abu Seif: Portrait of a Director," in *Catalogo della retrospettiva cinematografica "Il cinema secondo Salah Abou Seif"* (Naples: Cinemamed, 2002), 30, accessible at http://euromedi.org/home/azioni/pubblicazioni/artedanza/salah/ARISS.PDF.

30. For a more extensive treatment of his work see Farid, *al-Waqi'iyya al-jadida fi al-sinima al-misriyya*; Hashem al-Nahas, "Salah Abu Sayf wa tajkhir al-waqi'iyya wa-l-tanwir fi al-sinima al-misriyya" [Salah Abu Seif and the cultivation of realism and enlightenment in Egyptian cinema], *Alif: Journal of Comparative Poetics* 15 (1995): 6–21; Monique Hennebelle, "Les tribulations du néoréalisme égyptien: l'exemple de Salah Abou Seif" [The tribulations of Egyptian neorealism: The example of Salah Abou Seif], *L'afrique littéraire et artistique* 27 (1973): 76–86.

31. Cluny, *Dictionnaire des nouveaux cinemas arabes*, 101.

32. Greenberg, *The Aesthetic of Revolution in the Film and Literature of Naguib Mahfouz (1952–1967)*, xvi.

33. Hennebelle, "Les tribulations du néoréalisme égyptien," 80.

34. Smihi, "Anthropologie culturelle," 86.

35. Smihi, "Anthropologie culturelle," 86–87.

36. Smihi, "Anthropologie culturelle," 87.

37. Reda Bensmaïa, "A Cinema of Cruelty," in *Building Bridges: The Cinema of Jean Rouch*, ed. Joram Ten Brink (London: Wallflower, 2007), 73–85.

38. Steven Feld, "Editor's Introduction," in *Ciné-Ethnography*, ed. and trans. Steven Feld (Minneapolis: University of Minnesota Press, 2003), 17.

39. Rouch later recounted that this uncanny mix of improvisation and documentation proved fascinating to Roberto Rossellini and led him to proclaim the virtues of 16mm production and talk of collaboration with Rouch. Jean Rouch with Enrico Fulchignoni, "Ciné-Anthropology," in *Ciné-Ethnography*, 165.

40. Rouch with Fulchignoni, "Ciné-Anthropology," 165.

41. Feld, "Editor's Introduction," 20–21.

42. Abdelwahab Meddeb, "L'oeil féminin de la ville: *Chergui*" [The city's female eye: *Chergui*], *Cahiers du cinéma*, nos. 262/63 (1976): 104.

43. Peter Limbrick, "Moumen Smihi's Tanjawi/Tangérois/Tangerian Cinema," *Third Text* 26, no. 4 (2012): 450.

44. Moumen Smihi, "Moroccan Society as Mythology," 82, originally published as "La société marocaine comme mythologie" [Moroccan society as mythology], *Cinémaction* 14 (1981): 217–23.

45. Smihi, "Moroccan Society as Mythology," 79.

46. Schoonover, *Brutal Vision*, 15.

47. Colin MacCabe, "Realism and the Cinema: Notes on Some Brechtian Theses," *Screen* 15, no. 2 (1974): 7–27.

48. Smihi, "Moroccan Society as Mythology," 78, 79.

49. As I will discuss in chapter 3, the succession of seven opening doors is one of the film's many intertextual references. See Moumen Smihi, "La mémoire clandestine" [Clandestine memory], in *Écrire sur le cinema*, 24–25, originally published as "Moumen Smihi: Le silence violent" [Moumen Smihi: the violent silence], an interview with Noureddine Ghali, *Cinema 76*, no. 205 (January 1976): 92–101.

50. Rachel Gabara, "'A Poetics of Refusals': Neorealism from Italy to Africa," in *Italian Neorealism and Global Cinema*, ed. Laura E. Ruberto and Kristi M. Wilson (Detroit: Wayne State University Press, 2007), 194.

51. Gabara, "'A Poetics of Refusals,'" 196.

52. Roland Barthes, "The Third Meaning: Research Notes on Some Eisenstein Stills," in *Image, Music, Text*, trans. Stephen Heath (New York: Hill and Wang, 1972), 68.

53. Timothy Corrigan, *The Essay Film: From Montaigne, After Marker* (New York: Oxford University Press, 2011), 44.

54. MacCabe, "Realism and the Cinema," 49–50. MacCabe's point is not unrelated to Schoonover's intervention, which is to show that Rossellini's films allow the spectator to take for granted their humanist presence and response.

55. MacCabe, "Realism and the Cinema," 50.

56. MacCabe, "Realism and the Cinema," 54.

57. On realism and modernism, as well as Bloch et al., *Aesthetics and Politics*, cited above, see Fredric Jameson, "The Existence of Italy," in *Signatures of the Visible* (New York: Routledge, 1992), 155–229; Colin MacCabe, "Theory and Film: Principles of Realism and Pleasure," *Screen* 17, no. 3 (1976): 7–28; Rosalind Galt, *Pretty: Film and the Decorative Image* (New York: Columbia University Press, 2011), especially chapter 5.

58. Noa Steimatsky, *Italian Locations: Rehabiting the Past in Postwar Cinema* (Minneapolis: University of Minnesota Press, 2008), xxi.

59. Moumen Smihi, press materials for "Les récits de la nuit" [Tales of the Night], in *Écrire sur le cinéma*, 130.

60. Galt, *Pretty*, 15, 11.

61. On the tradition of textuality and the decorative in Arab-Islamic culture and their relationship to modernism see Laura U. Marks, *Enfoldment and Infinity: An Islamic Genealogy of New Media Art* (Cambridge, MA: MIT Press, 2011), esp. 49–52, 109–31, 219–51; Galt, *Pretty*, 164–70.

62. Galt, *Pretty*, 177, 178.

63. Jorge Sanjinés, "El cine político no debe abandoner su preocupación por la belleza" [Political cinema must not abandon its interest in beauty], in *Téoria y práctica de un cine junto al pueblo* [Theory and practice of a cinema with the people] (Mexico City: Veintiuno Editores, 1979), 156–57, cited in Galt, *Pretty*, 208.

64. Peter Limbrick, "Vernacular Modernism, Film Culture, and Moroccan Short Film and Documentary," *Framework* 56, no. 2 (2015): 388–413.

65. Galt, *Pretty*, 210.

66. Smihi, "Les récits de la nuit," 128.

CHAPTER TWO

1. The notion of filmmaking as research occurs at many points in Smihi's essays, for example "Anthropologie culturelle" [Cultural anthropology] (1984), in *Écrire sur le cinéma* (Tangier: Slaïki Frères, 2006), 76–89; "Cinema Arabiyya" [Arab cinema] (1993), in *Écrire sur le cinéma*, 90–106; "Lettre du Maroc," *Cinématograph* 109 (April 1985), 26–27, republished as "Choc de cultures" [Culture shock], in *Écrire sur le cinéma*, 133–36. It has likewise frequently been invoked in conversations with the author and in Q&As with audiences.

2. See for example Smihi, "Anthropologie culturelle," 88.

3. Moumen Smihi, "Avec Robert Bresson" [With Robert Bresson], in *Écrire sur le cinéma*, 9, 10, previously published as "Entretien avec Robert Bresson," *Image et son: la revue du cinema* 215 (January 1968): 68–71; Pierre Schaeffer, *In Search of a Concrete Music*, trans. Christine North and John Dark (1952; repr., Berkeley: University of California Press, 2012).

4. Michel Chion, *Sound: An Acoulogical Treatise*, trans. James A. Steintrager (Durham, NC: Duke University Press, 2016), 57.

5. Moumen Smihi, "Moroccan Society as Mythology," in *Film and Politics in the Third World*, ed. John Downing (New York: Praeger, 1987), 79.

6. Michel Chion, "Let's Have Done with the Notion of 'Noise,'" trans. James A. Steintrager, *Differences* 22, nos. 2/3 (2011): 245. Similarly, Chion also argued that the word "timbre" should be disassociated from its instrumentalist suppositions. Describing the timbre of a trombone as if it were a singular thing, he argues, overlooks the different sounds produced if we strike the trombone with a mallet versus play it as a wind instrument. The difference should not matter to the sound theorist; either technique can make a sound that is interesting in its own right. Michel Chion, "Dissolution of the Notion of Timbre," trans. James A. Steintrager, *Differences* 22, nos. 2/3 (2011): 238.

7. Moumen Smihi, "La mémoire clandestine" [Clandestine memory], in *Écrire sur le cinema*, 126–27, previously published as "Moumen Smihi: Le silence violent" [Moumen Smihi: the violent silence], interview with Noureddine Ghali, *Cinema 76*, no. 205 (January 1976): 92–101.

8. Smihi shot five of these one-minute actualities for GREC. Only two are currently available on video. See filmography for details.

9. Smihi, "Avec Robert Bresson," 12. Smihi is here paraphrasing a passage from Barthes's essay "L'art vocal bourgeois" [Bourgeois vocal art], which appears in his collection of essays published in French as *Mythologies* (Paris: Éditions de Seuil, 1957), 189–91, but not in the collected English translation published by Jonathan Cape. Barthes, suggesting that the

music of the baritone Gérard Souzay is the epitome of bourgeois art, states, "Cet art est essentiellement signalétique: il n'a de cesse d'imposer non l'émotion, mais les signes de l'émotion" [This art is essentially signaletic: it doesn't stop imposing not emotion but the signs of emotion] (189).

10. Moumen Smihi, "Science et émotion" [Science and emotion], in *Écrire sur le cinéma*, 182.

11. Moumen Smihi, "Les récits de la nuit" [Tales of the night], in *Écrire sur le cinéma*, 129.

12. Smihi, "Les récits de la nuit," 129.

13. R. Murray Schafer, *The Soundscape: Our Sonic Environment and the Tuning of the World* (Rochester: Destiny Books, 1993).

14. For more on the use of the term "acousmatic" in Chion and its development before him in the work of Pierre Schaeffer, see James A. Steintrager, "Introduction: Closed Grooves, Open Ears," in Michel Chion, *Sound: An Acoustological Treatise*, trans. James A. Steintrager (Durham, NC: Duke University Press, 2016), vii–xxvi.

15. Douglas A. Boyd, *Broadcasting in the Arab World: A Survey of Radio and Television in the Middle East* (Philadelphia: Temple University Press, 1982), 15–16.

16. Boyd, *Broadcasting in the Arab World*, 254.

17. Boyd, *Broadcasting in the Arab World*, 253–54.

18. Boyd, *Broadcasting in the Arab World*, 257.

19. For more on Ahmed Said see Boyd, *Broadcasting in the Arab World*, 26.

20. Kay Dickinson, *Arab Cinema Travels: Transnational Syria, Palestine, Dubai and Beyond* (London: British Film Institute, 2016), 69–70.

21. Ian Baucom, "Frantz Fanon's Radio: Solidarity, Diaspora, and the Tactics of Listening," *Contemporary Literature* 42, no. 1 (2001): 17.

22. Frantz Fanon, "This Is the Voice of Algeria," in *A Dying Colonialism*, trans. Haakon Chevalier (New York: Grove, 1965), 71, 74, 72–73, 92.

23. Rebecca P. Scales, "Subversive Sound: Transnational Radio, Arabic Recordings, and the Dangers of Listening in French Colonial Algeria, 1934–1939," *Comparative Studies in Society and History* 52, no. 2 (2010): 385, 415.

24. Umm Kulthum had been central to Egyptian radio since her debut in the 1920s. Even before the Voice of the Arabs and the Nasserite-period stations, Egyptian Radio (the government precursor to Nasser's stations, established in 1934) had developed musical programming that was hugely influential in cultural life. As Virginia Danielson recounts, the programming of Medhat Assem resulted in regular appearances by Mohammed Abdel Wahab and then Umm Kulthum, who eventually alternated with him in a Thursday-night programming spot. Her Thursday concerts "were the activity for which she was probably the most famous and which had the greatest impact on musical and social life in the Middle East." Virginia Danielson, *The Voice of Egypt: Umm Kulthum, Arabic Song, and Egyptian Society in the Twentieth Century* (Chicago: University of Chicago Press, 1997), 86. This importance was only to grow under the Nasserite period, when, as we have seen, the scope and impact of radio broadcasting increased dramatically. Abdel Wahab, a prolific composer who was responsible for writing some of the greatest hits for Umm Kulthum and Abdel Halim Hafez, another huge star, was for a time equally popular and, with Umm Kulthum, his songs narrated Arab nationalist messages, particularly during the early Nasser years.

25. Malek Khouri, *The Arab National Project in Youssef Chahine's Cinema* (Cairo: University of Cairo Press, 2010), xi.

26. As Khouri notes, while the political promise of pan-Arabism in the anti- and postcolonial period was lost, leading to "deep disillusionment with the entire pan-Arab modernizing project and a general despair among the masses," the cultural expressions of this movement as an "unfinished project" have continued. Khouri, *The Arab National Project in Youssef Chahine's Cinema*, 4–5. On Arab nationalist politics more generally see Elizabeth Suzanne Kassab, *Contemporary Arab Thought: Cultural Critique in Comparative Perspective* (New York: Columbia University Press, 2010).

27. For a fuller discussion and definition of the acousmatic see Michel Chion, *The Voice in Cinema*, trans. Claudia Gorbman (New York: Columbia University Press, 1999), 18–23.

28. Chion, *The Voice in Cinema*, 125.

29. Mary Ann Doane, "The Voice in the Cinema: The Articulation of Body and Space," *Yale French Studies* 60 (1980): 35; Chion, *The Voice in Cinema*, 33–35.

30. Chion, *The Voice in Cinema*, 21.

31. Chion, *The Voice in Cinema*, 23.

32. Chion describes the process of de-acoustamization as one that may be partial or by degree, with different attendant consequences. Chion, *The Voice in Cinema*, 27–29.

33. Short final vowels are usually dropped in Arabic conversation, but here they are pronounced in the more formal register of public speaking and recitation.

34. Roland Carrée, "Moumen Smihi: Grandir à Tanger," *Répliques* 9 (2017): 131.

35. This narration is voiced by Claude Pomme, also an assistant to the director and a costume creator for the film.

36. Viola Shafik, *Arab Cinema: History and Cultural Identity* (1998; repr., Cairo: American University in Cairo Press, 2016), 70–89.

37. Salah Ezzedine, "The Role of Music in Arabic Films," in *The Cinema in the Arab Countries*, ed. George Sadoul (Beirut: Interarab Centre of Cinema and Television, 1966), 47.

38. Adonis, *An Introduction to Arab Poetics*, trans. Catherine Cobham (London: Saqi, 1990), 13.

39. Charles Hirschkind, *The Ethical Soundscape: Cassette Sermons and Islamic Counterpublics* (New York: Columbia University Press, 2006), 50, 51.

40. Martin Stokes argues that in fact it was the intimacy of Nasser's closely miked voice that enabled his appeal to listeners. Nasser, he writes, had an impressive grasp of media possibility and "an exquisitely honed sense of what could be achieved by the amplified voice in a society attuned to the traditional arts of Islamic rhetoric and audition, the 'ilm al-balagha. . . . His was a quiet voice. . . . It was also a nuanced voice, one that relied greatly for its rhetorical effect on subtle changes of intensity, inflection, and emotional charge. Whether in large crowds, or listening to radio broadcasts or recordings, Egyptians responded to a voice that persuaded because it was intimate and proximate." Martin Stokes, "'Abd al-Halim's Microphone," in *Music and the Play of Power in the Middle East, North Africa and Central Asia*, ed. Laudan Nooshin (London: Routledge, 2009), 69.

41. Stokes and Hirschkind argue that Sadat was no match for Nasser's vocal legacy; for Hirschkind, this broken continuity meant that the rhetorical tradition of voice in politics

was taken up by *khutaba* (Muslim preachers, singular *khatib*) instead. Hirschkind, *The Ethical Soundscape*, 51.

42. Stokes, "'Abd al-Halim's Microphone," 60.

43. Danielson, *The Voice of Egypt*, 183, citing Raja al-Naqqash, "Liqa' ma'a Umm Kulthum" [A meeting with Umm Kulthum], in *Lughz Umm Kulthum* [The secret of Umm Kulthum] (Cairo: Dar al-Hilal, 1978), 41.

44. Danielson, *The Voice of Egypt*, 192. *Mashayikh* is the plural of the more recognizable *shaykh*.

45. Danielson, *The Voice of Egypt*, 138. Danielson notes that a series of Paris concerts lasted seven hours, until three o'clock in the morning, requiring special permission to delay the venue's closing time. Danielson, *The Voice of Egypt*, 137.

46. Nasser, like Umm Kulthum, was from a working-class background, and Danielson shows how the two together became recognizable as iconic and patriotic *fallahin* (peasants) and *abnaa' il-rif* (children of the countryside). Danielson, *The Voice of Egypt*, 166. On Umm Kulthum's relationship with Nasser and nationalist songs see Danielson, *The Voice of Egypt*, 164–67.

47. By contrast, the singer Asmahan's reported liaisons with men in the film industry tarnished her reputation in the eyes of some Egyptians. Danielson, *The Voice of Egypt*, 90–91.

48. Chion, *The Voice in Cinema*, 85.

49. Chion, *The Voice in Cinema*, 86.

50. Smihi, personal communication with the author, October 18, 2016.

CHAPTER THREE

1. This assessment of his films as "too difficult" and therefore "more French" or "intended for French viewers" is something I have frequently encountered in conversation while in Morocco; it is as much mythologized as written. But for a critical treatment that demonstrates the tendency to read textual complexity or critique as European or self-Orientalizing, see Lhoussain Simour, "Narrating Silence and (Re)locating Space: Cinematic Reflexions on Moumen Smihi's *al-Shergui awi* [sic] *al-samt al-anif (al-Shergui or the Violent Silence)*," *Film Matters* 3 (2010): 14–19.

2. Tarek El-Ariss, ed., introduction to *The Arab Renaissance: A Bilingual Anthology of the Nahda* (New York: Modern Language Association, 2018), xxi. The other works referred to are Ibrahim Abu-Lughod, *The Arab Rediscovery of Europe: A Study in Cultural Encounters* (1963; repr., London: Saqi, 2011); Albert Hourani, *Arabic Thought in the Liberal Age, 1798–1939* (1962; repr., Cambridge, UK: Cambridge University Press, 1983).

3. Robyn Creswell, *City of Beginnings: Poetic Modernism in Beirut* (Princeton, NJ: Princeton University Press, 2019), 20.

4. Elizabeth Suzanne Kassab, "Summoning the Spirit of Enlightenment: On the Nahda Revival in *Qadaya wa-shahadat*," in *Arabic Thought against the Authoritarian Age: Towards an Intellectual History of the Present*, ed. Jens Hanssen and Max Weiss (Cambridge, UK: Cambridge University Press, 2018), 312. In the same volume see Elias Khoury, who addresses the cultural *inqilab*, or overthrow of what he calls the "second Nahda" (during the Nasserite period), which included translation of foreign-language poetry into Arabic. Elias Khoury,

"For a Third Nahda," trans. Max Weiss with Jens Hanssen, in *Arabic Thought against the Authoritarian Age*, 363.

5. Laura U. Marks, *Hanan al-Cinema: Affections for the Moving Image* (Cambridge, MA: MIT Press, 2015).

6. Alexandre Astruc, "The Birth of a New Avant-Garde: La Caméra-Stylo," in *Critical Visions in Film Theory: Classical and Contemporary Readings*, ed. Timothy Corrigan and Patricia White with Meta Mazaj (Boston: Bedford/St. Martins, 2011), 350–54.

7. Delphine Bénézet, *The Cinema of Agnès Varda: Resistance and Eclecticism* (London: Wallflower, 2014), 111.

8. As Bénézet notes, Agnès Varda signed many of her films "cinécrit par Agnès Varda." Bénézet, *The Cinema of Agnès Varda*, 111.

9. Moumen Smihi, "Cinécriture d'Eisenstein" [Eisensteinian *cinécriture*], in *Écrire sur le cinéma* (Tangier: Slaïki Frères, 2006), 34, previously published as "Du cinéma à la cinécriture" [From cinema to cinécriture] in the journal *Intégral* 3/4 (1973): 50–52. The *Intégral* version of the essay is illustrated with stills from *Si Moh, the Unlucky Man* and *Colors on Bodies*, directly connecting Smihi's theoretical speculations to his films.

10. Robert Stam, Robert Burgoyne, and Sandy Flitterman-Lewis, *New Vocabularies in Film Semiotics: Structuralism, Post-Structuralism and Beyond* (London: Routledge, 1992), 191.

11. Moumen Smihi, "L'aventure structuraliste" [The structuralist adventure] (1970), in *Écrire sur le cinéma*, 28.

12. Moumen Smihi, "L'aventure structuraliste," 25.

13. Moumen Smihi, "Libé" [Liberation], in *Écrire sur le cinéma*, 69.

14. Moumen Smihi, "Les billes de flipper" [The pinballs], in *Écrire sur le cinéma*, 67.

15. Moumen Smihi, "Anthropologie culturelle" [Cultural anthropology], in *Écrire sur le cinéma*, 88.

16. Mohammed Hamdouni Alami, *Art and Architecture in the Islamic Tradition* (New York: I. B. Tauris, 2011), 2.

17. Naïma Boujibar and Mohamed Mezzine, "Andalusian Morocco," in *Andalusian Morocco: A Discovery in Living Art*, ed. Museum with No Frontiers (Rabat: Ministry of Cultural Affairs of the Kingdom of Morocco, 2002), 56.

18. Mohamed Mezzine, "A Day in the Life of a Taleb in Fez," in *Andalusian Morocco*, 91.

19. Mezzine, "A Day in the Life of a Taleb in Fez," 93.

20. Laura U. Marks, *Enfoldment and Infinity: An Islamic Genealogy of New Media Art* (Cambridge, MA: MIT Press, 2011), 53.

21. Marks, *Enfoldment and Infinity*, 62.

22. Marks, *Enfoldment and Infinity*, 63.

23. Moumen Smihi, "Le cercle flamboyant" [The blazing circle], *Intégral* 8 (1974): 42.

24. Smihi, "Le cercle flamboyant," 41.

25. Boujibar and Mezzine, "Andalusian Morocco," 57.

26. Moumen Smihi, "Riyah sharqiyya wa samt 'anif" [The East Wind and violent silence] (1978), in Mu'min al-Smihi, *Hadith al-sinima* [Conversations about cinema] (Tangier: Siliki Ikhwan, 2005), 1:14.

27. James E. Montgomery, *al-Jahiz: In Praise of Books*, Edinburgh Studies in Classical Literature (Edinburgh: Edinburgh University Press, 2013), 57.

28. Alami, *Art and Architecture in the Islamic Tradition*, 40.

29. For an English translation with comprehensive notes see Lenn Evan Goodman, *Ibn Tufayl's Hayy Ibn Yaqzan: A Philosophical Tale* (2003; repr., Chicago: University of Chicago Press, 2009).

30. Samar Attar, *The Vital Roots of European Enlightenment: Ibn Tufayl's Influence on Modern Western Thought* (Lanham, MD: Lexington, 2007), 4.

31. Goodman, *Ibn Tufayl's Hayy Ibn Yaqzan*; Antonio Pastor, *The Idea of Robinson Crusoe* (Watford, UK: Gongora, 1930).

32. Attar, *The Vital Roots of European Enlightenment*, 40–41.

33. See Kassab, "Summoning the Spirit of Enlightenment," 311–35; Elizabeth Suzanne Kassab, *Enlightenment on the Eve of Revolution: The Egyptian and Syrian Debates* (New York: Columbia University Press, 2019).

34. At the time of this writing, Smihi is in preproduction for a feature film, *Hayy Ibn Yaqzan*, to be shot in the Ouarzazate area of Morocco (host to many Hollywood productions) that adapts Ibn Tufayl's narrative for the screen.

35. "Ces artistes et ces écrivains étaient des Encyclopédistes, déjà, vertu qui manque cruellement aujourd'hui" [These artists and writers were already Encyclopedists, a virtue which is sorely missing today]. Moumen Smihi, "La nouvelle civilité" [The new civility], in *Écrire sur le cinéma*, 108–9.

36. Abu al-'Ala' al-Ma'arri, *The Epistle of Forgiveness, or A Pardon to Enter the Garden*, trans. Geert Jan Van Gelder and Gregor Schoeler (New York: New York University Press, 2016), xxiii.

37. Reynold Alleyne Nicholson, *Studies in Islamic Poetry* (Cambridge, UK: Cambridge University Press, 1921), 44, available at http://hdl.handle.net/2027/mdp.39015013514727.

38. Quoted in Nicholson, *Studies in Islamic Poetry*, 167.

39. This is my translation from the film's French subtitles. Smihi draws freely on the poems of al-Ma'arri collected in *Saqt al-zand* (Beirut: Dar al-Fikr, 1965). For another translation of these verses in context, see al-Ma'arri, *Saqt al-zand: the Spark from the Flint*, trans. Arthur Wormhoudt (Oskaloosa, IA: William Penn College, 1972), 53–54.

40. Elizabeth Kassab, *Contemporary Arab Thought: Cultural Critique in Comparative Perspective* (New York: Columbia University Press), 2010, 41. Hussein's book has never been translated into English. See Taha Hussein [Husayn], *Fi al-shi'r al-jahili* [On jahili poetry] (Cairo: Dar al-Nahr li-l-Nashra wa-l-Tawzi', 1996).

41. See Roger Allen, *The Arabic Novel: An Historical and Critical Introduction* (Syracuse, NY: Syracuse University Press, 1982).

42. Viola Shafik, *Arab Cinema: History and Cultural Identity* (1998; repr., Cairo: American University in Cairo Press, 2016), 128ff.

43. For the examples of *Palace Walk* (Bayn al-qasrayn, dir. Hassan al-Iman, 1956) or *Adrift on the Nile* (Tharthara fawq al-Nil, dir. Husayn Kamal, 1971) see Nathaniel Greenberg, *Aesthetic of Revolution in the Film and Literature of Naguib Mahfouz (1952–1967)* (Lanham, MD: Lexington, 2014), xxix.

44. Greenberg, *Aesthetic of Revolution in the Film and Literature of Naguib Mahfouz (1952–1967)*, xvii.

45. Frank Budgen, *James Joyce and the Making of Ulysses* (Bloomington: Indiana University Press, 1960), 124. The sentence in brackets, from Budgen's original text, is omitted in Smihi's on-screen quotation, which is translated into French.

46. See Paul Hegarty, "Violent Silence: Noise and Bataille's 'Method of Meditation,'" in *Negative Ecstasies: Georges Bataille and the Study of Religion*, ed. Jeremy Biles and Kent Brintnall (New York: Fordham University Press, 2015), 95–105. Smihi also discusses the multiple meanings of the subtitle in a 1976 interview with Amran El-Maleh where he states: "Le silence violent? C'est la violence du silence. Le silence violé. Le viol du silence. La loi du silence. La violence de la loi. S'y décrypte pour moi, dans une mythologie personelle, une lecture qui a été éprouvante, décisive: celle de Georges Bataille" [The violent silence? It's the violence of silence. Silence violated. The rape of silence. The law of silence. The violence of the law. For me it can also be interpreted in terms of a personal narrative, a reading that was illuminating and decisive for me: that of Georges Bataille]. Moumen Smihi, "Entretien avec Moumen Smihi. Chergui ou le silence violent" [Interview with Moumen Smihi: The East Wind or the violent silence], *Intégral*, no. 11 (1976), 33.

47. *Blek* was a bimonthly French adventure comic, or *bande dessinée*, that ran from 1963 to 1984. *Kiwi*, another French *bande dessinée*, appeared from 1955 to 2003.

48. Smihi, "Riyah sharqiyya wa samt 'anif," 1:17–18.

49. Mikhail Bakhtin, *Problems of Dostoevsky's Poetics*, ed. and trans. Caryl Emerson (Minneapolis: University of Minnesota Press, 1984).

50. Smihi, "Riyah sharqiyya wa samt 'anif," 1:9.

51. Interview with the author, July 5, 2010, Tangier. See also Roland Carrée, "Moumen Smihi: Grandir à Tanger," *Répliques* 9 (2017), 119.

52. Mohammed El-Fasi, *Chants anciens des femmes de Fes* [Ancient songs of the women of Fez] (Paris: Seghers, 1967), 7. *Aroubi* is an Arab-Andalusian genre of classical poetry and music.

53. El-Fasi, *Chants anciens des femmes de Fes*, 8.

54. See Peter Limbrick, "Vernacular Modernism, Film Culture, and Moroccan Short Film and Documentary," *Framework* 56, no. 2 (2015): 388–413.

55. Miriam Hansen, "Fallen Women, Rising Stars, New Horizons: Shanghai Silent Film as Vernacular Modernism," *Film Quarterly* 54, no. 1 (2000): 10–22.

56. The Egyptian artist Maha Maamoun explores the predominance of these pyramid scenes, including al-Tayeb's, in her compelling found-footage video *Domestic Tourism* (2009), available at https://vimeo.com/33387550.

57. For a cataloging of just the Tangier films—US and European—see Omar Berrada and Yto Barrada, eds., *Album—Cinémathèque de Tanger* (Tangier: Librarie des Colonnes, 2012).

58. Brian T. Edwards, *Morocco Bound: Disorienting America's Maghreb, from Casablanca to the Marrakech Express* (Durham, NC: Duke University Press, 2005). For an extensive analysis of how US cinema and culture has circulated and been used in the Middle East, see Brian T. Edwards, *After the American Century: The Ends of U.S. Culture in the Middle East* (New York: Columbia University Press, 2016).

59. See Ahmed Bouanani, La septième porte [The seventh gate], unpublished manuscript, n.p., private collection of Touda Bouanani; Ali Amahan, "Mohamed Osfour," *Lamalif* 189 (1987): 57; Janine Fabre, "Mohamed Osfour: auteur du *Trésor Infernal*" [Mohamed Osfour: author of the *Infernal Treasure*], *Lamalif* 189 (1987): 58–62.

60. Reflecting on Sternberg's *Morocco*, Smihi comments: "The fact that Sternberg, without having been to Morocco, filmed colonization as no director had filmed it, shocked me.

Here was a Hollywood director who touched on the truth of my culture and my society." Smihi, "Cinema Arabiyya" [Arab cinema] (1993), in *Écrire sur le cinéma*, 106.

61. That his film *Hayy Ibn Yaqzan* will be shot around Ouarzazate is in part an homage to Pasolini's use of the location in his *Oedipus Rex*.

62. Carrée, "Moumen Smihi: Grandir à Tanger," 122. In the film, Khalil dreams of a beautiful young woman, Rachida, whom he encounters the next day on the streets of Tangier. After they marry, she becomes obsessed with her reflection in the mirror, in which she appears in white. After their son is born she kills him and blames the figure in the mirror. Both seem to continue a descent into madness and Rachida eventually kills herself. Khalil moves to the country but continues to meet Rachida's doubled mirror figure, whom he agrees to marry.

63. Smihi, "Anthropologie culturelle," 88.

64. See Donald Richie, *Ozu* (Berkeley: University of California Press, 1974), esp. 115–18.

65. Richie, *Ozu*, 116.

66. Carrée, "Moumen Smihi: Grandir à Tanger," 132.

67. Keya Ganguly, *Cinema, Emergence, and the Films of Satyajit Ray* (Berkeley: University of California Press, 2010), 169–71.

68. Moinak Biswas, "In the Mirror of an Alternative Globalism: The Neorealist Encounter in India," in *Italian Neorealism and Global Cinema*, ed. Laura E. Ruberto and Kristi M. Wilson (Detroit: Wayne State University Press, 2007), 72–90.

CHAPTER FOUR

1. See Talal Asad, *Formations of the Secular: Christianity, Islam, Modernity* (Stanford, CA: Stanford University Press, 2003).

2. See Talal Asad, *Genealogies of Religion* (Baltimore: Johns Hopkins University Press, 1993); Saba Mahmood, *Politics of Piety: The Islamic Revival and the Feminist Subject* (Princeton, NJ: Princeton University Press, 2005). The latter work has been especially influential in its treatment of the Islamic revival and the politics of Islamic feminism.

3. For this critical position, see in particular Aziz al-Azmeh, *Islams and Modernities* (London: Verso, 2009). For a lengthy discussion of Asad's and al-Azmeh's arguments see Ali Mirsepassi and Tadd Graham Fernée, *Islam, Democracy, and Cosmopolitanism: At Home and in the World* (Cambridge, UK: Cambridge University Press, 2014). Another extensive critique of Asad and the post-secular critics is Aamir R. Mufti, "Why I Am Not a Postsecularist," *boundary 2* 40, no. 1 (2013): 7–19, and the other essays in that special issue of *boundary 2*, "Antinomies of the Postsecular."

4. Al-Azmeh, *Islams and Modernities*, 68.

5. Here I note Asad's distinction between "the secular" as ontology or epistemology and "secularism" as a political doctrine, a distinction that is developed extensively in *Formations of the Secular*. Asad eventually concludes that "the concept of 'the secular' today is part of a doctrine called secularism" (191).

6. Mayanthi L. Fernando, *The Republic Unsettled: Muslim French and the Contradictions of Secularism* (Durham, NC: Duke University Press, 2014), esp. 7–12.

7. I have already noted Smihi's recollections of this time in the introduction. Farida Benlyazid, another Moroccan filmmaker who grew up in the city, has similar recollections:

"We heard flamenco. At Christmas, the Spanish would come out and everybody would party. At Purim, the Jewish kids would walk from house to house offering pastries. A school, we celebrated Muslim and Christian holidays, and taking the day off was allowed on Jewish holidays." Hamid Aïdouni, "L'oeuvre au feminine," in Farida Benlyazid, Hamid Aïdouni, Ighodane, Bouchta Farqzaid, Fatim, Moulay Driss Jaïdi, and Suzanne Gauch, *L'Oeuvre cinématographique de Farida Benlyazid* [The cinematic oeuvre of Farida Benlyazid] (Rabat: Publications de l'Association Marocaine des Critiques de Cinéma, 2010), 28, cited in Florence Martin, *Screens and Veils: Maghrebi Women's Cinema* (Bloomington: Indiana University Press, 2011), 65.

8. Susan Gilson Miller, *A History of Modern Morocco* (New York: Cambridge University Press, 2013), 83.

9. *Mellah* refers to the Jewish quarter in a Moroccan city. See Emily Gottreich, *The Mellah of Marrakesh: Jewish and Muslim Space in Morocco's Red City* (Bloomington: Indiana University Press, 2007).

10. Ella Shohat's work is foundational for thinking about Sephardi or Arab Jews. See Ella Shohat, "Sephardim in Israel: Zionism from the Standpoint of Its Jewish Victims," *Social Text* 19/20 (1988): 1–35.

11. See Aomar Boum, *Memories of Absence: How Muslims Remember Jews in Morocco* (Stanford, CA: Stanford University Press, 2013); Jessica M. Marglin, *Across Legal Lines: Jews and Muslims in Modern Morocco* (New Haven, CT: Yale University Press, 2016); Gottreich, *The Mellah of Marrakesh*; Alma Rachel Heckman, "Fissures and Fusions: Moroccan Jewish Communists and World War II," in *The Holocaust and North Africa*, ed. Aomar Boum and Sarah Abrevaya Stein (Stanford, CA: Stanford University Press, 2018), 185–204; Alma Rachel Heckman, "Jewish Radicals of Morocco: Case Study for a New Historiography," *Jewish Social Studies* 23, no. 30 (2018): 67–100.

12. See Oren Kosansky and Aomar Boum, "The 'Jewish Question' in Postcolonial Moroccan Cinema," *International Journal of Middle East Studies* 44 (2012): 429; Michael Laskier, *Israel and the Maghreb: From Statehood to Oslo* (Gainesville: University Press of Florida, 2004).

13. As the authors note, there were accusations that the film was Zionist propaganda; Kosansky and Boum, "The 'Jewish Question' in Postcolonial Moroccan Cinema," 435. The film is illuminated extensively in Brian T. Edwards, *After the American Century: The Ends of U.S. Culture in the Middle East* (New York: Columbia University Press, 2016), 155–80. Valérie Orlando also discusses *Marock* and *Where Are You Going, Moshe?* in *Screening Morocco: Contemporary Film in a Changing Society* (Athens: Ohio University Press, 2011), 45–50, 66–70. Similar controversy accompanied a screening of *Tinghir-Jerusalem* at the Moroccan national film festival in 2013. See Jamal Bahmad, "Tinghir-Jerusalem-Tangier: The Jew, the Imam, and the Camera in Morocco," *Africultures*, February 12, 2013, http://africultures .com/tinghir-jerusalem-tangier-the-jew-the-imam-and-the-camera-in-morocco-11305/.

14. Kosansky and Boum note a similar scene in *Goodbye Mothers*: "*Adieu mères* begins with a scene of young street urchins throwing stones at the Jewish protagonists, giving graphic depiction to their insecurity even in the context of the amicable intimacy that generally characterizes the relationship between Muslims and Jews in the film." Kosansky and Boum, "The 'Jewish Question' in Postcolonial Moroccan Cinema," 435.

15. Circumcision in Islamic cultures is performed much later than in Judaism—at a time when the boy is old enough to remember it—which can, depending on circumstances, might

be between two and ten years of age, or even older. See Vincent Crapanzano, "Rite of Return: Circumcision in Morocco," *Psychoanalytic Study of Society* 9 (1981): 15–36; Abdelwahab Bouhdiba, *Sexuality in Islam*, trans. Alan Sheridan (2004; repr., London: Saqi, 2012), 174–87.

16. Indeed, we might see that shot and a subsequent one, where the women fawn over him and his brother, as making explicit the world of women that Larbi and Khalil are leaving, since circumcision traditionally marks the end of the period where boys could occupy women's space, including the hammam.

17. Jarrod Hayes's reading of *Halfouine* (dir. Férid Boughedir, 1990) notes a similar play between the cut of circumcision and the cut of montage. Jarrod Hayes, *Queer Nations: Marginal Sexualities in the Maghreb* (Chicago: University of Chicago Press, 2000), 261. The scene in Boughedir's film, however, is graphic to the point that (as Hayes notes) it is difficult to imagine that the circumcision did not actually take place for the boy actor. In this way, the scene is diametrically opposed to Smihi's method and presentation.

18. Bouhdiba argues that circumcision is in fact not ordained in the Qur'an and yet "is regarded preeminently as the mark of inclusion in Muslim society." Bouhdiba, *Sexuality in Islam*, 174.

19. The two practices, of course, have deep associations, since circumcision is an Abrahamic rite and the 'id al-adha or 'id al-kabir celebrates Abraham's willingness to sacrifice his son for God. As Robert Lang points out in a long discussion of the practice in the films of Nouri Bouzid, the story of the Abraham and Ishmael (or Isaac, for Jews and Christians) becomes "a lesson in 'castration' that every (male) Muslim and Jew learns early in his life." Robert Lang, *New Tunisian Cinema: Allegories of Resistance* (New York: Columbia University Press, 2014), 43.

20. We might compare this to the treatment of circumcision in Nouri Bouzid's films, which, as Lang cogently argues, perform a similar critique of patriarchal authority. Lang, *New Tunisian Cinema*, esp. 42–49. For a different reading of circumcision in Boughedir's film *Halfouine* (1990) see Hayes, *Queer Nations*, 241–61.

21. See Fait Muedini, "The Promotion of Sufism in the Politics of Algeria and Morocco," *Islamic Africa* 3, no. 2 (2012): 201–26.

22. Émile Durkheim, *The Rules of Sociological Method, and Selected Texts on Sociology and Its Method* (London: Macmillan, 1982).

23. Edward Westermarck, *Ritual and Belief in Morocco*, 2 vols. (London: Macmillan, 1926).

24. Catherine Bell, *Ritual: Perspectives and Dimensions*, rev. ed. (Oxford: Oxford University Press, 2009), 46–47, 52.

25. Bell, *Ritual*, 25.

26. For a consideration of the film as an initiation narrative see Martin, *Screens and Veils*, 63–84.

27. Crapanzano, "Rite of Return," 32.

28. Philip F. Kennedy, *Abu Nuwas: A Genius of Poetry* (Oxford: Oneworld, 2009).

29. Adonis, *An Introduction to Arab Poetics*, trans. Catherine Cobham (London: Saqi, 1990), 59–60.

30. Adonis, *An Introduction to Arab Poetics*, 81.

31. The controversies of recent years show some of the consequences of transgressions, most of which pale in comparison to Pasolini's. I have already mentioned the controversy

around *Marock*, with its scantily clad protagonist who mocks her Islamist brother and has a Jew for a boyfriend. The director (Nabil Ayouch) and lead actor (Loubna Abidar) of *Much Loved* (2015), which depicts Moroccan women as prostitutes, received death threats over the film (which was banned in Morocco); Abidar felt compelled to move to France. A few years earlier, actress Latefa Ahrarre received death threats from Islamists for exposing her leg on the red carpet at Marrakesh.

32. Smihi has made this claim in conversation with the author and in Q&As at screenings.

33. Moumen Smihi, "Cinema Arabiyya" [Arab cinema] (1993), in *Écrire sur le cinéma* (Tangier: Slaïki Frères, 2006), 92.

34. On the Nahda and the modernization of Arabic see Edward Said, "Living in Arabic," *al-Ahram Weekly*, no. 677 (February 12–18, 2004); Jens Hanssen and Max Weiss, eds., "Introduction: Language, Mind, Freedom and Time," in *Arabic Thought beyond the Liberal Age: Towards an Intellectual History of the Nahda* (Cambridge, UK: Cambridge University Press, 2016), 14–18. For a consideration of the relationship between the modernization of Arabic and colonial epistemologies see Jeffrey Sacks, *Iterations of Loss: Mutilation and Aesthetic Form, al-Shidyaq to Darwish* (New York: Fordham University Press, 2015).

35. The reference is to Raphael Patai, *The Arab Mind* (New York: Scribner, 1973). For a critique of such views on language see Hanssen and Weiss, "Introduction: Language, Mind, Freedom and Time," 14; Edward Said, *Orientalism* (New York: Vintage, 1979), 321.

36. In an interview, he notes that the term "Arab-Islamic" might describe the culture in the way that "Judeo-Christian" marks some discussions of European and US culture, without implying that all subjects need be observant. Smihi, "Cinema Arabiyya," 92.

37. Elizabeth Suzanne Kassab, *Contemporary Arab Thought: Cultural Critique in Comparative Perspective* (New York: Columbia University Press, 2010), 280.

38. Smihi recounts his family's genealogy in Daniel Rondeau, *Tanger* (Paris: Quai Voltaire, 1987), 51–63. 'Abdallah Gannun (Guennoun in the French transliteration used in Rondeau) is the author of many books on Maghribi literature, for example *Ahadith 'an al-adab al-maghribi al-hadith, wa hiya muhadarat al-qaha* [Conversations on modern Maghribi literature and lectures delivered] (Cairo: Dar al-Ra'id li-l-Taba'a, 1964).

39. Leyla Dakhli, "The Autumn of the Nahda in Light of the Arab Spring: Some Figures in the Carpet," in *Arabic Thought beyond the Liberal Age*, 361.

40. Nazira Zeineddine, "From *Unveiling and Veiling*," trans. Zeina G. Halabi, in *The Arab Renaissance: A Bilingual Anthology of the Nahda*, ed. Tarek El-Ariss (New York: Modern Language Association, 2018), 374. Brackets in the original.

41. Moumen Smihi, "La nouvelle civilité" [The new civility], in *Écrire sur le cinéma*, 110–11.

42. Albert Hourani, *Arabic Thought in the Liberal Age, 1798–1939* (1962; repr., Cambridge, UK: Cambridge University Press, 1983), 43–52.

43. Tarek El-Ariss, "Introduction," in *The Arab Renaissance*, xx–xxi; Tarek El-Ariss, *Trials of Arab Modernity: Literary Affects and the New Political* (New York: Fordham University Press, 2013). See also Hanssen and Weiss, *Arabic Thought beyond the Liberal Age*.

44. Hourani, *Arabic Thought in the Liberal Age, 1798–1939*, 68.

45. Hourani, *Arabic Thought in the Liberal Age, 1798–1939*, 148.

46. Consider Hourani's description of 'Abduh's personality and magnetism, which is compellingly similar to Sidi Ahmed's portrayal in the film: "A photograph taken on the

terrace of the House of Commons when he visited England in 1884 shows a handsome man, well built, dark of complexion, with a tranquil and almost melancholy charm that does not quite conceal the look of conviction in his eyes. In later years the gentleness increased, and those who knew him well were conscious of his kindness and intelligence and a certain spiritual beauty." Hourani, *Arabic Thought in the Liberal Age, 1798–1939*, 135.

47. Hourani, *Arabic Thought in the Liberal Age, 1798–1939*, 139.

48. For a fuller account see Sacks, *Iterations of Loss*, 123–24.

49. Hourani, *Arabic Thought in the Liberal Age, 1798–1939*, 327.

50. This text is one of few by Hussein that has been translated into English. Taha Hussein, *The Future of Culture in Egypt* (New York: Octagon, 1975).

51. Bassam Tibi further develops the term "semi-modernity" in *Islam between Culture and Politics* (Houndmills, UK: Palgrave, 2001), 6.

52. Moumen Smihi, "Les récits de la nuit [Tales of the night], in *Écrire sur le cinema*, 130.

53. See Tibi, *Islam between Culture and Politics*; Kassab, *Contemporary Arab Thought*, especially chapter 2, "Critique after the 1967 Defeat"; Samir Kassir, *Being Arab*, trans. Will Hobson (London: Verso 2006).

54. al-Azmeh, *Islams and Modernities*, 67.

55. Smihi notes that this denunciation may not seem shocking in a Western setting, but his fixed shot was to ensure that it carried an explosive charge in Morocco. Roland Carrée, "Moumen Smihi: Grandir à Tanger," *Répliques* 9 (2017): 133.

56. Sartre's positions on decolonization and the Arab world are comprehensively addressed in Yoav Di-Capua, *No Exit: Arab Existentialism, Jean-Paul Sartre, and Decolonization* (Chicago: University of Chicago Press, 2018).

57. The dialogue here (delivered in the film in French; I quote from the English subtitles prepared by Laurel Hirsch) appears in English in slightly different form in Sigmund Freud, *A General Introduction to Psychoanalysis*, trans. G. Stanley Hall (New York: Boni and Liveright, 1920), 246–47.

58. Kelley Conway, *Chanteuse in the City: The Realist Singer in French Film* (Berkeley: University of California Press, 2004), 29.

59. The French verses are: "Ils étaient vingt et cent, ils étaient des milliers / Nus et maigres, tremblants, dans ces wagons plombés / Qui déchiraient la nuit de leurs ongles battants / Ils étaient des milliers, ils étaient vingt et cent / Ils s'appelaient Jean-Pierre, Natacha ou Samuel / Certains priaient Jésus, Jéhovah ou Vishnou / D'autres ne priaient pas, mais qu'importe le ciel / Ils voulaient simplement ne plus vivre à genoux."

60. Kassab, *Contemporary Arab Thought*, 226, citing Fouad Zakariyya, *al-Haqiqa wa-l-wahm fi al-haraka al-islamiyya al-mu'assira* [Truth and illusion about the contemporary Islamic movement] (Cairo: Dar al-Fikr, 1986), 240.

61. Fatima Mernissi, *Islam and Democracy: Fear of the Modern World*, trans. Mary Jo Lakeland (Reading, MA: Addison-Wesley, 1992), esp. part I, "A Mutilated Modernity," 13–74.

62. Al-Azmeh, *Islams and Modernities*, esp. 71–73.

CHAPTER FIVE

1. Fatima Mernissi, *Dreams of Trespass: Tales of a Harem Girlhood* (Reading, MA: Addison-Wesley, 1994), 189.

2. Abdelwahab Meddeb, "L'oeil féminin de la ville: *Chergui*" [The city's female eye: *Chergui*], *Cahiers du cinéma* 262/263 (1976): 103–8, esp. 106.

3. On polygamy, for example, see Nawal El Saadawi, *The Nawal El Saadawi Reader* (London: Zed, 1997), 79–85; Leila Ahmed, *Women and Gender in Islam* (New Haven, CT: Yale University Press, 1992), esp. chapter 3, "Women and the Rise of Islam."

4. Ali Essafi correctly notes that there are a significant number of black Moroccans within Moroccan film history, but few women. Ali Essafi, "Les noirs dans le paysage visuel marocain" [Black people in the Moroccan visual landscape], in *The Africans,* ed. Omar Berrada (Rabat: Kulte Editions, 2016), 68–69.

5. See Chouki El Hamel, *Black Morocco: A History of Slavery, Race, and Islam* (New York: Cambridge University Press, 2013); Omar Berrada, ed., *The Africans* (Rabat: Kulte Editions, 2016).

6. Mernissi, *Dreams of Trespass,* 34, 35n3. For an excellent collection of diverse work on the harem see Marilyn Booth, ed., *Harem Histories: Envisioning Places and Living Spaces* (Durham, NC: Duke University Press, 2010).

7. Irvin Cemil Schick, "The Harem as Gendered Space and the Spatial Reproduction of Gender," in *Harem Histories,* 69–84; Teresa de Lauretis, *Technologies of Gender: Essays on Theory, Film, and Fiction* (Bloomington: Indiana University Press, 1987).

8. The Tangier branch of the famous French store was a fixture of the modernizing Rue Siaghine, the main commercial thoroughfare in Tangier before the Boulevard Pasteur in the *ville nouvelle* took over; Smihi recalls he'd never been to the Boulevard Pasteur until he was fourteen or fifteen. Smihi, personal communication with the author, August 9, 2019; Daniel Rondeau, "Une enfance dans la medina" [A childhood in the medina], in *Tanger* (Paris: Quai Voltaire, 1987), 59.

9. Marilyn Booth, "Between Harem and Houseboat: 'Fallenness,' Gendered Spaces, and the Female National Subject in 1920s Egypt," in *Harem Histories,* 366.

10. Fatima Mernissi, *Islam and Democracy: Fear of the Modern World,* trans. Mary Jo Lakeland (Reading, MA: Addison-Wesley, 1992), 130–48; Rondeau, "Une enfance dans la medina," 57. Rondeau's chapter, entirely enclosed in quotation marks, is Smihi's own account of his childhood, as related to Rondeau over dinner at Paul Bowles's house in Tangier in the early 1980s. Rondeau was there to interview Bowles and, by chance, met Smihi, who was bringing a tagine to Bowles as he would often do.

11. Iliya Abu Madi, "al-Masa'" [The Evening], in *al-Jadawil* [The Streams], 4th ed. (Beirut: Dar al-'Ilm li-l-Malayyin, 1963), 56–62.

12. Mernissi, *Dreams of Trespass,* 119, 120.

13. Nazira Zeineddine, "From *Unveiling and Veiling,*" trans. Zeina G. Halabi, in *The Arab Renaissance: A Bilingual Anthology of the Nahda,* ed. Tarek El-Ariss (New York: Modern Language Association, 2018), 375. For the original Arabic text of the passages there (on pp. 385–92) see Nazira Zeineddine, *al-Sufur wa-l-hijab* [Veiling and unveiling], ed. Buthaina Sha'ban (Damascus: Dar al-Mada, 1998), 45–53, 92–98.

14. Mernissi, *Dreams of Trespass,* 196, 197.

15. Mernissi, *Dreams of Trespass,* 180–81.

16. Translated as Qasim Amin, *The Liberation of Women: A Document in the History of Egyptian Feminism,* trans. Samir Sidhom Peterson (Cairo: American University of Cairo Press, 1992); Marilyn Booth, "Liberal Thought and the 'Problem' of Women: Cairo, 1890s,"

in *Arabic Thought beyond the Liberal Age: Towards an Intellectual History of the Nahda*, ed. Jens Hanssen and Max Weiss (Cambridge, UK: Cambridge University Press, 2016), 190, 189.

17. Hoda Elsadda, "al-Mar'a: mantiqat muharramat: qira'a fi 'amal Qasim Amin" [The woman: Taboo realm: A reading of the works of Qasim Amim], in *Hagar: Kitab al-mar'a* [Hagar: The book of the woman], ed. Hoda Elsadda and Salwa Bakr (Cairo: Sina li-l-Nashr, 1993), 1:144–59.

18. For a succinct summary of these debates see Elizabeth Suzanne Kassab, *Contemporary Arab Thought: Cultural Critique in Comparative Perspective* (New York: Columbia University Press, 2010), 91–113. See also Lila Abu-Lughod, ed., *Remaking Women: Feminism and Modernity in the Middle East* (Princeton, NJ: Princeton University Press, 1998), especially the introduction, "Feminist Longings," and part 1, "Rewriting Feminist Beginnings"; Jean Said Makdisi, Noha Bayoumi, and Rafif Rida Sidawi, eds., *Arab Feminisms: Gender and Equality in the Middle East* (London: I. B. Tauris, 2014).

19. Interview with the author, July 5, 2010, Tangier. See also Roland Carrée, "Moumen Smihi: Grandir à Tanger," *Répliques* 9 (2017): 115.

20. In that spirit of dissent see Nadia Yaqub and Rula Quawas, eds., *Bad Girls of the Arab World* (Austin: University of Texas Press, 2017), which analyzes many representations in contemporary culture and politics of transgressive and dissenting feminist voices from the region.

21. Viola Shafik, *Popular Egyptian Cinema* (Cairo: American University in Cairo Press, 2006), 256, 257.

22. Jean Said Makdisi, "Faten Hamama and Hind Rustom: Stars from Different Heavens," *al-Raida* 122/123 (2008): 28.

23. Shafik, *Popular Egyptian Cinema*, 218, see esp. the section titled "The Virgin-Whore Dichotomy," 218–27. Rania Stephan's film *The Three Disappearances of Soad Hosni* (2011) traces Hosni's place in Egyptian cinema from a montage of found VHS footage of her performances, including the slap in *Take Care of Zuzu* (dir. Hassan al-Imam, 1972). The cumulative effect of these scenes makes an argument for what Hosni suffered diegetically and non-diegetically.

24. Robert Lang, *New Tunisian Cinema: Allegories of Resistance* (New York: Columbia University Press, 2014), 21.

25. Brian T. Edwards, *After the American Century: The Ends of U.S. Culture in the Middle East* (New York: Columbia University Press, 2016). See also Roberto Pujante González, "Désir et sexualités non normatives au Maghreb et dans la diaspora" [Non-normative desire and sexualities in the Maghrib and the diaspora], *Expressions Maghrebines* 16, no. 1 (2017): 1–19; also see the other articles in the same special issue of *Expressions Maghrebines,* especially Madeleine Löning, "Un film qui 'trouble': Subversion des identités de genre et de la sexualité dans *Much loved* de Nabil Ayouch" [A film that 'disturbs:' the subversion of gender identities and sexuality in *Much Loved* by Nabil Ayouch], 183–99.

26. Florence Martin, *Screens and Veils: Maghrebi Women's Cinema* (Bloomington: Indiana University Press, 2011); Valérie Orlando, *Screening Morocco: Contemporary Film in a Changing Society* (Athens: Ohio University Press, 2011).

27. Suzanne Gauch, *Maghrebs in Motion: North African Cinema in Nine Movements* (New York: Oxford University Press, 2016), 18, 114–30.

28. Edward Said, *Orientalism* (1978; repr., New York: Vintage, 1979).

29. See for example Matthew Bernstein and Gaylyn Studlar, eds., *Visions of the East: Orientalism in Film* (1978; repr., New Brunswick, NJ: Rutgers University Press, 1997).

30. Jarrod Hayes, *Queer Nations: Marginal Sexualities in the Maghreb* (Chicago: University of Chicago Press, 2000), 185.

31. Massad is right on this point, although I cannot follow him to his larger conclusion: that the discourses of gay identities and rights in the Arab world are readable only as the neo-imperialist imposition of a "Gay International." See Joseph A. Massad, *Desiring Arabs* (Chicago: University of Chicago Press, 1987). For other explorations of gender and sexuality in the Arab and Muslim worlds see Afsaneh Najmabadi, *Women with Mustaches and Men without Beards: Gender and Sexual Anxieties of Iranian Modernity* (Berkeley: University of California Press, 2005); Abdelwahab Bouhdiba, *Sexuality in Islam*, trans. Alan Sheridan (2004; repr., London: Saqi, 2012); Kathryn Babayan and Afsaneh Najmabadi, eds., *Islamicate Sexualities: Translations across Temporal Geographies of Desire* (Cambridge, MA: Center for Middle Eastern Studies and Harvard University Press, 2008).

32. Hayes, *Queer Nations*, 285–86. See also Joseph Boone, *The Homoerotics of Orientalism: Mappings of Male Desire in Narratives of the Near and Middle East* (New York: Columbia University Press, 2014).

33. Rondeau, "Une enfance dans la medina," 53.

34. Brian T. Edwards, "Queer Tangier," in *Morocco Bound: Disorienting America's Maghreb, from Casablanca to the Marrakech Express* (Durham, NC: Duke University Press, 2005), 121–97.

35. See his op-ed a year after the start of the Arab Spring uprisings: Abdellah Taïa, "A Boy to Be Sacrificed," *New York Times*, March 24, 2012, https://www.nytimes.com/2012/03/25/opinion/sunday/a-boy-to-be-sacrificed.html.

36. The narrative presents the young masked woman as seeking out, flirting with, and willingly and laughingly submitting to at least two of the group (and, by implication, others). The film's protagonist, however, is traumatized by the act, which lends it more the register of a gang rape.

37. Eve Kosofsky Sedgwick, *Between Men: English Literature and Male Homosocial Desire* (New York: Columbia University Press, 1992).

38. See Lang, *New Tunisian Cinema*, 45–46. Hayes offers a quite different reading of the way that the Tunisian film *Halfaouine* (dir. Férid Boughedir, 1990) and two other Maghribi literary texts "offer a paradigm for understanding the challenge to Maghribian masculinity carried out through a cultivation of the joy of castration." Hayes, *Queer Nations*, 241. While I agree with his embrace of a feminized masculinity as a potential route to queer identifications, the emotional register of circumcision and the threat of castration in Smihi's and Bouzid's films remains, with Bouhdiba and Crapanzano, one of trauma. See Bouhdiba, *Sexuality in Islam*; Vincent Crapanzano, "Rite of Return: Circumcision in Morocco," *Psychoanalytic Study of Society* 9 (1981): 15–36.

39. Of course, in the Freudian account, fetishism is what allows the boy to avoid homosexuality. Here the equation is looser and, while constructing Larbi as something of a fetishist, the film also allows intimations of a more generalized queerness around its main character.

40. Philip F. Kennedy, *Abu Nuwas: A Genius of Poetry* (Oxford: Oneworld, 2009), 62.

41. One is reminded of Pasolini's reply to his Marxist critics that *Arabian Nights* was not political enough, a response cited (and put in its phallocentric context) by Boone in his

discussions of sex and Orientalism: "Ideology [is] really there, over [your] heads, in the enormous cock on the screen." Joseph Boone, "Framing the Phallus in the *Arabian Nights*: Pansexuality, Pederasty, Pasolini," in *Translations/Transformation: Gender and Culture in Film and Literature East and West*, ed. Valerie Wayne and Cornelia Moore (Honolulu: University of Hawaii Press, 1993), 28.

42. That combination might recall the depiction of 1968 in Paris in Bernardo Bertolucci's *The Dreamers* (2003).

43. Tarek El-Ariss, "Introduction," in *The Arab Renaissance*, xvii.

FILMOGRAPHY

Many of the films below are available for public, classroom, or research screening in a variety of formats and subtitled languages. For up-to-date information on availability, please see https://limbrick.sites.ucsc.edu.

Si Moh, the Unlucky Man [Si Moh, pas de chance], 1971, 17 min.

Colors on Bodies [Couleurs aux corps], 1972, 20 min.

The East Wind [al-Shergui wa samt al-'anif / El Chergui ou le silence violent: vent d'est], 1975, 80 min.

44, or Tales of the Night [44 aw usturat al-layl / 44, ou, les récits de la nuit], 1981, 110 min.

Caftan of Love [Quftan al-hub al-munaqat bi-l hawa / Caftan d'amour, constellé de passion], 1989, 90 min.

Egyptian Cinema: Defense and Illustration [Taqarir mujaza 'an al-sinima al-masriyya / Cinéma égyptien: défense et illustration], 1989, 52 min.

The Lady from Cairo [Sayyidat al-Qahira / La dame du Caire], 1991, 90 min.

With Matisse in Tangier [Avec Matisse à Tanger], 1993, 52 min.

The Medina of Paris: Supererogatory Prayer by a Muslim Dignatory—My Father—After Landing at Paris-Orly [La médina de Paris: Prière surérogatoire d'un dignataire musulman—mon père—après atterrissage à Paris-Orly], 1996, 1 min., https://vimeo.com/69467769.

The Medina of Paris: A Square during the Ramadan Market [La médina de Paris: Une place lors du souk de Ramadan], 1996, 1 min., https://vimeo.com/104704891.

Moroccan Chronicles [Waqa'a' maghribiyya / Chroniques marocaines], 1999, 70 min.

A Muslim Childhood [al-'Ayal: tufula mutamarrida / Le gosse de Tanger: une enfance rebelle], 2005, 83 min.

Girls and Swallows [al-Khuta'if 'adhara wa sununu / Les cris de jeune filles des hirondelles], 2008, 80 min.
The Sorrows of a Young Tangerian [Tanjawi, ahlam wa ahzan al-tanjawi al-shab al-'Arabi al-Salmi / Tanjaoui: peines de Coeur et tourments du jeune tanjaoui Larbi Salmi], 2013, 95 min.
With Taha Hussein [Avec Taha Hussein], 2015, 87 min.

BIBLIOGRAPHY

WORK BY MOUMEN SMIHI

English

"Moroccan Society as Mythology." In *Film and Politics in the Third World*, edited by John Downing, 77–87. New York: Praeger, 1987. Translation of an interview with Guy Hennebelle, first published as "La société marocaine comme mythologie" [Moroccan society as mythology]. *Cinémaction* 14 (1981): 217–23.

"Moumen Smihi, Poet of Tangier." Series of onstage conversations with the author after screenings at Tate Modern, May 18, 2014. https://www.tate.org.uk/context-comment/audio/moumen-smihi-poet-tangier-audio-recordings#open298637.

French

"L'atelier, l'agence, la villa." *Al Bayane*, March 20, 2017. http://albayane.press.ma/latelier-lagence-la-villa.html

"Le cercle flamboyant" [The blazing circle]. *Intégral* 8 (1974): 39–43.

"Un cinéaste marocain au Caire." *Égypte/Monde Arabe*, December 31, 1991, 49–62. https://journals.openedition.org/ema/1203. Republished as "Mythologies Arabes" [Arab mythologies], in *Écrire sur le cinéma* (Tangier: Slaïki Frères, 2006), 151–64.

"Du cinema à la cinécriture" [From cinema to cinécriture]. *Intégral* 3/4 (1973): 50–52. Republished as "Cinécriture d'Eisenstein" [Eisensteinian *cinécriture*], in *Écrire sur le cinéma* (Tangier: Slaïki Frères, 2006), 31–34.

Écrire sur le cinéma [Writing on cinema]. Tangier: Slaïki Frères, 2006.

"Entretien avec Moumen Smihi" [Interview with Moumen Smihi]. With Joel Farges. *Ça* 9 (1976): 53–57.

"Entretien avec Moumen Smihi" [Interview with Moumen Smihi]. With Guy Hennebelle. *Écran*, February 15, 1976, 46–47.

"Entretien avec Moumen Smihi. Chergui ou le silence violent" [Interview with Moumen Smihi: the east wind or the violent silence]. With Amran El-Maleh. *Intégral* 11 (1976): 31–33.

"Entretien avec Robert Bresson." *Image et son: la revue du cinema* 215 (January 1968): 68–71. Republished as "Avec Robert Bresson" [With Robert Bresson], in *Écrire sur le cinéma* (Tangier: Slaïki Frères, 2006), 9–13.

"Lettre du Maroc." *Cinématograph* 109 (April 1985): 26–27. Republished as "Choc de cultures" [Culture shock], in *Écrire sur le cinéma* (Tangier: Slaïki Frères, 2006), 133–36.

"Moumen Smihi et la distribution au Maroc: Le refus et le silence" [Moumen Smihi and distribution in Morocco: denial and silence]. Interview. *Lamalif* 82 (1976): 31–35.

"Moumen Smihi: Le silence violent" [Moumen Smihi: the violent silence]. Interview with Noureddine Ghali. *Cinema 76*, no. 205 (January 1976): 92–101. Republished as "La mémoire clandestine" [Clandestine memory], in *Écrire sur le cinema* (Tangier: Slaïki Frères, 2006), 121–27.

"Paris, notre mecque" [Paris, our Mecca]. *Cinémaction* 56 (1990): 136–39.

"Petite sociologie du cinema au Maroc" [A short sociology of cinema in Morocco]. *Intégral* 11 (1976): 27–30. Republished as "Qu'est-ce que le public?" [What is the audience?], in *Écrire sur le cinema* (Tangier: Slaïki Frères, 2006), 35–40.

"Le plateau comme autre scène: psychanalyse de la réalisation" [The set as other scene: the psychoanalysis of direction]. *Cinémaction* 50 (1989): 104–7.

"R. B., une maître savoureux." *Al Bayane*, March 23, 2015. http://albayane.press.ma/special-centenaire-roland-barthes.html.

"Les récits de la nuit [Tales of the night], in *Écrire sur le cinema* (Tangier: Slaïki Frères, 2006), 128–32.

"Si l'image arabe venait à disparaître" [If the Arab image just disappeared]. *Cinémaction* 43 (1987): 99–105. Republished as "Image de soi, pour soi, pour l'autre" [Image of the self, for the self and for the other], in *Écrire sur le cinema* (Tangier: Slaïki Frères, 2006), 137–45.

"La société marocaine comme mythologie" [Moroccan society as mythology]. Interview with Guy Hennebelle. *Cinémaction* 14 (1981): 217–23. Translated into English and republished as "Moroccan Society as Mythology," in *Film and Politics in the Third World*, edited by John Downing, 77–87. New York: Praeger, 1987.

"Un pays qui ne produit pas d'images est menacé de famine" [A country that does not produce images is threatened with famine]. Radio interview with Françoise Estève. France Culture, 1987. https://www.franceculture.fr/emissions/les-nuits-de-france-culture/moumen-smihi-un-pays-qui-ne-produit-pas-dimages-est-menace-de.

Arabic

(as Mu'min al-Smihi)

Abqariyat sinima 'iyya [Geniuses of cinema]. Translation of texts by Sergei Eisenstein, Jean Renoir, Roberto Rossellini, and Alfred Hitchcock, with preface by Moumen Smihi. Tangier: Siliki Ikhwan, 2011.

Fi al-sinima al-'arabiyya [On Arab cinema]. Tangier: Siliki Ikhwan, 2009.

Hadith al-sinima [Conversations about cinema]. 2 vols. Tangier: Siliki Ikhwan, 2005, 2006.

al-Zul al-dar [The shadow of the signifier]. Tangier: Siliki Ikhwan, 2013.

GENERAL BIBLIOGRAPHY

Abu-Lughod, Ibrahim. *The Arab Rediscovery of Europe: A Study in Cultural Encounters.* London: Saqi, 2011. First published 1963.

Abu-Lughod, Lila, ed. *Remaking Women: Feminism and Modernity in the Middle East.* Princeton, NJ: Princeton University Press, 1998.

Abu Madi, Iliya. *Al-Jadawil* [The Streams]. 4th ed. Beirut: Dar al-'Ilm li-l-Malayyin, 1963.

Adonis. *An Introduction to Arab Poetics.* Translated by Catherine Cobham. London: Saqi, 1990.

Ahmed, Leila. *A Quiet Revolution: The Veil's Resurgence, from the Middle East to America.* New Haven, CT: Yale University Press, 2012.

———. *Women and Gender in Islam.* New Haven, CT: Yale University Press, 1992.

Alami, Mohammed Hamdouni. *Art and Architecture in the Islamic Tradition.* New York: I. B. Tauris, 2011.

Allen, Roger. *The Arabic Novel: An Historical and Critical Introduction.* Syracuse, NY: Syracuse University Press, 1982.

Altman, Rick. *Sound Theory / Sound Practice.* London: Routledge, 1992.

Amahan, Ali. "Mohamed Osfour." *Lamalif* 189 (1987): 57.

Amin, Qasim. *The Liberation of Women: A Document in the History of Egyptian Feminism.* Translated by Samir Sidhom Peterson. Cairo: American University of Cairo Press, 1992.

Amine, Khalid, and Marvin Carlson. *The Theatres of Morocco, Algeria, and Tunisia: Performance Traditions of the Maghreb.* New York: Palgrave, 2012.

Andary, Nezar, and Samirah Alkassim. *The Cinema of Muhammad Malas: Visions of a Syrian Auteur.* Cham, Switzerland: Palgrave Macmillan, 2018.

Andrew, Dudley. "An Atlas of World Cinema." In *Remapping World Cinema: Identity, Culture and Politics in Film,* edited by Stephanie Dennison and Song Hwee Lim, 19–29. London: Wallflower, 2006.

al-Ariss, Ibrahim. "Salah Abu Seif on Salah Abu Seif: Portrait of a Director." In *Catalogo della retrospettiva cinematografica "Il cinema secondo Salah Abou Seif."* Naples: Cinemamed, 2002. http://euromedi.org/home/azioni/pubblicazioni/artedanza/salah/ARISS.PDF.

Armbrust, Walter. *Mass Culture and Modernism in Egypt.* Cambridge, UK: Cambridge University Press, 1996.

Armes, Roy. *Dictionary of North African Filmmakers.* Bilingual ed. Collection Camera des Trois Mondes. Paris: Editions ATM, 1996.

———. *New Voices in Arab Cinema.* Bloomington: Indiana University Press, 2015.

———. *Postcolonial Images: Studies in North African Film.* Bloomington: Indiana University Press, 2005.

———. *Roots of the New Arab Film.* Bloomington: Indiana University Press, 2018.

Asad, Talal. *Formations of the Secular: Christianity, Islam, Modernity.* Stanford, CA: Stanford University Press, 2003.

———. *Genealogies of Religion: Discipline and Reasons of Power in Christianity and Islam.* Baltimore: Johns Hopkins University Press, 1993.

Ashwika, Mohamad. *Fi Jumaliyat sinima Mu'min al-Smihi* [Moumen Smihi's cinema aesthetics]. In *Al-Sinima al-maghribia: rihanat al-hadatha wa wa'i al-that* [Maghribi cinema: the stakes of modernity and awareness of self]. Rabat: Dar al-Tawhidi li-l-Nashr, 2012.

Astruc, Alexandre. "The Birth of a New Avant-Garde: La Caméra-Stylo." In *Critical Visions in Film Theory: Classical and Contemporary Readings*, edited by Timothy Corrigan and Patricia White with Meta Mazaj, 350–54. Boston: Bedford/St. Martins, 2011.

Attar, Samar. *The Vital Roots of European Enlightenment: Ibn Tufayl's Influence on Modern Western Thought*. Lanham, MD: Lexington, 2007.

al-Azmeh, Aziz. *Islams and Modernities*. 3rd ed. London: Verso, 2009.

Babayan, Kathryn, and Afsaneh Najmabadi, eds. *Islamicate Sexualities: Translations across Temporal Geographies of Desire*. Cambridge, MA: Center for Middle Eastern Studies and Harvard University Press, 2008.

Badawi, M. M. *Modern Arabic Literature and the West*. London: Ithaca, 1985.

Bahmad, Jamal. "Tinghir-Jerusalem-Tangier: The Jew, the Imam, and the Camera in Morocco." *Africultures*, February 12, 2013. http://africultures.com/tinghir-jerusalem-tangier-the-jew-the-imam-and-the-camera-in-morocco-11305/.

Bakhtin, Mikhail. *Problems of Dostoevsky's Poetics*. Edited and translated by Caryl Emerson. Minneapolis: University of Minnesota Press, 1984.

Bakrim, Mohammed. "De Matisse à Taha Hussein" [From Matisse to Taha Hussein]. Interview with Moumen Smihi. *Al Bayane*, May 7, 2015. http://albayane.press.ma/de-matisse-a-taha-hossein.html.

———. "Du documentaire et de la fiction" [On documentary and fiction]. Interview with Moumen Smihi. *Al Bayane*, May 8, 2015. http://albayane.press.ma/du-documentaire-et-de-la-fiction.html.

Barthes, Roland. "L'art vocal bourgeois" [Bourgeois vocal art]. In *Mythologies*, 189–91. Paris: Éditions de Seuil, 1957.

———. *Image, Music, Text*. Translated by Stephen Heath. New York: Hill and Wang, 1972.

Bashkin, Orit. "Arabic Thought in the Radical Age: Emile Habibi, the Israeli Communist Party, and the Production of Arab Jewish Radicalism, 1946–1961." In *Arabic Thought against the Authoritarian Age: Towards an Intellectual History of the Present*, edited by Jens Hanssen and Max Weiss, 62–85. Cambridge, UK: Cambridge University Press, 2018.

Baucom, Ian. "Frantz Fanon's Radio: Solidarity, Diaspora, and the Tactics of Listening." *Contemporary Literature* 42, no. 1 (2001): 15–49.

Bazin, André. *What Is Cinema?* Translated by Hugh Gray. Berkeley: University of California Press, 1967.

———. *What Is Cinema? Volume II*. Translated by Hugh Gray. Berkeley: University of California Press, 1971.

Beinin, Joel. "Egyptian Workers in the Liberal Age and Beyond." In *Arabic Thought against the Authoritarian Age: Towards an Intellectual History of the Present*, edited by Jens Hanssen and Max Weiss, 233–61. Cambridge, UK: Cambridge University Press, 2018.

Bell, Catherine. *Ritual: Perspectives and Dimensions*. Revised edition. Oxford: Oxford University Press, 2009.

Bénézet, Delphine. *The Cinema of Agnès Varda: Resistance and Eclecticism*. London: Wallflower, 2014.

Benlyazid, Farida, Hamid Aïdouni, Ighodane, Bouchta Farqzaid, Fatim, Moulay Driss Jaïdi, and Suzanne Gauch. *L'Oeuvre cinématographique de Farida Benlyazid* [The cinematic oeuvre of Farida Benlyazid]. Rabat: Publications de l'Association Marocaine des Critiques de Cinéma, 2010.

Bensmaïa, Reda. "A Cinema of Cruelty." In *Building Bridges: The Cinema of Jean Rouch*, edited by Joram Ten Brink, 73–85. London: Wallflower, 2007.

Berman, Marshall. *All That Is Solid Melts into Air: The Experience of Modernity*. New York: Simon and Schuster, 1982.

Bernstein, Matthew, and Gaylyn Studlar, eds. *Visions of the East: Orientalism in Film*. New Brunswick, NJ: Rutgers University Press, 1997. First published 1978.

Berrada, Omar, ed. *The Africans*. Rabat: Kulte Editions, 2016.

Berrada, Omar, and Yto Barrada, eds. *Album—Cinémathèque de Tanger*. Barcelona: La Virreina Centre de la Imatge; Tangier: Librarie des Colonnes, 2012.

Berrah, Mouny, Victor Bachy, Mohand Ben Salama, and Férid Boughedir, eds. "Cinemas du Maghreb." Special issue, *Cinémaction* 14 (1981).

Bisani, Othman. "Al-Antrubuluji wa-l-untuluji fi *al-Sharqi aw al-samt al-'anif* [Anthropology and ontology in *The East Wind or the violent silence*]. In *Sinima Mu'min al-Smihi. Qalaq al-tajrib wa fa'iliyyat al-ta'sis al-nathri* [The cinema of Moumen Smihi: passion for experimentation and richness of theoretical foundation], edited by Jumiat al-qabas al-sinima wa-l-thaqafa [Al Qabas association for cinema and culture], 38–45. Errachidia, Morocco: Benlefqih, 2010.

Biswas, Moinak. "In the Mirror of an Alternative Globalism: The Neorealist Encounter in India." In *Italian Neorealism and Global Cinema*, edited by Laura E. Ruberto and Kristi M. Wilson, 72–90. Detroit: Wayne State University Press, 2007.

Bloch, Ernst, George Lukács, Bertolt Brecht, Walter Benjamin, and Theodor Adorno. *Aesthetics and Politics*. London: NLB, 1977.

Boone, Joseph. "Framing the Phallus in the *Arabian Nights*: Pansexuality, Pederasty, Pasolini." In *Translations/Transformation: Gender and Culture in Film and Literature East and West*, edited by Valerie Wayne and Cornelia Moore, 23–33. Honolulu: University of Hawaii Press, 1993.

———. *The Homoerotics of Orientalism: Mappings of Male Desire in Narratives of the Near and Middle East*. New York: Columbia University Press, 2014.

Booth, Marilyn. "Between Harem and Houseboat: 'Fallenness,' Gendered Spaces, and the Female National Subject in 1920s Egypt." In *Harem Histories: Envisioning Places and Living Spaces*, edited by Marilyn Booth, 342–73. Durham, NC: Duke University Press, 2010.

———. "Liberal Thought and the 'Problem' of Women: Cairo, 1890s." In *Arabic Thought beyond the Liberal Age: Towards an Intellectual History of the Nahda*, edited by Jens Hanssen and Max Weiss, 187–213. Cambridge, UK: Cambridge University Press, 2016.

Booth, Marilyn, ed. *Harem Histories: Envisioning Places and Living Spaces*. Durham, NC: Duke University Press, 2010.

Bou Ali, Nadia. "Collecting the Nation: Lexicography and National Pedagogy in *al-nahda al-'arabiyya*." In *Archives, Museums and Collecting Practices in the Modern Arab World*, edited by Sonja Mejcher-Atassi and John Pedro Schwartz, 33–56. Surrey, UK: Ashgate, 2012.

Bouanani, Ahmed. "An Introduction to Popular Moroccan Poetry." Translated by Robyn Creswell. In *Souffles-Anfas: A Critical Anthology from the Moroccan Journal of Culture and Politics*, edited by Olivia C. Harrison and Teresa Villa-Ignacio, 46–55. Stanford, CA: Stanford University Press, 2016.

———. "La septième porte" [The seventh gate]. Unpublished manuscript. Private collection of Touda Bouanani.

Bouhdiba, Abdelwahab. *Sexuality in Islam*. Translated by Alan Sheridan. London: Saqi, 2012. First published 2004.

Boujibar, Naïma, and Mohamed Mezzine. "Andalusian Morocco." In *Andalusian Morocco: A Discovery in Living Art*, edited by the Museum with No Frontiers, 50–63. Rabat: Ministry of Cultural Affairs of the Kingdom of Morocco, 2002.

Boukhari, Karim. "*Marock*: Le film de tous les tabous" [*Marock*: the film of all the taboos]. *TelQuel* 223 (2006): 40–47.

Boulanger, Pierre. *Le cinema colonial: de l'Atlantide à Lawrence d'Arabie* [The colonial cinema: from *Atlantis* to *Lawrence of Arabia*] (Paris: Éditions Segher, 1975).

Boum, Aomar. *Memories of Absence: How Muslims Remember Jews in Morocco*. Stanford, CA: Stanford University Press, 2013.

Bounfour, A., and Salim Jay. "*Chergui*: un film qui vous colle à la peau" [*The East Wind*: a film that sticks with you]. *Lamalif* 79 (1976): 42–43.

Bouthier, Marie. "Moumen Smihi et Tanger: des Femmes, une Histoire" [Moumen Smihi and Tanger: women, a history]. *Zamane*, April 2012, 94–97.

———. *See also* Pierre-Bouthier, Marie.

Bouzid, Nouri. "New Realism in Arab Cinema: The Defeat-Conscious Cinema." Translated by Shereen el-Ezabi. *Alif: Journal of Comparative Poetics* 15 (1995): 242–50.

Box, Laura Chakravarty. "North Africa's Performing Women: Notes from the Field." *Al-Raida* 122/123 (2008): 8–16.

Boyd, Douglas A. *Broadcasting in the Arab World: A Survey of Radio and Television in the Middle East*. Philadelphia: Temple University Press, 1982.

———. *Egyptian Radio: Tool of Political and National Development*. Journalism Monographs 48. Lexington, KY: Association for Education in Journalism, 1977.

Brahimi, Denise. *Cinémas d'Afrique francophone et du Maghreb* [Francophone and Maghribi cinemas]. Paris: Nathan, 1997.

Budgen, Frank. *James Joyce and the Making of Ulysses*. Bloomington: Indiana University Press, 1960.

Burkhalter, Thomas, Kay Dickinson, and Benjamin J. Harbert, eds. *The Arab Avant-Garde: Music, Politics, Modernity*. Middletown, CT: Wesleyan University Press, 2013.

Caminero-Santangelo, Byron. "Beyond Writing Back: Alternative Uses of Postcolonial Cultural Hybridity." In *African Fiction and Joseph Conrad: Reading Postcolonial Intertextuality*. Albany: State University of New York Press, 2005.

Carrée, Roland. "Moumen Smihi: Grandir à Tanger." *Répliques* 9 (2017): 112–43.

Carter, Sandra Gayle. *What Moroccan Cinema?: A Historical and Critical Study, 1956–2006*. Lanham, MD: Lexington, 2009.

Casanova, Pascale. *The World Republic of Letters*. Translated by M. B. DeBevoise. Cambridge, MA: Harvard University Press, 2004.

Chakrabarty, Dipesh. *Habitations of Modernity: Essays in the Wake of Subaltern Studies*. Chicago: University of Chicago Press, 2002.

———. *Provincializing Europe: Postcolonial Thought and Historical Difference*. Princeton, NJ: Princeton University Press, 2008. First published 2000.

Chion, Michel. *Audio-Vision: Sound on Screen*. Translated by Claudia Gorbman. New York: Columbia University Press, 1994.

———. "Dissolution of the Notion of Timbre." Translated by James A. Steintrager. *Differences* 22, nos. 2/3 (2011): 235–39.
———. "Let's Have Done with the Notion of 'Noise.'" Translated by James A. Steintrager. *Differences* 22, nos. 2/3 (2011): 240–48.
———. *Sound: An Acoulogical Treatise*. Translated by James A. Steintrager. Durham, NC: Duke University Press, 2016.
———. *The Voice in Cinema*. Translated by Claudia Gorbman. New York: Columbia University Press, 1999.
Chow, Rey. *Primitive Passions: Visuality, Sexuality, Ethnography, and Contemporary Chinese Cinema*. New York: Columbia University Press, 1995.
Cluny, Claude Michel. *Dictionnaire des nouveaux cinemas arabes* [Dictionary of the new Arab cinemas]. Paris: Sindbad, 1978.
Conway, Kelley. *Chanteuse in the City: The Realist Singer in French Film*. Berkeley: University of California Press, 2004.
Corrigan, Timothy. *The Essay Film: From Montaigne, after Marker*. New York: Oxford University Press, 2011.
Crapanzano, Vincent. "Rite of Return: Circumcision in Morocco." *Psychoanalytic Study of Society* 9 (1981): 15–36.
Creswell, Robyn. *City of Beginnings: Poetic Modernism in Beirut*. Princeton, NJ: Princeton University Press, 2019.
———. "Modernism in Translation: Poetry and Intellectual History in Beirut." In *Arabic Thought against the Authoritarian Age: Towards an Intellectual History of the Present*, edited by Jens Hanssen and Max Weiss, 113–42. Cambridge, UK: Cambridge University Press, 2018.
Dakhli, Leyla. "The Autumn of the Nahda in Light of the Arab Spring: Some Figures in the Carpet." In *Arabic Thought beyond the Liberal Age: Towards an Intellectual History of the Nahda*, edited by Jens Hanssen and Max Weiss, 351–71. Cambridge, UK: Cambridge University Press, 2016.
Danielson, Virginia. *The Voice of Egypt: Umm Kulthum, Arabic Song, and Egyptian Society in the Twentieth Century*. Chicago: University of Chicago Press, 1997.
Dayan, Daniel. "The Tutor Code of Classical Cinema." *Film Quarterly* 28, no. 1 (1974): 22–31.
De Lauretis, Teresa. *Technologies of Gender: Essays on Theory, Film, and Fiction*. Bloomington: Indiana University Press, 1987.
Dennison, Stephanie, and Song Hwee Lim, eds. *Remapping World Cinema: Identity, Culture and Politics in Film*. London: Wallflower, 2006.
Di-Capua, Yoav. "Changing the Arab Intellectual Guard: On the Fall of the *udaba'*, 1940–1960." In *Arabic Thought against the Authoritarian Age: Towards an Intellectual History of the Present*, edited by Jens Hanssen and Max Weiss, 41–61. Cambridge, UK: Cambridge University Press, 2018.
———. *No Exit: Arab Existentialism, Jean-Paul Sartre, and Decolonization*. Chicago: University of Chicago Press, 2018.
Dickinson, Kay. *Arab Cinema Travels: Transnational Syria, Palestine, Dubai and Beyond*. London: British Film Institute, 2016.

———. *Arab Film and Video Manifestos: Forty-Five Years of the Moving Image Amid Revolution*. Cham, Switzerland: Palgrave Macmillan, 2018.
Doane, Mary Ann. "The Voice in the Cinema: The Articulation of Body and Space." *Yale French Studies* 60 (1980): 33–50.
Durkheim, Émile. *The Rules of Sociological Method, and Selected Texts on Sociology and Its Method*. London: Macmillan, 1982.
Dwyer, Kevin. *Beyond Casablanca: M. A. Tazi and the Adventure of Moroccan Cinema*. Bloomington: Indiana University Press, 2004.
Edwards, Brian T. *After the American Century: The Ends of U.S. Culture in the Middle East*. New York: Columbia University Press, 2016.
———. *Morocco Bound: Disorienting America's Maghreb, from Casablanca to the Marrakech Express*. Durham, NC: Duke University Press, 2005.
El-Ariss, Tarek. *Trials of Arab Modernity: Literary Affects and the New Political*. New York: Fordham University Press, 2013.
El-Ariss, Tarek, ed. *The Arab Renaissance: A Bilingual Anthology of the Nahda*. New York: Modern Language Association, 2018.
El Hamel, Chouki. *Black Morocco: A History of Slavery, Race, and Islam*. New York: Cambridge University Press, 2013.
Elias, Chad. "The Libidinal Archive: A Conversation with Akram Zaatari." *Tate Papers*, no. 19 (Spring 2013): https://www.tate.org.uk/research/publications/tate-papers/19/the-libidinal-archive-a-conversation-with-akram-zaatari.
El Saadawi, Nawal. *The Nawal El Saadawi Reader*. London: Zed, 1997.
Elsadda, Hoda. "Al Mar'a: mantiqat muharramat: qira'a fi 'amal Qasim Amin" [The woman: taboo realm: a reading of the works of Qasim Amim]. In *Hagar: Kitab al-mar'a* [Hagar: the book of the woman], edited by Hoda Elsadda and Salwa Bakr, 1:144–59. Cairo: Sina li-l-Nashr, 1993.
Essafi, Ali. "Les noirs dans le paysage visuel marocain" [Black people in the Moroccan visual landscape]. In *The Africans*, edited by Omar Berrada, 64–69. Rabat: Kulte Editions, 2016.
Ezzedine, Salah. "The Role of Music in Arabic Films." In *The Cinema in the Arab Countries*, edited by George Sadoul, 46–53. Beirut: Interarab Centre of Cinema and Television, 1966.
Fabre, Janine. "Mohamed Osfour: auteur du *Trésor infernal*" [Mohamed Osfour: author of the *Infernal Treasure*]. *Lamalif* 189 (1987): 58–62.
Fanon, Frantz. "This Is the Voice of Algeria." In *A Dying Colonialism*, translated by Haakon Chevalier, 69–97. New York: Grove, 1965.
Farid, Samir. *Al-Waqi'iyya al-jadida fi al-sinima al-misriyya* [The new realism in Egyptian cinema]. Cairo: al-Haya al-Misriyya al-'Ama li-l-Kitab, 1992.
———. *Najib Mahfuz wa-l-sinima* [Najib Mahfouz and the cinema]. Cairo: al-Haya al-'Ama li-Qusur al-Thaqafa, 1990.
Farqzaid, Bouchta. "*El Chergui ou le silence violent*: Destin au pluriel ou la métaphore du chou romanesco" [*The East Wind or the Violent Silence*: plural destiny or the metaphor of the romanesco]. In *Sinima Mu'min al-Smihi. Qalaq al-tajrib wa fa'iliyyat al-ta'sis al-nathri* [The cinema of Moumen Smihi: passion for experimentation and richness of theoretical foundation], edited by Jumiat al-qabas al-sinima wa-l-thaqafa [Al Qabas association for cinema and culture], 6–18. Errachidia, Morocco: Benlefqih, 2010.

El-Fasi, Mohammed. *Chants anciens des femmes de Fes* [Ancient songs of the women of Fez]. Paris: Seghers, 1967.
Feld, Steven. "Editor's Introduction." In *Ciné-Ethnography*, edited and translated by Steven Feld, 1–25. Minneapolis: University of Minnesota Press, 2003.
Fernando, Mayanthi L. *The Republic Unsettled: Muslim French and the Contradictions of Secularism*. Durham, NC: Duke University Press, 2014.
Freud, Sigmund. *A General Introduction to Psychoanalysis*. Translated by G. Stanley Hall. New York: Boni and Liveright, 1920.
———. *Three Essays on the Theory of Sexuality*. Translated and edited by James Strachey. New York: Basic Books, 1975. First published 1962.
Gabara, Rachel. "'A Poetics of Refusals': Neorealism from Italy to Africa." In *Italian Neorealism and Global Cinema*, edited by Laura E. Ruberto and Kristi M. Wilson, 187–206. Detroit: Wayne State University Press, 2007.
Galt, Rosalind. *Pretty: Film and the Decorative Image*. New York: Columbia University Press, 2011.
Galt, Rosalind, and Karl Schoonover. "Introduction: The Impurity of Art Cinema." In *Global Art Cinema: New Theories and Histories*, edited by Rosalind Galt and Karl Schoonover, 3–27. London: Oxford University Press, 2010.
Galt, Rosalind, and Karl Schoonover, eds. *Global Art Cinema: New Theories and Histories*. London: Oxford University Press, 2010.
Ganguly, Keya. *Cinema, Emergence, and the Films of Satyajit Ray*. Berkeley: University of California Press, 2010.
Gannun, 'Abdallah. *Ahadith 'an al-adab al-maghribi al-hadith, wa hiya muhadarat al-qaha* [Conversations on modern Maghribi literature and lectures delivered]. Cairo: Dar al-Ra'id li-l-Taba'a, 1964.
Gaonkar, Dilip Parameshwar. "On Alternative Modernities." In *Alternative Modernities*, edited by Dilip Parameshwar Gaonkar, 1–23. Durham, NC: Duke University Press, 2001.
Gaonkar, Dilip Parameshwar, ed. *Alternative Modernities*. Durham, NC: Duke University Press, 2001.
Gauch, Suzanne. *Maghrebs in Motion: North African Cinema in Nine Movements*. New York: Oxford University Press, 2016.
González, Roberto Pujante. "Désir et sexualités non normatives au Maghreb et dans la diaspora" [Non-normative desire and sexualities in the Maghrib and the diaspora]. *Expressions Maghrebines* 16, no. 1 (2017): 1–19.
Goodman, Lenn Evan. *Ibn Tufayl's Hayy Ibn Yaqzan: A Philosophical Tale*. Chicago: University of Chicago Press, 2009. First published 2003.
———. *Islamic Humanism*. New York: Oxford University Press, 2003.
Gottreich, Emily. *The Mellah of Marrakesh: Jewish and Muslim Space in Morocco's Red City*. Bloomington: Indiana University Press, 2007.
Greenberg, Nathaniel. *The Aesthetic of Revolution in the Film and Literature of Naguib Mahfouz (1952–1967)*. Lanham, MD: Lexington, 2014.
Gunning, Tom. *The Films of Fritz Lang: Allegories of Vision and Modernity*. London: BFI, 2000.
Habermas, Jürgen. "Modernity—an Incomplete Project." Translated by Seyla Ben-Habib. In *The Anti-Aesthetic: Essays on Postmodern Culture*, edited by Hal Foster, 3–15. Port Townsend, WA: Bay Press, 1983.

Hansen, Miriam. "Fallen Women, Rising Stars, New Horizons: Shanghai Silent Film as Vernacular Modernism." *Film Quarterly* 54, no. 1 (2000): 10–22.

———. "The Mass Production of the Senses: Classical Cinema as Vernacular Modernism." In *Reinventing Film Studies*, edited by Christine Gledhill and Linda Williams, 332–50. London: Hodder Arnold, 2007.

Hanssen, Jens, and Max Weiss, eds. *Arabic Thought against the Authoritarian Age: Towards an Intellectual History of the Present*. Cambridge, UK: Cambridge University Press, 2018.

———. *Arabic Thought beyond the Liberal Age: Towards an Intellectual History of the Nahda*. Cambridge, UK: Cambridge University Press, 2016.

Harrison, Olivia C. *Transcolonial Maghreb: Imagining Palestine in the Era of Decolonization*. Stanford, CA: Stanford University Press, 2016.

Harrison, Olivia C., and Teresa Villa-Ignacio, eds. *Souffles-Anfas: A Critical Anthology from the Moroccan Journal of Culture and Politics*. Stanford, CA: Stanford University Press, 2016.

Hayes, Jarrod. *Queer Nations: Marginal Sexualities in the Maghreb*. Chicago: University of Chicago Press, 2000.

Heckman, Alma Rachel. "Fissures and Fusions: Moroccan Jewish Communists and World War II." In *The Holocaust and North Africa*, edited by Aomar Boum and Sarah Abrevaya Stein, 185–204. Stanford, CA: Stanford University Press, 2018.

———. "Jewish Radicals of Morocco: Case Study for a New Historiography." *Jewish Social Studies* 23, no. 30 (2018): 67–100.

Hegarty, Paul. "Violent Silence: Noise and Bataille's 'Method of Meditation.'" In *Negative Ecstasies: Georges Bataille and the Study of Religion*, edited by Jeremy Biles and Kent Brintnall, 95–105. New York: Fordham University Press, 2015.

Hennebelle, Monique. "Les tribulations du néoréalisme égyptien: l'exemple de Salah Abou Seif" [The tribulations of Egyptian neorealism: the example of Salah Abou Seif]. *L'afrique littéraire et artistique* 27 (1973): 76–86.

Hirschkind, Charles. *The Ethical Soundscape: Cassette Sermons and Islamic Counterpublics*. New York: Columbia University Press, 2006.

Hourani, Albert. *Arabic Thought in the Liberal Age, 1798–1939*. Cambridge, UK: Cambridge University Press, 1983. First published 1962.

Husayn, Taha [Taha Hussein]. *Fi al-shi'r al-jahili* [On jahili poetry]. Cairo: Dar al-Nahr li-l-Nashra wa-l-Tawzi', 1996. First published 1926.

Hussein, Taha. *The Days: His Autobiography in Three Parts*. Translated by E. H. Paxon, Hilary Wayment, and Kenneth Crag. Cairo: American University of Cairo Press, 1997.

———. *The Future of Culture in Egypt*. New York: Octagon, 1975.

———. *A Man of Letters*. Translated by Mona El-Zayyat. Cairo: American University of Cairo Press, 1994. Translation of *Adib*, by Taha Hussein (1935; Cairo: Dar al-Ma'arif, 1960).

Iampolski, Mikhail. *The Memory of Tiresias: Intertextuality and Film*. Berkeley: University of California Press, 1998.

Itbatu, Hamid. "Hawar ma'a Mu'min al-Smihi" [Dialogue with Moumen Smihi]. In *Sinima Mu'min al-Smihi. Qalaq al-tajrib wa fa'iliyyat al-ta'sis al-nathri* [The cinema of Moumen Smihi: passion for experimentation and richness of theoretical foundation], edited by Jumiat al-qabas al-sinima wa-l-thaqafa [Al Qabas association for cinema and culture], 46–98. Errachidia, Morocco: Benlefqih, 2010.

———. "Al-Qalaq al-nathri wa rihanat al-tajrib fi al-tajriba al-sinima'iyya li Mu'min al-Smihi" [Theoretical passion and the stakes of experimentation in Moumen Smihi's cinematic essay]. In *Sinima Mu'min al-Smihi. Qalaq al-tajrib wa fa'iliyyat al-ta'sis al-nathri* [The cinema of Moumen Smihi: passion for experimentation and richness of theoretical foundation], edited by Jumiat al-qabas al-sinima wa-l-thaqafa [Al Qabas association for cinema and culture], 1–32. Errachidia, Morocco: Benlefqih, 2010.

———. *Al-Sinima al-maghribia: qadia al-ibda' wa-l-hawiyya* [Maghribi cinema: issues of creativity and identification]. Tangier: Sigraf, 1999.

al-Jahiz. *Kitab al-bayan wa-l-tabiyyin* [Book of exposition and demonstration]. Cairo: al-Matba'a al-'ilmiyya, 1313. Available online at https://catalog.hathitrust.org/Record/100833294.

———. *Kitab al-hayawan* [Book of animals]. Cairo: Matba'at al-Hamidiyya al-Misriyya bi-Misr, 1905–7. Available online at https://catalog.hathitrust.org/Record/001880932.

Jaidi, Moulay Driss. *Le cinema au Maroc* [Cinema in Morocco]. Rabat: Collection al-Majal, 1991.

Jameson, Fredric. "The Existence of Italy." In *Signatures of the Visible*, 155–229. New York: Routledge, 1992.

———. *Postmodernism, or, The Logic of Late Capitalism*. Durham, NC: Duke University Press, 1999.

———. "Reflections in Conclusion." In Ernst Bloch, George Lukács, Bertolt Brecht, Walter Benjamin, and Theodor Adorno, *Aesthetics and Politics*, 196–213. London: Verso, 1980. First published 1977.

———. *A Singular Modernity*. London: Verso, 2002.

Jibril, Mohamed. "Silence, on tourne!" [Quiet on the set!]. *Lamalif* 117 (1980): 46–47.

Johnson, Rebecca C. "Foreword." In Ahmad Faris al-Shidyaq, *Leg over Leg*, translated by Humphrey Davies, 1:i–xxxvi. New York: New York University Press, 2015.

Jones, Christa. *Cave Culture in Maghrebi Literature: Imagining Self and Nation*. Lanham, MD: Lexington, 2012.

Jumiat al-qabas al-sinima wa-l-thaqafa [Al Qabas association for cinema and culture], ed. *Sinima Mu'min al-Smihi. Qalaq al-tajrib wa fa'iliyyat al-ta'sis al-nathri* [The cinema of Moumen Smihi: passion for experimentation and richness of theoretical foundation]. Errachidia, Morocco: Benlefqih, 2010.

Kassab, Elizabeth Suzanne. *Contemporary Arab Thought: Cultural Critique in Comparative Perspective*. New York: Columbia University Press, 2010.

———. *Enlightenment on the Eve of Revolution: The Egyptian and Syrian Debates*. New York: Columbia University Press, 2019.

———. "Summoning the Spirit of Enlightenment: On the Nahda Revival in *Qadaya wa-shahadat*." In *Arabic Thought against the Authoritarian Age: Towards an Intellectual History of the Present*, edited by Jens Hanssen and Max Weiss, 311–35. Cambridge, UK: Cambridge University Press, 2018.

Kassir, Samir. *Being Arab*. Translated by Will Hobson. London: Verso, 2006. First published as *Considérations sur le malheur arabe*. Paris: Actes Sud Sindbad, 2004.

Kennedy, Philip F. *Abu Nuwas: A Genius of Poetry*. Oxford: Oneworld, 2009.

Khalil, Andrea Flores. *The Arab Avant-Garde: Experiments in North African Art and Literature*. Studies in African Literature. Westport, CT: Praeger, 2003.

Khan, Mohamed. *An Introduction to the Egyptian Cinema*. London: Informatics, 1969.

Khatibi, Abdelkebir. "Double Criticism: The Decolonization of Arab Sociology." In *Contemporary North Africa: Issues of Development and Integration*, edited by Halim Barakat, 9–19. Washington, DC: Center for Contemporary Arab Studies, Georgetown University, 1985.

———. *Maghreb Pluriel*. Paris: Editions Denoël, 1983.

Khouri, Malek. *The Arab National Project in Youssef Chahine's Cinema*. Cairo: University of Cairo Press, 2010.

Khoury, Elias. "For a Third Nahda." Translated by Max Weiss with Jens Hanssen. In *Arabic Thought against the Authoritarian Age: Towards an Intellectual History of the Present*, edited by Jens Hanssen and Max Weiss, 357–69. Cambridge, UK: Cambridge University Press, 2018.

Khuri, Ra'if. *Modern Arab Thought: Channels of the French Revolution to the Arab East*. Translated by Ihsan Abbas. Princeton, NJ: Kingston, 1983.

Kosansky, Oren, and Aomar Boum. "The 'Jewish Question' in Postcolonial Moroccan Cinema." *International Journal of Middle East Studies* 44 (2012): 421–42.

Laâbi, Abdellatif. "Realities and Dilemmas of National Culture I." Translated by Olivia C. Harrison and Teresa Villa-Ignacio. In *Souffles-Anfas: A Critical Anthology from the Moroccan Journal of Culture and Politics*, edited by Olivia C. Harrison and Teresa Villa-Ignacio, 61–73. Stanford, CA: Stanford University Press, 2016.

Landau, Rom. *Portrait of Tangier*. London: Robert Hale, 1952.

Lang, Robert. *New Tunisian Cinema: Allegories of Resistance*. New York: Columbia University Press, 2014.

Laskier, Michael. *Israel and the Maghreb: From Statehood to Oslo*. Gainesville: University Press of Florida, 2004.

Lawrence, Amy. "Women's Voices in Third World Cinema." In *Sound Theory/Sound Practice*, edited by Rick Altman, 178–90. New York: Routledge, 1992.

Lenssen, Anneka, Sarah A. Rogers, and Nada M. Shabout, eds. *Modern Art in the Arab World: Primary Documents*. New York: Museum of Modern Art, 2018.

Limbrick, Peter. "Moumen Smihi's Tanjawi/Tangérois/Tangerian Cinema." *Third Text* 26, no. 4 (2012): 443–54.

———. "Vernacular Modernism, Film Culture, and Moroccan Short Film and Documentary." *Framework* 56, no. 2 (2015): 388–413.

Löning, Madeleine. "Un film qui 'trouble': Subversion des identités de genre et de la sexualité dans *Much loved* de Nabil Ayouch" [A film that disturbs: the subversion of gender identities and sexuality in *Much Loved* by Nabil Ayouch]. *Expressions Maghrebines* 16, no. 1 (2017): 183–99.

al-Ma'arri, Abu al-'Ala'. *The Epistle of Forgiveness, or A Pardon to Enter the Garden*. Translated by Geert Jan Van Gelder and Gregor Schoeler. New York: New York University Press, 2016.

———. *Saqt al-zand*. Beirut: Dar al-Fikr, 1965.

———. *Saqt al-zand: The Spark from the Flint*. Translated by Arthur Wormhoudt. Oskaloosa, IA: William Penn College, 1972.

MacCabe, Colin. "Realism and the Cinema: Notes on Some Brechtian Theses." *Screen* 15, no. 2 (1974): 7–27.

———. "Theory and Film: Principles of Realism and Pleasure." *Screen* 17, no. 3 (1976): 7–28.

Mahmood, Saba. *Politics of Piety: The Islamic Revival and the Feminist Subject*. Princeton, NJ: Princeton University Press, 2005.
Makdisi, Jean Said. "Faten Hamama and Hind Rustom: Stars from Different Heavens." *Al-Raida* 122/123 (2008): 24–31.
Makdisi, Jean Said, Noha Bayoumi, and Rafif Rida Sidawi, eds. *Arab Feminisms: Gender and Equality in the Middle East*. London: I. B. Tauris, 2014.
Mandelbaum, Jacques. "Chroniques marocaines: trois contes d'un cinéaste marocain radical" [*Moroccan Chronicles*: three tales by a radical Moroccan cinéaste]. *Le Monde*, November 17, 1999, 2.
Marglin, Jessica M. *Across Legal Lines: Jews and Muslims in Modern Morocco*. New Haven, CT: Yale University Press, 2016.
Marks, Laura U. *Enfoldment and Infinity: An Islamic Genealogy of New Media Art*. Cambridge, MA: MIT Press, 2011.
———. *Hanan al-Cinema: Affections for the Moving Image*. Cambridge, MA: MIT Press, 2015.
Martin, Florence. *Screens and Veils: Maghrebi Women's Cinema*. Bloomington: Indiana University Press, 2011.
Martin, Florence, and Patricia Call. "Reel Bad Maghrebi Women." In *Bad Girls of the Arab World*, edited by Nadia Yaqub and Rula Quawas, 167–84. Austin: University of Texas Press, 2017.
Massad, Joseph A. *Desiring Arabs*. Chicago: University of Chicago Press, 1987.
Meddeb, Abdelwahab. "L'oeil féminin de la ville: *Chergui*" [The city's female eye: *Chergui*]. *Cahiers du cinéma* 262/263 (1976): 103–8.
Mernissi, Fatima. *Dreams of Trespass: Tales of a Harem Girlhood*. Reading, MA: Addison-Wesley, 1994.
———. *Islam and Democracy: Fear of the Modern World*. Translated by Mary Jo Lakeland. Reading, MA: Addison-Wesley, 1992.
Mesnaoui, Mustafa. "Al-Sinima al-tarikh: *44 aw usturat al-layl* namuthja" [Historical cinema: the *44, or Tales of the Night* model]. *Dirassat Sinima'iyya* 12 (1990): 40–45.
Meyer, Stefan G. *The Experimental Arabic Novel: Postcolonial Literary Modernism in the Levant*. Albany: State University of New York Press, 2001.
Mezzine, Mohamed. "A Day in the Life of a Taleb in Fez." In *Andalusian Morocco: A Discovery in Living Art*, edited by the Museum with No Frontiers, 87–109. Rabat: Ministry of Cultural Affairs of the Kingdom of Morocco, 2002.
Mikdashi, Maya. "How Not to Study Gender in the Middle East." *Jadaliyya*, March 21, 2012. http://www.jadaliyya.com/Details/25434.
Millecam, Jean-Pierre. "Deep Morocco." *Lamalif* 114 (1980): 55–56.
Miller, Susan Gilson. *A History of Modern Morocco*. New York: Cambridge University Press, 2013.
Mirsepassi, Ali, and Tadd Graham Fernée. *Islam, Democracy, and Cosmopolitanism: At Home and in the World*. Cambridge, UK: Cambridge University Press, 2014.
Montgomery, James E. *Al-Jahiz: In Praise of Books*. Edinburgh Studies in Classical Literature. Edinburgh: Edinburgh University Press, 2013.
Moosa, Matti. *The Origins of Modern Arabic Fiction*. 2nd ed. Boulder, CO: Three Continents, 1997.
Mowitt, John. *Radio: Essays in Bad Reception*. Berkeley: University of California Press, 2011.

Mrabet, Mohammed. *The Big Mirror*. Translated by Paul Bowles. Santa Barbara, CA: Black Sparrow, 1977.

Muedini, Fait. "The Promotion of Sufism in the Politics of Algeria and Morocco." *Islamic Africa* 3, no. 2 (2012): 201–26.

Mufti, Aamir R. "Why I Am Not a Postsecularist." *boundary 2* 40, no. 1 (2013): 7–19.

Mufti, Aamir R., ed. "Antinomies of the Postsecular." Special issue, *boundary 2* 40, no. 1 (2013).

Muhaqiq, Nur al-Din. "Shi'riyyat al-hub wa hawas al-injidab qira'a fi film *al-Sharqi* li Mu'min al-Smihi" [The poetics of love and the madness of fascination: a reading of *The East Wind* by Moumen Smihi]. In *Sinima Mu'min al-Smihi. Qalaq al-tajrib wa fa'iliyyat al-ta'sis al-nathri* [The cinema of Moumen Smihi: passion for experimentation and richness of theoretical foundation], edited by Jumiat al-qabas al-sinima wa-l-thaqafa [Al Qabas association for cinema and culture], 33–37. Errachidia, Morocco: Benlefqih, 2010.

Nagib, Lúcia. "Towards a Positive Definition of World Cinema." In *Remapping World Cinema: Identity, Culture and Politics in Film*, edited by Stephanie Dennison and Song Hwee Lim, 30–37. London: Wallflower, 2006.

al-Nahas, Hashem. "Salah Abu Sayf wa tajkhir al-waqi'iyya wa-l-tanwir fi al-sinima al-misriyya" [Salah Abu Seif and the cultivation of realism and enlightenment in Egyptian cinema]. *Alif: Journal of Comparative Poetics* 15 (1995): 6–21.

Naji, Jamal Eddine. "Une problématique à ponctuer" [A problematic to punctuate]. *Lamalif* 80 (1976): 36–39.

Najmabadi, Afsaneh. *Women with Mustaches and Men without Beards: Gender and Sexual Anxieties of Iranian Modernity*. Berkeley: University of California Press, 2005.

al-Naqqash, Raja. "Liqa' ma'a Umm Kulthum" [A meeting with Umm Kulthum]. In *Lughz Umm Kulthum* [The secret of Umm Kulthum]. Cairo: Dar al-Hilal, 1978.

Nash, Geoffrey, Kathleen Kerr-Koch, and Sarah E. Hackett, eds. *Postcolonialism and Islam: Theory, Literatures, Culture, Society and Film*. Oxon: Routledge, 2014.

Nicholson, Reynold Alleyne. *Studies in Islamic Poetry*. Cambridge, UK: Cambridge University Press, 1921. Available at http://hdl.handle.net/2027/mdp.39015013514727.

Orlando, Valérie. *Francophone Voices of the "New" Morocco in Film and Print: (Re)presenting a Society in Transition*. New York: Palgrave, 2009.

———. *Screening Morocco: Contemporary Film in a Changing Society*. Athens: Ohio University Press, 2011.

Ouhiba, Insaf. "Zwoboda, André." In *Dictionnaire des orientalistes de langue française*, edited by François Pouillon, 987–88. Paris: Karthala, 2008.

Pandolfo, Stefania. "The Thin Line of Modernity: Some Moroccan Debates on Subjectivity." In *Questions of Modernity*, edited by Timothy Mitchell, 115–47. Minneapolis: University of Minnesota Press, 2000.

Pastor, Antonio. *The Idea of Robinson Crusoe*. Watford, UK: Gongora, 1930.

Patai, Raphael. *The Arab Mind*. New York: Scribner, 1973.

Pieprzak, Katarzyna. *Imagined Museums: Art and Modernity in Postcolonial Morocco*. Minneapolis: University of Minnesota Press, 2010.

Rastegar, Kamran. *Literary Modernity between the Middle East and Europe: Textual Transactions in Nineteenth-Century Arabic, English, and Persian Literatures*. Oxon, UK, and New York: Routledge, 2007.

Rhodes, John David. "Pasolini's Exquisite Flowers: The 'Cinema of Poetry' as a Theory of Art Cinema." In *Global Art Cinema*, edited by Rosalind Galt and Karl Schoonover, 142–63. London: Oxford University Press, 2010.
Richie, Donald. *Ozu*. Berkeley: University of California Press, 1974.
Rondeau, Daniel. *Tanger*. Paris: Quai Voltaire, 1987.
Rouch, Jean. *Ciné-Ethnography*. Edited and translated by Steven Feld. Minneapolis: University of Minnesota Press, 2003.
Rouch, Jean, with Enrico Fulchignoni. "Ciné-Anthropology." In *Ciné-Ethnography*, edited and translated by Steven Feld, 147–87. Minneapolis: University of Minnesota Press, 2003.
Ruberto, Laura E., and Kristi M. Wilson, eds. *Italian Neorealism and Global Cinema*. Detroit: Wayne State University Press, 2007.
Sacks, Jeffrey. *Iterations of Loss: Mutilation and Aesthetic Form, al-Shidyaq to Darwish*. New York: Fordham University Press, 2015.
Said, Edward. "Living in Arabic." *Al-Ahram Weekly*, no. 677 (February 12–18, 2004).
———. *Orientalism*. New York: Vintage, 1979. First published 1978.
Salazkina, Masha. *In Excess: Sergei Eisenstein's Mexico*. Chicago: University of Chicago Press, 2009.
———. "Introduction: Film Theory in the Age of Neoliberal Globalization." Introduction to the dossier "Geopolitics of Film and Media Theory." *Framework* 56, no. 2 (2015): 325–49.
Sanjinés, Jorge. "El cine político no debe abandonar su preocupación por la belleza" [Political cinema must not abandon its interest in beauty]. In *Téoria y práctica de un cine junto al pueblo* [Theory and practice of a cinema with the people]. Mexico City: Siglo Veintiuno Editores, 1979.
Scales, Rebecca P. "Subversive Sound: Transnational Radio, Arabic Recordings, and the Dangers of Listening in French Colonial Algeria, 1934–1939." *Comparative Studies in Society and History* 52, no. 2 (2010): 384–417.
Schaeffer, Pierre. *In Search of a Concrete Music*. Translated by Christine North and John Dark. Berkeley: University of California Press, 2012. First published 1952.
Schafer, R. Murray. *The Soundscape: Our Sonic Environment and the Tuning of the World*. Rochester: Destiny Books, 1993.
Schick, Irvin Cemil. "The Harem as Gendered Space and the Spatial Reproduction of Gender." In *Harem Histories: Envisioning Places and Living Spaces*, edited by Marilyn Booth, 69–84. Durham, NC: Duke University Press, 2010.
Schoonover, Karl. *Brutal Vision: The Neorealist Body in Postwar Italian Cinema*. Minneapolis: University of Minnesota Press, 2012.
Schoonover, Karl, and Rosalind Galt. *Queer Cinema in the World*. Durham, NC, and London: Duke University Press, 2016.
Sedgwick, Eve Kosofsky. *Between Men: English Literature and Male Homosocial Desire*. New York: Columbia University Press, 1992.
Sefrioui, Kenza. *La revue Souffles 1976–1973: Espoirs de révolution culturelle au Maroc* [The journal *Souffles* 1976–1973: hopes of cultural revolution in Morocco]. Casablanca: Éditions de Sirocco, 2013.
Séguin, Louis. "Paris, Tanger: Les deux amours de Moumen Smihi" [Paris, Tangier: Moumen Smihi's two loves]. *Cahiers du cinéma* 733 (2017): 70–72.

Shafik, Viola. *Arab Cinema: History and Cultural Identity*. Cairo: American University in Cairo Press, 2016. First published 1998.

———. *Popular Egyptian Cinema*. Cairo: American University in Cairo Press, 2006.

Sheehi, Stephen. *Foundations of Modern Arab Identity*. Gainesville: University of Florida Press, 2004.

al-Shidyaq, Ahmad Faris. *Leg over Leg*. Edited and translated by Humphrey Davies. Bilingual Arabic-English version. 4 vols. New York: New York University Press, 2014.

———. *Leg over Leg*. Translated by Humphrey Davies. 2 vols. New York: New York University Press, 2015.

Shohat, Ella. "Sephardim in Israel: Zionism from the Standpoint of Its Jewish Victims." *Social Text* 19/20 (1988): 1–35.

Simour, Lhoussain. "Narrating Silence and (Re)locating Space: Cinematic Reflexions on Moumen Smihi's *al-Shergui awi* [sic] *al-samt al-anif (al-Shergui or the Violent Silence)*." *Film Matters* 3 (2010): 14–19.

Spivak, Gayatri Chakravorty. "Can the Subaltern Speak?" In *The Post-Colonial Studies Reader*, edited by Bill Ashcroft, Gareth Griffiths, and Helen Tiffin, 28–37. Oxford: Routledge, 1995.

———. *A Critique of Postcolonial Reason: Toward a History of the Vanishing Present*. Cambridge, MA: Harvard University Press, 1999.

Stam, Robert, Robert Burgoyne, and Sandy Flitterman-Lewis. *New Vocabularies in Film Semiotics: Structuralism, Post-Structuralism and Beyond*. London: Routledge, 1992.

Steimatsky, Noa. *Italian Locations: Reinhabiting the Past in Postwar Cinema*. Minneapolis: University of Minnesota Press, 2008.

Steintrager, James A. "Introduction: Closed Grooves, Open Ears." In Michel Chion, *Sound: An Acoustological Treatise*, translated by James A. Steintrager, i–xxvi. Durham, NC: Duke University Press, 2016.

Stokes, Martin. "'Abd al-Halim's Microphone." In *Music and the Play of Power in the Middle East, North Africa and Central Asia*, edited by Laudan Nooshin, 55–73. London: Routledge, 2009.

Stuart, Graham H. *The International City of Tangier*. Stanford, CA: Stanford University Press, 1931.

al-Tahtawi, Rifa'a Rafi'. *An Imam in Paris: Account of a Stay in France by an Egyptian Cleric (1826–1831)*. Translated by Daniel L. Newman. London: Saqi, 2011.

Taïa, Abdellah. "A Boy to Be Sacrificed." *New York Times*, March 24, 2012. https://www.nytimes.com/2012/03/25/opinion/sunday/a-boy-to-be-sacrificed.html.

Taylor, Charles. "The Polysemy of the Secular." *Social Research* 76, no. 4 (2009): 1143–66.

Ten Brink, Joram, ed. *Building Bridges: The Cinema of Jean Rouch*. London: Wallflower, 2007.

Tibi, Bassam. *Islam Between Culture and Politics*. Houndmills, UK: Palgrave, 2001.

Traboulsi, Fawwaz. "Ahmad Faris al-Shidyaq (1804–87): The Quest for Another Modernity." In *Arabic Thought beyond the Liberal Age: Towards an Intellectual History of the Nahda*, edited by Jens Hanssen and Max Weiss, 175–86. Cambridge, UK: Cambridge University Press, 2016.

Wannous, Sa'dallah. *Sentence to Hope: a Sa'dallah Wannous Reader*. Translated by Robert Myers and Nada Saab. New Haven, CT: Yale University Press, 2019.

Welsh, Henry. "El Chergui." *Jeune Cinéma* 93 (1976): 32–33.
Westermarck, Edward. *Ritual and Belief in Morocco*. 2 vols. London: Macmillan, 1926.
White, Patricia. *Women's Cinema, World Cinema: Projecting Contemporary Feminisms*. Durham, NC: Duke University Press, 2015.
Yaqub, Nadia, and Rula Quawas, eds. *Bad Girls of the Arab World*. Austin: University of Texas Press, 2017.
Youssef, Adham. "Egypt's Cinematic Gems: *Cairo 30*." *Mada Masr*, December 13, 2014. https://madamasr.com/en/2014/12/13/feature/culture/egypts-cinematic-gems-cairo-30/.
Zaatari, Zeina. "From Women's Rights to Feminism: The Urgent Need for an Arab Feminist Renaissance." In *Arab Feminisms: Gender and Equality in the Middle East*, edited by Jean Said Makdisi, Noha Bayoumi, and Rafif Rida Sidawi, 54–65. London: I. B. Tauris, 2014.
Zakariyya, Fouad. *Al-Haqiqa wa-l-wahm fi al-haraka al-islamiyya al-mu'assira* [Truth and illusion about the contemporary Islamic movement]. Cairo: Dar al-Fikr, 1986.
Zeineddine, Nazira. *Al-Sufur wa-l-hijab* [Veiling and unveiling]. Edited by Buthaina Sha'ban. Damascus: Dar al-Mada, 1998.
———. "From *Unveiling and Veiling*." Translated by Zeina G. Halabi. In *The Arab Renaissance: A Bilingual Anthology of the Nahda*, edited by Tarek El-Ariss, 373–84. New York: Modern Language Association, 2018.

INDEX

Note: *fig.* refers to figures

Abdel Aziz, Lubna, 132–33
Abdel Salam, Shadi, 13, 100–101, 133, 156
Abdel Wahab, Mohammed, 87, 91, 101, 102–3, 104, 226n24
'Abduh, Muhammad, 168, 170, 173, 192
'Abdulhamid, 'Abdullatif, 89
About Some Meaningless Events (De quelques événements sans signification) (Derkaoui, 1974), 15
Abu-Lughod, Ibrahim, 108
Abu Madi, Iliya, 19, 190
Abu Nuwas, 9, 147, 159–60, 162–63, 181, 210
Abu Seif, Salah, 13, 37, 45, 52–54, 108, 132–33. *See also individual films*
Abu Tammam, 9, 160
Abu Yaq'ub Yusuf, 119
Abu Yusuf Yaq'ub al-Mansur, 119
acousmatic, 85, 93–94, 97, 101–2, 105, 226n14, 227n32. *See also* sound/tracks
acousmêtre, 97, 100
actuality films, 17–18, 31, 47
'*Adib* (A Man of Letters) (Hussein), 125
Adonis, 9, 21, 99, 159–60
Adorno, Theodor, 28
Afifi, Mohamed, 6, 64, 131
After the American Century (Edwards), 201
Ahl al-kahf (People of the Cave) (play), 125
Ahmed, Faeza, 102

Ahmed ou Moussa, Sidi, 1, 130, 213n2
Aïcha, Lalla (Moroccan princess), 192, 194
Alami, Mohammed Hamdouni, 112, 118
alcohol, 158–60, 165, 175–76
Alexandria, Why? (Chahine, 1979), 46
Algeria, 37, 70, 87, 89–90, 92, 100, 174, 214n9. *See also individuals*
Algerian FLN (Front de Libération Nationale), 87, 90
Alhazen (Ibn al-Haytham) (philosopher), 21, 115–16
Alkassim, Samirah, 15
Allen, Woody, 137, 146, 162
Amazigh culture, 2, 30, 32, 77, 83, 129, 150, 153, 213n3, 221n98
Ameur-Zaïmeche, Rabah, 38
Amin, Qasim, 195, 209
Amiralay, Omar, 21, 62–63
'*amiyyat* (dialects), 124, 128
Among the Ruins (Bain al-atlal) (Zulficar, 1959), 132–33
Andary, Nezar, 15
Andrew, Dudley, 3
Anfas (journal), 10, 21, 31
Anglophone film studies, 4, 14–15, 17, 28, 31, 33, 217n46
"Anthropologie culturelle" (Cultural Anthropology) (Smihi) (essay), 40, 54

INDEX

anthropologies, 40–41, 54–59, 66, 68, 72, 110, 129, 132, 144–45, 146, 151
Antonioni, Michelangelo, 41–42, 108, 129
Antun, Farah, 23
Arab Camera (Caméra arabe) (Boughedir, 1987), 37
Arab cinemas: Anglophone film studies, 17; Arab cultures, 3, 112, 116, 161; Arabic language, 101; Bouzid, Nouri, 37; colonialism, 3, 139; desire, 163; Egyptian cinema, 134; freedoms, 33, 211; images, 99; intertextuality, 32, 107, 108; Italian neorealism, 31; Kulthum, Umm, 90–91, 103; languages, 99, 112; literature, 108, 112; Marks, Laura U., 218n47; modernism, 3–4, 33, 39, 73, 107, 112; modernity, 2–3, 30, 139, 162; Moroccan cinema, 107; music, 112; the Nahda, 23; national cinemas, 17–21, 33; neorealism, 54; orality, 101, 112; Orientalism, 33, 107; politics, 37, 91; postcolonialism, 17, 37, 112; radio, 91; realism, 31, 36–39, 54–55; sacredness, 161; *The Seventh Gate* (Zwoboda, 1947), 19; sexuality, 163; Smihi, Moumen, 13, 17–21, 36, 39–40, 81, 107, 112, 138, 139, 211, 218n51; voices, 99–100, 101, 103; the West, 15, 17; women, 99, 103; world cinema, 3–4, 17–21, 32, 33, 108, 112, 211. *See also* New Arab Cinema
Arab cultures: Arab cinemas, 3, 112, 116, 161; Arab-Islamic architecture, 112, 115; El-Ariss, Tarek, 33; circumcision, 151; colonialism, 9, 91, 170–71; decorative, 69, 224n61; desire, 210; Ezzedine, Salah, 99; *44, or Tales of the Night* (Smihi, 1981), 116; gender, 32–33, 180; *hijabs*, 32; history, 170–71; homosexuality, 32–33, 181, 203–4, 205; Islam, 161, 163–64; languages, 9; literature, 210; Maghrib, 3, 112; Marks, Laura U., 33, 224n61; masculinities, 205; modernism, 3–4, 131–32, 211, 224n61; modernity, 30, 72, 163–64, 178, 200, 211; Moroccan cinema, 132; Morocco, 3, 73; music, 91, 99, 226n24; the Nahda, 2–3; nationalism, 90–91; orality, 99, 101; politics, 32–33, 170–71; postcolonialism, 3, 32; radio, 86, 91, 226n24; religion, 32–33, 162, 164; religious diversity, 211; sacrilege, 162; sexual identities, 32–33, 204, 239n31; sexuality, 180, 200, 210–11; Smihi, Moumen, 2, 5, 9, 11–12, 30, 32–33, 36, 41, 85, 91, 101, 109, 111–12, 116, 118, 122, 128, 130, 132, 144, 157, 180–81, 211, 218n51; sound/tracks, 73; spaces, 129; *With Taha Hussein* (Smihi, 2015), 2; Tangier, 167; textuality, 69, 224n61; Voice of the Arabs, 90–91; voices, 99, 101; the West, 2–3, 9,
23–24, 32–33, 178–79, 181; women, 32–33. *See also* pan-Arabism
Arab Enlightenment. *See* Nahda, the; new Nahda, the; *tanwir* (Enlightenment)
arabesques, 115. *See also* Arab-Islamic art; decorative
Arabian Nights (Pasolini, 1974), 106, 108, 137, 160, 181, 210, 239n41
Arabic language, 97–98, 100–101, 104, 122–27, 128, 163, 209. *See also* languages; voices; *individual dialects*; *individual languages*
Arabic Thought in the Liberal Age (Hourani), 23
Arab-Islamic architecture, 11, 112–22, 130, 141, 143, 181, 183, 214n12
Arab-Islamic art, 112–22, 124, 130, 163–64. *See also* decorative
Arab-Islamic philosophy, 11, 21, 112–22. *See also* individuals
Arab modernism. *See* modernism
Arab Spring, 91, 205
Arab worlds. *See* Arab cultures
architecture, 139–41. *See also* Arab-Islamic architecture
El-Ariss, Tarek, 22, 24, 25, 31, 33, 108, 165, 167, 211, 215n26
Armes, Roy, 12
art. *See* Arab-Islamic art
Art and Architecture in the Islamic Tradition (Alami), 112
art cinema, 2, 12–13, 30, 38–39, 40, 51, 61–62, 67, 72
Asad, Talal, 145, 232nn2,5
Asian cinema, 108, 132. *See also* Indian cinema; *individuals*; Japanese cinema
Asmahan, 132, 133, 228n47
Astruc, Alexandre, 109
Atlantis (L'Atlantide) (Feyder, 1921), 203
Atouna, Leila, 18
al-Atrash, Farid, 132, 133
Attar, Samar, 119
Aufklärung (Enlightenment), 123. *See also* European Enlightenment
auteurism, 12–17, 100–101, 109–10, 137, 143. *See also* individuals
auto-anthropologies, 41. *See also* anthropologies
auto-ethnographies, 41, 55, 73
autofiction, 5, 56, 98, 111. *See also* documentary fiction
avant-gardes, 20–21, 27–28, 31, 74, 80
"L'aventure structuraliste" (The Structuralist Adventure) (Smihi) (essay), 110

INDEX   263

Averroes. *See* Ibn Rushd (Averroes) (philosopher)
Avicenna (Ibn Sina) (philosopher), 115, 119, 163
Ayouch, Nabil, 200, 234n31
al-Azmeh, Aziz, 145, 163, 170–71, 178, 179

Baccar, Selma, 37
Bach, Johann Sebastian, 82, 83, 130
Badlands (Malick, 1973), 137
Badrakhan, Ali, 44
Baggiani, Guido, 80
Baker, Josephine, 79, 86, 162
Bakhtin, Mikhail, 129–30
Balzac, Honoré de, 120–21, 126, 128
Barber from the Poor Neighborhood, The (Le coiffeur du quartier des pauvres) (Reggab, 1982), 52
Barthes, Roland, 6–7, 8, 9, 15–16, 64, 80, 109–10, 118, 215n21, 225n9
Bashkin, Orit, 24, 219n75
Bataille, Georges, 127, 231n46
Battle of Algiers, The (Pontecorvo, 1966), 70
Battleship Potemkin (Eisenstein, 1925), 6, 155
Baucom, Ian, 89
Baudelaire, Charles, 9, 27–28, 160
Baudrillard, Jean, 108
Bazin, André, 40–41, 42, 44, 59, 61, 62
Beauvoir, Simone de, 174
Bedwin Hacker (El Fani, 2003), 201
Beethoven, Ludwig van, 82
Beginning and End (Bidaya wa nihaya) (Abu Seif, 1960), 52–53, 198
Beinin, Joel, 23
Beirut, 9, 11, 31, 108
Belarbi Alaoui, Moulay, 194
Bell, Catherine, 153–54
Ben Aïcha, Sadok, 15
Benani, Hamid, 205
Ben-Barka, Souheil, 14, 15
Benjamin, Walter, 27–28, 108
Benlyazid, Farida, 154, 201, 232n7
Bensmaïa, Reda, 55
Berber. *See* Amazigh culture
Berlin, Symphony of a City (Berlin: Die Sinfonie der Grosstadt) (Ruttman, 1927), 35–36
Berman, Marshall, 25, 27–28, 108
Beshara, Khairy, 37, 134
Bicycle Thieves (De Sica, 1948), 53, 60–61
Big City, The (Mahanagar) (Ray, 1963), 142
Big Mirror, The (Mrabet) (story), 11. *See also Caftan of Love* (Smihi, 1989)

Biswas, Moinak, 51, 143
Blek (comic series), 128, 231n47
Booth, Marilyn, 24, 188–89, 195
Bou Ali, Nadia, 24
Bouamari, Mohamed, 70, 89
Bouanani, Ahmed, 6, 8, 10, 14, 15, 18, 64, 71, 131–32, 217n46. *See also individual films*
Boughedir, Férid, 37
Bouhdiba, Abdelwahab, 234n18, 239n38
Boujibar, Naïma, 114, 116
Boulanger, Pierre, 19
Boum, Aomar, 149, 233n14
Bouzid, Nouri, 37, 181, 205, 206, 234nn19,20, 239n38
Bowles, Paul, 11, 32, 126, 204, 216n39, 237n10. *See also Caftan of Love* (Smihi, 1989)
Boyd, Douglas A., 87
Boy of the Jungle, The (L'enfant de la jungle) (Osfour, 1941), 18
Braunberger, Pierre, 7
Brecht, Bertolt, 39, 64, 66
Bresson, Robert, 42, 73–74, 84, 95, 129
Budgen, Frank, 117, 126–27
Buñuel, Luis, 5, 32, 126, 146, 160–62, 167, 210
Burroughs, William S., 11
Burton, Richard Francis, 203
Bus Driver, The (Suwaq al-atubus) (al-Tayeb, 1983), 133
al-Bustani, Butrus, 163, 195

café-concert, 175–77
Caftan of Love (Smihi, 1989), 11, 12, 13*fig.*, 32, 126, 139, 140*fig.*, 232n62, 241
Cahiers du cinéma, 8, 183
Cairo: Algerian FLN (Front de Libération Nationale), 87; Arab-Islamic art, 115; *Egyptian Cinema: Defense and Illustration* (Smihi, 1989), 134; Ibn al-Haytham (Alhazen) (philosopher), 115; Kulthum, Umm, 104; *The Night of Counting the Years* (Abdel Salam, 1969), 100–101; orality, 101; radio, 32, 88, 147; Radio Cairo, 32, 147; Smihi, Moumen, 11, 81, 134; *The Thug* (Abu Seif, 1957), 53; *The Will* (al-'Azima) (Selim, 1939), 52. *See also Lady from Cairo, The* (Smihi, 1991)
Cairo 30 (Abu Seif, 1966), 52, 53
Cairo Station (Bab al-hadid) (Chahine, 1958), 52, 133
calligraphy, 68–69, 80, 117, 124
Call of the Curlew, The (Hussein), 122, 125
camera-stylo, 109

Canterbury Tales, The (Pasolini, 1972), 137
capitalism, 25–26, 29
Casablanca, 17–18, 51–52, 69, 87–88, 106, 113, 131–32, 135, 194–95
Casablanca (Curtiz, 1942), 135
casbah, 120, 201–2, 207
Case 68 (al-Qadiyya 68) (Abu Seif, 1969), 54
Cassavetes, John, 137
Catholicism, 150, 160–61, 163–64, 188. See also Christianity
Centre cinématographique marocain (Moroccan National Cinema Center) (CCM), 8, 50, 131, 137
Centre national du cinéma (CNC), 7
Chahine, Youssef, 37, 38, 44, 46, 52, 91, 132, 133, 134, 196, 218n62
Chakrabarty, Dipesh, 26
chanson française (French song), 175–76, 177
Chants anciens des femmes de Fes (Ancient Songs of the Women of Fez), 131
Chaplin, Charlie, 5, 9
Charcoal Maker, The (Le charbonnier) (Bouamari, 1972), 70, 89, 91
Chebaa, Mohamed, 21
Chefchaouen, 67, 69, 170
chergui (east wind), 78–79, 128–29. See also *East Wind, The* (Smihi, 1975)
Cherkaoui, Ahmed, 21
Chickens, The (al-Dajaj) (Amiralay, 1977), 63
Chion, Michel, 74, 76, 95, 97, 105–6, 225n6, 227n32
Christianity: Buñuel, Luis, 160–61; colonialism, 149–50; *The Decameron* (Pasolini, 1971), 160; *The East Wind* (Smihi, 1975)/*Girls and Swallows* (Smihi, 2008), 150; Judeo-Christian culture, 162; al-Maʿarri, Abu al-ʿAlaʾ, 123; *Mamma Roma* (Pasolini, 1962), 161; the medina/*A Muslim Childhood* (Smihi, 2005)/Muslims, 150; Morocco, 149–51; Pasolini, Pier Paolo, 160–61; Smihi, Moumen, 116, 144, 171, 211, 232n7; *The Sorrows of a Young Tangerian* (Smihi, 2013), 147, 207; Tangier, 11, 149–50; Tangier trilogy, 146. See also Catholicism
cinécritique, 109
ciné-écriture/cinécriture (cinema-writing), 59, 73, 109, 111–12
ciné-ethnography. See ethnographic films
"Cinema Arabiyya" (Smihi) (essay), 162
cinéma colonial, 203–4
Cinémathèque française, 6, 8, 10–11, 137. See also French cinema

cinematic spaces. See spaces
circumcision: Bouzid, Nouri, 234n20, 239n38; *44, or Tales of the Night* (Smihi, 1981), 67, 151–52, 156–57; gender, 157; *Halfouine* (Boughedir, 1990), 234n17; Islam, 151–52, 233n15; Judaism, 233n15, 234n19; masculinities, 157, 205; montage, 234n17; *Moroccan Chronicles* (Smihi, 1999), 47–48, 151–52, 156–57; Morocco, 157; *A Muslim Childhood* (Smihi, 2005), 82, 104–5, 151–52, 156–57; Muslims, 234nn18,19; patriarchy, 151, 152, 157, 234n20; practices/rituals, 151–52; psychoanalysis, 157; Qurʾan, 234n18; religion, 146, 151–52; sacredness, 151; Smihi, Moumen, 157, 239n38; women, 151, 152, 157, 234n16
Cité internationale universitaire, 41, 222n15
cités universitaires, 6–7, 8, 222n15
city films, 35–36
Clair, René, 95
Clémenti, Pierre, 67, 95, 106
close-ups: *The East Wind* (Smihi, 1975), 43, 78, 147, 155–56; *44, or Tales of the Night* (Smihi, 1981), 70, 94, 127; *Girls and Swallows* (Smihi, 2008), 125; *With Matisse in Tangier* (Smihi, 1993), 138*fig.*; *Moroccan Chronicles* (Smihi, 1999), 50; *A Muslim Childhood* (Smihi, 2005), 132–33, 151, 206, 207; *Si Moh, the Unlucky Man* (Smihi, 1971), 34
Cluny, Claude Michel, 37, 53
Cocteau, Jean, 19
colonialism: actuality films, 31; Algeria, 89–90, 214n9; anthropologies, 55; Arab cinemas, 3, 139; Arab cultures, 9, 91, 170–71; Christianity, 149–50; desire, 208; *The East Wind* (Smihi, 1975), 57, 178; ethnographic films, 55; *44, or Tales of the Night* (Smihi, 1981), 1, 68–69, 91, 94, 130–31, 170, 178, 213n2; France, 1, 17–18, 19, 79–80, 89, 90, 149–50, 213n2, 214n9; Islam, 168; languages, 9–10; modernism, 128; modernity, 25–26, 80, 178; Moroccan cinema, 17–18, 132; Morocco, 1, 17–18, 19, 30–31, 68–69, 71, 80, 90, 94, 137, 213n2, 214n9, 231n60; *Othello* (Shakespeare), 126; politics, 88, 90; pretty images, 70; radio, 87–92; Ray, Satyajit, 143; *Si Moh, the Unlucky Man* (Smihi, 1971), 64; Smihi, Moumen, 20, 85, 90, 118, 131, 132, 138, 139, 143, 178; sound/tracks, 85; Tangier, 4, 79–80; Tangier trilogy, 208; Third Cinema, 62; Tibi, Mohammed, 170; Tunisia, 214n9; Voice of the Arabs, 87, 88; Zwoboda, André, 19. See also postcolonialism

INDEX 265

Color of Pomegranates, The (Parajanov, 1969), 139
Colors on Bodies (Smihi, 1972), 7, 241
Conway, Kelley, 176
Corrigan, Timothy, 64
Corso, Gregory, 11
court-métrages (short films), 31, 131
Crapanzano, Vincent, 157, 239n38
Creswell, Robyn, 24, 31, 108
cultural identities, 54, 116, 181
Curtiz, Michael, 135

Dakhli, Leyla, 23–24
Dananir (Badrakhan, 1940), 101
Danielson, Virginia, 103–4, 226n24, 228n45
darija (language), 5, 10, 98, 104–5, 106, 128, 148, 150, 214n13. See also *'amiyyat* (dialects); Arabic language; languages
Darwin, Charles, 173–74, 175, 178
Dauman, Anatole, 7
Day in My Life, A (Yawm min 'umri) (Salem, 1961), 132–33
Day of Despair (Oliveira, 1992), 142
Days, The (al-Ayyam) (Hussein), 5
Decameron, The (Pasolini, 1971), 137, 160
decorative: Arab cultures, 69, 224n61; *Art and Architecture in the Islamic Tradition* (Alami), 112; *The East Wind* (Smihi, 1975), 130; *44, or Tales of the Night* (Smihi, 1981), 69, 71fig., 114, 115, 116–17, 124, 183; Galt, Rosalind, 72; Marks, Laura U., 114–15, 116; Morocco, 69, 112; realism, 72; Smihi, Moumen/textuality, 69. See also individual decorative arts
Defoe, Daniel, 119
Degheidy, Inas El-, 134
de Lauretis, Teresa, 187–88
Deleuze, Gilles, 64, 115
Delon, Alain, 106
Derkaoui, Mustapha, 15
desacralization, 151, 154. See also sacrilege
Desert Wedding (Noces de sable) (Zwoboda, 1948), 18–19
De Sica, Vittorio, 53, 60–61
desire, 200–211; Arab cinemas, 163; Arab cultures, 210; colonialism, 208; femininities/masculinities, 201; *Girls and Swallows* (Smihi, 2008), 191, 207, 208–9, 214n17; *The Lady from Cairo* (Smihi, 1991), 197, 198–99; *Moroccan Chronicles* (Smihi, 1999), 189; *A Muslim Childhood* (Smihi, 2005), 206; the new Nahda, 180; Pasolini, Pier Paolo, 210; politics, 208; postcolonialism, 208; sexuality, 200–211; Smihi, Moumen, 33, 181, 200, 201, 210–11; *The Sorrows of a Young Tangerian* (Smihi, 2013), 103, 208, 209–10; Tangier trilogy, 201, 208; *Viridiana* (Buñuel, 1961), 160–61; women, 181, 208
dialects, 124, 128, 129
Diary of a Country Prosecutor (Yawmiyyat na'ib fi al-ariyaf) (Saleh, 1969), 54, 125, 133
DiCapua, Yoav, 24
Dickens, Charles, 82, 99, 118
Dickinson, Kay, 15, 89
Diderot, Denis, 122
diegesis: *Alexandria, Why?* (Chahine, 1979), 46; *44, or Tales of the Night* (Smihi, 1981), 84–85, 117; *The Lady from Cairo* (Smihi, 1991), 46; *Moroccan Chronicles* (Smihi, 1999), 92; music, 106; radio, 83, 86; *Si Moh, the Unlucky Man* (Smihi, 1971), 60; Smihi, Moumen, 83; *The Sorrows of a Young Tangerian* (Smihi, 2013), 125; sound/tracks, 58–59, 80–85, 86, 94–95, 97, 98, 100, 101, 104, 106; voices, 97, 98, 100, 101. See also voice-overs
Dietrich, Marlene, 137, 176
al-Dik, Bashir, 44, 134
Doane, Mary Anne, 95
documentaries: Amiralay, Omar, 62–63; Bazin, André, 42; Centre cinématographique marocain (Moroccan National Cinema Center) (CCM), 131; *The East Wind* (Smihi, 1975), 72, 78, 129; France, 17–18; Judaism, 147–48; *With Matisse in Tangier* (Smihi, 1993), 137–38; *Moroccan Chronicles* (Smihi, 1999), 72; New Arab Cinema, 37; *Si Moh, the Unlucky Man* (Smihi, 1971), 35–36, 41, 42–43, 72; Smihi, Moumen, 2, 35–36, 37, 42–43, 45–46, 50, 67, 102; *The Sorrows of a Young Tangerian* (Smihi, 2013), 56. See also individual documentary films
documentary fiction, 31, 41, 55–59, 60, 63–65, 71, 74, 76, 117, 223n39
domestic spaces, 57, 71, 181–91, 195. See also spaces
Door to the Sky, A (Benlyazid, 1989), 154, 201
Dostoevsky, Fyodor, 129–30, 174
"Double Criticism" (Khatibi) (essay), 10
Dragon Inn (King Hu, 1967), 142
Dreams of the City (Ahlam al-madina) (Malas, 1985), 89
Dreams of Trespass (Mernissi), 187
Duras, Marguerite, 95
Durkheim, Émile, 153–54

East Wind, The (Smihi, 1975): Amazigh culture, 129; Arab-Islamic architecture, 118, 181; Arab-Islamic art, 118, 130; Bataille, Georges, 127; Bazin, André, 42; Christianity, 150; close-ups, 43, 78, 147, 155–56; colonialism, 57, 178; *darija* (language), 150; decorative, 130; documentaries, 72, 78, 129; documentary fiction, 56, 57–59, 117; Egyptian cinema, 118; essay films, 64–65; Fez, 129; filmography, 241; *44, or Tales of the Night* (Smihi, 1981), 70; France, 8, 13–14, 79, 89, 118; gender, 180, 181–83; head and face coverings, 154–55; Hollywood, 118; Ibn Tufayl, 119–20; images, 58–59, 61, 63, 77, 78, 129, 147, 150, 155, 184*fig.*; intertextuality, 12, 128–29, 224n49; *istitrad* (digression), 117; Islam, 118, 146, 153; Italian neorealism, 60; al-Jahiz (philosopher), 118; languages, 128–29, 130, 147; literature, 118; long shots, 43–44; *lycée français*, 96–97, 119–20; the medina, 58, 61, 77–79, 129, 147, 155–56, 181; mise-en-scène, 61, 154–55; modernity, 78, 143; montage, 43–44, 61, 77, 129, 184*fig.*; *Moroccan Chronicles* (Smihi, 1999), 50, 130; Morocco, 8, 13–14, 43, 61, 130; music, 77, 84; *musique concrète*, 77–79; *A Muslim Childhood* (Smihi, 2005), 189; nationalism, 63, 129; neorealism, 43–44, 57, 60–61, 72; noise, 77–79, 103; Ozu, Yasujiro, 139–41; patriarchy, 180, 181, 183; postcolonialism, 63; practices/rituals, 152–54; prostitutes, 182; the protectorate, 63, 129; Qur'an, 147, 182; radio, 85–87, 89, 147; realism, 31, 61, 66, 75, 78, 80; religion, 119–20, 146; religious diversity, 120, 147, 150; Rif, 129; Rouch, Jean, 78; sacrilege, 153, 154; Smihi, Moumen, 7, 8, 67, 117, 128–29, 130; sound/tracks, 58–59, 61, 77–80, 85–87, 96–97, 103, 129, 147, 189; spaces, 43–44, 57, 61, 77, 96–97, 181–83, 189; Spain, 150; Tangier, 12, 43, 57–58, 60–61, 63, 78, 96–97, 103, 181, 182; Third Cinema, 63; *ville nouvelle*, 43, 57–58, 61, 154–55, 181, 183; voices, 77–79, 87, 96–97, 103, 129; wide shots, 78, 147; women, 43–44, 57, 103, 152–53, 154–56, 180, 181–83, 184*fig.*

Eclipse, The (L'éclisse) (Antonioni, 1962), 41–42
L'École pratique des hautes études, 6, 8, 10–11
Écrire sur le cinéma (Writing on Cinema) (Smihi), 54
écriture (writing), 107, 109. *See also ciné-écriture*/*cinécriture* (cinema-writing)
education, 114, 119–20, 189, 190, 194, 195. *See also lycée français*

Edwards, Brian T., 135, 201, 204, 217n46
Egypt: 'Abduh, Muhammad, 168; class, 52–53; Europe/France, 22, 169; *The Future of Culture in Egypt* (Hussein), 169; al-Hakim, Tawfiq, 125; Hussein, Taha, 124, 125, 169; Kulthum, Umm, 103–4; languages, 128; Mashriq, 216n30; modernity, 21; *The Monster* (Abu Seif, 1954) / *Raya and Sakina* (Abu Seif, 1953), 53; the Nahda, 21, 22, 134; Nasser, Gamal Abdel, 101–2, 227n40; Ottoman empire, 167; patriarchy, 189; politics, 22, 169; radio, 86, 102, 103, 226n24; Smihi, Moumen, 31, 45–47, 132–35; voices, 102; women, 188–89, 195. *See also Lady from Cairo, The* (Smihi, 1991)

Egyptian cinema: Arab cinemas, 134; auteurism, 100; *The East Wind* (Smihi, 1975), 118; *Girls and Swallows* (Smihi, 2008), 132; intertextuality, 133–34; *The Lady from Cairo* (Smihi, 1991), 44, 133, 196; literature, 125; modernism, 125; Moroccan cinema, 14, 18–19; Morocco, 18, 19; music, 80–81, 132, 133; *A Muslim Childhood* (Smihi, 2005), 20, 128, 132–33, 194, 206; neorealism, 40, 52, 54; non-diegesis, 81; realism, 36–38, 40, 52, 60, 125, 133; Smihi, Moumen, 5, 12–14, 19–20, 31, 37, 40, 52, 54, 80, 132–35, 143, 199, 241; Souissi studios, 18; sound/tracks, 80–81; Tangier, 132–33; veils, 5; women, 5, 197, 199. *See also individuals; individual Egyptian films*

Egyptian Cinema: Defense and Illustration (Smihi, 1989), 31, 37, 52, 134, 241
Eisenstein, Sergei, 6, 64, 109, 155
Elbardai, Hamza, 177
Elsadda, Hoda, 195
Elusive Corporal, The (Le Caporal épinglé) (Renoir, 1962), 142
Empty Pillow, The (al-Wasada al-khalia) (Abu Seif, 1957), 45, 102
Encyclopédie (Diderot), 122
Enlightenment. *See* European Enlightenment; *tanwir* (Enlightenment)
Essaouira, 47, 95, 103, 130, 136–37
essay films, 18, 59, 62–63, 64–65. *See also individual films*
Ethical Soundscape, The (Hirschkind), 101
ethnographic films, 55, 59, 73. *See also individual films*
"Étude aux chemins de fer" (Study for Railroads) (Schaeffer) (composition), 75
Europe: Egypt, 22, 169; film funds, 20; gender, 187; history, 178; Islam, 22, 163–64, 167–68;

Middle East, 23; modernity, 24–31, 167–68, 170, 175, 178, 187; Morocco, 194; Muslims, 22, 167–68; the Nahda, 2–3, 21–24, 108, 168; secularism, 145, 170; Smihi, Moumen, 118, 163–64, 181
Europe '51 (Europa 51) (Rossellini, 1952), 53
European cinema, 36, 59, 62, 70, 108, 129, 132, 138–39, 143, 160. *See also individuals;* Italian neorealism; world cinema; *individual films*
European Enlightenment, 5, 24–26, 119–20, 122, 123, 145, 147, 171, 174, 177–78. *See also* Nahda, the; *tanwir* (Enlightenment); West, the: modernity
Everyday Life in a Syrian Village (al-Hayat al-yawmiyya fi qaria suriyya) (Amiralay, 1974), 63
Ezzedine, Salah, 99

face coverings. *See* head and face coverings; veils
"Fallen Women, Rising Stars, New Horizons: Shanghai Silent Film as Vernacular Modernism" (Hansen) (essay), 29
Fanon, Frantz, 89–90
Fanon Edward, 108
Farid, Samir, 134
Faruk, King, 86
El-Fasi, Mohammed, 131
Fassi (dialect), 129
al-Fassi, Mohammed, 194
Fate's Stroke (Darbit al-qadar) (Wahbi, 1947), 197
Fatma (Badrakhan, 1947), 206
Fatma, the Mulatto Woman (painting), 138
Fawwaz, Zaynab, 195
Feld, Steven, 55, 56
Fellini, Federico, 5, 105–6, 130, 146
femininities, 102, 131, 183–84, 199, 201. *See also* domestic spaces; gender; women
feminism, 178–79, 181, 185, 192, 195, 209, 232n2. *See also individuals;* women's rights
Fernando, Mayanthi L., 145–46
Ferrat, Jean, 177
fetishism, 203, 207–8, 209*fig.*, 239n39
Fez: *Chants anciens des femmes de Fes* (Ancient Songs of the Women of Fez), 131; *The East Wind* (Smihi, 1975), 129; Fassi (dialect), 129; *44, or Tales of the Night* (Smihi, 1981), 67, 69, 70, 87, 97, 113*fig.*, 114–18, 123–24, 150, 170–71, 183, 184–85; *Girls and Swallows* (Smihi, 2008), 88; head and face coverings, 192; Merinid Fez, 114, 116–17; *Moroccan Chronicles* (Smihi, 1999), 47, 57, 92, 137; nationalism/the West, 192; orality, 131; the protectorate, 114; women, 123, 131, 192
Fi al-shiʿr al-jahili (On Jahili Poetry) (Hussein), 124–25, 169–70
Film-Essay on the Euphrates Dam (Muhawala ʿan wadi al-furat) (Amiralay, 1970), 62–63
film festivals, 5, 8, 14, 15, 51
Films of Fritz Lang: Allegories of Vision and Modernity, The (Gunning), 15–16
Finnegans Wake (Joyce), 66, 89
FIS (Islamic Salvation Front), 92
Flaherty, Robert, 117, 132
Flaubert, Gustave, 126, 203
Flood in Baʿath Country, A (Tufan fi balad al-baʿath) (Amiralay, 2003), 62–63
Ford, John, 5, 137, 215n21
Forest, The (La forêt) (Rechiche, 1970), 21
44, or Tales of the Night (Smihi, 1981), 66–72; anthropologies, 68; Arab cultures, 116; Arab-Islamic architecture, 113–14, 116, 181, 183; Arab-Islamic art, 116–17; calligraphy, 68–69, 80, 117; Christianity, 149–50; circumcision, 67, 151–52, 156–57; close-ups, 70, 94, 127; colonialism, 1, 68–69, 91, 94, 130–31, 170, 178, 213n2; *The Color of Pomegranates* (Parajanov, 1969), 139; decorative, 69, 71*fig.*, 114, 115, 116–17, 124, 183; diegesis, 84–85, 117; *The East Wind* (Smihi, 1975), 70; Fez, 67, 69, 70, 87, 97, 113*fig.*, 114–18, 123–24, 150, 170–71, 183, 184–85; France, 1, 14, 67, 120, 130–31, 149–50; gender, 97, 181, 183–86; Ibn Tufayl, 119; images, 66–72, 94, 116–17; inter/textuality, 69, 112, 117; *istitrad* (digression), 127; Islam, 117, 120; Joyce, James, 126–27, 130–31; literature, 133–34; long shots, 1, 94; *lycée français*, 170; al-Maʿarri, Abu al-ʿAlaʾ, 123–24; mise-en-scène, 66–67, 89, 113–14, 116, 139, 186; modernism, 66–72, 130–31; modernity, 67, 143, 170; *Moroccan Chronicles* (Smihi, 1999), 67; Morocco, 1, 66–69, 71, 131, 133–34, 139; music, 84–85; nationalism, 90, 127*fig.*; neorealism, 67; noise, 152; non-diegesis, 80–81; *Othello* (Shakespeare), 126, 127*fig.*; Pasolini, Pier Paolo, 137; patriarchy, 181, 185; poetics/poetry, 95, 97, 131; polygamy, 183, 184–85; postcolonialism, 67, 68, 170; practices/rituals, 154, 156–57; prizes, 14; the protectorate, 1, 67, 117, 130–31; Qurʾan, 69, 95, 114, 124; race, 183, 185–86; radio, 86–88, 89, 91; realism, 39, 66–67; *The Red and the White* (Jancsó, 1967), 139; religion, 120, 183; Rif, 1, 67, 114, 130–31,

44, or Tales of the Night (continued) 139, 150; on-screen/off-screen, 1, 97; Smihi, Moumen, 1–2, 12, 14, 66–67, 70, 116, 123–24, 130–31, 133–34, 139, 170, 184; sound/tracks, 39, 68, 80, 84–85, 86–88, 94, 106, 152; spaces, 71, 139, 181, 183–86; stories, 130–31, 150; voice-overs, 95, 123, 184; voices, 94, 95, 97, 106, 123; wide shots, 139; women, 71, 94, 97, 123, 131, 183–86, 203
Foucault, Michel, 6, 27
400 Blows, The (Les quatre cents coups) (Truffaut, 1959), 63, 142, 199–200
fqih (Islamic legal expert), 4–5, 148, 168–69, 188
France: Algeria, 89–90, 174; Arab-Islamic architecture, 113, 214n12; *café-concert*, 176–77; *cinéma colonial*, 203–4; colonialism, 1, 17–18, 19, 79–80, 89, 90, 149–50, 213n2, 214n9; documentaries, 17–18; *The East Wind* (Smihi, 1975), 8, 13–14, 79, 89, 118; Egypt, 22; European Enlightenment, 119–20; film funds, 12; *44, or Tales of the Night* (Smihi, 1981), 1, 14, 67, 120, 130–31, 149–50; *Girls and Swallows* (Smihi, 2008), 166, 214n17; *An Imam in Paris* (al-Tahtawi), 22; languages, 128; Maghrib, 11, 214n9; Maghribi cinema, 107; migration, 79; modernity, 80; Mohammed V, King, 87–88; *Moroccan Chronicles* (Smihi, 1999), 14, 92, 137; Morocco, 1–2, 6, 17–18, 19, 20, 46, 55, 63, 92, 94, 96–97, 98–99, 139, 149–50, 192, 214n12, 228n1; music/noise, 79–80, 177; Orientalism, 203; politics, 22; secularism, 145–46; sexual identities, 201; *Si Moh, the Unlucky Man* (Smihi, 1971), 34–35, 39, 74, 75–76, 79, 178; Smihi, Moumen, 5, 6–11, 14, 20, 34, 41, 78–80, 90, 107, 109, 118; *The Sorrows of a Young Tangerian* (Smihi, 2013), 20, 179; Tangier, 4, 10–11, 63, 79–80, 119–20, 237n8; Voice of the Arabs, 87; voices, 79–80. *See also* Baker, Josephine; *Medina of Paris* films; protectorate, the
freedoms, 180–211; Arab cinemas, 33, 211; Arab Spring, 205; gender, 33, 163; *Girls and Swallows* (Smihi, 2008), 192–93; *The Lady from Cairo* (Smihi, 1991), 99, 103, 196, 199–200; *A Muslim Childhood* (Smihi, 2005), 193–94; the Nahda, 24–25; queerness, 201, 204, 210; sexuality, 33, 163, 204; Smihi, Moumen, 11, 24–25, 32, 144, 146, 163, 165–66, 211; *The Sorrows of a Young Tangerian* (Smihi, 2013), 173, 175–79, 195–96; veils, 192; women, 193–94; Zeineddine, Nazira, 165–66

French cinema, 95, 105. *See also* art cinema; Cinémathèque française
French modernists, 105
French New Wave (*nouvelle vague*), 6, 8, 181
Freud, Sigmund, 5, 8–9, 111, 127, 175, 178, 181, 204, 207, 239n39
fusha (modern Arabic), 18, 124. *See also* Modern Standard Arabic (MSA)
Future of Culture in Egypt, The (Hussein), 169

Gabara, Rachel, 62
Galt, Rosalind, 20, 38–39, 68, 69–70, 71–72
Galuppi, Baldassare, 82
Gamal, Samia, 132–33, 198
Ganguly, Keya, 28–29, 142
Gannun, ʿAbdallah, 164–65
Gaonkar, Dilip Parameshwar, 27, 28–29
Gauch, Suzanne, 15, 201
gender, 180–211; Arab cultures, 32–33, 180; circumcision, 157; *The East Wind* (Smihi, 1975), 180, 181–83; Europe, 187; *44, or Tales of the Night* (Smihi, 1981), 97, 181, 183–86; freedoms, 33, 163; gender performativity, 202; *Girls and Swallows* (Smihi, 2008), 181, 188, 202–3, 207; harems, 187–88; Islam, 165; languages, 9; *Leg over Leg* (al-Saq ʿala l-saq fi ma huwa al-Fariyaq) (al-Shidyaq), 21–22; the medina, 182–83; modernity, 187; Mohammed V, King, 192; Morocco, 137, 181, 201; *A Muslim Childhood* (Smihi, 2005), 181, 187–88; the Nahda, 32; New Arab Cinema, 37; patriarchy, 180; politics, 192; public/spaces, 181–200; sexual identities, 203; sexuality, 180, 181; Smihi, Moumen, 33, 103, 144, 163, 180–211; *The Sorrows of a Young Tangerian* (Smihi, 2013), 181; Tangier trilogy, 186–87; voices, 103
General Introduction to Psychoanalysis, A (Freud), 127, 175
Genet, Jean, 204
Ghosh, Nemai, 51
Gide, André, 203
Ginsberg, Allen, 11, 126
Girls and Swallows (Smihi, 2008): Arabic language, 209; Arab-Islamic architecture, 118, 181; Christianity, 150; close-ups, 125; desire, 191, 207, 208–9, 214n17; documentary fiction, 56; Egyptian cinema, 132; feminism, 209; Fez, 88; filmography, 242; France, 166, 214n17; freedoms, 192–93; gender, 181, 188, 202–3, 207; Hafez, Abdel Halim, 102; harems, 188, 191; head and face coverings/veils, 165,

188, 192, 193, 194; homosexuality, 207; Hussein, Taha, 125, 209; Islam, 165–66, 169, 170; literature, 125, 126, 193; long shots/takes, 142, 190–91; the medina, 188, 202–3; mise-en-scène, 191; Morocco, 46, 192; music, 203; nationalism, 88, 166, 209, 214n17; the new Nahda, 209; non-diegesis, 46; Ozu, Yasujiro, 141; patriarchy, 181, 188, 190; poetics/poetry, 190; politics, 208; polygamy/postcolonialism, 188; practices/rituals, 165; pretty images, 72; queerness, 206–7; Qur'an, 188; radio, 46, 88; religious diversity, 147, 148–49, 150, 188; sacredness/sacrilege, 158–59, 166; science, 170; sexuality, 192–93; Smihi, Moumen, 5, 43, 72, 169, 214n17; sound/tracks, 76, 82, 83, 88, 203; spaces, 181, 188, 189–91, 193; Tangier, 12, 65, 76, 203*fig.*, 206; wide shots, 141, 190, 191; women, 188–93, 194, 209
Glass and a Cigarette, A (Mostafa, 1955), 198
global cinema. *See* world cinema
Global South, 26
Gnawa, 48, 50, 83–84, 108, 130, 156–57, 223n24
Godard, Jean-Luc, 8, 66, 95
Goethe, Johann Wolfgang von, 126
Goodbye, Dragon Inn (Tsai, 2003), 142
Goodbye Mothers (Ismaïl, 2007), 149, 233n14
Groupe de recherches et d'essais cinématographiques (Research and Cinema Experimentation Group) (GREC), 7, 48–49
Guattari, Félix, 115
guembri (instrument), 83, 84*fig.*
Gunning, Tom, 15–17
Gutiérrez Alea, Tomás, 62

Habermas, Jürgen, 27, 29
hadith (the words of the Prophet Muhammad), 69, 114, 168
Hafez, Abdel Halim, 81, 91, 101, 102–3, 128, 132–33, 226n24
haik (women's garment), 130, 189. *See also* head and face coverings
hakawati (storyteller), 48, 50, 130–31, 150
al-Hakim, Tawfiq, 124, 125, 133
Halfouine (Boughedir, 1990), 234n17, 239n38
al-halqa (story tradition), 32, 131, 221n105
Hamama, Faten, 5, 132–33
Hamed, Marwan, 196
Hanan al-Cinema (Marks), 108–9, 218n47
Handel, George Frideric, 160
Hansen, Miriam, 29, 132
Hanssen, Jens, 24

harems, 182–83, 186, 187–88, 191
Hassan II, King, 6–7, 91, 125, 149, 173–74
Hawks, Howard, 5, 9
hawma (the hood), 201, 205–6
Hayes, Jarrod, 204, 239n38
Hayy Ibn Yaqzan (Ibn Tufayl), 119–20, 126, 147, 230n34, 232n61
head and face coverings, 32, 146, 154–55, 165, 187, 192, 193. *See also jellabas* (garment); veils
Hellman, Monte, 137
Hennebelle, Guy, 59–60, 62
heteroglossia, 129–30
*hijab*s, 32. *See also* head and face coverings; veils
Hirschkind, Charles, 101, 227n41
Historia Animalium (Aristotle), 117
History of Modern Morocco, A (Miller), 30–31
Hitchcock, Alfred, 126, 135–36, 137, 138, 139
Hollywood, 135–37; *The East Wind* (Smihi, 1975), 118; homoeroticism, 203; modernism/modernity, 29; *Moroccan Chronicles* (Smihi, 1999), 137; Moroccan cinema, 18, 135; Morocco, 18, 135–37, 230n34; *A Muslim Childhood* (Smihi, 2005), 128; Orientalism, 135, 203; realism, 38, 40, 60, 62; *The Rose of the Souk* (La rose du souk) (Séverac, 1930), 18; Shanghai cinema, 29, 132; Smihi, Moumen, 11, 132, 135–37, 138, 143, 231n60; world cinema, 51. *See also individuals*; United States; *individual Hollywood films*
homoeroticism, 203, 204, 205, 210
homophobia, 33, 181, 204, 205
homosexuality, 32–33, 159, 181, 201–7, 239n39. *See also* gender; queerness; sexual identities
Hosni, Soad, 198, 238n23
Hourani, Albert, 23, 24, 108, 167, 168, 169, 235n46
Hsiao-Hsien, Hou, 142
Human Pyramid, The (La pyramide humaine) (Rouch, 1959), 55
Hussein, Taha: Egypt, 124, 125, 169; *Girls and Swallows* (Smihi, 2008), 125, 209; Islam, 124–25, 169–70; languages, 9, 124–25; literature, 170; modernity, 9, 21, 169–70; *A Muslim Childhood* (Smihi, 2005), 122, 170; Muslims, 169; the Nahda, 25, 26, 163, 169; politics, 169–70; Qur'an, 125, 169; science, 169; Smihi, Moumen, 2, 5, 6, 8–9, 11, 25, 32, 124–25, 126, 163, 169–70; Tangier trilogy, 125, 169. *See also individual works*
Hypothesis of the Stolen Painting (L'Hypothèse du tableau volé) (Ruiz, 1987), 142

I Am Free (Ana hurra) (Abu Seif, 1959), 45, 132–33
Ibn al-ʿArabi, 123
Ibn al-Haytham (Alhazen) (philosopher), 21, 115–16
Ibn Rushd (Averroes) (philosopher), 21, 23, 115, 118–19, 120, 122, 123, 124, 163
Ibn Sina (Avicenna) (philosopher), 115, 119, 163
Ibn Tamiyya, 168
Ibn Tufayl, 118–22, 123, 126, 147, 163, 230n34
ʿid al-adha (ʿid al-kabir) (festival), 152, 166, 234n19
identities, 137, 146, 164, 180–81. *See also* cultural identities; sexual identities
ijtihad (human judgment), 168
Image et son: la revue du cinema (journal), 73
images: Arab cinemas, 99; auteurism, 16; *The East Wind* (Smihi, 1975), 58–59, 61, 63, 77, 78, 129, 147, 150, 155, 184*fig.*; *44, or Tales of the Night* (Smihi, 1981), 66–72, 94, 116–17; modernism, 66–72, 107; *A Muslim Childhood* (Smihi, 2005), 65, 72, 142; *The Night of Counting the Years* (Abdel Salam, 1969), 100–101, 156; *Si Moh, the Unlucky Man* (Smihi, 1971), 34–35, 60, 63–64; Smihi, Moumen, 2, 30, 60, 63–65, 66–72, 73–74, 77, 85, 107, 111, 132, 143, 191; sound/tracks, 73–80, 84–85, 94–95, 111; Tangier trilogy, 65. *See also* pretty images; still images
Imam in Paris, An (al-Tahtawi), 22
Iman, Adel, 134
immigrants. *See* migration
Indian cinema, 51, 142–43
"In Paris" (song), 177–78
L'institut des hautes études cinématographiques (IDHEC), 6–8, 34, 73, 215n24
Intégral (journal), 21, 116
intertextuality, 107–43; Arab cinemas, 32, 107, 108; Arabic language, 122–27, 128; Arab-Islamic architecture/art/philosophy, 112–22; *The East Wind* (Smihi, 1975), 12, 128–29, 224n49; Egyptian cinema, 133–34; *44, or Tales of the Night* (Smihi, 1981), 112, 117; al-Jahiz (philosopher), 117; *The Lady from Cairo* (Smihi, 1991), 112, 133–34; languages, 122–27, 128, 130; literature, 122–27; Middle East, 32; modernism, 107–8, 112, 118, 128–43; *Moroccan Chronicles* (Smihi, 1999), 108, 112, 130; Moroccan cinema, 131–32; music, 82; *A Muslim Childhood* (Smihi, 2005), 12, 128; the new/Nahda, 107–8; phagocytosis, 111; polyphony, 129–30; Smihi, Moumen, 16–17,
32, 40, 65, 107–12, 117–18, 123–24, 132–43, 157, 160, 162, 189, 211; Tangier trilogy, 119, 120, 122, 125, 137; world cinema, 107, 128–43
Introduction to Arab Poetics (Adonis), 9
Iraq, 87, 216n30
al-Isfahani, Abu al-Faraj, 122, 125
istitrad (digression), 117, 127
Islam, 162–79; alcohol, 165; Almohad dynasty, 119; Arab cultures, 161, 163–64; Arabic language, 163; Asad, Talal, 145; al-Azmeh, Aziz, 179; *Chants anciens des femmes de Fes* (Ancient Songs of the Women of Fez), 131; circumcision, 151–52, 233n15; colonialism, 168; *The East Wind* (Smihi, 1975), 118, 146, 153; Europe, 22, 163–64, 167–68; European Enlightenment, 171; feminism, 232n2; FIS (Islamic Salvation Front), 92; *44, or Tales of the Night* (Smihi, 1981), 117, 120; gender, 165; *Girls and Swallows* (Smihi, 2008), 165–66, 169, 170; Hussein, Taha, 124–25, 169–70; languages, 124–25, 163, 168; al-Maʿarri, Abu al-ʿAlaʾ, 123; modernity, 144, 146, 162–79; Moroccan cinema, 172, 201; Morocco, 153; *A Muslim Childhood* (Smihi, 2005), 120–22, 158–59, 164–65, 166–67, 169, 170, 193–94; Muslims, 168; the Nahda, 24–25, 167; nationalism, 178, 219n75; Orientalism, 179; politics, 153, 163–64, 168, 169–70, 179; practices/rituals, 153, 165, 167–68; Qurʾan, 122; reformist Islam, 192; religion, 144; sacredness, 165; sacrilege, 158–59; science, 22, 114, 116, 158, 163, 167, 168, 170; secularism, 163, 178, 219n75; Smihi, Moumen, 4–5, 111, 116, 138, 144, 146, 158, 161, 162–79, 211; *The Sorrows of a Young Tangerian* (Smihi, 2013), 164, 169, 172–73; Sunni Islam, 146, 153; Tangier trilogy, 146, 164, 167–69; the West, 144, 145, 167, 178; women, 165, 195, 201. *See also* Arab-Islamic architecture; Arab-Islamic philosophy; Muslims
Islam and Democracy (Mernissi), 189
Islamophobia, 144, 167
Israel, 45–46, 89, 92, 101, 102, 147–48, 149
Italian cinema, 106
Italian Locations: Reinhabiting the Past in Postwar Cinema (Steimatsky), 67
Italian neorealism, 31, 37, 38, 40–41, 42, 51, 53, 60–62, 70. *See also individual directors; individual films*
Italy, 90, 160

Jaguar (Rouch, 1957–67), 55–57
jahiliyya (ignorance), 124–25, 126, 169–70

al-Jahiz (philosopher), 117–18, 124, 130–31
Jameson, Fredric, 25, 27, 28, 39, 108
Jancsó, Miklós, 139
Japanese cinema, 138–42
Jeanson, Francis, 174
jellabas (garment), 43, 70, 79, 113, 155, 187, 194. *See also* head and face coverings
Jemaa el-Fnaa, 48, 49*fig.*, 56–57, 131, 135, 156–57
Jetty, The (La jetée) (Marker, 1963), 64
Johnson, Rebecca C., 21–22
Joyce, James, 66, 89, 117, 126–27, 130–31, 133–34
Judaism, 147–49; circumcision, 233n15, 234n19; Freud, Sigmund, 8–9, 175; *Girls and Swallows* (Smihi, 2008), 188; Maghrib, 149; the medina, 150; *mellah* (Jewish quarter), 147–48; migration, 147–48, 149; Morocco, 147–49; Muslims, 233n14; *Othello* (Shakespeare), 136; Smihi, Moumen, 116, 144, 171, 211, 232n7; *The Sorrows of a Young Tangerian* (Smihi, 2013), 147; Tangier, 11, 147–48; Tangier trilogy, 146–49
Judeo-Christian culture, 162
Julien, Isaac, 89

Kamal, Husayn, 45, 54, 133
Kant, Immanuel, 119
Kassab, Elizabeth Suzanne, 22, 24, 26, 108, 164, 168, 178, 220n89
Kassir, Samir, 163
Kemal, Namik, 195
Kennedy, Philip F., 159
Kerouac, Jack, 11, 126
Khan, Mohamed, 52, 134
Khatibi, Abdelkebir, 10, 21
Khouri, Malek, 91, 218n62, 227n26
Khoury, Elias, 24
Kitab al-aghani (Book of Songs) (Isfahani), 122, 125
Kitab al-bayan wa-l-tabiyyin (Book of Exposition and Demonstration) (al-Jahiz), 117
Kitab al-hayawan (The Book of Animals) (al-Jahiz), 117–18
Kitabi (My Book), 5, 121*fig.*
Kiwi (comic series), 128, 231n47
Kosansky, Oren, 149, 233n14
Kuhle Wampe (Brecht, 1932), 66
Kulthum, Umm, 87, 89, 90–91, 101–5, 121, 132, 206, 226n24, 228n45
Kurosawa, Akira, 139
Kuwait, 15, 37

Laâbi, Abdellatif, 10, 21
Laamarti, Ahmed, 83

Lacan, Jacques, 6, 7, 8–9, 109, 111
Lady from Cairo, The (Smihi, 1991): acousmatic, 101–2; cinemas, 142; desire/sexuality, 197–200; al-Dik, Bashir, 134; Egypt, 45–46, 197; Egyptian cinema, 44, 133, 196; filmography, 241; freedoms, 99, 103, 196, 199–200; Giza pyramids, 133; intertextuality, 112, 133–34; literature, 126; mise-en-scène, 45; montage, 196; music, 81–82, 101–2, 103, 133, 197; Nasser, Gamal Abdel, 101–2; neorealism, 45, 46*fig.*; non/diegesis, 46, 80–81; patriarchy, 196, 199; prizes, 14; prostitutes, 197, 198; radio, 45–46, 81, 101–2; realism, 45; *sheikh*, 196; Smihi, Moumen, 12, 44–47, 196, 197, 198, 199; sound/tracks, 45, 80–82, 99, 101–2, 133, 199; Truffaut, François, 199–200; voice-overs, 46, 99, 103, 196, 199; voices, 99, 101–2, 103; wide shots, 199; women, 99, 103, 180, 196–200
Lady from Shanghai, The (Welles, 1947), 196
Lambert, Gavin, 11, 12, 216n39. *See also Caftan of Love* (Smihi, 1989)
Lamentation over the Dead Christ (Mantegna) (painting), 161
Lang, Fritz, 9, 15–17, 95, 137
Lang, Robert, 200, 201, 205, 206, 234nn19,20
Langlois, Henri, 6, 109
languages, 122–27; Arab cinemas, 99, 112; Arab cultures, 9; Arab-Islamic architecture, 112; Barthes, Roland, 118; *Caftan of Love* (Smihi, 1989), 140*fig.*; colonialism, 9–10; dialects, 124, 128, 129; *The East Wind* (Smihi, 1975), 128–29, 130, 147; *écriture* (writing), 109; Egypt/France, 128; gender, 9; Gunning, Tom, 16–17; Hussein, Taha, 9, 124–25; inter/textuality, 109, 122–27, 128, 130; Islam, 124–25, 163, 168; al-Jahiz (philosopher), 118; Joyce, James, 66; literature, 9–10; Maghrib/Morocco, 3, 10; Mahfouz, Naguib, 124; modernity, 124; *Moroccan Chronicles* (Smihi, 1999), 103; Moroccan cinema, 18–19; *A Muslim Childhood* (Smihi, 2005), 98; the Nahda, 163; pan-Arabism, 124; polyphony, 129–30; postcolonialism, 10, 92–93; radio, 90, 92–93; religion, 9, 122–23; sacredness, 122; secularism, 9; *The Seventh Gate* (La Septième porte) (Zwoboda, 1947), 19; sexuality, 9; Smihi, Moumen, 2, 5, 9–10, 11–12, 16–17, 18, 19, 40, 109, 122–27, 128, 163; Tangier, 11–12, 130; the West, 9–10. *See also* translations; *individual languages*
Laroui, Abdallah, 21
Latin American cinema, 62, 70, 108, 132
Léaud, Jean-Pierre, 142

Lebanon, 37. *See also* Beirut
Leg over Leg (al-Saq ʿala l-saq fi ma huwa al-Fariyaq) (al-Shidyaq), 21–22
Leopard, The (Visconti, 1963), 67, 106
lesbianism, 201. *See also* homosexuality; queerness
Lévi-Strauss, Claude, 6, 9, 41, 110–11, 130
"Libé" (Smihi) (essay), 111
Listener's Choice (Ma yatlubuhu al-mustamiʿun) (ʿAbdulhamid, 2003), 89
Liszt, Franz, 82, 130
literature: Arab cinemas, 108, 112; Arab cultures, 210; Beirut, 9, 11, 31; *The East Wind* (Smihi, 1975), 118; Egyptian cinema, 125; *44, or Tales of the Night* (Smihi, 1981), 133–34; *Girls and Swallows* (Smihi, 2008), 125, 126, 193; Indian cinema, 51; intertextuality, 122–27; *The Lady from Cairo* (Smihi, 1991), 126; languages, 9–10; Maghrib, 239n38; masculinities, 131; modernism, 3, 21, 31, 65, 122–27; modernity, 20–21, 51; *Moroccan Chronicles* (Smihi, 1999), 126, 130; Morocco, 20–21, 29–30; *A Muslim Childhood* (Smihi, 2005), 65, 120–22, 126, 128; pan-Arabism, 91; radio, 89; realism, 31, 37, 54–55, 66, 126; sacrilege, 160; sexuality, 201, 203; Smihi, Moumen, 5, 6, 11, 19, 54–55, 65, 108, 111–12, 122–28, 133–34, 143, 160; *The Sorrows of a Young Tangerian* (Smihi, 2013), 174, 209–10; Tangier trilogy, 137, 174; United States, 126; women, 188–89; world literature, 122–27. *See also* poetics/poetry; textuality; *individual works; individual writers*
long shots, 1, 34, 43–44, 49, 65, 94, 172, 190–91, 207
long takes, 59, 83, 105–6, 122, 139, 141–42, 172*fig.*, 208
Love Story, A (Hakayat hub) (Halim, 1959), 81, 102
Lukács, György, 39
Lumière brothers, 47, 48–49, 116, 162
Lyautey, Louis Hubert Gonzalve, 1, 117
lycée français: *The East Wind* (Smihi, 1975), 96–97, 119–20; *44, or Tales of the Night* (Smihi, 1981), 170; *A Muslim Childhood* (Smihi, 2005), 120, 122, 158, 214n17; Smihi, Moumen, 5, 6, 8; *The Sorrows of a Young Tangerian* (Smihi, 2013), 173–77; Tangier trilogy, 167, 168

al-Maʿarri, Abu al-ʿAlaʾ, 19, 21, 122–24, 133–34, 147, 160, 162, 163
MacCabe, Colin, 60, 66, 67, 224n54

madaris (*madrasa*) (educational institution), 113, 114–15
Maghreb Pluriel (A Plural Maghrib) (Khatibi), 10
Maghrib: Algeria, 214n9; *Anfas* (journal), 10; Arab cultures, 3, 112; *darija* (language), 128; film funds, 12; France, 11, 214n9; *al-halqa* (story tradition), 221n105; Judaism, 149; languages, 3, 10; literature/masculinities, 239n38; modernism, 13, 21; *Moroccan Chronicles* (Smihi, 1999), 92–93; Morocco, 214n9; Nasser, Gamal Abdel, 87; nationalism, 17; postcolonialism, 14; queerness, 204; radio, 87, 92–93; religion, 146, 153; *Screens and Veils* (Martin)/sexuality/women, 201; *Si Moh, the Unlucky Man* (Smihi, 1971), 34; Smihi, Moumen, 13, 59–60, 64–65, 72, 110, 146, 161; *The Sorrows of a Young Tangerian* (Smihi, 2013), 20, 175
Maghribi cinema, 14, 107, 201
Magnani, Anna, 161
Mahfouz, Naguib, 11, 37, 52, 53, 108, 124, 125–26, 195
Mahumud II (sultan), 167
Makariyus, Maryam, 195
Makdisi, Jean Said, 197
Malas, Mohammad, 21, 89
Malick, Terrence, 137
Mamma Roma (Pasolini, 1962), 161
Man of Ashes (L'homme des cendres) (Bouzid, 1986), 205
Mantegna, Andrea, 161
Man Who Knew Too Much, The (Hitchcock, 1956), 135–36, 138, 204
Man with a Movie Camera (Vertov, 1929), 35–36
marabouts (holy men), 43, 119, 129, 146, 153, 154, 183, 213n2
Maraini, Toni, 21
Marker, Chris, 64–65
Marks, Laura U., 15, 33, 108–9, 114–15, 116, 218n47, 224n61
Marock (Marrakchi, 2006), 149, 200–201, 234n31
Maʿrouf the Cairo Cobbler (Maʿarouf al-Iskafi / Maarouf, savetier du Cairo) (Mauran, 1947), 18
Marrakesh, 47, 48, 49*fig.*, 56–57, 135, 137. *See also* Jemaa el-Fnaa
Martin, Florence, 201
Marx, Karl, 25, 27–28
Marxism, 6, 39, 219n75, 239n41
masculinities, 103, 131, 157, 180–81, 199, 201, 204–5, 208, 239n38. *See also* gender; patriarchy
Mashriq, 10, 216n30

Massad, Joseph A., 204, 239n31
Matisse, Henri, 2, 32, 137–38, 186, 204. *See also* *With Matisse in Tangier* (Smihi, 1993)
Me, a Black Man (Moi, un noir) (Rouch, 1958), 55–56
Meddeb, Abdelwahab, 57, 183
Medi-FM, 86, 92. *See also* radio
medina, the: Christianity/Judaism/religious diversity, 150; *The East Wind* (Smihi, 1975), 58, 61, 77–79, 129, 147, 155–56, 181; gender, 182–83; *Girls and Swallows* (Smihi, 2008), 188, 202–3; *A Muslim Childhood* (Smihi, 2005), 47–48, 98, 104, 105, 120–21, 158, 201–2, 214n17; radio, 93; sexuality, 210; Smihi, Moumen, 4, 5; sound/tracks, 77–79; Tangier, 104–5; voices, 104–6
Medina of Paris: A Square during the Ramadan Market, The (Smihi, 1996), 48–49, 79
Medina of Paris: Supererogatory Prayer by a Muslim Dignatory—My Father—After Landing at Paris-Orly, The (Smihi, 1996), 79, 86, 162
Melehi, Mohamed, 21
mellah (Jewish quarter), 147–48
Memory 14 (Mémoire 14) (Bouanani, 1970), 18, 64
Merinid Fez, 114, 116–17
al-Mernissi, Fatima, 163, 178–79, 181, 182–83, 187, 189, 192, 194–95
Mesguich, Félix, 17–18
Metz, Christian, 94–95
Mezzine, Mohamed, 114, 116
Middle East, 17, 20, 23, 32–33, 37, 89, 226n24. *See also individual countries*
Midnight's Children (Rushdie), 89
migration: auteurism, 137; France, 79; *Jaguar* (Rouch, 1957–67), 55–57; Judaism, 147–48, 149; *The Medina of Paris: Supererogatory Prayer by a Muslim Dignatory—My Father—After Landing at Paris-Orly* (Smihi, 1996), 49, 162; *Moroccan Chronicles* (Smihi, 1999), 92–93; Morocco, 83; *A Muslim Childhood* (Smihi, 2005), 98; Rouch, Jean, 55–56; Smihi, Moumen, 60; spaces, 56; Tangier, 79. *See also Si Moh, the Unlucky Man* (Smihi, 1971)
Miller, Susan Gilson, 30–31, 147
mise-en-scène: Abu Seif, Salah, 53, 54; *Caftan of Love* (Smihi, 1989), 139; *The Charcoal Maker* (Le charbonnier) (Bouamari, 1972), 89; *The East Wind* (Smihi, 1975), 61, 154–55; *44, or Tales of the Night* (Smihi, 1981), 66–67, 89, 113–14, 116, 139, 186; *Girls and Swallows* (Smihi, 2008), 191; *The Lady from Cairo* (Smihi, 1991), 45; Latin American cinema, 62; *With Matisse in Tangier* (Smihi, 1993), 138; Morocco, 129; *A Muslim Childhood* (Smihi, 2005), 142, 148; radio, 85–86; *Si Moh, the Unlucky Man* (Smihi, 1971), 41–42; sound/tracks, 75
Mizoguchi, Kenji, 5, 139
modernism, 1–33, 59–72, 107–43; Afifi, Mohamed, 131; Arab cinemas, 3–4, 33, 39, 73, 107, 112; Arab cultures, 3–4, 131–32, 211, 224n61; El-Ariss, Tarek, 31; art cinema, 38–39, 62; Beirut, 31, 108; Bouanani, Ahmed, 131–32; colonialism, 128; Creswell, Robyn, 31; Egyptian cinema, 125; *44, or Tales of the Night* (Smihi, 1981), 66–72, 130–31; Ganguly, Keya, 28–29; Hansen, Miriam, 29; Hollywood, 29; images, 66–72, 107; intertextuality, 107–8, 112, 118, 128–43; literature, 3, 21, 31, 65, 122–27; Maghrib, 13, 21; modernity, 27–28; Morocco, 71; *A Muslim Childhood* (Smihi, 2005), 141; the Nahda, 108, 110–12; nationalism, 128, 132; neorealism, 67; New Arab Cinema, 38, 59–72; the new Nahda, 2, 25; Pasolini, Pier Paolo, 39–40; poetics/poetry, 21; politics, 21, 39; Ray, Satyajit, 28; realism, 36–41, 59–66, 67, 72; *Si Moh, the Unlucky Man* (Smihi, 1971), 39; Smihi, Moumen, 2–4, 13, 20, 30, 33, 36, 38–41, 60, 65–66, 72, 73, 93, 107–11, 118, 128, 130, 132, 143, 144, 211; sound/tracks, 31–32, 74, 77, 80, 107; Third Cinema, 62, 63; United States, 62; vernacular modernism, 29, 128–43; Visconti, Luchino, 67; the West, 21, 25, 28, 41, 118; world cinema, 3, 107, 108, 128–43, 147. *See also* French cinema
modernist cinema, 10, 29, 30, 66
modernity, 144–79; Abdel Salam, Shadi, 100; Anglophone film studies, 28; Arab cinemas, 2–3, 30, 139, 162; Arab cultures, 30, 72, 163–64, 178, 200, 211; El-Ariss, Tarek, 18–19, 25, 31; capitalism, 25–26; *ciné-écriture/cinécriture* (cinema-writing), 111; colonialism, 25–26, 80, 178; *The East Wind* (Smihi, 1975), 78, 143; Egypt, 21; Enlightenment, 26; Europe, 24–31, 167–68, 170, 175, 178, 187; *44, or Tales of the Night* (Smihi, 1981), 67, 143, 170; France, 80; Freud, Sigmund, 175; *fusha* (modern Arabic), 124; Gaonkar, Dilip Parameshwar, 27; gender, 187; al-Hakim, Tawfiq, 125; Hollywood, 29; Hussein, Taha, 9, 21, 169–70; Indian cinema, 142–43; Islam, 144, 146, 162–79; languages, 124; *Leg over Leg* (al-Saq ʿala l-saq fi ma huwa al-Fariyaq) (al-Shidyaq), 21–22;

modernity *(continued)*
literature, 20–21, 51; *The Medina of Paris: Supererogatory Prayer by a Muslim Dignatory—My Father—After Landing at Paris-Orly* (Smihi, 1996), 162; modernism, 27–28; Moroccan cinema, 29–30; Morocco, 20–21, 30–31, 80, 135, 143; *A Muslim Childhood* (Smihi, 2005), 187–88; Muslims, 168; the Nahda, 9, 22, 24, 91, 111; nationalism, 30; the new Nahda, 25; pan-Arabism, 227n26; postcolonialism, 26, 30–31; radio, 85, 86; Ray, Satyajit, 28, 142–43; religion, 144–79; Saleh, Tawfik, 133; secularism, 144–79; sexual identities, 204; sexuality, 200; *Si Moh, the Unlucky Man* (Smihi, 1971), 143; Smihi, Moumen, 2–3, 21–33, 61–62, 78–80, 111, 118, 119, 132, 139, 142–43, 144, 162–79, 200; *The Sorrows of a Young Tangerian* (Smihi, 2013), 164, 174–75; sound/tracks, 74; Syria, 62–63; Tangier, 78–79; Tangier trilogy, 167–69, 179; United States, 25, 26–28; voices, 106; the West, 22, 25–31, 178–79; women, 195; world cinema, 138–39; Zeineddine, Nazira, 165

Modern Standard Arabic (MSA), 5, 18, 124
Mohammad, Oussama, 89
Mohammed III, King, 136
Mohammed V, King, 46, 63, 87–88, 104, 105*fig.*, 129, 192, 214n17
Mohammed VI, King, 149, 153
Monster, The (al-Wahsh) (Abu Seif, 1954), 45, 52–53.
montage: Amiralay, Omar, 63; *Battleship Potemkin* (Eisenstein, 1925), 155; circumcision, 234n17; *The East Wind* (Smihi, 1975), 43–44, 61, 77, 129, 184*fig.*; *Egyptian Cinema: Defense and Illustration* (Smihi, 1989), 134; *Film-Essay on the Euphrates Dam* (Amiralay, 1970), 62–63; *The Lady from Cairo* (Smihi, 1991), 196; Latin American cinema, 62; *A Muslim Childhood* (Smihi, 2005), 82, 121–22, 148, 158; realism, 64; *Si Moh, the Unlucky Man* (Smihi, 1971), 34, 60; Smihi, Moumen, 64; *The Thug* (Abu Seif, 1957), 53; Vertov, Dziga, 21
Montgomery, James E., 117
Morin, Léa, 15
Moroccan Cafe (painting), 138
Moroccan Chronicles (Smihi, 1999), 46–51; Algeria, 92; circumcision, 47–48, 151–52, 156–57; close-ups, 50; desire/*haik* (women's garment), 189; diegesis, 92; documentaries, 72; documentary fiction, 56–57; *The East Wind* (Smihi, 1975), 50, 130; Essaouira, 136; Fez, 47, 57, 92, 137; filmography, 241; *44, or Tales of the Night* (Smihi, 1981), 67; France, 14, 92, 137; Gnawa, 48, 50, 130, 156–57; *hakawati* (storyteller), 50, 130; *al-halqa* (story tradition), 131; Hollywood, 137; Ibn Tufayl, 118; intertextuality, 108, 112, 130; languages, 103; literature, 126, 130; long takes, 83; Maghrib/migration, 92–93; *The Man Who Knew Too Much* (Hitchcock, 1956), 135–36; Morocco, 83, 92; music, 50, 82, 103, 130; neorealism, 42, 47–48, 50–51, 57, 72; orality, 130; *Othello* (Welles, 1951), 136; patriarchy/sexuality/veils, 189; practices/rituals, 47, 156–57; public spaces, 49–50, 57; radio, 86, 92–93; Smihi, Moumen, 46–51, 126, 130, 136; sound/tracks, 48, 82, 83, 95, 130; Tangier, 12, 50, 57, 92, 137; voice-overs, 83, 92; voices, 95, 126; the West, 92, 130; women, 92, 103, 126

Moroccan cinema: Arab cinemas, 107; Arab cultures, 132; colonialism, 17–18, 132; Egyptian cinema, 14, 18–19; Hollywood, 18, 135; important figures, 6; intertextuality, 131–32; Islam, 172, 201; languages, 18–19; Marks, Laura U., 15, 218n47; modernity, 29–30; Orientalism, 107; Osfour, Mohammed, 135; postcolonialism, 4, 17–18, 29–30, 135; the protectorate/world cinema, 17–18; race, 186, 237n4; "La septième porte" (The Seventh Gate) (Bouanani), 18; sexuality/women, 201, 237n4; Smihi, Moumen, 2, 6, 13–15, 17–20, 111, 131; Torres, Mohamed, 7–8; United States, 14, 19, 131–32; the West, 15; Zwoboda, André, 19. *See also* Centre cinématographique marocain (Moroccan National Cinema Center) (CCM); *individual Moroccan films*

Morocco: alcohol, 158–59; Arab cultures, 3, 73; Arab-Islamic architecture, 130, 214n12; calligraphy, 117; Christianity, 149–51; circumcision, 157; colonialism, 1, 17–18, 19, 30–31, 68–69, 71, 80, 90, 94, 137, 213n2, 214n9, 231n60; *darija* (language), 5, 128, 214n13; decorative, 69, 112; *The East Wind* (Smihi, 1975), 8, 13–14, 43, 61, 130; Egyptian cinema, 18, 19; ethnographic films, 55; Europe, 194; feminism, 192; film funds, 12; *44, or Tales of the Night* (Smihi, 1981), 1, 66–69, 71, 131, 133–34, 139; France, 1–2, 6, 17–18, 19, 20, 46, 55, 63, 92, 94, 96–97, 98–99, 139, 149–50, 192, 214n12, 228n1; gender, 137, 181, 201; *Girls and Swallows* (Smihi, 2008), 46, 192; Gnawa, 83, 84; Hassan II, King, 6–7, 91, 173; *Hayy Ibn*

INDEX   275

Yaqzan (Ibn Tufayl), 230n34; *A History of Modern Morocco* (Miller), 30–31; Hollywood, 18, 135–37, 230n34; homosexuality, 181; Islam, 153; Judaism, 147–49; languages, 3; literature, 20–21, 29–30; Maghrib, 214n9; Matisse, Henri, 2; migration, 83; mise-en-scène, 129; modernism, 71; modernity, 20–21, 30–31, 80, 135, 143; *Much Loved* (Ayouch, 2015), 234n31; music, 84; *A Muslim Childhood* (Smihi, 2005), 98–99; national cinemas, 18; nationalism, 5, 86, 88, 90, 91, 192; Orientalism, 135, 138; *Othello* (Shakespeare), 126; Pasolini, Pier Paolo, 137, 232n61; patriarchy, 137, 188; politics, 6–7, 39, 195; polygamy, 188; postcolonialism, 10, 20–21, 29–30, 31, 39, 90–91, 92–93; practices/rituals, 153; queerness, 204, 206, 210; race/slavery, 186, 237n4; radio, 86, 90; realism, 37; religion, 144, 146, 153, 164; religious diversity, 147–51; sacredness/sacrilege, 157–58; secularism, 32, 144, 167; sexual identities, 201; sexuality, 159, 200–201, 211; *Si Moh, the Unlucky Man* (Smihi, 1971), 8, 34, 74; Smihi, Moumen, 2, 3–4, 13–14, 15, 17, 19, 31, 41, 47, 59, 69, 70, 73, 74, 129, 136–38, 141, 143, 167, 180–81, 195, 211; *The Sorrows of a Young Tangerian* (Smihi, 2013), 20, 177, 236n55; sound/tracks, 73, 74, 84, 86; Spain, 98–99; *tanwir* (Enlightenment), 173, 178; *Tarfaya, or a Poet's Walk* (Tarfaya, ou, la marche d'un poète) (Bouanani, 1966), 71, 131–32; veils, 154; Voice of the Arabs, 87, 90–91; the West, 163; *With Matisse in Tangier* (Smihi, 1993), 137–38; women, 154, 189, 191–92, 194–95. *See also* Amazigh culture; *Moroccan Chronicles* (Smihi, 1999); *individual places*

Morocco (von Sternberg, 1930), 135, 137, 176, 203, 204, 231n60
Mourad, Leila, 5, 196, 197
Mrabet, Mohammed, 11, 140*fig.*
Mubarak, ʿAli, 195
Much Loved (Ayouch, 2015), 200, 234n31
Mufti, Aamir R., 163
Muhammad ʿAbduh, 23
Muhammad ʿAli Pasha, 22, 23
multivocality, 12, 32, 69, 105–6, 130, 171. *See also* polyphony; voices
Munif, ʿAbd al-Rahman, 26
Musa, Salama, 19
music: Amazigh culture, 129; Arab cinemas, 112; Arab cultures, 91, 99, 226n24; Barthes, Roland, 80, 225n9; *café-concert*, 175–76; *The East Wind* (Smihi, 1975), 77, 84; Egyptian cinema, 80–81, 132, 133; *44, or Tales of the Night* (Smihi, 1981), 84–85; France, 79–80, 177; *Girls and Swallows* (Smihi, 2008), 203; instruments, 83, 84*fig.*; intertextuality, 82; *The Lady from Cairo* (Smihi, 1991), 81–82, 101–2, 103, 133, 197; *The Medina of Paris: Supererogatory Prayer by a Muslim Dignatory—My Father—After Landing at Paris-Orly* (Smihi, 1996), 79; *Moroccan Chronicles* (Smihi, 1999), 50, 82, 103, 130; Morocco, 84; *A Muslim Childhood* (Smihi, 2005), 82, 83–84, 104–5, 206; non/diegesis, 106; *Omar Gatlato* (Allouache, 1976), 100; orality, 101; pan-Arabism/postcolonialism, 91; Qurʾanic *hadaʾith* (classical Arabic songs), 128; radio, 85, 86, 91, 226n24; realism, 81; *Si Moh, the Unlucky Man* (Smihi, 1971), 74–76; Smihi, Moumen, 76–77, 80–85, 91, 111, 112, 132; *The Sorrows of a Young Tangerian* (Smihi, 2013), 59, 175–78, 208; sound/tracks, 74, 79, 80–85; Tangier, 11, 79–80, 84; Tangier trilogy, 83–85, 137; Voice of the Arabs, 87; voices, 101, 102–3. *See also* Gnawa; *individuals*; Western classical music; *individual songs*
musique concrète, 75–80
Muslim Childhood, A (Smihi, 2005): alcohol, 158–59; Arabic language, 97–98; Arab-Islamic architecture, 118, 181; Christianity, 150; cinemas, 142; circumcision, 82, 104–5, 151–52, 156–57; close-ups, 132–33, 151, 206, 207; *darija* (language), 98, 104–5, 106, 148; desire, 206; diegesis, 133; documentary fiction, 56; *The East Wind* (Smihi, 1975), 189; Egyptian cinema, 20, 128, 132–33, 194, 206; fetishism, 207–8; filmography, 241; freedoms, 193–94; gender, 181, 187–88; Gnawa, 83–84; head and face coverings, 187, 193; Hollywood, 128; homosexuality, 239n39; Hussein, Taha, 170; Ibn Tufayl, 120–22; images, 65, 72, 142; intertextuality, 12, 128; Islam, 120–22, 158–59, 164–65, 166–67, 169, 170, 193–94; *jellabas* (garment), 187; Kulthum, Umm, 104–5, 121, 206; languages, 98; literature, 65, 120–22, 126, 128; long shots, 65, 207; *lycée français*, 120, 122, 158, 214n17; the medina, 47–48, 98, 104, 105, 120–21, 158, 201–2, 214n17; migration, 98; mise-en-scène, 142, 148; modernism, 141; modernity, 187–88; montage, 82, 121–22, 148, 158; Morocco, 98–99; music, 82, 83–84, 104–5, 206; non-diegesis, 65, 82–83; offscreen, 98, 206; patriarchy, 181, 187; poetics/poetry, 99; politics, 122; polygamy, 164, 189; practices/rituals, 156–57; prostitutes, 120–21, 159, 165,

Muslim Childhood (continued)
193, 202, 205–6; queerness, 201–2, 203, 204–6, 207, 239n39; Qur'an, 120, 166, 194; radio, 86; religion, 121–22, 151; religious diversity, 147–51; Rif, 98–99; sacredness, 158–59; sacrilege, 158–59, 164–65, 172–73; science, 170; sexuality, 159, 193, 201–2, 207; Smihi, Moumen, 5, 65, 72, 98, 105, 122, 141, 158, 169, 214n17; sound/tracks, 82, 83, 86, 94–95, 97–99, 104–5; spaces, 141, 181, 189, 192–94; Spain, 158; Tangier, 12, 65, 98, 105, 120, 158; Truffaut, François, 142; United States, 82; *ville nouvelle*, 98, 187; voice-overs, 65, 94–95, 98–99, 120, 148, 150, 151, 158, 187, 201–2, 206; voices, 94–95, 97–99, 104–5; wide shots, 207; women, 97–99, 187–88, 189, 192–94

Muslims: Christianity, 150; circumcision, 234nn18,19; *The East Wind* (Smihi, 1975), 147; Europe, 22, 167–68; *Girls and Swallows* (Smihi, 2008), 166; homosexuality, 204, 205; Hussein, Taha, 169; Judaism, 233n14; *Marock* (Marrakchi, 2006), 149; masculinities, 205; modernity, 168; religion, 144; Smihi, Moumen, 144, 232n7; *The Sorrows of a Young Tangerian* (Smihi, 2013), 147, 172; Sufi Muslims, 153, 154, 213n2; Tangier, 11; *tanwir* (Enlightenment), 178–79; the West, 167–68, 181. See also Islam

"Mythologies Arabes" (Arab Mythologies) (Smihi) (essay), 19

Nagib, Lúcia, 3
Naguib, Mohammed, 86
Nahda, the, 21–31; Arab cinemas, 23; Arab cultures, 2–3; Arabic/languages, 163; El-Ariss, Tarek, 108, 211; Chahine, Youssef, 218n62; debates, 26; Egypt, 21, 22, 134; Enlightenment, 24–26, 119; Europe, 2–3, 21–24, 108, 168; feminism, 192, 195; freedoms, 24–25; gender, 32; globalism, 108; Hussein, Taha, 25, 26, 163, 169; intertextuality, 107–8; Islam, 24–25, 167; *Leg over Leg* (al-Saq 'ala l-saq fi ma huwa al-Fariyaq) (al-Shidyaq), 21–22; modernism, 108, 110–12; modernity, 9, 22, 24, 91, 111; nationalism, 24, 218n62; politics/religion, 168; secularism, 26, 146, 163; Smihi, Moumen, 2–3, 21–31, 91, 107–8, 143, 167; translations, 107–8; veils, 165; the West, 9, 21–31, 215n26; women, 165–66, 195

Nascimbene, Mario, 100–101
Nasrallah, Yousry, 196
Nasser, Gamal Abdel, 45, 81, 86–87, 90, 91, 101–2, 104, 226n24, 227n40, 228n45

national cinemas, 17–21, 33, 51. See also Arab cinemas; *individual countries' cinemas*
nationalism: the new/Nahda, 24, 218n62; Abdel Wahab, Mohammed, 91; Algerian FLN (Front de Libération Nationale), 87, 90; Arab cultures, 90–91; Chahine, Youssef, 91; *The East Wind* (Smihi, 1975), 63, 129; feminism, 192; Fez, 192; *44, or Tales of the Night* (Smihi, 1981), 90, 127*fig.*; *Girls and Swallows* (Smihi, 2008), 88, 166, 209, 214n17; Hafez, Abdel Halim, 226n24; Islam, 178, 219n75; Italy/Spain, 90; Kulthum, Umm, 104; Maghrib, 17; modernism, 128, 132; modernity, 30; Mohammed V, King, 129; Morocco, 5, 86, 88, 90, 91, 192; pan-Arabism, 90, 124; politics, 91; postcolonialism, 17; radio, 86–92, 226n24; Sartre, Jean-Paul, 9; secularism, 178; Smihi, Moumen, 19, 63, 91, 192; *The Sorrows of a Young Tangerian* (Smihi, 2013), 20, 177; Tangier, 147; Tangier trilogy, 90, 208; Tibi, Mohammed, 170; veils/women, 192, 194, 195; Voice of the Arabs, 87–88, 92–93

Necipoglu, Gülrü, 115–16
neo-imperialism, 145. See also postcolonialism
neorealism, 41–54; Algeria, 70; Arab cinemas, 54; *The Barber from the Poor Neighborhood* (Reggab, 1982), 52; Bazin, André, 62; Biswas, Moinak, 51; *Cairo 30* (Abu Seif, 1966), 53; *The East Wind* (Smihi, 1975), 43–44, 57, 60–61, 72; Egyptian cinema, 40, 52, 54; *44, or Tales of the Night* (Smihi, 1981), 67; Indian cinema, 51, 143; *The Lady from Cairo* (Smihi, 1991), 45, 46*fig.*; Latin American cinema, 62; modernism, 67; *Moroccan Chronicles* (Smihi, 1999), 42, 47–48, 50–51, 57, 72; New Arab Cinema, 41–54; politics, 70; pretty images, 68, 69–70; Schoonover, Karl, 60; *Si Moh, the Unlucky Man* (Smihi, 1971), 41–43, 72; Smihi, Moumen, 40–43, 45, 47–48, 51–55, 57, 60–61, 67, 73; *Spring Sunshine* (Lahlou, 1970), 51–52; *The Thug* (Abu Seif, 1957), 53; Visconti, Luchino, 67; world cinema, 51, 52. See also documentary fiction; Italian neorealism

New Arab Cinema, 34–72; art cinema, 38–39; documentaries, 37; gender/sexuality/women, 37; modernism, 38, 59–72; neorealism, 41–54; realism, 38, 59–66; Syria, 37; as term, 37–38. See also *individuals*

new Nahda, the, 2–3, 20–21, 24, 25, 108, 144, 180, 209, 211. See also Nahda, the
Nietzsche, Friedrich, 173

Night of Counting the Years, The (al-Momia) (The Mummy) (Abdel Salam, 1969), 100–101, 133, 156
Nights of the Jackal (Layali ibn awa) ('Abdulhamid, 1988), 89
noise, 74–80, 84, 85, 103, 106, 152. *See also musique concrète*
non-Arab cinemas, 33. *See also* Hollywood; world cinema; *individual cinemas*
non-diegesis: Egyptian cinema, 81; *44, or Tales of the Night* (Smihi, 1981), 80–81; *Girls and Swallows* (Smihi, 2008), 46; *The Lady from Cairo* (Smihi, 1991), 46, 80–81; music, 106; *A Muslim Childhood* (Smihi, 2005), 65, 82–83; *Si Moh, the Unlucky Man* (Smihi, 1971), 60; Smihi, Moumen, 80; *The Sorrows of a Young Tangerian* (Smihi, 2013), 208; sound/tracks, 32, 80–83, 94, 106; voices, 94
nonsynchronous, 35, 75–76, 95. *See also* sound/tracks
North Africa, 17, 18, 20, 37, 62, 89, 132, 201, 213n3, 214n9. *See also individuals;* Maghrib
North African cinema, 17, 63, 70
Nothing but Time (Rien que les heures) (Cavalcanti, 1926), 35–36
nouvelle vague (French New Wave), 6, 8, 181. *See also* French cinema; *individuals*
novels. *See* literature
"Nuit et brouillard" (Night and Fog) (song), 177

Obsession (Ossessione) (Visconti, 1943), 67
Oedipus Rex (Pasolini, 1967), 137, 232n61
Of Flesh and Steel (De chair et d'acier) (Afifi, 1959), 64
offscreen, 1, 60, 81, 83–84, 93–94, 96–98, 100, 125, 206
Oliveira, Manoel de, 142
Omar Gatlato (Allouache, 1976), 99, 100
One Thousand and One Nights (tale), 48, 92, 127, 133, 160
1001 Hands (Les mille et une mains) (Ben-Barka, 1972), 14
on-screen, 60, 81, 83, 84, 93, 96–97
On the Origin of Species (Darwin), 173
orality, 99, 101, 111, 112, 130, 131. *See also* voices
Orientalism, 19, 30, 107, 135, 138, 179, 203–4, 211, 239n41
Orientalism (Said), 203
Orientalists, 25, 32–33, 163, 190, 204, 211
Orlando, Valérie, 201
Osfour, Mohammed, 18, 135
Othello (Shakespeare), 103, 126, 127*fig.*, 136–37

Othello (Welles, 1951), 136–37, 138
Ottoman empire/rule, 22, 167, 170
Ouhiba, Insaf, 19
Ouled Sidi Ahmed ou Moussa, the, 1, 130
Ozu, Yasujiro, 57, 139–41, 190

Palestine, 12–13, 37, 45, 82, 92
pan-Arabism, 3, 9, 19, 32, 86–88, 90, 91, 104, 124, 227n26. *See also* Arab Spring
pansexuality, 181, 210
Parajanov, Sergei, 139
Paris. *See* France
Pasha, Muhammad 'Ali, 167
Pasolini, Pier Paolo: desire, 210; modernism/poetics/poetry, 39–40; Morocco, 232n61; politics, 160, 239n41; religion, 137, 146, 160–61; sacrilege, 137, 160–62; sexuality, 160, 181, 210; Smihi, Moumen, 32, 106, 108, 146, 160–62, 167, 210, 234n31; Steimatsky, Noa, 67. *See also individual films*
Pather Panchali (Ray, 1955), 142–43
patriarchy, 33, 137, 151–52, 157, 180–81, 183, 185–90, 196, 199, 234n20
Pépé le Moko (Duvivier, 1937), 203
Perdicaris Park (Tangier), 102–3, 177–78
phagocytosis, 111–12
Pinal, Silvia, 160–61
Pisier, Marie-France, 184
poetics/poetry: Adonis, 9, 99; classic Arabic, 159; Creswell, Robyn, 31; femininities/masculinities, 131; *Fi al-shi'r al-jahili* (On Jahili Poetry) (Hussein), 124–25, 169–70; *44, or Tales of the Night* (Smihi, 1981), 95, 97, 131; *Girls and Swallows* (Smihi, 2008), 190; Introduction to Arab Poetics (Adonis), 9; modernism, 21; *A Muslim Childhood* (Smihi, 2005), 99; orality, 101; Pasolini, Pier Paolo, 39–40; *Problems of Dostoevsky's Poetics* (Bakhtin), 129–30; Smihi, Moumen, 6, 8, 112, 160; *Tarfaya, or a Poet's Walk* (Tarfaya, ou, la marche d'un poète) (Bouanani, 1966), 71, 131–32; translations, 108; women, 123. *See also* literature
"Political Cinema Must Not Abandon Its Interest in Beauty," 70
politics, 34–72; Algeria, 89–90; Arab cinemas, 37, 91; Arab cultures, 32–33, 170–71; *Arabian Nights* (Pasolini, 1974), 239n41; Arab-Islamic architecture, 112; El-Ariss, Tarek, 33, 167; colonialism, 88, 90; desire, 208; Egypt, 22, 169; France, 22; gender, 192; *Girls and Swallows* (Smihi, 2008), 208; Hussein, Taha, 169–70; Islam, 153, 163–64, 168, 169–70, 179;

politics *(continued)*
Italian neorealism, 62, 70; Kassab, Elizabeth Suzanne, 164; Marks, Laura U., 33; masculinities, 181; modernism, 21, 39; Morocco, 6–7, 39, 195; *A Muslim Childhood* (Smihi, 2005), 122; the Nahda, 168; nationalism, 91; neorealism, 70; the new Nahda, 24; orality, 101; pan-Arabism, 91, 227n26; Pasolini, Pier Paolo, 160, 239n41; pretty images, 69–70, 72; queerness, 201, 210; radio, 86, 88–91; religion, 24, 32, 145–46, 150–51, 211; secularism, 145, 232n5; sexuality, 201, 208, 210; Smihi, Moumen, 6–7, 10–11, 24, 32, 34, 39, 72, 91, 101, 103, 160, 163, 210; *The Sorrows of a Young Tangerian* (Smihi, 2013), 59, 103, 172, 173, 174, 177, 179, 195–96, 209, 214n17; sound/tracks, 32; Syria, 62–63; Third Cinema, 62, 72; veils, 192; Voice of the Arabs, 90–91; voices, 102, 227n41. *See also individuals*
polygamy, 19, 164, 180, 182–85, 188, 189
polyphony, 105, 129–30, 136–37. *See also* multivocality; voices
Pomme, Claude, 175–76, 227n35
postcolonialism: anthropologies, 55; Arab cinemas, 17, 37, 112; Arab cultures, 3, 32; desire, 208; *The East Wind* (Smihi, 1975), 63; *44, or Tales of the Night* (Smihi, 1981), 67, 68, 170; *Girls and Swallows* (Smihi, 2008), 188; harems, 188; languages, 10, 92–93; Maghrib, 14; modernity, 26, 30–31; Moroccan cinema, 4, 17–18, 29–30, 135; Morocco, 10, 20–21, 29–30, 31, 39, 90–91, 92–93; music, 91; nationalism, 17; North Africa, 70; pan-Arabism, 227n26; queerness, 203–4; radio, 89, 91–92; Ray, Satyajit, 51; realism, 68; Smihi, Moumen, 4, 11, 14, 23, 31, 33, 51, 63, 91; sound/tracks, 92; Syria, 62–63; Tangier trilogy, 208; veils, 188
Postman, The (al-Bustagi) (Kamal, 1968), 45, 54, 133
post-secularism, 145, 232n3. *See also* secularism
practices/rituals, 2, 40, 47, 107, 146, 151–58, 165, 167–68. *See also individual practices*
pretty images, 66–72. *See also* images
Problems of Dostoevsky's Poetics (Bakhtin), 129–30
profane. *See* sacrilege
prostitutes, 120–21, 159, 165, 176, 182, 193, 197–98, 202, 205–6, 234n31
protectorate, the, 1, 17–18, 63, 67, 114, 117, 129, 130–31, 214n12. *See also* colonialism; France
Protestantism, 163–64
Proust, Marcel, 82, 99, 118

psychoanalysis, 10, 55, 72, 127, 157, 175. *See also* Freud, Sigmund
public spaces: *The Barber from the Poor Neighborhood* (Reggab, 1982), 52; *The East Wind* (Smihi, 1975), 43–44, 61, 182–83; gender, 181, 191–200; *The Medina of Paris: A Square during the Ramadan Market* (1996), 48–49; *Raya and Sakina* (Abu Seif, 1953), 53; *Moroccan Chronicles* (Smihi, 1999), 49–50, 57; *A Muslim Childhood* (Smihi, 2005), 192–94; *Si Moh, the Unlucky Man* (Smihi, 1971), 34–36, 41–42, 56, 64; Smihi, Moumen, 196; Tangier trilogy, 191, 196; women, 181, 191, 196, 211. *See also* spaces

Qadaya wa-shahadat (journal), 26, 108
al-Qarawiyyin mosque and university, 67, 95, 114, 170, 194
queerness, 32–33, 201–2, 203–8, 210, 239nn31,39. *See also* homosexuality; sexuality
Qur'an: Arabic language, 163; circumcision, 234n18; *The East Wind* (Smihi, 1975), 147, 182; *44, or Tales of the Night* (Smihi, 1981), 69, 95, 114, 124; *Girls and Swallows* (Smihi, 2008), 188; Hourani, Albert, 168; Hussein, Taha, 125, 169; Islam, 122, 164; *A Muslim Childhood* (Smihi, 2005), 120, 166, 194
Qur'anic Arabic, 104, 122, 124–25, 163
Qur'anic *hada'ith* (classical Arabic songs), 128

Rabat, 70, 113
race, 6, 136, 183, 185–86, 237n4
radio, 32, 45–46, 81, 83, 85–93, 101–6, 147, 162, 226n24, 227n40
Radio-Alger, 89–90
Radio Bari, 90
Radio Cairo, 32, 147
Rashid, Harun al-, 210
Ray, Nicholas, 137
Ray, Satyajit, 28–29, 51, 126, 142–43
Raya and Sakina (Raya wa Sakina) (Abu Seif, 1953), 52–53
realism, 34–72; Abu Seif, Salah, 52–54; Amiralay, Omar, 63; Arab cinemas, 31, 36–39, 54–55; art cinema, 38–39; Biswas, Moinak, 51; *Cairo Station* (Bab al-Hadid) (Chahine, 1958), 52; city films, 35–36; decorative, 72; *The East Wind* (Smihi, 1975), 31, 61, 66, 75, 78, 80; Egyptian cinema, 36–38, 40, 52, 60, 125, 133; *44, or Tales of the Night* (Smihi, 1981), 39, 66–67; Hollywood, 38, 40, 60, 62; Joyce, James, 66; *The Lady from Cairo* (Smihi, 1991), 45; literature, 31, 37, 54–55, 66, 126; MacCabe,

Colin, 66; Mahfouz, Naguib, 124; Marxism, 39; modernism, 36–41, 59–66, 67, 72; *The Monster* (Abu Seif, 1954) / *Raya and Sakina* (Abu Seif, 1953), 53; montage, 64; music, 81; New Arab Cinema, 38, 59–66; postcolonialism, 68; pretty images, 68, 69; radio, 86; Ray, Satyajit, 142; Rossellini, Roberto, 66; *Si Moh, the Unlucky Man* (Smihi, 1971), 31, 34–36, 39, 60, 66, 74, 80; Smihi, Moumen, 31, 36, 38–41, 45, 54–55, 60, 62, 64, 65–66, 69, 72, 75, 82, 133, 157, 211; sound/tracks, 74, 75; Tangier trilogy, 65; textuality, 69; *The Thug* (Abu Seif, 1957), 53; world cinema, 142. *See also* Italian neorealism; neorealism

"Realism and the Cinema" (MacCabe), 66

Rechiche, Abdelmajid, 6

Red and the White, The (Jansco, 1967), 139

Reggab, Mohammed, 52

religion, 144–79; Abu Nuwas, 159, 163; Allen, Woody, 137; anthropologies, 146; Arab cultures, 32–33, 162, 164; Arab-Islamic architecture, 112–15, 118; Buñuel, Luis, 160–62; *café-concert*, 177; circumcision, 146, 151–52; *The Decameron* (Pasolini, 1971), 160; Durkheim, Émile, 154; *The East Wind* (Smihi, 1975), 119–20, 146; Enlightenment, 119, 145, 171, 178; *Fi al-shi'r al-jahili* (On Jahili Poetry) (Hussein), 125; *44, or Tales of the Night* (Smihi, 1981), 120, 183; *Hayy Ibn Yaqzan* (Ibn Tufayl), 120; head and face coverings, 154; Ibn Tufayl, 119; identities, 146, 164; Kulthum, Umm, 104; languages, 9, 122–23; Maghrib, 146, 153; Marks, Laura U., 114–15; modernity, 144–79; Morocco, 144, 146, 153, 164; *A Muslim Childhood* (Smihi, 2005), 121–22, 151; Muslims, 144; the Nahda, 168; Orientalism, 107; Pasolini, Pier Paolo, 137, 146, 160–61; politics, 24, 32, 145–46, 150–51, 211; practices/rituals, 146, 151–58; queerness, 204; sacredness/sacrilege, 158–62; secularism, 171–79; Smihi, Moumen, 24, 32, 113–14, 116, 119, 120, 137, 144–47, 157, 160–64, 169–70, 211; *The Sorrows of a Young Tangerian* (Smihi, 2013), 105–6, 122, 123, 142, 164, 171–79, 209, 214n17; Tangier, 11; Tangier trilogy, 158–60, 167–68, 179; the West, 145; women, 183. *See also* Muhammad 'Abduh; *individual religions*

religious diversity, 11, 120, 144, 146–51, 167, 171, 177, 188, 211, 232n7

Rélili, Abdallah, 6

Renan, Ernest, 23

Rendezvous with a Stranger (Mawa'id ma' al-majul) (Salem, 1959), 132–33

Renoir, Jean, 5, 142

Return to Agadir (Retour à Agadir) (Afifi, 1967), 21, 64

Rhodes, John David, 39–40

Richie, Donald, 141

ricotta, La (Pasolini, 1963), 161

Rif, 1, 67, 98–99, 114, 129, 130–31, 139, 150

Risalat al-ghufran (Epistle of Forgiveness) (Abu al-'Ala' al-Ma'arri), 123

rituals. *See* practices/rituals

River, The (Tsai, 1997), 142

Rivette, Jacques, 8

Rocha, Glauber, 62

Roche, Natalie, 13*fig.*

Rohmer, Éric, 8

Room of One's Own, A (Woolf), 126, 136–37

Roos, Astrid, 177

Rose of the Souk, The (La rose du souk) (Séverac, 1930), 18

Rossellini, Roberto, 42, 44, 51, 53, 60–61, 66, 67, 108, 129, 223n39

Rostom, Hind, 132, 197–98

Rouch, Jean, 7, 41, 54–59, 78, 108, 132, 223n39

Rousseau, Henri, 5

Rousseau, Jean-Jacques, 122, 172, 174, 175, 178

Ruiz, Raúl, 142

Rushdie, Salman, 89

Saab, Jocelyne, 37

Sacks, Jeffrey, 24

sacredness, 32, 122, 146, 151, 154, 157–62, 165, 166, 169. *See also* religion

Sacrifices (Sunduq al-dunya) (Mohammad, 2002), 89

sacrilege, 32, 137, 146, 153, 154, 157–62, 172–73. *See also* religion

Sadat, Anwar, 45, 46, 102, 227n41

Said, Ahmed, 88, 102

Said, Edward, 33, 203

Said, Frantz, 108

Sakini, Abdesslam, 41, 56. *See also Si Moh, the Unlucky Man* (Smihi, 1971)

Saleh, Tawfik, 15, 37, 52, 54, 125, 133–34

Salih, Tayeb, 25

Sanjinés, Jorge, 70, 71–72

Saqt al-zand (Abu al-'Ala' al-Ma'arri), 123–24

Sartre, Jean-Paul, 5, 6, 9, 174, 195, 215n18

satire, 161

Scales, Rebecca, 90

Schaeffer, Pierre, 74, 75, 108

Schafer, R. Murray, 85

Schick, Irvin Cemil, 187–88

Schoonover, Karl, 20, 38–39, 42, 60, 224n54
Schubert, Franz, 82–83, 130
science, 22, 114, 116, 117, 120, 158, 163, 167–70, 174–75
Screening Morocco (Orlando), 201
Screens and Veils (Martin), 201
second cinema, 62
secularism, 144–79; anthropologies, 144–45; Antun, Farah, 23; *A Door to the Sky* (Benlyazid, 1989), 154; Europe, 145, 170; France, 145–46; Freud, Sigmund, 175; history, 164; Islam, 163, 178, 219n75; languages, 9; *The Medina of Paris: Supererogatory Prayer by a Muslim Dignatory—My Father—After Landing at Paris-Orly* (Smihi, 1996), 162; al-Mernissi, Fatima, 194; modernity/religion, 144–79; Morocco, 32, 144, 167; the Nahda, 26, 146, 163; nationalism, 178; politics, 145, 232n5; postsecularism, 145, 232n3; sacrilege, 32; Smihi, Moumen, 24, 32–33, 144, 163, 167, 178, 211; *The Sorrows of a Young Tangerian* (Smihi, 2013), 171–79; *talib* (university student), 114; Tangier trilogy, 158–60; *tanwir* (Enlightenment), 171; United States/universalism/the West, 145
Sedgwick, Eve Kosofsky, 205
Sefrioui, Kenza, 31
Seif, Mohamed Abu, 45, 102, 126, 134
Selim, Kamal, 52, 54, 133
Selim III (sultan), 167
semi-diegesis, 94–95, 99, 103
"septième porte, La" (The Seventh Gate) (Bouanani), 18
Seqqat, Mohammed, 6
Seventh Gate, The (La Septième porte) (Zwoboda, 1947), 18–19
Séverac, Jacques, 18
sexual desire. *See* desire
sexual identities, 32–33, 201, 203–4, 239n31. *See also* gender; homosexuality; queerness
sexuality, 180–211; Abu Nuwas, 159–60, 210; Arab cinemas, 163; Arab cultures, 180, 200, 210–11; Arab Spring, 205; *The Decameron* (Pasolini, 1971), 160; femininities/masculinities, 201; freedoms, 33, 163, 204; French New Wave, 181; gender, 180, 181; *Girls and Swallows* (Smihi, 2008), 192–93; *The Lady from Cairo* (Smihi, 1991), 197–200; languages, 9; literature, 201, 203; al-Ma'arri, Abu al-'Ala', 160; Maghrib/Maghribi cinema, 201; *Mamma Roma* (Pasolini, 1962), 161; the medina, 210; modernity, 200; *Moroccan Chronicles* (Smihi, 1999), 189; Moroccan cinema/Tangier, 201; Morocco, 159, 200–201, 211; *A Muslim Childhood* (Smihi, 2005), 159, 193, 201–2, 207; New Arab Cinema, 37; the new Nahda, 180; Orientalism, 203–4, 239n41; *Orientalism* (Said), 203; Pasolini, Pier Paolo, 160, 181, 210; politics, 201, 208, 210; Smihi, Moumen, 32–33, 144, 163, 180–81, 200, 201, 203, 210–11; *The Sorrows of a Young Tangerian* (Smihi, 2013), 210; Tangier trilogy, 201; Tunisian cinema, 200; *ville nouvelle*, 210; *Viridiana* (Buñuel, 1961), 160–61; the West, 203–4; women, 198. *See also* desire; prostitutes
Sha'arawi, Huda, 163
Shadia (actress), 5, 196, 197
Shafik, Viola, 37–38, 99, 101, 125, 197–98
Shafiqa the Copt (Shafiqa al-qibtiyya) (al-Imam, 1963), 198
Shahrazad (al-Hakim) (play), 125
Shakespeare, William, 103, 126, 127fig., 136–37
Shanghai cinema, 29, 132
Sharif, Omar, 132–33, 197
al-Sharqawi, 'Abd al-Rahman, 125
Shawqi, Farid, 53
Sheehi, Stephen, 24
sheikh, 196, 197, 199
Shenna, Leila, 8, 43–44, 57
al-Shidyaq, Ahmad Faris, 21–22
al-Siddiq, Khalid, 15, 38
Silences of the Palace, The (Samt al-qusur) (Tlatli, 1994), 89, 91, 99–100
Si Moh, the Unlucky Man (Smihi, 1971): close-ups, 34; colonialism, 64; diegesis/non-diegesis, 60; documentaries, 35–36, 41, 42–43, 72; documentary fiction, 56, 60, 74, 76; essay films, 64–65; filmography, 241; France, 34–35, 39, 74, 75–76, 79, 178; GREC, 48–49; images, 34–35, 60, 63–64; long shots, 34; migration, 34–35, 39, 41, 42–43, 49, 56, 60, 64, 74, 76; mise-en-scène, 41–42; modernism, 39; modernity, 143; montage, 34, 60; Morocco, 8, 34, 74; music, 74–76; *musique concrète*, 80; neorealism, 41–43, 72; noise, 74–80; off-screen/on-screen, 60; public spaces, 34–36, 41–42, 56, 64; radio, 85; realism, 31, 34–36, 39, 60, 66, 74, 80; Smihi, Moumen, 7, 8, 41–43, 60, 67; sound/tracks, 34, 35, 39, 60, 74–80, 85, 95; voices, 34, 75, 76, 95
sintar (instrument), 83, 84fig.
6 and 12 (6 et 12) (Bouanani, 1968), 21, 64, 131–32
slavery, 185–86. *See also* race
Smihi, Moumen, 1–33; Abdel Salam, Shadi, 100–101; Abu Seif, Salah, 54, 108; acousmatic,

97, 105; as actor, 1–2, 46, 65, 88, 98, 131; Allen, Woody, 137, 162; Anglophone film studies/scholarship, 5, 14–17, 217n46; anthropologies, 40, 41, 55, 66, 72, 110, 129, 132, 151; Antonioni, Michelangelo, 108; Arab cinemas, 13, 17–21, 36, 39–40, 81, 107, 112, 138, 139, 211, 218n51; Arab cultures, 2, 5, 9, 11–12, 30, 32–33, 36, 41, 85, 91, 101, 109, 111–12, 116, 118, 122, 128, 130, 132, 144, 157, 180–81, 211, 218n51; Arab-Islamic architecture, 112–22, 141, 143, 181; Arab-Islamic art, 116–17; Arab-Islamic philosophy, 114–22, 143; art cinema, 40, 51, 61–62, 67, 72; auteurism, 12–17, 110, 143; autofiction, 5, 98; Barthes, Roland, 6–7, 8, 9, 109, 110, 118, 215n21; Beshara, Khairy, 134; Biswas, Moinak, 51; Bowles, Paul, 11, 32, 126, 237n10; Bresson, Robert, 42, 73–74, 84; Buñuel, Luis, 5, 32, 126, 146, 160–62, 167, 210; Cairo, 11, 81, 134; Chahine, Youssef, 91; Christianity, 116, 144, 171, 211, 232n7; *cinécritique*, 109; *ciné-écriture/cinécriture* (cinema-writing), 59, 73, 109, 111–12; Cinémathèque française, 10–11; cinephilia, 5–7, 130, 142, 143; circumcision, 157, 239n38; colonialism, 20, 85, 90, 118, 131, 132, 138, 139, 143, 178; *court-métrage* (short film), 31; decorative, 69; desire, 33, 181, 200, 201, 210–11; diegesis, 83; al-Dik, Bashir, 134; documentaries, 2, 35–36, 37, 42–43, 45–46, 50, 67, 102; documentary fiction, 31, 56, 57–59, 117; early years, 4–12; Egypt, 31, 45–47, 132–35; Egyptian cinema, 5, 12–14, 19–20, 37, 40, 52, 54, 80, 132–35, 143, 199, 241; Eisenstein, Sergei, 109; employment, 7, 215n24; Enlightenment, 5, 119, 122, 147, 163, 220n89; essay films, 64–65; essays, 10, 12, 19, 40, 54, 109–10, 111, 116, 162; Europe, 118, 163–64, 181; European cinema, 59, 108, 129, 132, 160; feminism, 192, 195; film funds, 7–8, 12, 137, 141, 215n24; as filmmaker, 5–8, 32, 73; Flaherty, Robert, 117, 132; France, 5, 6–11, 14, 20, 34, 41, 78–80, 90, 107, 109, 118; freedoms, 11, 24–25, 32, 144, 146, 163, 165–66, 211; gender, 33, 103, 144, 163, 180–211; Gnawa, 108; Gunning, Tom, 16–17; Hafez, Abdel Halim, 102–3, 132; al-Hakim, Tawfiq, 124; Hollywood, 11, 132, 135–37, 138, 143, 231n60; Hussein, Taha, 2, 5, 6, 8–9, 11, 25, 32, 124–25, 126, 163, 169–70; Ibn al-Haytham (Alhazen) (philosopher), 115–16; Ibn Tufayl, 118–22; identities, 137, 180–81; IDHEC, 6–8, 34, 73; images, 2, 30, 63–65, 66–72, 73–74, 77, 85, 107, 111, 132, 143, 191; influences, 5–8, 10–12, 214n16; L'institut des hautes études cinématographiques (IDHEC), 34, 73; intertextuality, 16–17, 32, 40, 65, 107–12, 117–18, 123–24, 132–43, 157, 160, 162, 189, 211; Islam, 4–5, 111, 116, 138, 144, 146, 158, 161, 162–79, 211; al-Jahiz (philosopher), 117–18; Judaism, 116, 144, 171, 211, 232n7; Kamal, Husayn, 133; Kulthum, Umm, 104, 132; Lacan, Jacques, 6, 7, 8–9, 109, 111; Lambert, Gavin, 11, 12; Langlois, Henri, 6, 109; languages, 2, 5, 9–10, 11–12, 16–17, 18, 19, 40, 109, 122–27, 128, 163; Lévi-Strauss, Claude, 6, 110–11; literature, 5, 6, 11, 19, 54–55, 65, 108, 111–12, 122–28, 133–34, 143, 160; long takes, 139, 141–42; *lycée français*, 5, 6, 8; al-Maʿarri, Abu al-ʿAlaʾ, 123–24, 133–34; MacCabe, Colin, 66; Maghrib, 13, 59–60, 64–65, 72, 110, 146, 161; Mahfouz, Naguib, 37, 124, 126; masculinities, 180, 199; the medina, 4, 5; Middle East, 32, 89; migration, 60; modernism, 2–4, 13, 20, 30, 33, 36, 38–41, 60, 65–66, 72, 73, 93, 107–11, 118, 128, 130, 132, 143, 144, 211; modernity, 2–3, 21–33, 61–62, 78–80, 111, 118, 119, 132, 139, 142–43, 144, 162–79, 200; montage, 64; Moroccan cinema, 2, 6, 13–15, 17–20, 111, 131; Morocco, 2, 3–4, 13–14, 15, 17, 19, 31, 41, 47, 59, 69, 70, 73, 74, 129, 136–38, 141, 143, 167, 180–81, 195, 211; multivocality, 12, 171; music, 76–77, 80–85, 91, 111, 112, 132; Muslims, 144, 232n7; the Nahda, 2–3, 21–31, 91, 107–8, 143, 167; national cinemas, 17–21; nationalism, 19, 63, 91, 192; neorealism, 40–43, 45, 47–48, 51–55, 57, 60–61, 67, 73; New Arab Cinema, 8, 37–38; the new Nahda, 20–21, 24, 108, 144, 211; *The Night of Counting the Years* (Abdel Salam, 1969), 156; noise, 74, 76–77, 80, 85, 106; non-diegesis, 80; orality, 111; Orientalism, 30, 204, 211; Ozu, Yasujiro, 57, 139–42, 190; pan-Arabism, 3, 19; Pasolini, Pier Paolo, 32, 106, 108, 146, 160–62, 167, 210, 234n31; patriarchy, 33, 180–81; phagocytosis, 111–12; poetics/poetry, 6, 8, 112, 160; politics, 6–7, 10–11, 24, 32, 34, 39, 72, 91, 101, 103, 160, 163, 210; polyphony, 130; postcolonialism, 4, 11, 14, 23, 31, 33, 51, 63, 91; practices/rituals, 2, 154, 157; prizes, 14; psychoanalysis, 10, 72; queerness, 33, 203–4, 210; race, 186; radio, 83, 85–93; Ray, Satyajit, 51, 126; realism, 31, 36, 38–41, 45, 54–55, 60, 62, 64, 65–66, 69, 72, 75, 82, 133, 157, 211; religion, 24, 32, 113–14, 116, 119, 120, 137, 144–47, 157, 160–64, 169–70, 211; religious diversity, 11, 144, 146, 147–51, 211, 232n7; Rossellini, Roberto, 51, 108; Rouch, Jean, 41, 55, 59, 108, 132;

Smihi, Moumen *(continued)*
  sacredness, 32, 122, 146, 157; sacrilege, 32, 146, 161; Saleh, Tawfik, 133–34; Sartre, Jean-Paul, 9; secularism, 24, 32–33, 144, 163, 167, 178, 211; Seif, Mohamed Abu, 134; Selim, Kamal, 133; sexuality, 32–33, 144, 163, 180–81, 200, 201, 203, 210–11; slavery, 186; sound/tracks, 2, 30, 31–32, 72, 73–106, 108, 111, 132, 143, 157, 211; spaces, 41–43, 57, 129, 181–91, 196; structuralism, 8, 9, 10, 72, 109, 110, 111; Tangier, 4–5, 10–12, 20, 32, 74, 109, 126, 130, 147, 191, 204; Tangier trilogy, 5; *tarikh* (Islamic calendar), 189; Tazi, Mohamed, 8; Tazi, Mohamed Abderrahman, 215n21; textuality, 64, 69, 107, 109, 110, 116, 120, 124, 130; Third Cinema, 62; United States, 8, 11, 14, 59, 70, 108, 109, 138; Vertov, Dziga, 117; *ville nouvelle*, 4; Visconti, Luchino, 106, 108; visibility, 13–15, 217n46; voice-overs, 93; voices, 76–79, 80, 85, 88, 93–106, 136–37; von Sternberg, Josef, 137, 231n60; the West, 8, 14–15, 59, 108–9, 110, 118, 130, 132, 138, 144, 158, 163, 181; women, 33, 103, 126, 181, 183, 190, 191, 194–96, 211, 222n19; world cinema, 2–3, 17–21, 30, 32–33, 40, 51–52, 61–62, 108–9, 132–43, 145–46, 211; as writer, 8–10, 12, 54, 109, 124, 215n24; Zwoboda, André, 19. *See also individual films*
Snake Charmer, The (Gérôme) (painting), 203
Sorrows of a Young Tangerian, The (Smihi, 2013): Arab-Islamic architecture, 118, 181; *café-concert*, 175–77; Christianity, 147, 207; *darija* (language), 106; Darwin, Charles, 173–74; desire, 103, 208, 209–10; diegesis/offscreen, 125; documentary fiction, 56; Enlightenment, 122, 173, 174, 177–78; fetishism, 207–8, 209*fig.*; filmography, 242; France, 20, 179; freedoms, 173, 175–79, 195–96; gender, 181; Hafez, Abdel Halim, 102–3; Islam, 164, 169, 172–73; literature, 174, 209–10; long shots, 172; long takes, 59, 105–6, 122, 142, 172*fig.*, 208; *lycée français*, 173–77; Maghrib, 20, 175; masculinities, 103, 208; modernity, 164, 174–75; Morocco, 20, 177, 236n55; music, 59, 175–78, 208; Muslims, 147, 172; nationalism, 20, 177; non-diegesis, 208; Ozu, Yasujiro, 139–41; patriarchy, 181; politics, 59, 103, 172, 173, 174, 177, 179, 195–96, 209, 214n17; pretty images, 72; psychoanalysis, 127, 175; queerness, 208; radio, 86, 91, 102–3; religion, 105–6, 122, 123, 142, 164, 171–79, 209, 214n17; religious diversity, 147, 150, 177; Renoir, Jean, 142; Rouch, Jean, 59; sacredness/sacrilege, 158–59; science, 174–75;
secularism, 171–79; sexuality, 210; *Shahrazad* (al-Hakim) (play), 125; Smihi, Moumen, 4–5, 20, 72, 105–6, 125, 166, 171, 173, 214n17; sound/tracks, 82, 83, 86, 102–3, 105–6, 208; spaces, 181; Tangier, 12, 65, 125, 127, 181; textuality, 127; veils, 196; *ville nouvelle*, 214n17; voices, 102–3, 105–6; wide shots, 173; women, 195–96
Souffles (journal), 10, 21, 31
Souissi studios, 18–19
Soundscape: Our Sonic Environment and the Tuning of the World, The (Schafer), 85
sound/tracks, 73–106; Arab cultures, 73; auteurism, 16; Bresson, Robert, 73–74; Chion, Michel, 74, 76, 95, 97, 225n6; colonialism, 85; diegesis, 58–59, 80–85, 86, 94–95, 97, 98, 100, 101, 104, 106; *The East Wind* (Smihi, 1975), 58–59, 61, 77–80, 85–87, 96–97, 103, 129, 147, 189; Egyptian cinema, 80–81; *44, or Tales of the Night* (Smihi, 1981), 39, 68, 80, 84–85, 86–88, 94, 106, 152; *Girls and Swallows* (Smihi, 2008), 76, 82, 83, 88, 203; images, 73–80, 84–85, 94–95, 111; Kulthum, Umm, 104; *The Lady from Cairo* (Smihi, 1991), 45, 80–82, 99, 101–2, 133, 199; *Ma'rouf the Cairo Cobbler* (Ma'arouf al-Iskafi /Maarouf, savetier du Cairo) (Mauran, 1947), 18; the medina, 77–79; *The Medina of Paris: A Square during the Ramadan Market* (Smihi, 1996), 79; *The Medina of Paris: Supererogatory Prayer by a Muslim Dignatory—My Father—After Landing at Paris-Orly* (Smihi, 1996), 79, 162; mise-en-scène, 75; modernism, 31–32, 74, 77, 80, 107; modernity, 74; *Moroccan Chronicles* (Smihi, 1999), 48, 82, 83, 95, 130; Morocco, 73, 74, 84, 86; music, 74, 79, 80–85; *A Muslim Childhood* (Smihi, 2005), 82, 83, 94–95, 97–99, 104–5; *The Night of Counting the Years* (Abdel Salam, 1969), 100–101, 156*fig.*; noise, 74–80, 84; non-diegesis, 32, 80–83, 94, 106; offscreen, 81, 83, 84; politics, 32; postcolonialism, 92; radio, 85–93; realism, 74, 75; on-screen, 81, 83, 84, 96–97; *Si Moh, the Unlucky Man* (Smihi, 1971), 34, 35, 39, 60, 74–80, 85, 95; Smihi, Moumen, 2, 30, 31–32, 72, 73–106, 108, 111, 132, 143, 157, 211; *The Sorrows of a Young Tangerian* (Smihi, 2013), 82, 83, 102–3, 105–6, 208; Tangier, 74, 79–80, 84, 88; Tangier trilogy, 83–85; voices, 74, 77–79, 84, 93–106. *See also individual sounds*
spaces: Abu Seif, Salah, 54; Amiralay, Omar, 63; Antonioni, Michelangelo, 129; Arab cultures, 129; *The East Wind* (Smihi, 1975),

43–44, 57, 61, 77, 96–97, 181–83, 189; *44, or Tales of the Night* (Smihi, 1981), 71, 139, 181, 183–86; gender, 181–200; *Girls and Swallows* (Smihi, 2008), 181, 188, 189–91, 193; harems, 187–88; Marks, Laura U., 115; migration, 56; *A Muslim Childhood* (Smihi, 2005), 141, 181, 189, 192–94; *The Night of Counting the Years* (Abdel Salam, 1969), 156; Ozu, Yasujiro, 139–41; radio, 86; *Si Moh, the Unlucky Man* (Smihi, 1971), 56; slavery, 186; Smihi, Moumen, 41–43, 57, 129, 181–91, 196; *The Sorrows of a Young Tangerian* (Smihi, 2013), 181; Tangier trilogy, 141, 186–87, 191, 196; voices, 95; women, 185. See also domestic spaces; public spaces

Spain, 4, 90, 98–99, 118–19, 149–50, 158

Spring Sunshine (Shams al-rabi'a / Soleil de printemps) (Lahlou, 1970), 51–52

Steimatsky, Noa, 67

Stein, Gertrude, 27–28

Step by Step (Khutwa khutwa) (Mohammad, 1978), 89

Stern, Arno. See *Colors on Bodies* (Smihi, 1972)

still images, 41, 63–65, 142. See also images

Stokes, Martin, 227n40,41

stories. See *hakawati* (storyteller); *al-halqa* (story tradition)

Straub, Jean-Marie, 95

structuralism, 8, 9, 10, 72, 109–10, 111

Struggle on the Nile (Salem, 1959), 197–98

Sufi Muslims, 153, 154, 213n2

Sunni Islam, 146, 153

Syria, 21, 26, 37, 62–63, 89, 108, 122–24, 195

Syrian films, 89

S/Z (Barthes), 118

tafsir (theological treatise), 165

Tahrir al-mara'a (Liberation of Women) (Amin), 195

al-Tahtawi, Rifa'a Rafi', 22–23, 163, 167, 195

Taïa, Abdellah, 201, 205

Take Care of Zuzu (al-Imam, 1972), 198

talib (university student), 114

Tamazight language, 128, 214n13

Tangier: Arab cultures, 167; Arab-Islamic architecture/philosophy, 11; casbah, 120; Christianity, 11, 149–50; colonialism, 4, 79–80; *The East Wind* (Smihi, 1975), 12, 43, 57–58, 60–61, 63, 78, 96–97, 103, 181, 182; Egyptian cinema, 132–33; films set in, 12; France, 4, 10–11, 63, 79–80, 119–20, 237n8; *Girls and Swallows* (Smihi, 2008), 12, 65, 76, 203*fig.*, 206; history of, 4; Judaism/Muslims/religion, 11; Kulthum, Umm, 103–4; Lambert, Gavin, 216n39; languages, 11–12, 130; the medina, 104–5; migration, 79; modernity, 78–79; *Moroccan Chronicles* (Smihi, 1999), 47, 50, 57, 92, 137; music, 11, 79–80, 84; *A Muslim Childhood* (Smihi, 2005), 12, 65, 98, 105, 120, 158; nationalism, 147; noise, 79–80; Perdicaris Park, 102–3, 177–78; polyphony, 130; queerness, 201, 204, 205–6; religious diversity, 147–51, 171; sexuality, 201; Smihi, Moumen, 4–5, 10–12, 20, 32, 74, 109, 126, 130, 147, 191, 204; *The Sorrows of a Young Tangerian* (Smihi, 2013), 12, 65, 125, 127; sound/tracks, 74, 79–80, 84, 88; Tanjawi (dialect), 129; United States, 4; voices, 79–80, 84, 98. See also *With Matisse in Tangier* (Smihi, 1993)

Tangier American Legation Institute of Moroccan Studies (TALIM), 4

Tangier trilogy: colonialism, 208; desire, 201, 208; domestic spaces, 186–87, 191; fetishism, 207; gender/patriarchy, 186–87; Hussein, Taha, 125, 169; images, 65; intertextuality, 119, 120, 122, 125, 137; Islam, 146, 164, 167–69; literature, 137, 174; *lycée français*, 167, 168; modernity, 167–69, 179; music, 83–85, 137; nationalism, 90, 208; postcolonialism, 208; queerness, 201, 206, 210; realism, 65; religion, 158–60, 167–68, 179; religious diversity, 146–51, 167; Rouch, Jean, 56–57; sacredness/sacrilege/secularism, 158–60; sexuality, 201; Smihi, Moumen, 5; sound/tracks, 83–85; spaces, 141, 186–87, 191, 196; voices, 97, 103, 106; women, 186–87, 191, 194–96. See also *individual films*

Tanjawi (dialect), 129

tanwir (Enlightenment), 26, 119, 122, 147, 163, 171, 173, 178–79, 220n89. See also European Enlightenment; Nahda, the

Tarfaya, or a Poet's Walk (Tarfaya, ou, la marche d'un poète) (Bouanani, 1966), 71, 131–32

tarikh (Islamic calendar), 172, 189

Tashilhit language, 128

Tati, Jacques, 95, 106

al-Tayeb, Atef, 133

Taymur, 'A'isha, 195

Tazi, Mohamed, 8

Tazi, Mohamed Abderrahman, 6, 215n21

Teguia, Tariq, 38

Telemsani, Tarek, 47*fig.*

Tel Quel (literary magazine), 109

textuality: Arab cultures, 69, 224n61; Arab-Islamic architecture, 112–15; decorative, 69; *44, or Tales of the Night* (Smihi, 1981), 69; languages, 109; Marks, Laura U., 114–15; realism, 69; Smihi, Moumen, 64, 69, 107, 109, 110, 116, 120, 124, 130; *The Sorrows of a Young Tangerian* (Smihi, 2013), 127; *S/Z* (Barthes), 118; world cinema, 128. *See also* intertextuality; literature

They Were Promised the Sea (Wazana, 2012), 147–48

Third Cinema, 62–63, 72

"This Is the Voice of Algeria" (Fanon), 89–90

Thug, The (al-Futuwa) (Abu Seif, 1957), 53–54

Tibi, Bassam, 170, 178, 179

Tibi, Mohammed, 163

tiles. *See zellij* (mosaic tiles)

Tinghir-Jerusalem: Echoes of the Mellah (Hachkar, 2012), 147–48

Tlatli, Moufida, 37, 89, 91, 99–100

Tolstoy, Leo, 108, 126

Torres, Mohamed, 7–8

Tout Va Bien (Godard, 1972), 66

Traboulsi, Fawwaz, 22, 24

Traces (Benani, 1970), 205, 239n36

translations, xiii, 9–10, 30, 107–8

Truffaut, François, 6, 8, 63, 126, 142, 199–200

Tsai Ming-liang, 142

Tunisia, 15, 37, 87, 89, 214n9

Tunisian cinema, 12–13, 15, 200, 205, 206, 239n38

Turkey, 195

Two-Lane Blacktop (Hellman, 1971), 137

Ugetsu (Mizoguchi, 1953), 139

Ulysses (Joyce), 66, 127

United States: Bouanani, Ahmed, 131–32; literature, 126; al-Mernissi, Fatima, 194–95; modernism, 62; modernity, 25, 26–28; *Moroccan Chronicles* (Smihi, 1999), 92; Moroccan cinema, 14, 19, 131–32; *A Muslim Childhood* (Smihi, 2005), 82; *Orientalism* (Said), 203; Ozu, Yasujiro, 141; secularism, 145; Smihi, Moumen, 8, 11, 14, 59, 70, 108, 109, 138; Tangier, 4; *tanwir* (Enlightenment), 178; Voice of America, 86, 92; world cinema, 118. *See also* Hollywood; *individuals*; West, the

Unveiling and Veiling (al-Sufur wa-l-hijab) (Zeineddine), 192

Uprooted (Chinnamul) (Ghosh, 1950), 51

urban spaces. *See* public spaces

Varda, Agnès, 109

veils, 5, 154, 155*fig.*, 161, 165–66, 187–89, 192–94, 196, 201

vernacular modernism, 29, 128–43. *See also* modernism

Vertigo (Hitchcock, 1958), 139, 232n62

Vertov, Dziga, 21, 35–36, 117

Vigo, Jean, 95

ville nouvelle, 4, 43, 57–58, 61, 98, 154–55, 181, 183, 187, 194, 210, 214n17, 237n8

Viridiana (Buñuel, 1961), 160–61

Visconti, Luchino, 67, 95, 106, 108

vococentrism, 76–77. *See also* orality

Voice of America, 86, 92

Voice of the Arabs, 86–88, 90–91, 92–93, 226n24. *See also* radio

voice-overs: *Desert Wedding* (Noces de sable) (Zwoboda, 1948), 19; *44, or Tales of the Night* (Smihi, 1981), 95, 123, 184; *The Lady from Cairo* (Smihi, 1991), 46, 99, 103, 196, 199; *Me, a Black Man* (Moi, un noir) (Rouch, 1958), 56; *Moroccan Chronicles* (Smihi, 1999), 83, 92; *A Muslim Childhood* (Smihi, 2005), 65, 94–95, 98–99, 120, 148, 150, 151, 158, 187, 201–2, 206; *The Silences of the Palace* (Samt al-qusur) (Tlatli, 1994), 99–100; Smihi, Moumen, 93. *See also* diegesis

voices, 93–106; acousmatic, 93–94, 97; *acousmêtre*, 97; Arab cinemas, 99–100, 101, 103; Arab cultures, 99, 101; Bresson, Robert, 95; Chion, Michel, 95, 105, 106, 227n32; diegesis, 97, 98, 100, 101; *The East Wind* (Smihi, 1975), 77–79, 87, 96–97, 103, 129; Egypt, 102; Fellini, Federico, 105–6; *44, or Tales of the Night* (Smihi, 1981), 94, 95, 97, 106, 123; France, 79–80; French cinema, 95, 105; gender, 103; Hafez, Abdel Halim, 102; Kulthum, Umm, 101, 102, 103–5, 228n45; *The Lady from Cairo* (Smihi, 1991), 99, 101–2, 103; the medina, 104–6; modernity, 106; *Moroccan Chronicles* (Smihi, 1999), 126; *Moroccan Chronicles* (Smihi, 1999), 95; multivocality, 105–6, 130; music, 101, 102–3; *A Muslim Childhood* (Smihi, 2005), 94–95, 97–99, 104–5; Nasser, Gamal Abdel, 227nn40,41; *The Night of Counting the Years* (Abdel Salam, 1969), 100–101; non-diegesis, 94; nonsynchronous, 95–96; off/on-screen, 93, 94, 96–97; *Omar Gatlato* (Allouache, 1976), 99, 100; politics, 102, 227n41; polyphony, 129–30, 136–37; radio, 85, 93, 106; semi-diegesis, 94–95, 99, 103; *The Silences*

of the Palace (Tlatli, 1994), 99–100; *Si Moh, the Unlucky Man* (Smihi, 1971), 34, 75, 76, 95; Smihi, Moumen, 76–79, 80, 85, 88, 93–106, 136–37; *The Sorrows of a Young Tangerian* (Smihi, 2013), 102–3, 105–6; sound/tracks, 74, 77–79, 84, 93–106; spaces, 95; Tangier, 79–80, 84, 98; Tangier trilogy, 97, 103, 106; women, 97–100, 103; world cinema, 106
Voltaire, 5, 122, 172, 174, 175, 178
von Sternberg, Josef, 9, 135, 137, 203, 231n60
von Stroheim, Erich, 9

Wahby, Youssef, 133, 197
Wannous, Sa'adallah, 21, 26
waqi'iyya. *See* realism
Watani al-kabir (My Great Nation) (song), 91
Weber, Max, 27
Weiss, Max, 24
Welles, Orson, 2, 103, 136–37, 138, 196
West, the: Arab cinemas, 15, 17; Arab cultures, 2–3, 9, 23–24, 32–33, 178–79, 181; documentary fiction, 117; *A Door to the Sky* (Benlyazid, 1989), 154; Fez, 192; harems, 187, 191; Islam, 144, 145, 167, 178; languages, 9–10; Middle East, 23; modernism, 21, 25, 28, 41, 118; modernity, 22, 25–31, 178–79; *Moroccan Chronicles* (Smihi, 1999), 92, 130; Moroccan cinema, 15; Morocco, 163; Muslims, 167–68, 181; the Nahda, 9, 21–31, 215n26; queerness, 203–4; religion/secularism, 145; sacrilege, 162; sexuality, 203–4; Smihi, Moumen, 8, 14–15, 59, 108–9, 110, 118, 130, 132, 138, 144, 158, 163, 181; *tanwir* (Enlightenment), 178–79; women, 181, 195; world cinema, 118. *See also* Anglophone film studies; European Enlightenment; *individual countries*
Westermarck, Edward, 153
Western classical music, 32, 80, 82–83, 108. *See also individuals*
What Time Is It There? (Ming-liang, 2001), 142
Where Are You Going, Moshe? (Benjelloun, 2007), 149
wide shots, 78, 139, 141, 147, 173, 190, 191, 199, 207
Will, The (al-'Azima) (Selim, 1939), 52, 53, 54, 133
Williams, Raymond, 28
Williams, Tennessee, 11, 126
Wind of the Aurès (Vent d'Aurès) (Lakhdar-Hamina, 1966), 70
With Matisse in Tangier (Smihi, 1993), 2, 12, 137–38, 186, 241
With Taha Hussein (Smihi, 2015), 2, 32, 242

women: Arab cinemas, 99, 103; Arab cultures, 32–33; Booth, Marilyn, 188–89; *café-concert*, 176; *Caftan of Love* (Smihi, 1989), 139; *Chants anciens des femmes de Fes* (Ancient Songs of the Women of Fez), 131; *cinéma colonial*, 203; circumcision, 151, 152, 157, 234n16; *The Decameron* (Pasolini, 1971), 160; desire, 181, 208; *A Door to the Sky* (Benlyazid, 1989), 154; *The East Wind* (Smihi, 1975), 43–44, 57, 103, 152–53, 154–56, 180, 181–83, 184*fig.*; education, 194, 195; Egypt, 188–89, 195; Egyptian cinema, 5, 197, 199; "Fallen Women, Rising Stars, New Horizons: Shanghai Silent Film as Vernacular Modernism" (Hansen) (essay), 29; Fez, 123, 131, 192; *44, or Tales of the Night* (Smihi, 1981), 71, 94, 97, 123, 131, 183–86, 203; freedoms, 193–94; *Girls and Swallows* (Smihi, 2008), 188–93, 194, 209; *haik* (women's garment), 130, 189; harems, 191; homosexuality, 207; Islam, 165, 195, 201; *The Lady from Cairo* (Smihi, 1991), 99, 103, 180, 196–200; literature, 188–89; al-Ma'arri, Abu al-'Ala', 160; Maghrib, 201; modernity, 195; Mohammed V, King, 192; *Moroccan Chronicles* (Smihi, 1999), 92, 103, 126; Moroccan cinema, 201, 237n4; Morocco, 154, 189, 191–92, 194–95; *A Muslim Childhood* (Smihi, 2005), 97–99, 187–88, 189, 192–94; the Nahda, 165–66, 195; nationalism, 192, 194, 195; New Arab Cinema, 37; orality, 131; Orientalists, 190; patriarchy, 181; poetics/poetry, 123; public spaces, 181, 191, 196, 211; religion, 183; sexuality, 198; Smihi, Moumen, 33, 103, 126, 181, 183, 190, 191, 194–96, 211, 222n19; *The Sorrows of a Young Tangerian* (Smihi, 2013), 195–96; *Tahrir al-mara'a* (Liberation of Women) (Amin), 195; Tangier trilogy, 186–87, 191, 194–96; *Ugetsu* (Mizoguchi, 1953), 139; virgin-whore dichotomy, 198; voices, 97–100, 103; the West, 181, 195. *See also* domestic spaces; gender; head and face coverings; *individuals*; prostitutes; veils
women's rights, 165, 195–96, 208. *See also* feminism
Woolf, Virginia, 126, 130, 136–37
world cinema, 1–33, 128–43; Arab cinemas, 3–4, 17–21, 32, 33, 108, 112, 211; Hollywood, 51; Indian cinema, 51, 143; inter/textuality, 107, 128–43; modernism, 3, 107, 108, 128–43, 147; modernity, 138–39; Moroccan cinema, 17–18; Nagib, Lúcia, 3; national cinemas, 17–21; neorealism, 51, 52; realism, 142; Reggab,

world cinema *(continued)*
    Mohammed, 52; Smihi, Moumen, 2–3, 17–21, 30, 32–33, 40, 51–52, 61–62, 108–9, 132–43, 145–46, 211; textuality, 128; United States/the West, 118; voices, 106. *See also individuals;* non-Arab cinemas; *individual films*
world literature, 122–27. *See also individuals;* literature; *individual titles*

Yarmolinsky, Benjamin, 80
Yasmina (Lordier, 1946), 18

You Are My Love (Inta habibi) (Chahine, 1957), 132
Young Soul Rebels (Julien, 1991), 89
Yousra (actress), 14, 44, 134, 196, 223n21

Zakariyya, Fouad, 178
Zaki, Ahmed, 134
Zeineddine, Nazira, 165–66, 192
zellij (mosaic tiles), 70–71, 113–14, 115, 118
Zinet, Mohamed, 15, 38
Zohra, Lalla Fatima (Moroccan princess), 192
Zohra Standing (Matisse) (painting), 138
Zwoboda, André, 18–19

Founded in 1893,
UNIVERSITY OF CALIFORNIA PRESS
publishes bold, progressive books and journals
on topics in the arts, humanities, social sciences,
and natural sciences—with a focus on social
justice issues—that inspire thought and action
among readers worldwide.

The UC PRESS FOUNDATION
raises funds to uphold the press's vital role
as an independent, nonprofit publisher, and
receives philanthropic support from a wide
range of individuals and institutions—and from
committed readers like you. To learn more, visit
ucpress.edu/supportus.

www.ingramcontent.com/pod-product-compliance
Lightning Source LLC
Chambersburg PA
CBHW030526230426
43665CB00010B/781